D1457298

Webs of Power

Webs of Power

International Cartels
and the World Economy

Kurt Rudolf Mirow and Harry Maurer

HOUGHTON MIFFLIN COMPANY · BOSTON

1982

Library of Congress Cataloging in Publication Data

Mirow, Kurt Rudolf.
Webs of power.

Includes bibliographical references and index.
1. International business enterprises.   2. Trusts,
Industrial.   I. Maurer, Harry.   II. Title.
HD2755.5.M58   338.8'81   81-6771
ISBN 0-395-30536-5   AACR2
Printed in the United States of America

S 10 9 8 7 6 5 4 3 2 1

For Barbara;
and for Robert, Charlotte, and Charlo.

Contents

Appendixes

Acknowledgments

THIS book could not have been written without the aid and advice of many friends and colleagues — too many, in fact, to be listed here. Those who gave essential help in assembling the material, correcting facts, criticizing theory, and smoothing out rough spots in the prose include the European authorities Helmut Arndt, Hans Ulrich Horm. Stoltz, Colin Greenhill, Emil Herbolzheimer, and Claes Brundenius; in the United States, Richard Newfarmer, Mike Locker, Robert Engler, Kai Bird, Horace de Podwin, Barbara Durr, and David Gardner; in Buenos Aires, Carlos Maria Vilas; and in Brazil, Luiz Alberto Moniz Bandeira. Dozens of Brazilians collaborated on the Brazilian version of the book by providing documents and interviews about the activities of cartels in that country; and the coverage provided by numerous Brazilian journalists was indispensable in rescuing the book from the censors after the government seized it. We are also indebted to Barbara Epstein, pioneer researcher of the electrical cartel, who was unfailingly generous with her time and insights. A special salute goes to Jeff Frieden, a friend whose energy is infectious and who was never too busy to track down a source or a contact. Milly Klingman, George Hagman, Terri Schultz, and Benito Romano gave good advice, some of which struck home. And deep thanks go to Diana Gubbay and Maria Barbara Mirow, who shared the ups and downs, giving support in all the ways it's needed.

Our agent, Heidi Lange of Sanford Greenburger Associates, believed in the book and worked hard to make it happen. Jonathan Galassi, who took on the project for Houghton Mifflin, and John Russell, who finished it, are editors who embody the best of the old school; they care about writing and have a delicate touch with writers. The book's final shape owes a great deal to John Russell's editorial acumen.

Finally, Harry Maurer is indebted to two institutions that provide inexpensive workspace where writers can escape the distractions of home: the Frederick Lewis Allen Memorial Room in the New York Public Library, and the Writers Room, on Broadway and 42nd Street in New York. To good friends from both places, who always offered encouragement when the spirit was flagging; to the staff of the great Public Library; to the band of pioneering scribes who organized the Writers Room; and to the kindly Abby Schaefer, who keeps it running: many thanks. There should be more such havens.

Webs of Power

Introduction: The Death and Life of a Book

ASH WEDNESDAY, February 23, 1977, 3:00 P.M. Throughout Brazil the raucous sounds of the Carnival celebration are fading, and most revelers have left the streets by the time the military police begin to surround the bookstores. The operation is well coordinated: jeeps arrive almost simultaneously at the Sulina bookstore in the southern state capital of Pôrto Alegre; at the Sete bookstore in Recife, 2500 miles away on the northern coast; at Entrelivros and other stores in Rio de Janeiro; at the Siciliano bookstore in São Paulo; and at shops in Brasília, Belo Horizonte, and nearly every other major city in the country. The police are heavily armed with submachine guns and tear gas grenades, as though expecting violent resistance. They need not have worried; the target of their assault surrenders peaceably and is soon carted off into custody. The prisoner is a book — *A Ditadura dos Cartéis (The Cartel Dictatorship)* by Kurt Rudolf Mirow. The generals who rule Brazil have deemed it a menace to the state and condemned it to languish in oblivion along with some four hundred other banned titles.

As the generals are soon to realize, they have made a political mistake of historic proportions.

Their first blunder was in seizing the book too late. *A Ditadura dos Cartéis* had arrived in the stores only on Friday the 18th, but by Wednesday eight hundred copies had been sold. Xerox machines soon transformed the hundreds into thousands, which circulated rapidly. Even more disastrous, though, was the decision to make an example of Mirow. A week after banning the book, the minister of justice, Armando Falcão, announced that Mirow would be tried in military courts for violating the National Security Law. From the start, it was as though Falcão's attempt was hexed. The military prosecutor general declined to bring the case before the Supreme Military Tribunal in Brasília, declaring that he saw no legal grounds for doing so. He was replaced, and a new prosecutor general decided to hold a court-martial in an air force court in Rio, where Mirow lives and his publisher is located. Two local air force prosecutors then demonstrated *their* lack of enthusiasm for the case by requesting transfer or vacation time in order to avoid filing a complaint. Finally a newly appointed prosecutor drew up a complaint in Brasília, but this only caused Falcão further embarrassment; the complaint was based on a copy of the manuscript stolen from Mirow in 1976, and many of the passages cited as seditious were not even in the book as finally published.

Mirow was charged with violating Article 16 of Decree-Law 898 of the military government, which declares it a crime "to divulge by any social medium of communications any false or tendentious report, or any true fact truncated or distorted in such a way as to dispose the public against the constituted authorities." The government alleged that the book included "passages which describe the Brazilian economy in a distorted and tendentious manner, compromising and discrediting, in the eyes of the public, the Government and the guiding principles of the revolutionary movement of '64,"* and that thereby the author had committed "a violent libel against the federal government, as though attempting to discredit it internationally."[1] Mirow based his defense on the Brazilian Constitution, particularly the passage stating that the fundamental principle of the country's economic policy shall be the "repression of abuse of economic power, characterized by market domination, the elimination of competition, and the arbitrary increase of profits." Mirow also declared himself ready to prove every assertion in the book, a point he dramatized by showing up on the first day of the hearing accompanied by porters carrying five trunks holding more than four hundred pounds of documents.

Mirow's trial was front-page news, Brazilian newspapers being largely free of censorship, but his attempt at defense was regarded as quixotic. In military-ruled Brazil his conviction by court-martial was thought to be a foregone conclusion. But the case had been unpredictable from the start, and it continued that way. On September 18, 1977, the judges voted 4–1 to acquit Mirow, with the only civilian on the panel casting the sole vote for conviction. After another air force court confirmed the verdict, the pros-

---

* That is, the military *coup d'état* of March 31, 1964, against the elected government of President João Goulart.

ecution appealed the case to Brasília for final judgment by the Supreme Military Tribunal.

If the acquittals in Rio came as a surprise, demonstrating a hitherto unknown degree of independence on the part of the military judges, the outcome in Brasília stunned the country. On April 7, 1978, the ten officers and five civilians who constituted the Supreme Military Tribunal ruled unanimously that Mirow was not guilty of violating the National Security Law. The written opinions were sharply worded, indignant, and resoundingly critical of the government. "I read the book twice. It is a notable work which brings honor to the economic literature of the nation. I am astonished that a defendant of this ilk can be brought to be judged by this court. It is sad," wrote General Rodrigo Octávio. Another judge, Rui Lima Pessoa, observed that the book "reflects the advance of the great international economic organizations, showing that they make use of corruption to succeed in the unrestrained elimination of small and medium-sized businesses, including those owned by Brazilians, and even those owned by the state." "Far from striking against the National Security Law, [the book] will fortify national security," said General Deoclécio Lima de Siqueira. And Justice Jacy Pinheiro advised, "All Brazilians should read and think about this book."[2]

Which is exactly what Brazilians did. The order banning *A Ditadura dos Cartéis* was lifted two weeks after the ruling in Mirow's case — the first time since 1893 that the courts had voided a censorship order in Brazil. A new printing was rushed to the bookstores, and *Ditadura* shot to the top of the best-seller lists, remaining there for eleven months. To date some 125,000 copies have been sold, an unprecedented number in Brazil, where the reading public is a tiny minority of the population. Mirow's second book, *Condenados ao Subdesenvolvimento?* (*Condemned to Underdevelopment?*) also became a best seller when it appeared in 1979. Following Mirow's victory in the courts, three other authors immediately brought suit to liberate their books from the censor's ban — and won. The government then abandoned its policy of censoring books (with the exception of pornography), and dozens were liberated. The attempt to silence Mirow thus ended by seriously damaging the apparatus of the dictatorship itself.

✦   ✦   ✦

What was it the junta found so terrifying about a book with the odd title *The Cartel Dictatorship?* What led the government to miscalculate so severely the results of its move against Mirow? In part the answer lies in the peculiarities of a specific moment in Brazilian history, a moment of plummeting prestige for the military, swelling demands for a return to democracy, economic crisis, and intense resentment of transnational corporations in Brazil. The atmosphere was charged with political energies that had been accumulating for years, and Mirow's book acted as a light-ning rod. But the battle over the book was not purely the product of a transitory political situation. It was not simply that *Ditadura* caught the generals at a weak moment and caused them to overreact. What made the book so threatening was that it dared discuss a highly sensitive topic: pri-vate economic cartels.

It was a subject the author knew through bitter personal experience. Mirow's family has been in Brazil since 1863, when Kurt's great-grandfa-ther, Hermann Stoltz, emigrated from Germany and established himself in Rio de Janeiro. He founded an import–export firm, Herm. Stoltz, which still exists. The firm specialized in commerce between Germany and Bra-zil, and in the 1920s began to import small electrical apparatus — genera-tors, water-wheel turbines, transformers, motors. The family built a fac-tory to produce water wheels, but the Brazilian government seized it in 1942, when anyone in Brazil with German ancestry and strong ties to Ger-many was viewed as a potential Nazi agent. In 1957 the Mirows founded a new company called Codima, Máquinas e Acessórios, S.A., and built an-other factory to make the types of electrical equipment the family had formerly imported. Codima was a success, manufacturing, among other products, the first motors for use in shipboard winches and cranes ever produced in Brazil and employing, at its peak, 750 workers.

But the prosperity was short lived. The firm had been born during a pe-riod of explosive growth in the Brazilian electrical industry. This postwar spurt was nurtured by a policy of "import substitution," that is, the impo-sition of high tariffs on imports to encourage local production. Brazilian firms like Codima benefited from the policy, but so did transnational cor-porations (TNCs) that built (or acquired) factories in Brazil. Indeed, in 1955, two years before Codima was founded, the government enacted a law known as Instruction 113, the currency exchange provisions of which granted extremely favorable terms to foreign companies, giving them an advantage over local firms. The goal of Instruction 113 was to attract for-eign investment, and so it did. By 1960 the foreign-owned share of Brazil's electrical industry had expanded enormously. Of the hundred largest electrical firms, thirty-one were foreign-owned. These tended to be the largest, holding 66 percent of the one hundred firms' total assets and in-cluding four of the five biggest. Among the TNCs established in Brazil were many of the giants of the industry: General Electric and ITT of the United States, ASEA and Ericsson of Sweden, AEG and Siemens of Ger-many, Philips of the Netherlands, Brown Boveri of Switzerland, and Pirelli of Italy. Later the great Japanese firms — Hitachi, Toshiba, Mitsubishi, and others — entered Brazil as well.

Through the 1960s Codima and other small Brazilian companies came under intense pressures as the transnationals moved aggressively into the market. Many local firms failed or were forced to associate themselves with foreign companies in order to survive. The recession that struck the country between 1963 and 1967 accounted for some failures, but foreign competition was also a major factor — competition so ferocious that its only result could be to drive the weakest firms from the field. The mid-1960s brought repeated rounds of price cutting, leading to numerous complaints that foreign firms were selling their products below cost. Codima was hurt by the Brazilian subsidiary of the Swiss transnational Brown Boveri which, according to Codima's calculations, was selling small generators and rotating motors for up to 30 percent less than the lowest possible cost of production.

In 1966 Codima was forced into receivership and did not recover fully until 1968, when the receivership was lifted. By that time market conditions had brightened somewhat. But in 1970 the price cutting began again. Finally, in 1971, Mirow believed he had enough evidence of predatory competition to present a complaint to Brazil's tiny antitrust agency, the Administrative Council for Economic Defense, or CADE. The CADE investigators approved the complaint and charged the Brown Boveri subsidiary with "dumping" its products — that is, selling them below cost — between 1962 and 1972, in a successful effort to increase its market share. CADE's case rested largely on the fact that Brown Boveri absorbed large losses in Brazil during four out of five years between 1966 and 1970, the total loss amounting to some $20 million, which was supplied by the parent firm in Switzerland. CADE also provided examples of Brown Boveri sales at extremely low prices. Brown Boveri denied the dumping charges and insisted that its losses were due to investment in plant expansion. After a trial, the CADE council of judges acquitted Brown Boveri due to lack of sufficient evidence.[3]

The CADE decision was a disappointment to Codima, but during the trial something happened that dwarfed the case in importance. In June 1972 Kurt Mirow received a call from a man who worked for Induselet, the Brazilian subsidiary of the Belgian electrical firm ACEC (Atéliers de Constructions Electriques Charleroi), which since 1970 has been owned by Westinghouse. The man said he had some documents Mirow might find interesting. The papers proved to be copies of an agreement between members of a trade association innocuously called the Institute for the Study of Exports of Heavy Electrical Equipment (IBEMEP). On reading the agreement, it immediately became obvious that IBEMEP was in reality the cover for a sophisticated cartel.

IBEMEP, Mirow discovered, had been established in 1964. Of the companies present at the founding meeting on March 14 of that year, all but two were corporate offspring of powerful transnational parents: ACEC, AEG, ASEA, Brown Boveri, General Electric, and Siemens. Three other firms joined soon afterward: Marini Daminelli, a Westinghouse subsidiary; ALCACE, owned by H. K. Porter and later Harvey Hubbel of Great Britain; and COEMSA, an affiliate of the Italian firm Ansaldo San Giorgio. Of the two token Brazilian firms, ITEL and Line Material, the latter was taken over almost immediately by Hitachi. Thus the cartel consisted of ten TNC subsidiaries and one local firm.

The face IBEMEP presented to the community was highly public-spirited. The organization's stated purpose was to "actively promote the development of exports" and "to promote within the law by means within its disposal the intra-American and international exchange of ideas, laws, and information, technical or not, considered useful for the development and prosperity of the heavy electrical industry." In other words, the IBEMEP companies claimed that their intention was to compete with their parent firms for the heavy equipment market, not only in Brazil but abroad. The institute also announced it would carry out other programs of public interest, including studies of the market, the establishment of trade schools for workers, support for research, and organization of conferences.[4]

Oddly enough, however, almost none of these proposed activities came to fruition. Despite years of uninterrupted work, including weekly meetings of company representatives, aided by a secretary-general, two secretaries, two telephone lines, and ample office space in downtown São Paulo, and despite innumerable progress reports conveyed to the parent companies with which it supposedly was competing, the IBEMEP group had failed utterly in its stated goal of increasing Brazilian exports of heavy electrical equipment. Nor had its scientific and educational programs been carried out. Instead, its main result seems to have been the sharp increase of *imports* of electrical equipment into Brazil, the collapse or absorption of various Brazilian firms, and thus the steady denationalization of the Brazilian electrical industry.

The documents supplied to Mirow included Regulation 2/67, or "Brazilian Agreement for Large Transformers," and Regulation 10, covering small transformers, which strongly suggested that IBEMEP had intentions other than those announced. In fact, the documents describe the workings of a classic private cartel, aimed at tight control of the market and the elimination of competitors. Article 1 of Regulation 2/67 states flatly, "These regulations establish the rules to be observed in negotiations within the Brazilian internal market for transformers and auto-transformers . . . with power above 7.5 MVA and/or with voltage above 69 KV." Article 2 establishes that the agreement will apply to companies designated by the letters A, B, C, D, E, G, H, and I; that is, ITEL, AEG, Brown Boveri, Induselet, ASEA, Siemens, General Electric, and Hitachi. There follow detailed provisions for notifying the IBEMEP secretary-general whenever a member is invited to bid on an order for transformers. Once notified, the secretary calls a meeting at which it is decided which company shall get the contract. The firms are to take turns receiving orders according to procedures outlined in the regulation. They also agree on the price to be bid by each firm, with the "winning" firm naturally offering the equipment at the lowest price.

Article 24 of the regulation is especially interesting. It reads, "The final sales prices agreed upon during the meeting will include two percent payable by the winning member to a 'reserve for combat purposes.' " Article 26: "By using purchase orders received, the secretary will keep a record of individual members' credits in the 'reserve for combat purposes.' " Article 27: "If the need for combat [that is, for driving another firm out of business by slashing prices] arises, it will be taken up first by the company that has accumulated the largest amount of reserves." The section on enforcement of the agreement is also intriguing:

> Non-observance of any provision of these regulations, particularly where such conditions are expressly mentioned, will be considered an infringement; the same applies to the nonobservance of prices, discounts and commissions, payments conditions, delivery dates without readjustment, rotation, price lists or any other acts undertaken by a member and whose effects, voluntary or not, are harmful to the other members.

An infringement, says the next article, may be punished by a fine of 20 percent of the bid. Finally, the regulation issues a chilling warning to possible miscreants: "In case any member leaves this program, he will be systematically combatted by all the others, who will alternate in the combat."

According to Mirow's informants, Regulation 2/67 went into effect in 1967, and was still operative at least through 1972. (Regulation 10, the agreement covering small transformers, reportedly was suspended in 1970.) "Working group meetings" were held on the average of once a week to decide which member should get which orders, and at what price. "Executive meetings" took place once a month and were attended by high-level officers of the firms. They approved the decisions of the working group and made the more important ones — often after consultation with the parent corporations — such as how to allocate unusually large orders, how to settle serious quarrels between the members, and when to enter into combat with outsider firms.

One can only guess at the cartel's direct impact on its competitors. Its internal records remain secret, and there is no way to tell which cases of price cutting were actually "combats" financed by IBEMEP. But a look at the shifting market shares in transformers is certainly suggestive. By the mid-1970s the IBEMEP firms had taken over the entire large transformer market, and their market share for small and medium-sized transformers had also risen sharply, to more than 80 percent. At least seven Brazilian

producers of power and distribution transformers went out of business between 1960 and 1974, some of them long-established firms.[5]

The rout of local enterprises was not confined to the transformer market. In almost every branch of the electrical industry where Brazilians had
held a sizable market share before 1964 — from consumer durables like
televisions and refrigerators to heavy equipment like generators, turbines,
and motors — the advance of foreign firms had been overwhelming. Nor
was dumping the only tactic the cartel used, as Mirow and his Codima associates learned when they began to make inquiries. Again and again they
heard horror stories from colleagues in other branches of the industry:
stories of boycotts, sudden shortages of essential supplies, crippling delays
in delivery of components, price discrimination, and political influence by
TNC subsidiaries over key agencies empowered to grant or deny import
and export licenses. The stories were reflected in the business press, which
printed melancholy accounts of the demise of one firm after another. Codima itself survived, but only as a skeleton of its former self, operating at a
fraction of capacity.

Not long after receiving the IBEMEP papers, Mirow made his next discovery: the Brazilian cartel was but a minor branch of the central electrical industry cartel. Based outside Lausanne, Switzerland, but operating
world-wide, the organization has an appropriately nondescript name: the
International Electrical Association. The IEA was founded (under another
name) in 1930, largely suspended during the war, and reconstituted after
1945. It is nothing less than a private association of most of the world's
largest corporations in the electrical industry, organized with the express
purpose of dividing up markets, fixing prices, and regulating competition
on a world scale. Its activities, which would appear to be contrary to law
in many countries, affect the shape and pace of economic development
throughout the West, and yet the IEA operates virtually unknown to the
public. The association has been implicated by various nations in investigations of suspicious patterns in the electrical trade, yet the IEA functions
unhindered by government oversight. Executives of IEA firms meet
monthly in luxury hotels in such cities as London, Zurich, Frankfurt, Biar-
ritz, Taormina (Italy), and Kyoto (Japan) to apportion orders worth $2 bil-
lion per year. Small wonder, then, that the transnational electrical firms
organized a mini-cartel in Brazil — they were past masters at cartel practices. Mirow learned that of the eight founding members in IBEMEP,
five — AEG, ASEA, Brown Boveri, General Electric, and Siemens — were
also founders, in 1930, of the cartel that eventually became the IEA.
Mirow's informant also revealed that the IBEMEP regulations had come
from the parent firms in Europe and were modeled on IEA agreements
covering trade in the same products.

Sensing that he had found the key not only to the traumas of his family's
company but also to Brazil's distorted pattern of industrial development,

Mirow began an intense search for more data. In 1975 his complaint led CADE to file an unprecedented antitrust suit against both the IEA and IBEMEP, causing a stir in European and U.S. electrical industry circles; executives who had left Brazil, as well as other top-level officers from the firms' headquarters, were called to testify. The suit, one of the most complex filed anywhere against an international cartel, still has not been settled. But by the time it was filed Mirow was already looking ahead. Prevailing expert opinion held that the cartels which controlled the bulk of world trade during the 1930s had vanished after World War II. But if the electrical cartel reorganized itself shortly after the war, might not other cartels have done so as well?

A Ditadura dos Cartéis was written to answer that question in the affirmative. For the fact is that the cartels never vanished; they simply went underground. In various key industries, including steel, chemicals, petroleum, and man-made fibers, the cartels that flourished prior to the war either resumed operations with barely a hitch or regrouped in new forms during the 1950s. In these industries today, the manipulation of markets by associations of private firms remains so prevalent that unrestricted competition is the exception rather than the rule. Raw materials and commodities trades, too, are infested with cartels — some organized with government backing, some private. In many other manufacturing fields, cartel schemes arise intermittently and then lapse when they are no longer needed. The IEA, in short, is by no means unique. It is simply one among a multitude of cartels, which assume an enormous variety of forms. Some cartels operate so subtly as to be virtually undetectable; others are so ponderous and clumsy as to guarantee eventual discovery and disintegration. A cartel may try to influence only one small factor in a market or may subject an entire industry to tight controls. It may involve no more than two firms or twenty. It may survive six months or fifty years. But what all these cartels have in common is the use of concentrated economic power to suppress the workings of the market's "invisible hand" — with consequent impact on trade balances, patterns of investment, employment growth, tax structures, and technological progress. And in developing countries like Brazil, where cartels undermine local industry and hasten foreign penetration of the economy, that impact can be devastating.

It was this message that the Brazilian military rulers found distasteful — so much so that they embarked on their ill-fated attempt to obliterate the book that bore the bad tidings.

*   *   *

The curious story of *A Ditadura dos Cartéis* could have taken place in any one of numerous Third World nations where dictatorial regimes are closely allied with foreign corporations and where criticism of the latter is viewed as an attempt against the former. What makes the tale unusual in the Third World context is that it had a relatively happy ending. But how is it relevant to the industrialized Western nations? How are they affected by the cartel activities of their own firms? Do cartels bring in earnings that offset their drawbacks? The present volume addresses these questions. Based on the information collected for *A Ditadura dos Cartéis*, this book also incorporates the mass of new data on cartels that has emerged since 1978 — including major leaks from within the IEA — as well as the fruits of further research undertaken by the authors in the United States and Europe.

We will leave our conclusions for the chapters to come. Here we will simply suggest that it is imperative for the wealthy nations to face the facts about cartels and do something to counteract them. This is true, we believe, for two fundamental reasons. First, since World War II an ever larger share of global trade has come under the control of a few hundred huge transnational firms. Both scholars and the general public have grasped the importance of this development. But it is not widely recognized that the transnationals, by nature of their history and present circumstances, tend to collaborate with each other at least as readily as they compete. And, as world trade becomes concentrated in fewer hands, every cartel scheme operated by the transnationals has more extensive impact. In short, national governments trying to retain some degree of control over trade and monetary policy can ill afford to ignore the machinations of international cartels.

Second, there is evidence that the world is entering a new "Age of Cartels," as some writers dubbed the 1930s. The natural tendency of large corporations to smother competition is now being exacerbated by the permanent recession that has settled upon the Western economies. Sluggish growth causes firms to struggle to keep their share of a declining market — precisely the conditions that most often give rise to cartels. It is no accident that the first great outburst of cartels came during the Depression, nor that pressures for cartelization of "troubled" industries are rising today, particularly in Europe.

We believe, then, that it would be foolhardy for the West to persist in its habitual refusal to take seriously the restrictive business practices of its own transnational firms. The world in the 1980s is rapidly becoming a more dangerous place. Economic weather has turned foul, and protectionist pressures are rising. Rich and poor nations are daily becoming more dependent on each other and at the same time are more bitterly at odds. Yet the power to shape economic events around the globe is increasingly falling to huge private firms whose loyalty to any particular nation, political system, or international order is extremely tenuous. There is no way to check the growth of that power, or even comprehend it, until we understand how and why the transnationals collaborate for their own greater good.

1

"A Conspiracy Against the Public"

"PEOPLE of the same trade seldom meet together, even for merriment and diversion, but the conversation ends in a conspiracy against the public, or in some contrivance to raise prices," remarks Adam Smith in a famous passage from *The Wealth of Nations*. Smith, of course, was describing the new breed of trader emerging during the latter years of the eighteenth century: the capitalist. But the quip by the apostle of capitalism also describes businessmen of earlier eras. The impulse to suppress competitors is as old as competition itself and has given rise to feats of inventiveness in techniques of trade restraint almost as diverse as those in technology. The history of such "conspiracies" and "contrivances" — reaching their apotheosis in the modern international cartel — is long indeed.

Cartels, in fact, have been defended on the grounds that they are as natural and permanent on the landscape as mountains and rivers. Various forms of price cartels existed in ancient Egypt, Phoenicia, Palestine, and India as long ago as 3000 B.C.[1] There were also numerous cartel-like combines in the Middle Ages in Europe.[2] And there is record of one Renaissance cartel that included so many modern features that it is worth describing in detail. The agreement was signed on June 11, 1470, by Pope Paul II and King Ferdinand of Naples, who owned alum mines in the Papal State and on the island of Ischia, respectively. The two sovereigns were forthright about their intentions. Prices were fixed, and profits shared. The market was divided, and each party received a predetermined quota of sales. Marketing was performed by common sales agents, and uniform terms governing credit and other conditions of sale were established. Heavy fines were to be paid should violations of the agreement be proven. Statistical information was exchanged, and each party was granted the right to make inspection tours of the other's storehouses to guard against cheating. The cartel even had a "combat clause" establishing procedures for doing battle against outsiders. Among the combat features was an unusual one that today's cartels might well find enviable: the Pope pledged to issue an order at least once a year forbidding all Christendom to buy alum from the mines of the Pope's infidel competitors, the Turks. Turkish alum, in effect, was anathema, and could be seized by any upstanding Christian. The Pope also committed himself to use his profits from alum to pay for religious wars against Moslems and Protestants.[3]

Aside from this creative use of religious authority for commercial purposes, one finds here many elements of the modern cartel, including the possibility of political influence, one which came to terrible fruition in the 1930s, when cartels dominated by German firms gave the Nazis indispensable support in preparing for *their* war against infidels. But the deal struck between Pope Paul II and King Ferdinand was essentially an agreement between sovereign states and thus differs in character from the contemporary cartels that are the focus of this book. The alum cartel was definitely a forebear, but some four hundred years were to pass before its descendants, the "classic" international cartels, could be born.

What is a cartel, exactly? The term itself has its roots in the Latin word *charta*, which means a paper, writing, or letter. In English it came to be associated with communication involving combat or the military: a "cartel of defiance" was a challenge sent to a rival, and a "cartel" could be an agreement relating to an exchange of prisoners or even a ship used in the exchange.[4] The first public use of the word in its current commercial sense is thought to have occurred in Germany in 1879, to describe dealings among rail, truck, and locomotive producers.[5] The term did not filter into popular American usage until some thirty years later,[6] although its short life has not prevented *cartel* from meaning different things to Americans at different points during the century. But in its military lineage the essence of the word is revealed: it springs from the notion of a truce or agreement between hostile powers.

In the commercial sphere the public often does not look kindly upon such truces, and that fact has imposed on the word *cartel* an evil aura, or "a demonic force," as one writer labeled it.[7] Since the word came into common usage, Americans with little idea of what it means have known at least that a cartel is something bad; and at times, particularly during the late 1930s and 1940s, cartels were widely felt to have the sort of vast, secret, almost occult economic power that is ascribed to multinational corporations today. In the United States the word's negative connotation was bolstered by xenophobia. Because cartels first developed in Europe, the notion had a nasty alien quality; the popular American prejudice in the early 1900s was that cartels involved an Old World deviousness to which upright entrepreneurs would never stoop — although the owners of General Electric and Standard Oil already knew better. The foreign tinge to the word *cartel* was reinforced in the 1970s, when the term, which had fallen into relative disuse, made a tremendous popular comeback, this time identified with Arabs and oil.

The problem in precisely defining the term *cartel* lies in the great variety of forms cartels can assume. Because of that ability, the standard definitions tend to be extremely broad. George Stocking and Myron Watkins, in their 1946 book *Cartels or Competition?* wrote: "A cartel is an arrangement among, or on behalf of, producers engaged in the same line of business, with the design or effect of limiting or eliminating competition between them."[8] Another standard work, Ervin Hexner's *International Cartels,* defines a cartel as "a voluntary, potentially impermanent, business relationship among a number of independent, private entrepreneurs, which through coordinated marketing significantly affects the market of a commodity or service."[9] The elusiveness of the definitions testifies to the elusiveness of the phenomenon. But Hexner usefully narrows the basic concept of the classic cartel. He argues that a cartel must be voluntary — thus eliminating, for example, the organization of Chilean nitrate producers that was forced by the government in the 1930s — and be made up of private firms, thus leaving out OPEC. An arrangement between a parent firm and its subsidiary does not constitute a cartel, but a joint venture set up by two independent firms may well act as a cartel or as part of an overall cartel strategy. "Coordinated marketing," of course, can encompass almost any technique for manipulating trade, including the simple exchange of data that would allow supposed competitors to set common prices or target sales efforts more accurately. To Hexner's definition, then, we would add only that the cartels we are concerned with are *international,* that is, they have members based in two or more countries. Cartels can (and often do) exist within national, regional, or even local markets. But the subject of this book is those cartels, usually dominated by transnational corporations, which take the entire world as their sphere of influence.

The Coming of Cartels

The reason major cartels did not appear until the late nineteenth century is simply that the structure of the world economy would not support them before then.

Prior to the Industrial Revolution, production in agriculture and manufacturing, although growing, took place on a small scale. Markets for most
commodities were limited; of the goods consumed by a typical family, the
bulk were made at home. Production, therefore, was extremely decentral-
ized, spread among innumerable small producers, and international trade,
or even commerce between different sections of the same country, was restricted by the small size of the market. Also, the state played a central
role in commerce; the practice of trade was inseparable from public policy. Although the importance of private financial, manufacturing, and
trading companies grew steadily, throughout Europe they were intimately
linked to governments which regulated their activities. The main purpose
of trade was to strengthen the nation, although the merchant class did get
rich as a result.

The Industrial Revolution, however, changed economic life fundamentally. The scale of production expanded at a dizzying pace. Markets
mushroomed almost as quickly, and trade grew. A new class of industrialists with new ideas about politics and economics began their rise to power
in Western Europe. *The Wealth of Nations*, which appeared in 1776, became the classic statement of their outlook: private entrepreneurs, competing in a "free market," and relatively unencumbered by state controls,
would bring about economic growth much more rapidly than state-
directed enterprises. The flow of investment and the distribution of goods
and services through society should be governed by the "invisible hand" of
the market — not by government.

Modern cartels, however, were not born with capitalism; nor did they
arise during its youthful phase, which lasted for perhaps a century after
the appearance of Smith's treatise. During the eighteenth and early nineteenth centuries, competition in most capitalist economies was intense,
the number of producers in each branch of industry remaining relatively
high. But by the late 1800s, somewhat to the surprise of many classical
economists — but not to others, like Smith, Ricardo, and Marx, who had
predicted it — the process of competition had itself spawned a new trend
toward economic concentration. Increasingly, large companies had the
power to destroy or absorb their smaller competitors, and they did not
hesitate to use it. Technology rapidly became more complex and costly;
the size of productive facilities — factories, farms, and so forth — grew
immensely as businessmen tried to gain competitive advantages offered by
economies of scale. These new realities meant that fewer and fewer people could raise the capital or master the advanced technology necessary to
enter many fields of manufacture; and ease of entrance is one essential for
the capitalist ideal of "perfect competition."

In the United States, the most spectacular outgrowth of the trend toward concentration was the trust movement, which began with the orga-

nization of the Standard Oil trust by the innovative John D. Rockefeller in 1882. The Standard Oil model, which was copied in other industries, placed the administration but not the ownership of several competing companies in the hands of a "trustee" or group of trustees. By running the companies cooperatively, the officers who control the trust achieve the effect of one large firm. The trustee device was soon outlawed by U.S. courts, and after 1890 it was never used again. But one year before that date an even more effective device for industrial consolidation was bestowed on American industrialists. Prior to 1889, it was illegal (except in special circumstances) for a corporation to own the stock of another corporation. When New Jersey became the first state to legalize such ownership, the "holding company" was born: a firm whose assets consist largely (or entirely) of the stock of other corporations. When the holding company owns controlling interest in the various firms that dominate an industry, it is in effect a trust; the competing firms are merged into one unit. In 1899 Standard Oil was reorganized as Standard Oil of New Jersey, a massive holding company. United States Steel, one of the most gigantic trusts of all, was put together by J. P. Morgan in 1901; it was built principally around Morgan's purchase of the Carnegie Steel Company, which itself controlled twenty-six subsidiaries. Other important trusts organized around 1890 included American Sugar Refining, Diamond Match, American Tobacco, United States Rubber, General Electric, and United States Leather.[10] In the five years after the Supreme Court's famous 1895 decision in *U.S.* v. *E. C. Knight Co.*, which effectively eviscerated the antitrust laws for some time to come by absolving the American Sugar Refining trust of any violations, about three hundred trusts were formed.

The development of what is often called the age of monopoly capitalism provoked alarm and opposition from Americans subject to all the abuses attendant upon "imperfect competition": the swallowing up of small firms by giants, followed by price gouging, stock market manipulations, artificial shortages, bribery of entire legislatures, and other market distortions.[11] The trust movement thus gave rise to the antitrust movement, first embodied in the Sherman Antitrust Act of 1890, and later by the Clayton Act and the Federal Trade Commission Act of 1914. As Richard Hofstadter has pointed out, however, the Sherman Antitrust Act from the beginning "was recognized by most of the astute politicians of that hour as a gesture, a ceremonial concession to an overwhelming public demand for some kind of reassuring action against the trusts."[12] It was rarely enforced at first; indeed, during its early years it was used most often to repress labor unions attempting to organize or negotiate better conditions. In 1905 the Roosevelt administration began a much overrated "trust-busting" effort which, combined with a recession, slowed for some years the pace of mergers and conglomerations. But trust busting did not long remain a priority for presidents, and even the most spectacular cases — such as the breakup of Standard Oil in 1911 — had only a minor effect on the general trend toward concentration, a trend which has remained strong until today.

The passing of industry into fewer hands was not confined to the United States. The same process took place throughout the advanced capitalist world, most particularly in Great Britain and Germany, the other two leading industrial states. England, the birthplace of the liberal ideology of free trade and vigorous competition, found itself falling behind the United States and Germany in various key fields by the late nineteenth century, and one response was to consolidate companies in order better to meet the challenge. The process in England was slower than in the other two countries, but by 1919 it had progressed far enough that the Committee on Trusts of the Reconstruction Ministry could state in a report: "There is at the present time in every important branch of industry in the United Kingdom an increasing tendency to the formation of Trade Associations and Combinations, having for their purpose the restriction of competition and the control of prices." The committee predicted that such combinations "may within no distant period exercise a paramount control over all important branches of British trade." A minority of the committee added, "The fact is that Free Competition no longer governs the business world . . . We find that capitalist combination, in one or another form, and at one or another stage of production, transportation, and distribution, now loads in varying degrees the price of practically everything we purchase."[13]

In certain ways the situation in Germany was the opposite of that in England. The British, with their early lead in the techniques of modern industrial production, had held a preeminent position in world commerce by the early 1800s. Their philosophy of free trade and unfettered competition thus reflected the fact that they held all the advantages in such trade. Germany, on the other hand, was a latecomer both economically and politically.[14] Upon unification, the German people retained the authoritarian, communitarian outlook that reflected a strong feudal inheritance; and the German leaders, notably Bismarck, faced with the problem of thrusting a new, relatively weak nation into the modern world, espoused an ideology that emphasized the supremacy of the state and the subordination of the individual. For German leaders the goal of economic growth was not the increased well-being of individuals but the aggrandizement of the nation, a policy sometimes termed "neo-mercantilism."

Nor did a modern, large-scale industrial plant develop gradually in Germany. Factories, machinery, and techniques were bought wholesale, usually from England, and implanted during the late 1800s. The country never experienced the years of intense competition among numerous steadily growing producers. Rather, huge companies and conglomerations were created almost overnight and were subjected, far more than in England or the United States, to the economic direction of the state. Economic concentration and cooperation were seen as the natural way of things. "Neither the German state nor German businessmen accepted free competition as a method of organizing production, controlling prices, and making economic adjustments," write Stocking and Watkins. "At the outset of Germany's industrialization both resorted to collective controls."[15]

The form taken by such controls was the cartel. Some of the earliest cartels were in the mining industry, and they usually involved price-fixing alliances between state-owned and privately owned mines, with the cartel being imposed by the state. But cartels were also encouraged in fields where the state had less direct interests. Since the German domestic market was relatively underdeveloped, it was crucial for German private companies — and thus for the state they served — to win markets abroad, and export cartels of German producers were seen as a particularly useful weapon in such trade combat. It is generally thought that the 1870s saw the birth of the modern cartel "movement" in Germany. As noted above, it was in 1879 that the word *cartel* was first used in its current sense — by a liberal German deputy, Eugen Richter, in a speech before the Reichstag attacking a combination of rail, truck, and locomotive producers who were charging higher prices on domestic than on foreign markets. The first book on modern cartels was written by an Austrian, Friedrich Kleinwachter; its title was *Die Kartelle*, and it appeared in Innsbruck in 1883. For several decades afterward most of the major works on the subject were written by Germans, and the phenomenon was viewed as peculiarly German, much the same way that trusts were considered a U.S. invention. In the late 1800s the German economy was already thoroughly organized into national cartels. A government study in 1904 showed 385 domestic cartels covering nearly all the major industries, among them coal, iron, metals, chemicals, textiles, leather, rubber, wood, paper, and glass. Seven years later a monthly magazine devoted to cartels, the *Kartell-Rundschau*, estimated that there were between 550 and 600 domestic cartels in Germany.[16]

By the turn of the century, then, the most important fields of industry in the great industrial nations had to a large degree come under the sway of consolidated groups. Whether in the form of trusts, cartels, oligopolies, or outright monopolies, these groups had reduced competition to a minimum — or eliminated it altogether. *International cartels did not arise in any significant number until these national consolidations were complete.*

*   *   *

International cartels are an outgrowth of the age of monopoly and an extension of that phenomenon to the global sphere. They could not have developed previously because cartels governing international trade have little chance of success unless domestic markets are under control, that is, unless the companies that might undersell the cartel on foreign markets have been destroyed or absorbed. The very success of the monopolists on the national level gave impetus to the international cartel movement. If restraint of competition worked so well at home, why waste resources in competing for foreign markets with powerful interests from other nations?

Naturally enough, the Germans took the lead in the effort. Robert Liefmann, one of the first authorities on cartels, published a study in 1897 describing some forty products subject to cartel agreements in international trade. The majority of the accords were between Germans and firms of another nationality: twenty-two involved German and English producers; thirteen, German and Austrian; ten, German and Belgian; nine, German and French.[17] Largely because Germany developed an extremely strong position in the chemicals industry, many of the first cartels — and later some of the most formidable mature cartels — involved chemicals. The Bismuth Syndicate, for example, was organized at the very dawn of the cartel epoch, in the 1870s, and was cited by Liefmann as one of the first "solidly organized international syndicates."[18] Borax, quinine, acetic acid, and carbide were also subject to early cartels.

Probably the most comprehensive early chemical cartel covered high explosives, and here the lead came from an English and an American company. In Europe, production of explosives was dominated by the Nobel Dynamite Trust, uniting the interests of the inventor of dynamite, Alfred Nobel. Nobel built a network of companies in Europe, Asia, Africa, and South America and organized most of them into two trusts: the Nobel Dynamite Trust Company, which joined the English and German firms; and the Société Centrale de Dynamite, which covered the French, Swedish, Italian, Spanish, and South American firms. Englishmen, Germans, and Frenchmen held most of the power on the boards of directors, but each country with a Nobel company in one of the trusts was allowed at least one director.

Meanwhile, U.S. gunpowder producers united under the aegis of the E. I. du Pont de Nemours Company — thus following the usual pattern of establishing "order" within national markets — which led to a cartel agreement signed in 1897 by the American group, headed by du Pont, and the Europeans, led by the Nobel Dynamite Trust and a German company, the Vereinigte Köln-Rottweiler Pulverfabriken of Cologne. The cartel barred both groups from building factories in the other's territories. It also divided the world into four sales territories for high explosives. The du Pont group received as its exclusive province the United States and its possessions, Central America, Colombia, and Venezuela (the other countries in South America were to be shared); the Nobel group received the rest of the world, with the exception of certain territories where free competition was allowed.[19]

Steel was another industry in which cartelization began very early, when such products as merchant bars and steel rails came under controls. Indeed, the history of the International Rail Makers Association (IRMA) illustrates how resilient some of the early cartels were. The IRMA was formed in 1883 by British, Belgian, and German producers who wanted to regulate their exports of steel rails. The need for the cartel arose from an overcapacity that developed after the first great wave of railroad construction in Europe. Under the terms of the accord, Britain was allotted 66 percent of the total export trade, Germany 27 percent, and Belgium 7 percent. These were soon adjusted to 63.5, 29, and 7.5 percent, respectively. Disputes over quotas persisted, however, and in 1886 the cartel collapsed. In 1904 it was reorganized, with French producers included as members. The American Steel Rail Makers group also joined that year, having successfully demanded as a precondition that the British give up their exclusive rights to Canada and Newfoundland. The IRMA later made arrangements with Spanish, Italian, Austro-Hungarian, and Russian rail makers as the situation required. In 1907 the IRMA was renewed for five years, and in 1912 for another three. By that date the changing relative importance of the various national industries was reflected in drastically altered quotas, as follows: Great Britain, 33.63 percent, United States, 23.13; Germany, 23.13; Belgium, 11.11; and France, 9.0. World War I brought an end to the cartel, and it was not reorganized until 1926.[20]

The Modern Cartel

The cartels in high explosives and steel rails, both in operation before the turn of the century, already included most of the features of the classic modern cartel's profile. The centerpiece of such a cartel is almost always the *home market protection agreement*. This establishes that the country where each member of the cartel is located shall be regarded as that member's exclusive territory; the other members agree not to sell their products there. (If one member already has a share of another's home market, the former may promise not to increase that share; or, as in the explosives cartel, all members may undertake not to underbid each other for sales at home.) Home market protection may seem innocuous enough, but in fact it causes an enormous reduction of competition on a world scale. Once a producer is freed from the fear that foreign competitors will be able to manufacture goods more cheaply and invade his home market, he is left with only domestic competitors — usually smaller firms — to worry about. With the home market protected, the cartel member not only has a secure, relatively predictable source of profit but can reap extraordinary gains by raising prices without risk of being undersold.

The counterpart to the home market protection agreement is the *hunting ground agreement*, which spells out the degree of competition that cartel members plan to allow in all parts of the world where they operate. Members often receive, besides their home market, exclusive "hunting grounds," which tend to correspond to traditional spheres of commercial and political interest: U.S. firms usually receive the nations lying in or around the Caribbean Sea; British firms, the Commonwealth countries; French firms, present and former French colonies; German firms, northern and Eastern Europe; Japanese firms, East and Southeast Asia; and so on. Other hunting grounds may be shared by the members, or declared "open" territory.

In addition to sharing out hunting grounds, most classic cartels have some mechanism for *fixing prices and quotas* in "open" markets. In the case of a mass-produced, uniform commodity such as steel rails or many chemicals, the members may simply decide that each shall have a set share of sales to a certain market and that all members shall quote the same price. In the case of sophisticated machinery or equipment, which is usually contracted for on the basis of competing bids, the system must be more complicated, with bids rigged so that each firm will "win" enough orders to account for its predetermined share of the market.

The electrical industry offers the best examples of another device central to modern cartels: the *agreement to exchange technology*, usually by trading rights to patents (cross-licensing) or by setting up patent pools. The power of the great electrical corporations was based originally on monopolies created by patents on new technological advances — and the monopolies earned such huge profits for the companies that they have been able to maintain their preeminent positions on national and international markets until today. In the United States, for example, the foundation for the structure of the entire industry was laid on January 27, 1880, when Thomas Alva Edison was granted a patent on the first commercially successful incandescent lamp. Edison, an inventor of genius, allied himself with J. Pierpont Morgan, a financier of genius, and the union bore fruit in 1882, when Morgan put together the General Electric Company, consolidating the Edison General Electric Company and its rival, the Thomson-Houston Company.

The next crucial step in the cartelization of the industry was the cross-licensing agreement between the new giant GE and the Westinghouse Electric and Manufacturing Company. George Westinghouse, owner of GE's chief rival, had at first refused to come to terms with the trust but was forced to submit after several years of brutal competition had caused Westinghouse stock to plummet. The battle was fought with the usual tactics of slashing prices, bribing politicians for government contracts, wooing away distributors, and so on, but it was also a war over technology, with each firm bringing patent infringement suits against the other. Finally, in 1896, the two companies agreed to recognize all of each other's patents in the electric lamp field and to trade rights to them, and this cease-fire in the technological conflict enabled the firms to agree on matters of price and market share. With its only significant domestic competitor now a cohort, GE could easily gobble up smaller lamp-producing firms. In 1911, GE, Westinghouse, and a few other companies were convicted of antitrust violations, but the paltry penalties in the case left their market control unbroken: GE held an overwhelming 80 percent of U.S. lamp output; Westinghouse held 13 percent; and independents clung to 7 percent.[21]

In Germany and England, the two countries whose electrical industries were strong enough to rival America's, the pattern of national consolidation was similar. Important cross-licensing agreements occurred in Germany as early as 1883, when the two leading German companies — the Telegrafenbauanstalt Siemens & Halske, which arose from the numerous inventions of Werner von Siemens, and the Deutsche Edison Gesellschaft (later AEG), founded on Edison patents — decided to share patents and divide the market. Some years later these two firms and a third, the Deutsche Gasluhlichtgesellschaft (later Auergesellschaft), organized a patent pool called the Drahtkonzern, or Filament Trust. (A patent pool differs from cross-licensing in that the participating firms place the patents they hold into common hands — usually a jointly owned subsidiary created for that purpose — instead of merely trading exclusive licenses.) Shortly afterward, in 1913, the four firms that dominated the English electrical industry formed a similar group called the Tungsten Lamp Association, with patent exchange and market quotas its main goals.

Naturally, the electrical companies did not limit themselves to agreements on the national level; international networks based on patent rights took shape at the turn of the century as well. The English Tungsten Lamp Association, for example, was in reality an international alliance, since two of the four members were linked to foreign firms: British Thomson-Houston, controlled by GE, and Siemens Brothers, Ltd., the British branch of the German firm. GE was participating in at least three major international patent accords by 1905: with the French Thomson-Houston Company, with the Tokyo Electric Company (which GE bought in 1905), and with British Thomson-Houston. The three leading German producers signed agreements with British companies in 1912, with French Thomson-Houston the same year, and with Philips of Holland, Watt of Vienna, and United Incandescent Lamp & Electricity of Hungary in 1913.[22] Earlier, the German firms took the lead in organizing one of the first formal international electrical cartels, which lasted from 1903 to 1914 and included Austrian, Hungarian, Italian, Dutch, and Swiss lamp producers in price-fixing agreements.

By the outbreak of World War I, then, the necessary conditions for the spread of international cartels had been met, most importantly the concentration of industry into trusts and monopolies on the national scale. Some industries had already experienced thirty years of intermittent cartelization, and the fundamental techniques of classic cartels — home market protection, hunting ground agreements, price fixing, market division, and technological accords — had been established. However, the industries we have discussed are only a few of those subject to cartel controls before the war. Trade in various metals and minerals, including lead, zinc, aluminum, and sulphur, was influenced by international cartels that attempted to reduce output when stocks on world markets rose too high. Tobacco products were tightly controlled in much of the world by a cartel of U.S. and British companies. Liefmann's list of cartels functioning before 1900 mentions such products and services as coal, textiles, ceramics, paper and pulp, and shipping. One German expert compiled a list of 112 international cartel accords as of 1912.[23]

The exigencies of war caused many of the cartels in existence in 1914, most of which were centered in Europe and primarily affected European markets, to disband. But the collapse did not last long; after the war the firms either resumed their old ties or created new ones. The trend toward private marketing controls in the world economy was already too well established for a few years of warfare to check it; and, in any case, the effect of the war was just the opposite. For several reasons, it encouraged the effusion of cartels that took place during the following decade.

One reason was the experience with wartime mobilization. During the hostilities, governments forced businessmen to standardize their products, coordinate output from scattered plants throughout entire industries, exchange technical expertise, and otherwise cooperate closely in pursuit of national aims. Particularly in Britain and the United States, they found that such cooperation often brought about striking increases in productivity. With the arrival of peace, industrialists were not eager to remain under the official controls that had prevailed during wartime, but neither were they eager to give up the advantages of collaboration. Having glimpsed the possibilities in centralized planning and coordination, industrialists were inclined to pursue them — but only according to their own designs.

World War I also left most advanced nations with industrial structures ill suited to peacetime. For certain products — particularly armaments, of course — there was tremendous overcapacity; for others, such as many consumer goods, capacity fell short of demand. The existence of huge war-related stockpiles of many strategic metals and other materials threatened the producing countries with disastrous price collapses as the stockpiles were sold off, glutting the markets. In other words, the war left in its wake economies that were maladjusted to peace, and the reconversion promised to be painful. In addition, the two decades following the war were plagued by political and economic instability, one result of which was monetary disturbance that put a great strain on international trade. Both these factors, industrial maladjustment and monetary instability, caused businessmen to long for the cushioning effects and long-term price security that market controls might bring.

The economic residue of the war inevitably dealt another blow to the ideology that vigorous competition is the best way to regulate production and distribution. American businessmen became perhaps the most vociferous advocates of "self-government in industry," that is, cooperation among ostensibly competing firms so as to create "orderly" markets.[24] This new entrepreneurial wisdom soon produced important political results. In 1918 the U.S. Congress passed the Webb-Pomerene Act, which allowed U.S. corporations to form export associations to market American goods jointly abroad — an activity which hitherto had been forbidden by the antitrust laws. In 1916 and 1920, respectively, the Shipping Act and the Merchant Marine Act were passed, permitting shipping companies to form cartels and jointly set rates. The year 1920 also brought a Supreme Court ruling in *U.S.* v. *United States Steel Corp.* that effectively halted any serious attempt to enforce the Sherman or Clayton acts for years to come. Proclaiming that "size is no offense," the Court absolved the world's greatest trust of any violations — and thus opened the door to an epoch of mergers that rivaled that of the turn of the century.

In Britain and France the same tendencies were in evidence. French industry continued its drive toward greater concentration by means of the *comptoirs,* or business syndicates, that were organized in one field after another. British businessmen, eager to regain their prewar standing in world trade, pointed out that in other countries industries were consolidating with official support and that Britain could not afford to be an exception. By the early 1920s the government had gotten the message and was energetically spurring amalgamation in coal, steel, shipbuilding, textiles, and other industries. Here as elsewhere "cooperation" was the watchword; for example, the extremely powerful Iron and Steel Federation worked closely with the government and through forty subordinate trade associations to set quotas and write up price schedules for its members.[25] At the same time, in younger, more vigorous industries, trusts were still being formed. The most important was Imperial Chemical Industries, created in 1926 from the union of four huge companies. Under the leadership of Sir Charles Mond, ICI ruled the British chemicals field and became a weighty influence on world markets as well through its cartel agreements with U.S. and German companies.

German industrialists soon followed suit. Although catastrophic inflation until 1924 undermined effective price cartels, the period saw the rise of immense private industrial conglomerates put together by such magnates as Fritz Thyssen and Hugo Stinnes. Criticism of the abuses of such monopolies led to an emergency decree issued on November 9, 1923, supposedly establishing some public supervision of the combines, including a Cartel Court. In fact, however, the court busied itself primarily with helping enforce cartel agreements, thus affording them further legitimacy.[26] After 1924, the policy of the German Republic, like the policy of the Empire before, was even more favorable to "rationalization" and cartelization of the economy than were those of Britain or the United States. The proudest example of the new German cartels was the Interessengemeinschaft Farbenindustrie A.G. (known as I. G. Farben, or simply IG), a chemicals trust formed in 1925 that combined the "big six" German producers. IG not only dominated the chemicals industry of Germany but also, in many branches, of the world; it was later to become a symbol of cartel perfidy.

It was during the 1920s that some of the most famous (or infamous) international cartels were organized. Although more complete discussion of them will be reserved for later chapters, those in several major industries should be mentioned here. The first comprehensive steel cartel was founded in 1926, with members from France, Germany, Belgium, Luxembourg, and the Saar, who among themselves accounted for two-thirds of all world exports of steel. Known as the Entente Internationale de l'Acier (EIA), the cartel operated mainly by setting production quotas and fining members who exceeded them. But the scheme was only partially successful, and the EIA (in this, its first incarnation) disbanded in 1931. A more durable cartel was formed in the petroleum industry in 1928, with the signing of the Achnacarry Agreement by the heads of the three largest oil companies of the time: Standard Oil of New Jersey (now Exxon), the Anglo-Persian Oil Company (now British Petroleum, or BP), and Shell. The crux of Achnacarry was that the companies agreed to preserve the status quo: they would not attempt to increase their market shares at the expense of the others; they pledged not to increase production faster than the growth of demand; and they promised to refrain from using surplus oil from one geographical market to drive down prices in another.

GE was the prime mover behind an extremely sophisticated cartel that controlled lamp production in much of the world. Founded in 1924, the cartel operated through a Swiss company, the Phoebus S.A. Compagnie Industrielle pour la Développement de l'Eclairage, whose members included Hungarian, British, German, Dutch, French, and U.S. firms, along with a number of GE's foreign subsidiaries. Phoebus, whose complex structure and administrative procedures were the forerunners of today's equally intricate electrical industry cartels, operated by fixing prices and market quotas for its members, standardizing quality, supervising the exchange of patents, and carrying out research, advertising, and statistical functions. Phoebus prospered until World War II, when the cartel went into recess.

In the chemicals industry cartel accords achieved during the 1920s have shaped the structure of the industry ever since. Many of these affected specific products, such as alkalies. But the most spectacular of all cartel agreements signed prior to the Depression was the Grand Alliance between du Pont and Imperial Chemicals Industries. Negotiated in 1929, on the eve of the economic cataclysm that was to bring about the "cartel decade," it bound the two firms in virtual partnership. Du Pont and ICI were already linked by agreements covering certain product sectors such as explosives. But the 1929 pact, known as the Patents and Processes Agreement, went much further. It established home market protection, division of territory, and exchange of licenses and know-how *for nearly every chemical product that both firms made,* including plastics, paints, acids, fertilizers, dyestuffs, insecticides, and disinfectants — to name just a few.[27] This quasi-merger of two of the world's three largest chemical firms (both of which made their peace with I. G. Farben by other means) was a harbinger of things to come.

The Golden Age of Cartels

The New York Stock Exchange collapse of October 1929 and the subsequent world-wide depression gave impetus to a cartel movement that already had the flow of economic history behind it, and for the next ten years cartels more or less openly ruled international trade. At first, however, the Depression had a rather contradictory effect on cartels. Many cartels that had existed at the time of the crash were not able to withstand the pressures of plummeting demand in 1930–31; cartel discipline broke down as members scrambled to undersell each other, and the agreements were abandoned. At the same time, however, the Depression convinced more industrialists and politicians than ever before that free competition was not the ideal arbiter of commerce, and the latter tendency proved stronger in the long run. What one source calls the "new converts to the philosophy of economic restrictionalism"[28] soon engineered a proliferation of new cartels, while most of the cartels destroyed by the impact of the crash had regrouped by the mid-1930s. Even the lip service usually paid to liberal principles of free trade was largely set aside; what was at stake was survival (one aspect of which was preparation for the next war), and if cartels would bring calm to the perilous seas of international trade, then competition be damned. Never before or since the Depression have so many espoused cartel practices so openly.

One result of the Depression was that governments became more directly involved in cartels — particularly governments of nations that depended heavily on the export of raw materials. When demand for most goods plummeted in 1930–31, such nations found themselves with tremendous overcapacity. Producers, usually private businessmen or farmers, began to clamor for protection against the ruinous price wars that would surely result if every country tried to dump its full production on sagging international markets. Governments responded, and the result was a series of agreements regulating trade in various commodities. The first international wheat agreement dates from 1933; it involved an agreement by the United States, Canada, Australia, and Argentina to limit their exports, while thirteen importing nations in Europe promised not to increase their domestic capacity. In 1931, under the so-called Chadbourne Plan, negotiators for the sugar industries of all the major producing countries agreed to set specified tonnage limits on exports for the next five years. In 1933 tea producers, who had been trying to build effective market controls since 1920, finally achieved their goal. Similar arrangements — the basic ingredient of which was to restrict production and/or exports — were reached in tin (1931), rubber (1934, following a less successful program in the 1920s), meat (1936, as regarded exports to Great Britain), and others.

Government involvement of quite another sort was to be found in Germany after the Nazi takeover of 1933. Epitomizing the German tendency to scorn free competition and regard industry as the handmaiden of the state, the Nazis reorganized German business into even more concentrated groups than had existed before and brought its operations under much closer official supervision. Some of the new super-units formed by the Nazis were essentially the old national cartels with new names, but there were important changes: membership in the industrial groups was made compulsory, and domestic price competition was largely eliminated. Under the Nazis, private industrial decisions, particularly regarding foreign trade, became indistinguishable from state policy — and cartels were very much favored by the regime as a means of asserting German economic power abroad and of gaining access to foreign technology.

Private cartels also flourished during the 1930s. The petroleum companies solidified their control over marketing by setting up local cartels in most of the important consuming countries. Agreements signed in 1930, 1933, and 1934 described, each with greater precision, just how these local cartels were to function, and by the mid-1930s they were efficiently fixing prices and market quotas. Within the United States, the oil companies during this period erected a system of controls — under the rubric *conser-*

vation — that meshed neatly with the international cartel system created by the Achnacarry Agreement. The Phoebus cartel had considerable success in maintaining high prices on most markets during the Depression years (although competition from outsiders, notably the Japanese, took its toll in some countries, the United States among them). New alliances between chemical producers, including important pacts between du Pont and I. G. Farben, supplemented the basic ones signed in the 1920s, but a large number of major new cartels sprang up as well. In 1931 Alcoa and I. G. Farben reached an agreement governing the production and marketing of magnesium in the United States. Dow Chemical, the other major producer, joined the cartel in 1934, and it lasted until 1941, when the members pleaded nolo contendere to an antitrust suit filed by the Justice Department. The first world-wide comprehensive cartel of nitrogen producers was formed in 1930; although the Depression caused it to collapse in 1931, the next year it was reorganized, and it had good success until World War II broke it up. A comprehensive international cement cartel was founded in Europe in 1937. World trade in sheet and plate glass were cartelized in the 1930s. Phosphate rock came under control in 1933, with U.S. producers, acting through a Webb-Pomerene association, playing a major role in the cartel.

A further, more astounding illustration of how far Western industrialists had progressed toward complete abandonment of competitive tenets is the Düsseldorf Agreement of 1939. This was nothing less than an accord between the largest British and German capitalists, *acting in unison and with the approval and assistance of their governments,* to join their entire industrial systems together into a single, all-embracing cartel governing their international trade, that is, both trade between the two countries and exports to third countries. The agreement was signed by representatives of the Reichsgruppe Industrie and the Federation of British Industries on March 16, after a conference in Düsseldorf.[29] It included the following provisions:

> 4. The two bodies are agreed that the objective to be attained is that the export of all countries should be conducted in such a way as to ensure a fair return for the products of those countries. Hence it is agreed that it is essential to replace destructive competition wherever it may be found by constructive cooperation, designed to foster the expansion of world trade, to the mutual benefit of Great Britain, Germany, and all other countries.
> 10. ... They are encouraged in this task owing to the fact that a considerable number of agreements between individual German and British industrial groups are already in existence.... They are glad to state that approximately a further fifty industrial groups have already signified their willingness in principle to negotiate at an early date.

These sentiments were endorsed just five months before Germany's invasion of Poland plunged the two signatories into war.

It was not only the war that put a stop to the rampant cartelization epitomized by the Düsseldorf Agreement. Public opposition to trusts and cartels had been rising throughout the 1930s, particularly in the United States, where the Depression had provoked a strong antibusiness mood. In 1938–39 inquiries of the Temporary National Economic Committee (TNEC) into economic concentration fueled the public's outrage. Other investigations arising from wartime problems heightened it still further. Out of one of these — an antitrust case brought by Thurman Arnold, President Roosevelt's assistant attorney general in charge of the Justice Department's Antitrust Division — came the story that inflamed Americans most and thus was most directly responsible, in the political sense, for the sharply anticartel position of the U.S. government after the war: the I. G. Farben–Standard Oil (New Jersey) agreement restricting the development of synthetic rubber.

The complex tale of synthetic rubber can only be summarized briefly here.[30] It involves three companies: IG, du Pont, and Standard Oil. In the 1920s the first two had discovered separate methods of producing commercially viable synthetic rubber. Du Pont's type was called Neoprene; I. G. Farben's was known as Buna. IG feared that du Pont's product was superior and therefore was eager to enter into a cross-licensing agreement that would give IG the German rights to Neoprene; but du Pont, having the same confidence in its own product, resisted turning it over to IG. On the other hand, IG did possess other patented chemical processes and know-how that du Pont actively desired. Standard Oil, which was primarily interested in the realms of the chemical industry that affected petroleum refining, was desperately eager to get rights to IG's spectacular advances in the techniques of making gasoline from coal. This conjunction of interests gave IG the opportunity to play the two American firms against each other, which IG did masterfully for more than a decade.

First, IG signed agreements with Standard in 1929 and 1930 accomplishing two basic goals: the companies agreed to stay out of each other's industrial territories, that is, IG would not move into the petroleum industry, and Standard would stay out of chemicals, thus freeing Standard from the threat of IG's coal hydrogenation process; and they set up a joint subsidiary, Jasco, in order to exploit together any "new chemical processes" either might discover in the borderline area between the oil and chemicals industries. Synthetic rubber was one such area, and Standard Oil soon began pressuring IG to give Jasco the U.S. rights to produce Buna rubber. Throughout the 1930s IG stalled, citing government opposition. The Nazi regime certainly was reluctant to turn over Buna technology to a U.S. company, but an additional reason seems to have been that IG wanted to maintain control over Buna as a bargaining chip in its continuing attempts to get Neoprene technology from du Pont. For several crucial years the situation remained unchanged: Standard could not get access to Buna; and du Pont restricted production of Neoprene, apparently out of a desire to reach some accord with IG before risking full-scale development. In 1938 du Pont and IG compromised by exchanging certain essential processes but not the rights to produce the other's brand of synthetic rubber; yet IG still would not turn over Buna to Standard. In 1939, with the outbreak of war, IG finally released the Buna patents (a move that was then unavoidable, since as enemy property the patents were seized in Britain) but withheld know-how and imposed restrictive terms for the United States that made them essentially useless. Therefore, thanks to IG's manipulations and the deep desire of du Pont and Standard to have all markets securely cartelized before embarking on any risky ventures, the United States found itself in December 1941 with "only the rudiments" of a synthetic rubber industry — at a time when the Japanese seizure of Southeast Asian rubber plantations made rubber substitutes among the most essential of all materials for the war effort.

To an aroused American public the IG–Standard Oil case became an infuriating symbol of how cartels had been used — particularly by the Germans, but with the cooperation of U.S. companies — to undermine the Allies' economies and leave them unprepared for war. "American business houses, in conspiracy among themselves and in alliance with foreign commercial interests ... suppressed the production of critical materials, deprived the allies of weapons of war, and unwittingly divulged military secrets and vital production data to foreign governments," wrote Thurman Arnold and J. Stevens Livingston in the *Harvard Business Review*.[31] The Standard Oil antitrust case was settled with a slap on the wrist for the defendants, but the matter was soon brought into the public forum again by Senator Harry Truman's Special Committee to Investigate the National Defense Program. During the hearings Truman off-handedly stated that he felt Standard Oil's officials were guilty of treason.[32]

Damage to national security was not the only argument — although during the war it may have been the most persuasive — advanced against cartels. Americans were increasingly aware of the broad scope of cartels in foreign trade and of the fact that cartels cost them money. The revulsion against two decades of spreading commercial collusion amounted to a new political atmosphere in which the previous government tolerance of, or open support for, private cartels was replaced by hostility. Between 1939 and 1945, the Justice Department initiated 52 antitrust proceedings against international cartels, and of the 165 companies involved as defendants only 36 were foreign.[33] Also, a flood of books, pamphlets, articles, and studies of cartels began to appear in the United States. In addition to the TNEC and the Truman Committee, major hearings disclosing cartel practices were staged by the Senate Committee on Patents under Senator

Homer T. Bone and by the Senate Special Committee on War Mobilization, headed by Senator Harley M. Kilgore. For the first time the details of
many cartel operations were widely publicized.

The chorus of American opposition to cartels was not entirely political
in origin; it also reflected the stronger position of U.S. industry. By 1944 it
was apparent that the United States would emerge from the war as the
world's most powerful nation. To some businessmen and politicians this
meant that the country's interest lay in competition rather than cooperation or restriction, and, although opposition did arise in some quarters,
there is no doubt that America's economic predominance made the need
for cartels appear much less pressing.

In early September 1944, President Roosevelt made clear what the postwar U.S. position on cartels would be. The year before he had named an
Inter-Departmental Executive Committee, known as the Cartel Group,
and headed by Dean Acheson, then assistant secretary of state, to make a
study of cartels and relay recommendations. But before the group's report
was even released, Roosevelt made public a letter he had written to Secretary of State Cordell Hull in which he pointed out that cartels contra-
vened the spirit of approved U.S. commercial practice, as embodied in the
antitrust laws, and said that "cartel practices which restrict the free flow
of goods in foreign commerce will have to be restricted," perhaps through
action by the United Nations. He also called for the "eradication" in Germany of "these weapons of economic warfare." The *New York Times,* in
reporting on Roosevelt's letter, observed, "The program would have other
nations subscribe, in effect, to the philosophy of our antitrust laws in international trade, with the exception of some Government-regulated
commodities."[34] Roosevelt was cautious not to go too far in asserting
America's right to impose the anticartel outlook on others — for example,
our British allies — but that was clearly what the administration intended
to do as far as it was practicable.

With the end of the war, the United States embarked on its anticartel
campaign, achieving fairly good results. U.S.-sponsored resolutions
containing anticartel language (or, more vaguely, criticism of restrictive
business practices) passed in international forums such as the 1945 Inter-
American Conference on Problems of War and Peace. The Truman administration proposed the foundation of an International Trade Organization under U.N. auspices, the functions of which would include to "prevent business practices which restrain competition, restrict access to
markets or foster monopolistic control in international trade"; the State
Department's suggested charter for the ITO spelled out the mechanisms
to be employed in such a task. (However, the charter was never ratified,
and the ITO never became a reality.[35]) In occupied Germany, the Allied
Control did its best to break up the German cartels; in the U.S. zone addi-

tional measures were enacted limiting the size of German firms to 10,000 employees. And, at home, the Supreme Court ruled in a landmark case in 1949 that U.S. Webb-Pomerene export cartels may not take part in international arrangements.[36]

Indeed, as the years passed it almost seemed that American antitrust beliefs had triumphed around the world. The treaty establishing the Organization for Economic Cooperation and Development mentioned control of cartels as one of its goals, and the Treaty of Rome founding the European Economic Community included strong antitrust clauses. By the mid-1960s, Germany and twelve other European nations had anticartel legislation on the books.[37] It appeared that the cartel stranglehold on international trade had been broken.

That was not the case, however — and not only because Europe's weaker enthusiasm for antitrust precepts made cartel laws there generally ineffective. Neither national legislation nor international resolutions could keep the cartels from regrouping and adjusting to the new shape of the postwar world. In the final analysis, the U.S. government's short-lived crusade never amounted to much more than an attempt to halt with words the process of economic concentration.

The Postwar Resurgence

The destruction wrought by the war upon productive facilities in Europe and Japan was so extensive that in many industries cartelization immediately after 1945 was either impossible or unnecessary. The established patterns of international trade that had been worked out so laboriously during the 1920s and 1930s could not be resumed, simply because many participants had been so severely damaged. With most of the advanced Western nations engaged in a strenuous effort to rebuild, those firms — many of them American, naturally — which had survived with their capacities intact had little trouble finding markets and satisfactory prices for their products. Along with the new political atmosphere in the postwar decade, these circumstances caused something of a hiatus in cartel activity.

Gradually, however, as recovery progressed cartels revived. Often the impetus was overcapacity as new plants were built. Postwar cartels, however, differed in important respects from their predecessors. Because the bulk of this book concerns the workings of postwar cartels, we will not recount their history in any detail here, but certain basic changes undergone by cartels after 1945 should be noted.

Essentially, the strategy of international cartels in the postwar period has been to perfect their camouflage, to become, insofar as possible, invisible and intangible. Both public opinion and the spread of antitrust laws have made the relatively open cartelization of the 1930s an impossibility. The cartels have been forced to find less obvious forms for collective market controls, and they have succeeded. In a few countries, Switzerland being the most notable example, the laws are friendly enough that formal international cartels can still find a safe and secret haven for their administrative headquarters. Corporations also make use of the international export cartels that are legal in such nations as Great Britain and Germany. Although such cartels are meant to affect only export markets, they frequently serve as a cover for schemes that regulate home markets as well.[38] Finally, cartels have relied increasingly on apparently innocent commercial and technological links such as patent exchange, cooperation in research, and joint ventures, which can discreetly muffle competition.[39]

In some industries the regulation of competition since the war has been accomplished largely on the basis of gentlemen's agreements, or even unspoken understandings, which often maintain the effect of an old cartel that was allowed to lapse or was declared illegal. Such arrangements do not involve the standard cartel apparatus: written accords, regular meetings, an administrative staff. The degree of active collusion varies widely. Firms may never actually *agree* to restrict competition but may simply refrain from attempts to undersell each other or alter market shares. Often, in an oligopoly of this type, the largest firm exercises "price leadership," with the others setting identical prices in response to the leader's moves. Somewhat less nebulous (although not necessarily any more effective) is the case in which the companies actually reach an informal, verbal agreement. This does constitute a cartel and has the advantage of being extremely difficult to detect.

One industry that has been heavily influenced by such informal or tacit arrangements is aluminum. Prior to the war, trade in aluminum was controlled by a cartel headed by a Canadian firm, Aluminum, Ltd. (now Alcan), the largest exporter. Alcan represented its erstwhile parent firm, the Aluminum Company of America (Alcoa), in the cartel; the home market protection this afforded Alcoa helped the company preserve its monopoly over aluminum production in the United States until 1939. After the war the cartel was broken up, partly as a result of an antitrust case won by the U.S. Justice Department. But the system of price coordination survived; in producing countries, the price set by local producers was respected; and Alcan remained the price leader in markets where there was little or no local production. Except for rare occasions, Alcan did not try to raise its exports to the U.S. market by cutting prices — and Alcoa reciprocated by matching Alcan's prices on foreign markets. These arrangements, supplemented by joint ventures and research agreements among the major firms, regulated the aluminum trade without need for a formal cartel at least until the 1970s, when the entry of new producers brought more competition into the industry.[40]

The postwar hostility to cartels led other industries to rely chiefly on agreements involving technology. The best examples here come from the various branches of the chemicals industry. Companies manufacturing industrial chemicals and pharmaceuticals, whose fortunes ride on the constant development of new products and processes, have long practiced cross-licensing of patents to avoid competition. But in the 1920s and 1930s the industry also was cartelized on the basis of comprehensive agreements between the giant firms, such as the Grand Alliance of ICI and du Pont, or the pact between I. G. Farben and Standard Oil. Accords of this type, dividing up markets for the entire range of products manufactured by the firms, are relatively rare today. Instead, cartels in chemicals work on a product-by-product basis, through innumerable patent licenses that the major firms tend to grant only to each other, excluding smaller outsiders (see Chapter 5). Also important to such industries as chemicals and electronics are joint research projects; when powerful firms agree to share the cost and fruits of technological discoveries, the resulting market control can be every bit as effective as a cartel fixing prices and quotas.

This is not to say that formal cartels have expired entirely — or even that they are an endangered species. In fields such as oil, steel, and electrical equipment, classic cartel structures either emerged from the war unscathed or were reassembled not long afterward. The International Electrical Association, now a half-century old, stands as a monument to the durability of classic cartels in the modern age. In the years since the war, dozens of other cartels have taken shape, manipulated their respective markets for varying periods of time, and then fallen apart, sometimes as a result of public exposure. Secret international cartels have been discovered affecting trade in such diverse goods as quinine, nitrogen, rayon, linoleum, electrical cables, sugar, and uranium. Hundreds of export cartels, many of which include members from more than one country, are on register in the industrialized nations. How many cartel contracts remain secret is impossible to judge.

The general trend for cartels in the postwar period has been toward subtler methods of collusion. This trend goes hand in hand with another critical development: the expansion of transnational corporations. The link between cartels and TNCs is not new, of course; many of the firms involved in early cartels already fit the OECD's definition of a transnational as "an enterprise which carries out operations, such as production of goods or the provision of services, in more than one country through component units which are subject to some measure of central control."[41] What is new is the enormous growth of direct foreign investment by these firms since 1945, and their growing share of the capitalist world's economy.

U.S. corporations led the initial wave of TNC expansion. In 1946 the total book value of U.S. direct foreign investment was $7.2 billion; by 1975 it had shot up to $137 billion, trebling between 1950 and 1960, and trebling again between 1960 and 1971.[42] Foreign affiliates of American TNCs also more than trebled between 1950 and 1966, from about 7000 to 23,000. Later, in the 1970s, German and Japanese firms began to expand abroad even faster than the Americans, and other countries, particularly the United Kingdom, France, and Switzerland, also had large stocks of direct foreign investment.[43] The grand total of TNC investment abroad rose from $105 billion in 1967 to $287 billion in 1976 (although these figures exaggerate the increase somewhat because they do not account for inflation or exchange rate fluctuations).[44] In 1971 the total production of transnational firms amounted to an astonishing 20 percent of the entire capitalist world's combined gross national products.[45]

This unprecedented growth has naturally brought a sharp increase in economic concentration and centralization of power. Even *among* the transnationals, concentration is marked. In 1973 there were some 10,000 firms that possessed at least one foreign affiliate and thus could be considered "transnational." Yet a U.N. report that year noted that under 300 American firms accounted for 70 percent of all U.S. direct foreign investment. In the United Kingdom 165 companies held over 80 percent of foreign investment, and in Germany a mere 82 firms controlled more than 70 percent.[46] As these few hundred largest firms enlarge their operations and spread their investments to more countries, a greater portion of *all economic activity* comes under their control.[47] Perhaps the most outstanding trait of transnational firms is their tendency to centralize power. Indeed, it is often argued that the key to the global firms' success is their ability to process information and streamline management so that far-flung networks of subsidiaries are run from central headquarters as highly integrated units rather than as collections of semi-autonomous fiefdoms.[48]

Concentration and centralization — both these trends have implications for cartels. The fewer the firms vying for any particular market, the easier it is to organize them, particularly if they have plentiful experience with restrictive agreements. Once again, the agreements need not be detailed cartel contracts; with a small number of firms involved, patent exchanges and joint ventures may be the ideal methods for avoiding competition. The close control exercised by transnationals over their subsidiaries can also make a cartel more efficient. A transnational corporation is actually a system of linked firms, often extending through dozens of countries, and its policies are quickly transmitted through the system. An agreement to restrict competition among several TNCs thus can be put into practice around the world by subsidiaries *in situ*, using their knowledge of local conditions to good advantage. Subsidiaries judge the best mix of local production and imports from parent firms abroad; they report on local politics; they evaluate potential local competitors; and they can be used to set up mini-cartels within specific markets, as with IBEMEP in Brazil. An international cartel that operates solely by means of exports must work at a distance from its markets — and distance creates uncertainty and risk. The new transnational structure of industry has given cartels the power to "organize" markets in the postwar decades more effectively than ever before.

The history of cartels since 1945, then, has been one of changes in form but not in essence. From a political standpoint the changes have been completely successful, as cartels (with the exception of OPEC) have vanished from public consciousness as a problem. Corporation executives, government officials, and many economists deny that cartels have any impact on today's world. In the following chapters, however, we will demonstrate the contrary.

2

Electrical Connections: The Classic Cartel

OUR discussion must begin with the cartel that today epitomizes the classic breed: the International Electrical Association. No other organization so perfectly embodies what one might imagine an ideal cartel to be; and other IEA attributes make it a fascinating object of study as well. In the first place, it has lasted for half a century in much the same form as when it was founded. It governs trade throughout the world in a branch of manufacturing — heavy electrical equipment — of high importance to developed and developing countries alike. It includes virtually all the industry's major corporations. It is a completely private group, handling annual sales of about $2 billion. Yet it pretends to be a simple trade association and camouflages its real activities behind a facade of statistical and market research. Its officers and member firms, on the rare occasions when they will talk about the IEA at all, refuse to admit it is a cartel, even when confronted with documentary evidence that leaves no doubt as to the truth.[1]

Ironically, the very existence of that evidence is another fact that makes the IEA worthy of extended attention. Private cartels, for obvious reasons, are totally secretive. Except for the rare instances when they become the object of government investigations, or the even more unusual cases when information leaks to journalists or other private citizens, cartels operate in obscurity. The sheer longevity of the IEA, however, probably made it inevitable that the group's wall of secrecy would be breached — as it has been, more than once. And although the breaches have been infrequent, they have been serious, especially the most recent. Most of what is known

36

about the IEA before the war is contained in a Federal Trade Commission report published in 1948, the result of an antitrust case against the cartel.[2] In 1957 a British government report offered a few details on the association's postwar activities.[3] In 1965 Dr. Barbara Epstein, an economist working for the New York consulting firm of Horace J. DePodwin Associates, obtained a copy of the basic agreement covering Section H (transformers) of the IEA, along with financial data on prices and sales in that section.[4] Five years later Kurt Mirow received the agreements of the cartel's branch in Brazil. In 1977 Dr. Richard Newfarmer, an economist at Notre Dame University, obtained from industry sources copies of the contracts covering nine IEA product sections. Then, two years later, there came a massive leak. A former cartel staff member passed to Mirow some three hundred documents, filling some two thousand pages, from internal IEA files: contracts, letters, memoranda, price formulas, minutes of meetings, and so forth. The sum of these revelations is a picture of IEA operations that, although not complete, is uncommonly rich in detail.

 ⁂

The range of products manufactured in the many branches of the electrical industry is extremely broad, and the products themselves are increasingly complex. From light bulbs to turbines, from electric shavers to communication systems for supersonic bombers, from Waring blenders to spaceships — the industry plays a direct or indirect part in virtually every aspect of our daily lives.

But the most striking aspect of the electrical industry is that, despite its many ramifications, it remains largely the province of a few corporations founded on the inventions of equally few American and European men at the end of the nineteenth century. The greatest of the inventors were Thomas Edison, George Westinghouse, Werner von Siemens, Elihu Thomson, and Joseph Swan. When these names are joined by a handful of others — Charles Parsons, Sebastian Ferranti, Charles Brown, Walter Boveri, Gustav de Laval, Escher Wyss, and Jonas Wenstrom — we have the fathers of the giant multinationals that today dominate world trade in most important branches of the industry.[5] With the sole exception of the Japanese companies, which rose to their current position on the basis of technology developed after the basic U.S. and European patents expired — and on the basis of cheap labor and strong government support — it has proved difficult for new firms of any but insignificant size to break into the industry. (The few powerful new firms that have arisen did so by developing entirely new product sectors: for example, IBM in computers, Xerox in copying machines, and several companies in the still very youthful semiconductor industry.)

The difficulty of entry into the established sectors of the electrical industry has a number of causes. One is the continuous and rapid-paced technical innovation that is required for survival, demanding astronomical research and development investments that only the giant firms can afford. Another is the efficiency that can be achieved through large-scale operations, thus giving big firms a competitive edge over ambitious but smaller ones. This factor operates with particular force in the capital goods division of the industry — the production of machinery that produces and transmits electrical power — where, for example, it has been shown that a huge power plant employing huge generators can be considerably more efficient than a smaller plant using machinery that could be built by smaller firms. But along with economies of scale and technological innovation there is still another reason that the major firms have maintained their hold on the electrical industry: their extensive use of restrictive business practices.

For purposes of clarity it is helpful to separate the electrical industry into its two components: capital goods and consumer goods. Electrical industry cartels have tended to operate in either one or the other branch, although most of the biggest firms — those which manufacture a full line of products, from transistor radios to nuclear reactors — belong to cartels in both branches, so one may presume a good deal of cross-fertilization takes place.

We mentioned in Chapter 1 the most famous prewar cartel in the consumer goods branch of the industry: the Phoebus incandescent lamp association. Phoebus had its roots in two events that took place in 1919. The first was the birth of a German firm known as Osram, which resulted from the merger of the lamp operations of the three major German producers: AEG, Siemens, and Auergesellschaft. Osram soon acquired other companies as well, leaving only one concern of any size to oppose it in Germany. Also in 1919, GE created a subsidiary, International General Electric, to handle the company's foreign interests — and in the process to protect GE's domestic market, because the firm was worried that European producers might attempt to invade its lucrative American preserve. International GE promptly entered into patent and process-sharing accords with most major foreign producers. But GE was concerned to develop an even more secure method of suppressing the vagaries of a competitive market. When a European lamp producers' cartel that Osram founded in 1921 collapsed in 1924, International GE opened a round of intensive talks with the Europeans in order to hammer out a more durable union. GE thus became the prime mover behind the cartel that was formed on December 24, 1924, with the signing of a document innocuously called the Convention for the Development and Progress of the International Incandescent Electric Lamp Industry.[6]

The Phoebus cartel, named after the Swiss firm created to administer it, established three market regions: home territories, British overseas territories, and "common" territories. Markets in the home territories, amounting to twelve countries, were, of course, largely reserved for the companies based there who already held a preponderant share of the trade. British overseas territories were the province of British lamp manufacturers, although other companies were allowed minor shares. The rest of the world, except the United States and Canada (which were tacitly left to the GE–Westinghouse group) was common territory. Each member of Phoebus was given a quota of sales within each of the three types of territory. With its home market reserved, the member was free to use its common territory sales quota anywhere in that territory. However, the members paid fines for overselling their quotas, and the money was redistributed to members who had undersold theirs. Also, members agreed to pool all their lamp patents and open their plants to inspection by any other members. In other words, there was almost no incentive to compete, except in the negotiations leading to determination of market shares. Home markets were protected from invasion. Nothing could be gained from pursuing an aggressive sales policy in the common territory because fines would have to be paid on any sales exceeding the quota. Even if a company made a striking technological advance, it would have to share it (although it could charge a licensing fee to be determined by negotiation or arbitration) or pull out of the cartel, with all the risks that action entailed.

Although neither General Electric, its wholly owned subsidiary, International GE, nor its close American associate, Westinghouse, formally belonged to the Phoebus cartel, there is not the slightest doubt that all three companies formed an integral part of the cartel's operations.[7] The impetus for the organization of Phoebus came originally from J. M. Woodward, who was in charge of International GE's light bulb business in Europe. Subsidiaries of GE based in England, Brazil, China, and Mexico belonged to the cartel and were known as the "overseas group."[8] American producers were linked to cartel members through agreements that scrupulously respected the cartel's general market policies or fleshed them out even further: for example, although Phoebus did not explicitly assign South America to GE as a captive territory, its members recognized the American combine as the leading power there, with "rights" to set prices and conditions of sale for goods covered under the agreements.

Phoebus left control over prices to the respective national associations, which tended to set them higher or lower depending on the level of competition presented by noncartel members. In Holland, for example, where Philips overwhelmingly monopolized lamp sales, prices for 25-watt, 40-watt, and 60-watt metal filament lamps in 1938 were 32, 59, and 70 cents, respectively. In Germany, where Osram held sway, the equivalent prices were 30, 36, and 48 cents. However, in Sweden, where the Swedish Cooperative Union built a lamp production plant and undersold Phoebus companies, prices were only 23, 27, and 33 cents. And in the United States all three types sold for 15 cents. Part of the reason for GE's low prices was that the huge U.S. market allowed the company to achieve major economies of scale so that the lamps were simply cheaper to produce. But another reason was the threat of competition from Japan, where 1938 lamp prices were one-half those in the United States and whose exports of lamps to the United States rose dramatically during the 1930s. General Electric battled against the Japanese lamps by cutting prices and threatening patent infringement suits against wholesalers that handled Japanese lamps. But while GE's prices were relatively low, its profits remained very high during the 1930s. In the years for which data are available, GE's lamp profits never sank below 20 percent on its average capital investment in that division, and between 1935 and 1939 those profits ranged between 33 and 47 percent.[9]

Another intriguing aspect of Phoebus's operations involved quality control — which in this case seems to have meant attempts to produce lamps of shorter life. The cartel's stated goal was to standardize lamps, which might have brought certain benefits; but Phoebus neglected to publicize the fact that its idea of standardization also meant more lamp sales because the bulbs burned out sooner. Almost immediately after its formation the cartel stipulated a standard life for incandescent bulbs of 1000 hours, despite the fact that firms were capable of producing, at a somewhat lower output, bulbs lasting 2500 hours.[10] Documents obtained by the U.S. government in its antitrust suit against GE allow glimpses of executives highly annoyed by companies, including some cartel members, that insisted on producing long-life lamps. J. M. Woodward set the tone in a letter of September 19, 1924: "All manufacturers are committed to our program of standardization, as well as the adoption of our formulae for arriving at the economic life of lamps. . . . This is expected to double the business of all parties within five years, independently of all other factors tending to increase it."[11]

By 1934, however, the effects of the Depression were being felt, and apparently some companies could not resist the temptation to cheat a little by selling lamps built for high voltages, which at normal voltages would burn longer. The head of Philips protested to an executive of International General Electric:

> This . . . is a very dangerous practice and is having a most detrimental influence on the total turnover of the Phoebus Parties. Especially with a view to the strongly decreased prices in many countries, this may have serious consequences for Phoebus and after the very strenuous efforts we made to emerge from a period of long-life lamps, it is of the greatest importance that we do not sink back into the same mire by paying no attention to voltages and supplying lamps that will have a very prolonged life.[12]

GE, while insisting that lamp life was only one factor in the complicated variables determining lamp efficiency (that is, the amount of light delivered for each watt of power consumed), repeatedly did its best to conceal from consumers any reduction in lamp life. Witness a 1937 letter from a GE official to the Champion Lamp Works: "Decision has just been made to change the life of the 200-watt 110–120 volt PS30 bulb lamp from 1000 hours design and published to 750 hours design and published. . . . (W)e are giving no publicity whatever to the fact that the change is contemplated."[13]

The Phoebus agreement withstood the severe test of the Depression: it lasted until war broke out in 1939. Even during the war, while formal collaboration between companies from Axis and Allied countries was impossible, the firms did their best not to let the entire framework collapse. In fact, two parallel cartels soon formed, one of which included Philips, the British, and the American "overseas group."[14] But in 1941 came the beginning of the end for Phoebus as an all-embracing cartel: that year the U.S. government filed an antitrust suit against GE, Westinghouse, Philips, and several other firms, alleging numerous illegal restraints of trade, including activities associated with the Phoebus cartel. In 1949, GE and Philips were found guilty of violating the Sherman Act by operating the cartel and protecting GE's near monopoly in the U.S. lamp market. Westinghouse was not convicted but was included in the consent decree barring further violations.[15]

Cartelizing Capital Goods

Just six years after founding Phoebus, six of its members, along with three other firms, agreed to cartelize the capital goods branch of the electrical industry as well.

In some ways the market situation for heavy equipment was the opposite of that for lamps. Lamps can be produced with relative ease by small concerns; thus it is more difficult to "discipline" the market. The major firms were faced with the constant threat of competition, even if only minor harassment, in their home markets. For that reason the protection of home markets, allowing the large firms to stop worrying about invasion from abroad and concentrate on the elimination of pesky competitors at home, was the most important aspect of the cartel agreements governing lamps. Heavy equipment producers, on the other hand, had an easier time of it at home.[16] The high costs of manufacturing heavy machinery make it impossible for small firms to enter the business, and most countries practice a policy of urging purchasers of such machinery to "buy national" so

that the home market, in a sense, protects itself.[17] By and large, prices for
heavy equipment in the home markets were acceptably high. It was the
export market that posed problems, especially when demand began to
drop in the industrialized countries in the late 1920s, leaving some plants
with excess capacity. With companies willing to sell abroad at cost in
order to keep their factories running at capacity, savage competition hit
the export markets. The companies naturally reacted by doing what had
worked for them before: they formed a cartel.

On December 13, 1930, the International Notification and Compensation Agreement was signed in the Paris offices of International General
Electric.[18] The original signatories were nine of the most important producers of electrical capital goods in the world: AEG and Siemens, from
Germany; British Thomson-Houston, British Electric, The General Electric Co., Ltd., and Metropolitan Vickers, from Great Britain; Brown Boveri, from Switzerland; and Westinghouse and GE, from the United
States. Two months later the latter two firms organized a Webb-Pomerene
association called the Electrical Apparatus Export Association, whose
purpose was to coordinate the North American export business with the
cartel's policies.

The provisions of the INCA accord were every bit as detailed and complicated as those governing Phoebus. Notification and compensation were
in fact significant aspects of the agreement, but it extended considerably
further. Because home markets were relatively secure, the cartel only covered territories outside Western Europe, the Soviet Union, Japan, the
United States, Canada, and French and Spanish colonies, all of which were
considered the exclusive territory of one member or another.[19] The basic
process of the cartel worked as follows: when any member company was
invited to bid on a contract for heavy electrical equipment in a country
covered by the agreement, the company was obliged to inform the INCA
secretary of the invitation. The secretary would then notify all the prospective bidders of who their "competitors" were. Having talked the matter over, the companies, with the guidance of the secretary, would decide
who was to get the contract and at what price. The other companies
would then submit higher bids.

The INCA agreement also provided that the winning company would
pay a certain percentage of the contract price as "compensation" into a
fund administered by INCA. One of the fund's purposes was to reimburse
the other bidders for their costs in preparing bids. Naturally, the winning
bid was always padded by the amount that was to be paid in compensation
so that the winning company would not have to shave its profit margin.
This meant that the unsuspecting purchaser was not only the victim of
collusive bidding and the resulting high prices but also was being forced to
pay for the maintenance and administrative expenses of the cartel that
was gouging him.

By 1936 the original nine members of the heavy equipment cartel had expanded to thirty, and the organization had been restructured so that each specific type of apparatus was covered by a separate accord. In 1936 INCA itself was replaced by a new, more formal entity charged with administering the cartel and looking after the common interests of the members of all the sections: the International Electrical Association, whose first headquarters were in Zurich.

Like Phoebus, the IEA remained in full-scale operation until the war broke out. Indeed, just three weeks before Hitler invaded Poland a new quota system was worked out that met German demands for a larger market share.[20] Westinghouse dropped out altogether; General Electric agreed to continue notifying other members of bids but not to pay compensation. Britain's Trading with the Enemy Act of 1939 made it illegal for compensation from the fund to be paid to any foreign members, and changes in currency regulations in 1942 forbade British companies to pay compensation directly to foreigners. At the end of the war only a few active members remained: the British companies, which maintained the agreement in full effect among themselves; two Swiss firms; one Swedish company; and International GE.[21] A decade was to pass before the cartel would regain its former power.

*   *   *

Although the war disrupted cartel operations in the capital goods and consumer goods sectors alike, the peace affected them differently. The IEA eventually revived in a form closely resembling the original, but the Phoebus cartel did not. In 1945 General Electric withdrew from the group of firms from Allied countries that had maintained the Phoebus accords, claiming that it feared antitrust prosecution. Antitrust rulings in Britain weakened the postwar European lamp cartel arrangements,[22] and finally in 1955 further legal action brought them to an end altogether.[23] However, Richard Newfarmer notes that formal collusion has now been replaced by new systems — parallel pricing and international forbearance — that achieve an "only slightly less stable equilibrium."[24] In other words, the major lamp-producing firms, having established mutually exclusive bailiwicks and mutually satisfactory market shares before the war, have been able to preserve them without resort to a central organization like Phoebus. Instead a network of *national* cartels, maintained by the major firms' reluctance to invade each others' territory, has arisen.

Investigations during the 1950s, 1960s, and 1970s uncovered cartels operating on the national level in several developed and developing countries. The cartels employed the usual array of restrictive practices and bore distinct resemblance to their international forebears. Serious competition over prices or quality was rare; the British Monopolies Commission, for example, noted in 1968 that "there has been considerable uniformity of prices and discounts for main-brand lamps and changes have been introduced almost simultaneously."[25] In France, agreements signed in 1943 and renewed in 1951 established fixed market shares, combat procedures for the elimination of outsiders, and fines for infractions of the cartel rules.[26] In Canada, the three firms that controlled almost all lamp production — Canadian General Electric, Westinghouse Canada, and GTE Sylvania — were convicted in 1976 of collusive tendering on bids and of carrying out identical and simultaneous price changes from 1959 to 1967.[27] But the most intriguing aspect of the lamp industry is the degree to which a tacit system of home market protection seems to remain from the days of Phoebus. In the United States, for example, no European firm made any serious attempt to compete until 1974, when Philips acquired the lamp production plants of ITT. Similar conditions prevail in England, where, despite relatively high lamp prices and the absence of a protective tariff, European firms have made no substantial effort to enter the market. Aside from lamps supplied by Philips, a firm that long before the war owned an "established" share of the British market, imported lamps account for a minuscule portion of sales in Britain.[28]

Local lamp cartels are not limited to the developed countries. In India, the electric lamp industry was dominated from 1938 until the mid-1970s by a cartel originally organized by Philips and three British firms. These companies created a joint venture known as the Electric Lamp Manufacturers (India) Private Ltd., or ELM, whose primary function was to make lamps that were to be sold under the four brand names of the ELM owners. They also agreed to purchase all machinery, equipment, and parts from Philips (with the exception of lamp caps, which were bought either from an Indian firm or from a British company controlled by one of the members). This arrangement virtually eliminated price competition on the Indian market, the few independent manufacturers apparently following the price lead of the cartel.[29] In Brazil, where lamp producers appear to be locked in a fierce competitive struggle, market shares have remained mysteriously constant for many years: 50 percent for GE, 30 percent for Philips, and the remaining 20 percent for Osram and GTE.[30]

Radio, Television, and the ICDC

Another branch of the electronics consumer goods industry — radio and television — was cartelized largely on the basis of patent pools. Because radios and TVs can be manufactured by small firms, making entry into the industry relatively easy and thus threatening perpetual intense competition, the most effective way to control markets in this branch was to limit access to technology. As far back as the 1920s the companies that dominated radio technology — including many that belonged to cartels in other branches of the industry — began to pool their patents through a jointly owned subsidiary in order to end competition among themselves and keep outsiders at bay. The first important patent pool in the electrical industry was set up under the aegis of the Radio Broadcasting Company of America, RCA, which was first a subsidiary of GE and then became a joint venture of GE and Westinghouse. Although RCA was formally split from its two parents as a result of antitrust action in 1932, it continued to act as the administrator for a gigantic patent pool in the radio field which by the mid-1930s embraced more than four thousand patents. Outsiders who wished to enter the industry were forced to pay royalties on the patents, which were sold only as a group, a policy which often made entry prohibitively expensive.[31] As similar pools were set up in other countries, patent pooling neatly divided the world market for radio into distinct national markets, each ruled by the parties operating there.

This system worked excellently until 1965, when the feisty Zenith Corporation, one of the few independent national companies left in the U.S. consumer electronics industry, was sued for patent infringement by Hazeltine Research Inc., which had been formed to handle the patent pools administered by RCA. Zenith had invited the suit by refusing to accept a patent license to the Hazeltine patents. Besides revealing details of the system as it worked in the United States, the suit exposed the network of patent pools in Canada, Great Britain, and Australia, involving subsidiaries of General Electric, Philips, RCA, AT&T, and the English companies EMI and Marconi.[32] These pools all operated in the same manner. The Canadian pool, for example, was called Canadian Radio Patents, Ltd. (CRPL), and it controlled the rights to about five thousand patents in the 1960s. The members of the pool naturally had access to all these patents. Nonmembers, however, were granted only "package licenses" to the whole group of patents; and because CRPL's patent position was so strong, covering the entire range of radio and TV apparatus, this meant that no nonmember could make or even import such equipment in Canada without buying the expensive rights to the CRPL package. Also, licenses granted to nonmembers limited them strictly to manufacture and sale of their products within Canada. The goal of these measures, and the similar ones operating in Great Britain and Australia, was to seal off these markets from imports.[33]

Within the United States there was no patent pool *as such* because of antitrust legislation, but the same effect was achieved by indirect means. Two companies, RCA and Hazeltine, commanded the field, with Hazeltine alone controlling some five hundred patents and patent applications.

The major U.S. competitors — GE, Westinghouse, AT&T, and others —
acknowledged RCA's leadership in 1954 by agreeing either to license their
patents to RCA or to license other firms only on terms effectively dictated
by RCA. Hazletine followed the same policy. As did CRPL, Hazeltine and
RCA only granted licenses to their patents as a package, and with the
usual restrictions on imports and exports. Both Hazeltine and RCA were
linked to foreign patent pools, as follows: a Hazeltine subsidiary belonged
to the Australian pool; Hazeltine exchanged exclusive licenses with CRPL
and with a member of the British pool; and RCA had a cross-licensing pact
with the Germany company Telefunken in which both pledged to impose
the same restrictive terms on third-party licensees. Thus RCA and Hazeltine managed to control the U.S. market and shield it from foreign competition for many years, just as the foreign patent pools kept the other
major countries insulated from one other. But as a result of the 1971 decision in *Hazeltine Research, Inc.* v. *Zenith Radio Corp.* American firms
were enjoined from belonging to radio and TV patent pools whose purpose was to exclude other firms from specific markets.[34]

*   *   *

Before turning to our examination of the contemporary IEA, mention
should be made of a closely related cartel, the International Cable Development Corporation (ICDC) — both because its existence indicates the
scope of cartelization in the industry and because certain details of its operations are especially intriguing. Most of what is publicly known about
the ICDC is the result of an investigation by London *Times* reporters
Maurice Corina and Malcolm Brown, who developed sources within the
cartel.

The ICDC was founded in 1928, and was registered in Vaduz, Liechtenstein, in 1931. At the time it consisted of fifteen national groups with
nearly ninety member companies, including European, Canadian, Japanese, and U.S. firms. As usual, home market protection agreements were
the basis of cooperation. The cartel was disrupted by the war but in 1947
made new interim agreements to fit postwar circumstances.[35] According
to the London *Times*, though, it was not until the 1960s that the cartel
began to grow steadily, eventually accommodating members from twenty
nations by 1975.[36]

The goal of the cartel was to control commerce in electric cables up to
30 KV capacity, and it appears they had considerable success: the cartel's
own statistics indicate that in 1974 two-thirds of the export business mon-
itored by ICDC was conducted at or above price levels set by the "guiding
price list." Although registered in Liechtenstein, the ICDC's working
headquarters were in London, and its various committees — the price
committee, the factory committee, the export committee — met periodi-

cally in hotels in Hamburg, Turku, Monte Carlo, Lausanne, Helsinki, and Amsterdam, among other cities. The factory committee's reported task was "to vet and to control development of any new cable-making plant, especially in the developing world."

In the early 1970s complaints arose from various national groups, particularly the British, that ICDC procedures were too inflexible to be of much use in turbulent market conditions. After intense negotiations through a series of meetings in 1974, a new framework was set up, dividing the world into three types of export territory: the Soviet bloc (and China), a group of twelve developing countries known as the "low price territories," and all other export markets. As before, whenever a member was invited to tender a bid, he was obligated to inform the ICDC general secretary. Three weeks before bids were due, the secretary would propose which company should win the contract. If other members felt the decision was unfair, they could claim compensation from the cartel pool; or, if the contract was from a Soviet bloc country, they could make a wildcat bid. In the low price territories the general secretary could make a mandatory allocation.

Furthermore, under the new bylaws the provisions for battling outsiders were strengthened, apparently at the insistence of British members. Potential competitors were to be considered either "general" or "specific"; the former were thought to be susceptible to cartel pressure, and the latter were not. The general secretary was given the power to declare a "fight" against specific outsiders, designate the national group that was to serve as "fighting leader," and set the level of prices at which combat would be carried out.

Another sidelight on the ICDC was that the subsidiaries of ITT in Europe, reportedly including the Standard Telephone and Cable Company of Great Britain, pulled out of the cartel in 1973. ITT, it seems, was worried that ICDC operations would eventually become the target of European antitrust authorities. (ITT also may have sensed that the ICDC's tenure in London would become insecure once Britain joined the Common Market.) The *Times* reported that the ITT break with the cartel was "total," although other members claimed ITT had indicated it would follow a policy of "peaceful coexistence." Two years after it supposedly left the ICDC, Standard Telephone and Cable admitted that it had taken part in a nine-year cartel scheme governing sales of cable to the British Post Office. The other members of the cartel were Pirelli General Cable Works (a subsidiary of the Italian firm, Pirelli), British Insulated Callender's Cables, and Telephone Cables, Ltd. Between 1969 and 1974, the latter firm obtained annual return on capital invested of as much as 53.5 percent, and never lower than 38.6 percent — compared with the national average of 13.6 percent. If the other cartel members made similar enormous profits

on their telephone cable sales, the overcharges to the Post Office during
the cartel's life probably amounted to more than $50 million.[37]

*   *   *

Lucrative as its operations may be, however, the ICDC pales in comparison with its giant cousin, the IEA.

On June 5, 1945, less than a month after World War II ended in Europe,
the IEA was formally reborn. The cartel incorporated in London and filed
new Articles of Association,* essentially the same as those which govern
the IEA today. But owing to its nearly complete breakdown during the
war — and to the vast differences between the world of the late 1940s and
that of the 1930s — the IEA did not recover its full strength for some
years. The industrial plant of Europe, and particularly of Germany, had
been devastated, and the German firms were under the control of the Allied government of the occupied zones. Under these circumstances, the
intricate compensation agreements that had been in force during the
1930s, but had been suspended in 1942, could not be resurrected, nor
could the even trickier cartel devices such as minimum common prices
and strict market quotas. Another major difference was that the U.S. firms
were forced by their government to leave the cartel.[38] Westinghouse had
withdrawn from membership in the IEA during the war; GE now did so as
well.

Little is known of the cartel's inner workings during the decade following the war — perhaps because its relative insignificance allowed it a res-
pite from investigations. However, around 1955 demand for heavy equipment in the home countries began to decline, prices slipped, and worried
manufacturers increasingly began to look to export markets for sales.[39] In
order to maintain the proverbial "orderly" conditions, they pressed for resumption of the IEA agreements, particularly those involving allocations
of orders and compensation by winning bidders to other member firms. In
a short time, the "new" IEA operated as a replica of the "old."[40] The great
Japanese companies joined the cartel in the late 1960s, immeasurably increasing its market power. In 1977, the latest date for which full information is available, the IEA was composed of fifty-five members from twelve
countries.[41]

Like all cartels, the IEA exists for two purposes: to keep prices for its
products as high as possible; and to keep its members' share of the market

* Documents cited in this chapter can be found in Barbara Epstein and Richard Newfarmer, *International Electrical Association: A Continuing Cartel,* Report Prepared for
the Use of the Committee on Interstate and Foreign Commerce and Its Subcommittee on
Oversight and Investigations, U.S., Congress, House, 96th Cong., 2d sess., 1980. Kurt
Mirow collaborated with Epstein and Newfarmer in assembling the documentation for
the report. Certain documents are reprinted in the appendixes to this book.

as large as possible. That sounds simple enough. But for a cartel whose goal is to monopolize markets in scores of countries and whose products are heterogeneous, costly, and technologically complex, the obstacles to success are formidable. Fifty years is a very long life span for a formal cartel of such scope. How has the IEA managed to flourish for so long? The secret of its success is that the fundamental agreements of the cartel establish principles that apply to every situation, but the accords covering specific products are highly flexible. The cartel can change to fit changing circumstances, and so it has.

But the agreements themselves can also be deceptive. With few exceptions they are limited specifically to export markets in the less-developed countries. The IEA's field of operations thus would appear to exclude the members' home countries — most of Europe and Japan — as well as the United States, for reason of antitrust law. In fact, however, the cartel's reach extends much further than the agreements indicate. The territorial limits actually reflect the old system of home market protection that was established long before even the INCA was created. The cartel members tacitly agree not to invade one another's local markets. Whereas, as we shall show later, there is evidence that the cartel has seriously harmed the American electrical industry since GE and Westinghouse were forced to become "outsiders" after the war. The major U.S. firms reportedly find themselves at a sharp disadvantage in competing against cartel members for exports of heavy equipment, and there are indications that in recent years the loss of competitive edge has even weakened American firms at home, allowing the European and Japanese cartel members to take over important sectors of the U.S. market.

In arguing this case we confront a dilemma that will crop up again: the difficulty of assessing with any precision specific *effects* of the cartel. Leaked documents tell us what the IEA hopes to accomplish and how it plans to do so; but information revealing the degree of its success remains fragmentary. Nevertheless, we believe there is enough evidence to support the view that the IEA's impact on the world's heavy electrical industry both in developed and Third World countries is substantial.

❂　❂　❂

Let us begin with the question of prices. The IEA agreements make it obvious that the organization's primary goal is price maintenance — or price gouging, depending on one's point of view. Therefore the most immediate evidence that the cartel has kept prices higher than they would have been otherwise is simply its survival. The IEA would hardly have lasted fifty years had its members not felt they were being rewarded for the considerable effort they put into the cartel — the countless meetings, weighty administrative costs, and periodic rewriting of the agreements, often in order to make them more restrictive. Running a cartel is hard work, and belonging involves a major sacrifice of freedom. One must presume that the members know their best interests.

A second argument also rests on the logic of the market. The collusive agreements in the IEA allow members to achieve international price discrimination — selling products to different buyers at widely differing prices — something not usually possible in a competitive market. IEA members, meeting in advance of tendering bids, are able to discuss exhaustively the unique nature of each order, including such factors as the presence of "outside" competition, the sophistication and bargaining power of the buyer, and the general level of world demand. Having already eliminated a major source of uncertainty — competition among themselves — they are able to reduce their margin of error, or "fine-tune" their bids, that is, fit them exactly to the circumstances, bidding low enough to get the order but no lower than necessary. Cartel prices can be sharply cut when outsiders are also bidding or when demand is slack; and they can be hiked when the members have the field to themselves or when the buyer is poorly informed.

That this is exactly what happens is indicated by the single example of detailed commercial accounting that has leaked from the cartel to date. This document, obtained by Dr. Barbara Epstein, lists the orders obtained under Agreement P(H)C (the pooling and compensation accord for Section H, transformers) from May 19, 1965, through December 31, 1967, and the conditions under which those orders were won (see Appendix V). The figures in the P(H)C document permit a reasonably accurate measure of the effects of the cartel's restrictive practices on transformer prices.

Cartel members dominated the market during the years in question: in 1965 they captured 77 percent of the world exports; in 1966, 72 percent; and in 1967, 86 percent.[42] Their sales also evidence a consistent pattern of higher prices to buyers in the Third World than to those in developed countries. New Zealand, for example, placed ten orders during the period, although prices are available for only nine. On only two of those orders did the buyer pay more than the reference price (the cartel's ideal minimum). For the other seven, the prices paid averaged less than 75 percent of the reference price. Other developed countries also usually paid less than the reference price. Kuwait, on the other hand, placed five orders for a total of twenty-seven large transformers and paid an average of over 20 percent more than the reference price. Venezuela bought seventy-nine transformers, with only nineteen of them discounted below the reference price — and the discounts were tiny. The other sixty were acquired at a premium, often a hefty one; seven of the transformers, for example cost 238 percent of the reference price. Korea, Yugoslavia, the Philippines, and India were similarly overcharged. Interestingly, Brazil between 1965 and 1967 bought thirteen transformers (all in one order) and paid only 78 percent of the reference price for them, thus countering the pattern for Third World countries. This may be accounted for by the fact that Brazil from 1965 through 1967 was in a deep recession, with capital in short supply, and therefore unwilling or unable to pay high prices for capital goods. Another factor, however, could be the founding of the subcartel in Brazil in 1964; the members there might well have had an interest in selling cheaply to undercut local competitors.

The transformer order lists also make it possible to measure the effect of different competitive situations on the cartel's prices. Beside the notation for each order there is a space either marked PC, OT, or SA or left blank. The code letters reveal the type of agreement in operation on each order. PC stands for "pool canceled," a measure taken when outsiders are also bidding and the cartel members feel the necessity to lower their prices by dispensing with the 7 percent pool payments. SA means "special arrangement," something undertaken in Section H when the members are determined to win an order at any cost and face dangerous outside competition; it involves, in other words, even more drastic price cutting than when the pooling arrangement is simply canceled. OT means "only tenderer," indicating that only one firm has been invited to bid. When the space is left blank it means that normal procedures prevail: the pool is in operation, and the members have reached agreement on how to bid the order.

These different situations would lead one to expect higher or lower prices according to the degree of competition. Prices would tend to be lowest when special arrangements are in effect, reflecting the cartel's resolve to underbid outsiders. Pool canceled arrangements would lead to somewhat higher prices, since the cartel members face outsiders but have not chosen (or have not been able) to adopt a policy of all-out attack by jointly slashing prices; therefore they are likely to bid close to what they think the order is actually worth. When normal cartel arrangements are in effect the price would be expected to be higher still, because it must include the cost of the pool, compensation payments, and whatever extra profits the members feel they can achieve by colluding on the bid. But the highest price of all would come on orders for which there is only one bidder, who is free to charge whatever the market will bear.

In fact, as the table illustrates, the prices obtained by Section H conform almost perfectly to these predictions. On pool canceled bids, which most closely approximate what competitive conditions would be in the absence of a cartel, the average price paid was almost identical to the reference price: 98.3 percent of it, to be exact. Prices dropped sharply for deals concluded under special arrangements, rose when the pool was in effect, and were extremely high when only one bidder was involved, averaging

Effects of the Cartel on Prices of Transformers, 1965–67

Average Price Paid[a] as Percent of Reference Price Under:

	Special Arrangements		Pool Canceled		Pool in Effect		Only One Tenderer		All Orders	
	Price	No.[b]	Price	No.[b]	Price	No.[b]	Price	No.[b]	Price	No.[b]
All Countries:	87.7	4	98.2	40	116.4	58	148.1	31	117.4	133
Developed Countries[c]	93.2	2	87.5	21	106.1	21	114.1	9	99.6	53
Developing Countries[d]	82.3	2	110.0	19	122.2	37	162.0	22	129.3	80

a Price f.o.b.

b Number of bidding situations.

c Includes Australia, New Zealand, South Africa, Spain, Denmark, Greece, Israel, and Ireland.

d Includes India, Pakistan, Rhodesia, Zambia, Nigeria, Ivory Coast, Hong Kong, Malaysia, Jamaica, Brazil, Paraguay, Chile, Colombia, Venezuela, Panama, Formosa (Taiwan), China, Korea (South), Iran, Kuwait, Iraq, Romania, Yugoslavia, Philippines, Indonesia, Saudi Arabia, Syria, Lebanon, and Morocco.

Source: U.S., Congress, House, Committee on Interstate and Foreign Commerce, Subcommittee on Oversight and Investigations, *International Electrical Association: A Continuing Cartel*, prepared by Barbara Epstein and Richard Newfarmer, 96th Cong., 2d sess., 1980.

148.2 percent of the reference price. It is also worth noting that, no matter what the situation, developing countries paid much more than advanced countries for transformers — an average of 129.4 percent of the reference price as opposed to 97.2 percent for the latter group.

The data from Section H suggest that the IEA succeeded in raising prices on its sales by some 15 to 20 percent. Unfortunately, these figures are now fifteen years old, and no more recent accounts of orders taken and prices paid have been obtained. There is no way of knowing whether price increases achieved by the cartel today are of the same magnitude, or smaller, or even larger. Also, the figures outlined above apply to only one of ten sections, so they may or may not be representative. But if we assume for the moment that they are and assume likewise that the total annual value of sales covered by IEA agreements has remained at the $1.5 billion level indicated by Secretary Hughes in 1976, then we may conclude that the "price maintenance" practiced by the cartel costs the world some $225 to $300 million per year, most of it paid by the less-developed countries.[43]

Specific instances of cartel overpricing tend to surface, of course, only when something goes disastrously wrong. There apparently was one such instance recently in Saudi Arabia. Ever since the OPEC price increases of 1973, the Middle East has been the most important growth market for heavy electrical equipment in the world, and Saudi Arabia, with the possible exception of Iran under the Shah, has been the leading consumer nation in the area, not only of electrical equipment but of other large-scale industrial and civil engineering projects. After some years of liberal spending, however, the Saudis came to feel they were being regularly cheated by firms that inflated their prices. The resentment finally erupted in 1977, when the Saudis were planning a huge enlargement of their electrical power sysem and invited tenders for transformers, power lines, diesel generating sets, and switchgear, all covered by contracts of the IEA or the ICDC, the cable cartel. Of the eight firms invited to bid, six — GEC, Hawker Siddeley, Siemens, Brown Boveri, Hitachi, and Mitsubishi — were members of the IEA. The Saudi consultants estimated the value of the equipment at some $1.4 billion. The exact amounts of the bids are not known, but the Saudis revealed that they ranged from two to four times the independent estimates.[44]

On February 23, 1977, the Saudi Council of Ministers issued a stinging denunciation of the companies involved, which, said the ministers, "have agreed to fix the price of their bids to share in illegal profit" of the winners. The eight original bidders were eliminated from consideration for the projects, and the Saudi minister of industry and electricity pointedly toured the Far East looking for other bidders. He eventually awarded the contracts to companies in India, Pakistan, South Korea, and Taiwan, whose bids were markedly lower than the lowest of the first round. Dr. Feisal Bashir, acting deputy minister of planning, expressed hope that the European and Japanese firms would learn a lesson from the experience and would in future be aware, as he put it, that "we are not easy meat."

But usually matters are not so clear-cut; the indications of cartel action on any particular contract are rarely so marked — and are not aired in public. The circumstances that led Saudi Arabia to react so strongly were probably unique, the most important being the bargaining power bestowed on the Saudis by their oil wealth. Few other Third World countries are in a position to offend rich and powerful transnational corporations that are the traditional (and often the only) source of sorely needed technology and that customarily pay huge "commissions" to local "agents" who help them win contracts. Cartel activity in such nations can only be ascertained by examining patterns of investment, trade, price, and development, patterns which will support educated guesses as to their causes. In the case of the electrical industry, the country from which we have gathered extensive data is, of course, Brazil, where we have the added advantage of knowing that a formal cartel was in operation at least until the early 1970s. Precisely what the cartel did we do not know, but it is possible to trace the activities of its members during the critical growth years of the industry.

Combat in Brazil

As we noted in the Introduction, the Brazilian electrical industry, including both consumer and capital goods, was dominated by foreign investment as far back as 1960. Of the one hundred largest firms in the industry (which accounted for all but 10 to 15 percent of production), thirty-one were foreign-owned, and these tended to be the largest: they held 66 percent of the one hundred firms' total assets, and included four of the five biggest. Many had been established by the purchase of a controlling interest in local companies.[45] By 1974, after the recession of the mid-1960s and the boom years of the "economic miracle" engineered by the military government, the foreign share had grown even larger. Of the one hundred largest electrical enterprises in that year, fifty-seven were foreign-owned, and they controlled 75 percent of the assets. There were no Brazilian firms among the largest five, only two among the largest fifteen, and only five among the largest twenty-five. And the degree of concentration in the industry was high: the top twenty-five firms held nearly three-quarters of the total assets of the one hundred largest.[46]

The foreign takeover of the industry affected virtually all product sectors, from televisions to massive hydroelectric generating plants. It was particularly rapid and extensive in the market for transformers, which happens to be the product covered by the IBEMEP cartel accords that were leaked in 1972 (see Appendix VI). The IBEMEP agreements demonstrate the transnational firms' capacity to create, in a major Third World country, a sophisticated cartel that was the near perfect copy of the parent. Following time-tested IEA methods, IBEMEP provided for notification, allocation, rigged bids, and stiff fines for members who took orders out of turn or otherwise violated the rules. According to sources with firsthand knowledge, IBEMEP's daily operations also were patterned after those of the IEA. But perhaps the most interesting articles of the IBEMEP agreement, because of what they suggest about the members' designs on the market, are those relating to "combat":

> Article 24: The final sales prices agreed upon during the meeting will include 2 percent payable by the winning member to a "reserve for combat purposes."
> Article 27: If the need for combat arises, it will be taken up first by the company that has accumulated the largest amount of reserves.
> Article 50: In case any member leaves this program, he will be systematically combatted by all the others who will alternate in the combat.

The general purpose of these provisions is clear: the reserve fund was meant to finance predatory price wars in order to drive enemy firms out of the market. Unfortunately, we do not know all the firms that were formally "combatted," or for how long, or the details of how combats worked. But sources report that one major target was the Brazilian firm Marongoni. Beginning in 1968, members of the IBEMEP allegedly decided to take away Marongoni's share of the large transformer market at all costs. Tenders had been solicited for an order of 150 transformers, and Induselet was chosen to do battle. Having analyzed Marongoni's past bidding history, Induselet was able to bid 10 percent lower than what it calculated to be the Brazilian firm's minimum possible price. Such predatory bidding was directed against Marongoni and another Brazilian firm, Gordon, for a number of years. Marongoni finally filed bankruptcy papers and entered receivership. By the mid-1970s neither firm was receiving anything but small orders from minor buyers of transformers.[47]

But the decline of Marongoni and Gordon was by no means extraordinary. Numerous Brazilian transformer manufacturers were wiped out altogether during the late 1960s and early 1970s. Those which survived were generally small regional firms outside the major markets. In short, the cartel's assault was a total success: IBEMEP firms took over the entire large transformer market, with Brown Boveri and ASEA winning about 25 percent each; and they captured more than 80 percent of the market for small and medium-sized transformers.

Newfarmer notes the extremely interesting fact that this foreign take-over of the transformer market was accompanied by a sharp rise in imports of transformers.[48] From 1955 to 1963, the value of imported transformers remained constant at about $4 million per year. The recession brought a dip in all industrial imports, which then recovered briskly after the economy picked up again. But from 1965 (the year after the IBEMEP cartel was installed) to 1972, imports of transformers increased at a rate nearly twice that of other manufactured goods: 47.9 percent per year as opposed to 26.7 percent. Transformer imports also grew much faster than imports of other electrical material, and faster than all types of machinery. Yet Brazilian firms were technologically capable of producing all but the largest sizes of transformers and during the late 1960s were operating far below capacity.

Why the rise in transformer imports and the steady denationalization of the Brazilian industry? What did the foreign firms, including the cartel members, have to gain from such a trend? For the answer one must look beyond Brazil to the countries where the parent firms are headquartered — that is, to the home ground of the IEA. In a period during which there is world-wide excess capacity for a certain product, the typical transnational firm often must choose between idling its plants at home or idling plants run by subsidiaries abroad. Will greater profits accrue from producing transformers in Brazil for the Brazilian market or from building them in Germany (for example) and exporting them to Brazil? Often the firm finds that to produce at home and export is more profitable in the long run and more popular politically at home as well. The home plants are usually the most modern, with great amounts of capital absorbed in the most advanced equipment, whereas plants in Third World countries often employ machinery that is outdated, perhaps secondhand, and in many cases already depreciated and written off. It is therefore much more expensive to shut down the home plant than the plant abroad.

The behavior of General Electric's Brazilian subsidiary, GE do Brasil, provides a good example of this tendency. In 1975 the company announced that its long-established Campinas plant would no longer produce large transformers because the Brazilian market was "well served by existing producers and now has excess capacity."[49] The GE do Brasil spokesman also claimed that "due to the lack of skilled personnel which results in limiting our ability to expand all product lines simultaneously, GE was forced to concentrate its efforts in the expansion of generators, turbines, motors and locomotives." But the news took on quite a different cast when it appeared in the American trade publication *Electrical Week*,[50] which cited officers of the parent corporation as saying that the Brazilian market — supposedly suffering from such excess capacity that it made no sense for GE to produce locally — would be supplied from GE plants in Massachusetts and Georgia. It was hardly coincidental that this shift came at a time when the United States was mired in a deep recession that had caused demand for heavy electrical equipment to drop. The resulting excess capacity *in the United States* could only be employed by increasing exports to countries like Brazil.

This pattern applies not only to transformers but to most sectors of the industry in Brazil: once the transnationals have established themselves in a market, usually by building or buying local production facilities, they shift production to their home plants whenever economic or political circumstances make doing so advantageous. However, in order for this strategy to work, the TNCs must be sure that when subsidiary plants are shut down local competitors do not take up the slack in the market and prevent the transnationals from achieving their export goals. For that reason they may wish to ensure that there *is* no potential local competition. It is worth examining briefly some of their methods for achieving this.

The simplest is to buy out local firms, and to a great extent that is what happens. Often a transnational's first move into a foreign market will be the acquisition of an established company. A Harvard University study showed that U.S. TNCs in the electrical industry used acquisition as their "mode of entry" 42 percent of the time in Latin America between the years 1958 and 1968, and 64 percent of the time in Brazil during those years.[51] Another study found that approximately 90 percent of the growth in the foreign share of Brazil's electrical industry from 1960 to 1974 came about through acquisitions of established firms. Among the Brazilian companies acquired were many of the largest, oldest, most profitable, and technologically most proficient.[52]

What would lead such firms to sell to foreign competitors? Occasionally an offer may be so attractive as to be irresistible. But more often, we suspect, the local firms cannot resist various pressures to sell. The mere threat of competition from such a giant as GE or Siemens can be a powerful inducement to sell out while there is still a chance of getting a reasonable price. If intimidation does not suffice, the threat can be made good. Subsidiaries of TNCs can expect to win bitter and prolonged price wars because they have the resources of the parent firms backing them. Such wars, as we have seen, may be financed by a cartel combat fund, as in the case of the IBEMEP firms, or the TNCs may resort to "cross-subsidization," which means the use of profits earned in one sector of the firm (on the home market, say) to cover losses taken elsewhere in the attempt to capture new markets.

This appears to have been a standard tactic of transnational electrical firms in Brazil during the crucial years of the foreign takeover. In a study of the profit performance of forty-four large electrical firms between 1966 and 1974, nine were found to have recorded losses during five of seven consecutive years. All nine were subsidiaries of transnational corporations. Not one Brazilian firm lost money in five of seven years and survived until 1974.[53] The Swiss firm Brown Boveri, as we noted in the Introduction, absorbed particularly heavy losses in its drive to gain a major share of Brazil's market for generators, electric motors, and transformers. In fact, the firm's Brazilian subsidiary was kept from bankruptcy only by loans from the parent totaling some $36 million between 1960 and 1974. But such efforts by Brown Boveri and other TNCs paid off; the Brazilian share of the market for medium-sized electric motors fell from 51 to 22 percent between 1966 and 1972, partly because the Brazilian firm Arno, unable to compete against motors that were being dumped by TNC subsidiaries, was forced to merge with ASEA, the Swedish firm. The Brazilian share of the generator market fell from 17 to 3 percent for similar reasons, mainly through the absorption of Irmaos Negrini by Toshiba.[54] The consumer electronics market, too, was almost completely taken over by foreign firms.[55]

* * *

Somewhat more devious than predatory pricing as a means of attack on local firms is the manipulation of supplies. Most TNC subsidiaries, linked to the largest electrical manufacturers in the world, have direct access to components, test equipment, and other essential materials, whereas their independent competitors do not. Creative withholding of supplies, then, can be a formidable weapon. And it has the advantage of being difficult to prove. In 1969, for example, Brazilian firms began to complain about sporadic shortages of copper wire, a vital material in most electrical machinery, while the members of IBEMEP were experiencing no such problems, having bought up large supplies of wire. Two Brazilian firms later claimed that the shortages of copper wire contributed to their exit from the market; one, an appliance manufacturer, was absorbed by Philips, and the other went bankrupt.[56] The evidence is circumstantial, but such stories were common enough in Brazil during the period of foreign takeover as to arouse suspicion.

Another example from the late 1960s involved a firm called Resilan. The company was founded by a Brazilian businessman to produce bushings, the expensive porcelain pieces that are an essential component of transformers. Before Resilan was established, Brazil imported all its bushings. Brown Boveri ordered fifty bushings rated at 138 KV from Resilan, under a contract that specified severe penalties should Resilan fail to deliver in time. However, to produce the bushings Resilan required a special device only obtainable from Brown Boveri's parent firm in Switzerland; and Resilan's owner (who, ironically, had once been a director of Brown Boveri in Brazil) neglected to stipulate penalties should the Swiss company not deliver the device promptly. There were long delays before it arrived from

Switzerland, and as a result Resilan could not meet its deadlines. The heavy penalties eventually led to Brown Boveri's acquisition of Resilan, and Brown Boveri began importing all high-voltage bushings, limiting Resilan's production to lower voltages — an unnecessary technological constraint on Brazil's domestic production.[57]

One final aspect of the foreign takeover of Brazil's electrical industry should be mentioned here: the growing control of the TNCs over the actual legal processes of decision making as to whether electrical equipment will be produced locally or imported. Brazilian laws dating from the 1950s allow imports of essential capital equipment to benefit from preferential exchange rates or to enter the country duty-free. Theoretically, though, under another law known as the Law of Similars, no capital equipment is to be imported if similar goods are available within Brazil. This naturally leads to endless wrangles over what constitutes "similarity." The government agency that issues import permits has given local businessmen the right to decide whether equipment specified in orders can be produced in the country or should be imported. In the electrical industry, these decisions are made under the auspices of the trade association known as ABINEE (the Brazilian Association of Electrical and Electronic Industry). The only problem with the system is that, as independent Brazilian producers have been driven out of business or have sold out to the transnationals, the latter have gained preponderant influence within ABINEE and now find themselves in the enviable position of adjudicating the Law of Similars for themselves.[58] Those eager to increase imports from their parent firms can simply draw their technical or financial specifications in such a way that they can claim the goods can only be supplied from abroad, and as likely as not the foreign-dominated ABINEE will certify the claim. This situation has led to innumerable cases of equipment and machinery being imported when goods similar in all but minor details could have been produced in Brazil.

Impact on the United States

In one important developing country, then, the activities of cartelized transnational firms in the electrical industry have brought about the decline — or complete disappearance — of local enterprise and the increase of the country's dependence upon foreign sources of supply. Other evidence — notably the cartel agreements of the IEA, the comparative price data on transformers, and the Saudi Arabian experience — indicates that the developing countries pay a premium for electrical equipment whenever the cartel firms achieve solid control over a specific territory or order.

But what of the cartel's impact on the developed countries, and in particular on the largest market of all: the United States?

For reasons decribed in Chapter 1, the cartel agreements have little if
any *direct* effect on the members' home country markets. By and large, the
principles of home market protection set down decades ago in the first
cartel and cross-licensing accords still apply and are reinforced by various
measures: high tariffs; "buy national" policies; licensing arrangements
under which companies agree not to invade each others' territories; and
tacit mutual forbearance. A number of the home country markets are
controlled by purely national cartels. In fact, the policy held to by most
developed nations of maintaining a complete line of heavy power equipment production is one reason for the persistent overcapacity in the world
industry, which in turn creates the need for an international cartel to keep
export prices high. Whatever the wisdom of the policy, though, the de
facto home market protection that prevails in the nations of the major European producers and Japan apparently insulates them from the cartel's
price-fixing and market allocation provisions.

The position of the United States is considerably more ambiguous. The
legal situation is clear enough: U.S. companies cannot belong to international cartels, and in fact the American members of the IEA — notably
GE and Westinghouse, two founding members — were forced to withdraw in 1947. Any international cartel activity, should it affect the American market, would be illegal under U.S. antitrust law — so the IEA specifically excludes the United States from the territory covered by cartel
agreements. Does this mean that U.S. firms are regarded as hostile "outsiders" by the cartel and must battle the IEA members for export sales? Or do
the Americans secretly cooperate with the cartel?

Certain facts might offer a basis for the latter conclusion. The two U.S.
firms that are contenders for export markets in the full range of electrical
equipment are, of course, GE and Westinghouse. The subsidiaries of both
belonged to the IBEMEP cartel in Brazil, and GE is the dominant power
in the small group of TNCs (amounting to an informal cartel) that has
fixed prices and maintained market shares constant in the Brazilian electric lamp market since at least the 1950s. It seems highly unlikely — although not impossible — that the subsidiaries act without the full knowledge of their parent firms, and this naturally raises the question of what
ties GE and Westinghouse might have to their foreign competitors in
other Third World countries. Also, both firms have very long histories of
engaging in restrictive business practices. The most serious recent incident
came to light in the "Philadelphia cases" of the early 1960s, when most of
the United States' major producers of electrical equipment were found to
be participating in a domestic cartel. In what was certainly one of the
greatest business scandals in the country's history, no less than twenty-

nine companies were convicted and thirty-one executives received jail sentences for having engaged in massive market- and price-fixing schemes covering the supply of heavy equipment for power plants.* In this case, 1880 civil suits were filed against the offending firms, and more than $300 million in damages were paid.[59]

Bolstering the mistrust created by the companies' criminal record is the curious fact that neither GE nor Westinghouse seems to have made the slightest effort to expose the cartel and thereby destroy its effectiveness. One would think that American firms hoping to win export orders, and facing a well-organized cartel of virtually all the world's other major producers, would protest on the grounds of unfair competition. Yet GE and Westinghouse remain silent and passive. When asked directly about the IEA, their spokespeople merely seem embarrassed and deny any substantive knowledge of the cartel's activities.

However, other evidence suggests that the U.S. firms do indeed find themselves in the position of "outsiders" and that the U.S. electrical equipment industry is being weakened as a result, both by loss of export markets and by foreign entry into the U.S. market itself.

The consensus among industry sources is that American firms are increasingly being shut out of markets in the developing world. Unfortunately, there are no statistics available to measure the decline. Because only two firms sell significant amounts of heavy power equipment abroad; and the publication of figures covering only two firms would reveal to each how much the other is selling, the U.S. government does not publish statistical analyses of exports in these product groups, following the principle that export data are trade secrets. Thus, for statistical purposes, heavy electrical equipment is lumped together with other product groups. The government does publish export data on a group titled "electrical power machinery," which covers some heavy equipment but also such items as small motors. Analysis of these figures shows that U.S. exports declined from 40.2 percent of all world exports in 1964–65 to 33 percent in 1974–75, a noteworthy drop but one which may or may not be significant in terms of heavy equipment.[60] Nevertheless, insiders admit that the American export performance in products covered by IEA agreements is poor.

The reasons for this competitive disadvantage are undeniably complex and involve questions of politics, credit terms, sales tied to foreign aid grants, traditional spheres of influence, labor costs in different countries, and levels of technological development. But cartel activity is also an important factor. As we have seen, the IEA accords set out formal procedures for concluding "special arrangements" among members when they

---

* Twenty-four jail sentences were suspended.

are bidding against outsiders. These arrangements allow members to bid so low that they make sure their competitors do not get orders. The cartel firms may take a loss in the process, but they are in a position to recoup those losses, both by fixing prices on cartel-controlled sales when no "outsiders" are involved and from the high profits they earn in their protected home markets. Thus the outsiders, who have no such means to cross-subsidize losses taken in order to preserve a market share, may be systematically barred from export markets, as appears to have happened to the Americans.

The consequences of America's inability to compete in these export markets are serious, going far beyond mere loss of income from abroad.[61] A once powerful national industry that loses its ability to sell its products world-wide may be gravely damaged, in terms of both its financial health and its comparative position in the race for technological leadership. Sales of heavy electrical equipment are highly cyclical; that is, the volume of orders in any particular country tends to rise sharply during periods of economic growth and then fall equally sharply during downturns. Export markets provide a means of keeping large capital-intensive plants operating at relatively high capacity through slack times at home. The loss of exports, on the other hand, exposes the company to costly periods of plant idleness, which sap its overall financial strength. Even more serious, perhaps, is the loss of the chance to achieve the economies of scale that are increasingly required to maintain a competitive edge in the technological field. Technical developments in the industry have generally been in the direction of larger and larger equipment size. To produce these huge products in the most economically efficient manner, plants must grow larger. But firms that are losing markets also lose incentive to make the investments necessary to keep up with the state of the art. This process, of course, soon becomes a vicious circle, as the firms' outdated technology causes them to lose more markets, which in turn causes them to drop further behind. If this downward spiral continues, the firms' markets in their own country will inevitably be threatened.

In fact, there are indications that this is already happening in the United States. Industry observers believe that since the early 1970s the members of the IEA have taken a new attitude toward the American domestic market. That is, they have sensed the weakness of U.S. firms and moved to exploit it, abandoning their long-established general policy of forbearance. Evidence is fragmentary, and the shift (assuming it has taken place) is still in its early stages, so it is too early to draw final conclusions. But, as with the Brazilian market, certain events when viewed in conjunction and combined with what is known about the cartel suggest a pattern.

In April 1972, the U.S. Tariff Commission ruled that producers from five IEA countries — France, Italy, Japan, Switzerland, and the United Kingdom — had been dumping large power transformers on the United States market, and that American companies had been substantially injured as a result. "If these dumping practices [were] allowed to continue," the commission stated, "there is adequate capacity among these nations to threaten the continued existence of the [American] large-power-transformer industry."[62] Yet the ruling did not prevent three of the eight American producers of such transformers from quitting the field: Central Moloney (a subsidiary of Colt Industries) in 1973; the Wagner Electric Corporation (a subsidiary of Studebaker-Worthington) in 1976; and, in the same year, Allis-Chalmers, which announced it was replacing its domestic production of transformers with imports from Germany, made by Siemens.

There is only one remaining U.S. firm with its own up-to-date technology for producing power circuit breakers: Westinghouse. The others have all entered into cooperative ventures in which the Americans are relegated largely to the role of distributor for products made by members of the IEA. GE and Hitachi share a joint venture in which the U.S. firm imports the main parts for circuit breakers from Hitachi, assembles them, and sells them in the United States. Allis-Chalmers participates in a joint venture with Siemens, and Brown Boveri recently acquired I-T-E, a former branch of Gould, Inc. The French IEA member, Merlin-Gerin, has distributed its circuit breakers through an American firm, the High Voltage Power Corporation.

Both Brown Boveri and Siemens have in the past decade made additional moves into the U.S. market. The Brown Boveri North American Group now includes among its interests a gas turbine division, acquired in 1977 from Studebaker-Worthington; the joint venture with I-T-E to produce circuit breakers; a turbine servicing facility; and 49 percent of Howden-Parsons, a turbine manufacturing operation in Canada, which Brown Boveri bought in 1979. Siemens's move has come by means of its alliance with Allis-Chalmers. The German firm owns 50 percent of a joint venture called Siemens-Allis, created in 1978, which sells a full line of "engineered electrical equipment" built either in the United States or Germany. Thus far, it is Siemens that has produced the firm's supply of turbines and generators, and Allis-Chalmers has canceled its plans to rebuild its own turbine-generator facilities.

What these developments indicate is that U.S. heavy equipment firms may have begun to lose the technological superiority — or at least equality — that would enable them to compete successfully against their European and Japanese counterparts and that consequently foreign firms are entering the American market as never before. It remains to be seen whether the trend will persist. Of course, foreign entry as such is not a bad thing. In theory, the added competition brought to the market by foreign firms can bring consumers (in this case, utility companies) lower prices and a wider range of choices among products and technologies. But, as we pointed out in the case of Brazil, there are two possible means by which foreign firms may enter a market, and one brings considerably fewer competitive benefits than the other. When the entrant builds a new plant, expands an existing one, or even embarks on a drive to import its products into the new market, competition sharpens. But when the foreign firm simply buys out an established domestic company or enters into a joint venture, competition increases marginally if at all. No new capacity is created; established market shares are not necessarily challenged; and the number of potential competitors is actually reduced. Unfortunately, the foreign firms entering the U.S. electrical equipment market seem to prefer the latter method, which only leads to replacement of American goods by foreign ones — or to continued American production, but under foreign control — and to a more highly concentrated industry.

Again it must be stated that the currents underlying this trend are complex. We have no evidence — other than Agreement Y, signed in 1974, which provides for the gathering of information on orders taken in the United States — that the IEA cartel is now directly involved in the American market. But consideration of the industry's history since World War II gives rise to troubling questions. After the war, the U.S. electrical equipment firms were the strongest in the world, and they maintained a healthy volume of exports, thanks in part to the abundant credit offered in various forms to foreign buyers by the U.S. government. The rise of the Europeans and the Japanese — strengthened, we have every reason to believe, by their collusion through the IEA — began to close the Americans out of export markets. Recently the IEA members have moved in force into the American market, raising the possibility of a gradual foreign takeover as occurred in Brazil. We must ask, then: Is it conceivable that the members of the cartel, who rig the market for orders taken in almost every other part of the world, will practice unfettered competition on the U.S. market alone?

We do not find that a very likely prospect.

3

The Real Oil Cartel

The men who flocked to the oil regions [of Pennsylvania] in the first years . . . soon discovered another fact about the new industry: that it was subject — far more than coal, or gold — to disastrous over-production, leading to sudden collapses in the price. It was here that the ominous phrase was first coined: "the bottom fell out of the market."

Anthony Sampson, *The Seven Sisters*

The day of combination is here to stay. Individualism has gone never to return.

John D. Rockefeller

MENTION the oil cartel to almost any American today, and he or she immediately thinks of the Organization of Petroleum Exporting Countries (OPEC), a group of oil-rich Third World nations, many of them Arab. Prevailing opinion has it that OPEC's sudden discovery in 1973 of its power over an increasingly scarce and vital natural resource and the organization's untrammeled abuse of that power are largely responsible for the parlous state of the economies of the United States, Japan, and most countries of Western Europe. But the very fact that the word *cartel* is now so closely associated with greedy Arabs in reality is only the latest indication of the much longer-standing, although somewhat less obvious, power of the *original* oil cartel, dominated by the gigantic oil companies commonly known as the Seven Sisters. During the decades that the Sisters held unchallenged sway over a cartel that ruled the world market for oil, the public rarely heard the term. The oil companies for some time have been the target of a healthy mistrust, but their point of view has so thoroughly dominated public debate over what has come to be known as the "energy crisis" that most people are not aware that OPEC in all likelihood would not have survived without the vigorous support of the private companies acting in consort. In employing their ability to set prices unilaterally and restrict production to support those prices, the OPEC countries are merely taking advantage of machinery laboriously created by the companies since the 1920s. In other words, the oil-exporting nations spent many years as the unwilling pupils of the oil cartel; finally, when circumstances had changed, they promoted themselves into partnership.

*   *   *

Like the electrical industry, the oil industry has been cartelized almost since its inception — which might be dated to 1859, when "Colonel" Edwin Drake drilled the first oil well near the town of Titusville, Pennsylvania. But oil has always presented unique difficulties to those who would control the industry, difficulties that stem from one fundamental fact: petroleum is a raw material rather than a manufactured good. Certainly in the many forms it reaches the consuming public, ranging from heating oil to rocket fuel to petroleum jelly to plastics, it has undergone extremely complicated forms of processing. But the oil cartel has not generally relied on a monopoly over the technology necessary to transform the raw material into its manufactured forms. Rather, the basis of the cartel has been its increasingly sophisticated methods of restricting production.

The reason the cartel has taken this direction is that for a hundred years the petroleum industry has found itself constantly hovering on the brink of overabundance. On the occasions when the feared gluts have materialized, the resulting competitive struggles (usually termed "catastrophic" or "chaotic" by oil executives, although the public may view them differently) have wreaked havoc with petroleum company profits until the oversupply could be contained. The companies have long complained that their profits are not sufficient because the costs of exploring and drilling for new oil are very high. It is hard to know how much credence their claims deserve; most data available on production, costs, and certainly profits come from the companies themselves, and, as we shall see, the history of the industry shows that the companies are not above keeping oil fields out of production in order not to disrupt their carefully constructed world-wide balance of supply and demand. Many of the great discoveries of new fields, in fact, have been made by small companies or independent wildcatters operating on a shoestring. But even if one lends full credence to the claim of high exploration costs, it is well known that once a field is found, the cost of extracting the oil and transporting it is low — in some cases, such as most Middle Eastern fields, ridiculously low.[1] In other words, oil flows cheaply; but if the market is sufficiently "orderly" it can be sold dearly. The companies make most of their profits from the actual *production* of crude oil; until very recently, the transport, refining, and marketing of petroleum products yielded relatively little gain, merely serving to support the tremendous profits that were being turned at the wellhead.[2] It was this contrast between the very low cost of extracting a barrel of oil from the ground and the good price it would fetch that made the control of production the key to any effective petroleum cartel. The point was to keep the oil in the ground and release it in quantities that would meet but not exceed the companies' estimate of probable demand. When combined with other devices common to most cartels — home market protection, pricing agreements, control over technology, and occasional wars on outsiders who menaced the tidy market — the Sisters' ability to increase or decrease the flow of oil to a dependent world placed them among the most wealthy and powerful institutions in the world.

* * *

It was overproduction that gave rise to the first great national oil monopoly, the Standard Oil Trust; and it was overproduction that indirectly led to the first international agreements upon which the oil cartel is based. Following Drake's successful attempt to produce oil by means of a drilling rig and a pump in 1859, an oil rush took place in western Pennsylvania that was as violent and chaotic as the most spectacular gold rushes. By the mid-1860s petroleum was gushing from hundreds of little rigs and flowing across the continent to fuel lamps and stoves and lubricate machines. There was no way to limit production during the early years of the industry; it was simply too easy to break into the business, and there were too many scrappy individual prospectors, each producing a few barrels a day. There were times, as Anthony Sampson notes, when "a barrel of oil was literally cheaper than a barrel of water."[3] With each new discovery, the price dropped dizzily until demand could catch up.

But there was one man, John D. Rockefeller, who glimpsed a way to make a fortune from oil and avoid the possibility of ruination due to wild swings in price. Ironically, given the future shape of the oil cartel, Rockefeller's strategy had nothing to do with limiting production; in fact, he gained his hold on the industry *because* there was too much oil. Rockefeller sensed that in a glutted market the key to control was the transport and refinement of oil. That is, with more oil available than the nation needed, only some of it would get refined and transported to market; Rockefeller determined that if he could control the bottleneck — the refineries — and then win favorable terms for the oil products he had refined, he would occupy an unassailable competitive position.[4] In 1865 he bought his first refinery, in Cleveland, and rapidly bought up others, often keeping his acquisitions secret so it would appear that the Rockefeller refineries were still competing with each other. At the same time he negotiated secret rebates with the railroads so that his oil was transported more cheaply than anyone else's. As his ownership of refining capacity expanded, Rockefeller was in a position to dictate the price he would pay for crude oil. Although the producers did attempt to organize and set their own price, their large number prevented any effective unity, and their associations never lasted long before some desperate or greedy producer would begin to undercut the agreed price. In this buyer's market, Rockefeller made himself the most important buyer; and, thanks to the rebates he received from the railroads, he could add a considerable markup to his refined products and still undersell his competitors.

In less than twenty years Rockefeller rose to dominate the petroleum industry in the United States. With the large profits from his early operations he was able to buy his own oil fields and build his own pipelines, thus making Standard Oil the first "integrated" oil company, controlling all phases of its business from production to transport to refining to retail marketing. In 1882 Rockefeller organized the Standard Oil Trust, which grouped a number of companies under central administration (in which Rockefeller, of course, had preponderant influence) as a means to reduce competition among them. Companies that would not submit to Standard Oil by selling out or at least accepting Rockefeller's mandates on prices and market division were ruthlessly driven out of business.[5] This was the classic case of monopolization on the national level; Rockefeller's methods at the same time made him the envy of and model for other tycoons, while among the public he was perhaps the most unpopular American alive. Finally, in 1911, a federal antitrust case brought about the breakup of the Standard Oil (New Jersey) holding company, which held shares in all the components of the trust and effectively ran them as one firm. But because the court ordered that Standard be divided into its constituent companies and the Rockefellers and their aides by that time had acquired large holdings in many of those companies, the family for some time continued to dominate the industry through the thirty-eight successors to Standard Oil.[6] Three of the successors — Standard Oil of New Jersey (now Exxon), Standard Oil of New York (now Mobil), and Standard Oil of California (now Socal) — later became known as three of the Seven Sisters that ran the international cartel.

o   o   o

Rockefeller, of course, did not restrict his ambitions to North America; he wanted to be the foremost oil man in the world, and for some time it appeared that he might well achieve preeminence abroad as well as at home. During the late 1800s he built up marketing networks in Europe and Asia; and, although the discovery of rich oil fields in the Russian Caucasus on a concession owned by the Nobel and Rothschild families forced Standard Oil to agree to share Europe with those interests, Rockefeller's Asian markets appeared impregnable. However, in 1892, a British entrepreneur named Marcus Samuel began shipping Russian oil through the Suez Canal to Far Eastern markets, and the advantage he thus gained by shortening the distance between wellhead and market allowed him to compete with Rockefeller. For fourteen years Samuel's company, called Shell, engaged Standard Oil in a series of ferocious price wars, with Shell challenging not only in Asia but in Europe and even the United States. Somewhat miraculously, Shell survived, but the company was so weakened that in 1906 it was forced into a merger with a Dutch firm called Royal Dutch, which was using its discovery of abundant oil fields in Indonesia as a basis from which to chip away at Rockefeller's Asian monopoly. With the formation of Royal Dutch Shell, Standard Oil suddenly was faced with an international rival large enough to be truly dangerous.

The third company that eventually helped lay the foundations for the international oil cartel was the Anglo-Persian Oil Company (now BP, or British Petroleum), which was founded in 1909 as a union between the Burmah Oil Company, a British firm with holdings in Burma, and William Knox D'Arcy, an adventurer who in 1901 had acquired a concession in Persia that proved to be fabulously rich in oil. In 1914 the British government, eager to obtain a reliable source of oil for its navy and reluctant to depend on the Standard Oil companies or Shell, purchased a 51 percent share of Anglo-Persian. With its control over the huge Persian fields, its government backing, and its assured volume of sales to the navy, Anglo-Persian also loomed large on the international scene.

By the 1920s, then, three companies controlled the lion's share of international trade in oil: Exxon, Shell, and BP.* There were also four American firms of smaller but nevertheless substantial size that held certain market positions abroad: the old Standard Oil companies, Mobil and Socal; and two independents founded on discoveries of oil in Texas in the early 1900s, Gulf and Texaco. By and large, the strength of the U.S. companies rested on their control of oil deposits at home, whereas Shell and BP were thoroughly international, drawing their crude from fields scattered all over the world. World War I and the fast-growing popularity of the automobile had illustrated to all nations that future prosperity and power rested on supplies of oil to an extent that few had guessed before;

---

* Hereinafter we will refer to the companies by the names under which they are known today.

and in the early 1920s the United States, which (along with Mexico) still produced more than 80 percent of the world's oil, was swept by the alarming (and false) notion that the country's reserves were fast being depleted.[7] Intense interest therefore began to focus on access to new sources of oil, particularly in the Middle East, where the Seven Sisters (and the governments supporting them) confronted each other, battled, and finally worked out the form of coexistence that was to serve as the basis for the oil cartel ever since: the joint production agreement.

The immediate issue after World War I was the oil fields that were thought to exist in the Mosul and Baghdad regions along the Tigris River. The territory had belonged to the Ottoman Empire, which had been defeated in the war; and the oil concession belonged to Calouste Gulbenkian, a tough and sagacious Armenian whose unshakable belief in the potential riches to be uncovered there proved well founded. In 1919, the victors in the Middle East, Britain and France, divided up the former Ottoman Empire between them, adding a special oil agreement under which ownership of the Turkish Petroleum Company was distributed as follows: nearly 50 percent for BP; nearly 25 percent for Shell; another 25 percent for the French; and 5 percent for Gulbenkian. However, upon hearing of this agreement the U.S. government protested bitterly, arguing for what it called an "open door" policy under which any companies from nations that had contributed to the Allied victory in the war should have access to Middle East oil fields. After years of political pressure and protracted negotiations the Europeans capitulated, and in 1928 the TPC (now known as the Iraq Petroleum Company, the region in question having been included in the new state of Iraq) was reconstituted. Exxon and Mobil were allowed a 23.75 percent share, to be divided equally between them. BP, Shell, and the Compagnie Française Petrole (CFP), which is sometimes referred to as an "eighth sister," each received a 23.75 percent share. The remarkable Gulbenkian retained his 5 percent. Only months after drilling began, the great Iraqi oil fields were discovered — just where Gulbenkian had predicted they would be.

The fact that the IPC brought together four of the Seven Sisters in a common venture was not the only landmark aspect of the 1928 agreement. Gulbenkian also insisted on a clause under which all the companies pledged not to pursue any other concessions within the former Ottoman Empire — as defined by Gulbenkian, who drew a red line on a map around the area he had in mind — *except through the IPC*. This meant that none of the IPC companies could exploit new wells in most of the Middle East without sharing the finds according to the agreed percentages. The famous Red Line Agreement completely contradicted the open door policy so heatedly insisted upon by the U.S. government and under which companies were supposed to have unfettered access to the area. Apparently, however, once Exxon and Mobil had gone through the door, the Americans were quite content for it to close again.[8]

The IPC consortium served as a model for the joint production agreements that burgeoned throughout the Middle East. In the 1930s Socal won concessions in Bahrain and Saudi Arabia and then sold a half interest in each to Texaco. Gulf and BP shared the rich Kuwait concession. The IPC companies held concessions in Qatar, Oman, the Trucial States, and Dhofar. Through all these ventures the fortunes of supposedly competing companies were inextricably linked, and it became increasingly possible for the companies to impose "orderly" conditions on world markets by common determination of desirable production levels.

*   *   *

But the joint production ventures, while providing the bedrock for the international oil cartel, were not the only form it took in the years before World War II. We have already seen (in Chapter 1) that the oil industry, like most others, also set up formal cartel machinery in order to eliminate competition among the majors. The Achnacarry Agreement of 1928, first signed by the heads of BP, Shell, and Exxon and later ratified by fifteen other companies, including the other four Sisters — Gulf, Texaco, Socal, and Mobil — was in fact a statement of principles that the firms agreed should govern the industry.[9] Certainly the most important was the first principle: "the acceptance by the units of their present volume of business and their proportion of any future increases in consumption." In other words, the companies agreed that, insofar as possible, the market would remain forever apportioned as it was in 1928, and that they would not try to expand their shares of it at the expense of other cartel members. Reduction of competition was also to be pursued by not expanding production facilities faster than demand and by supplying each market from the nearest producing area.

Of course, the "big three" companies understood that the successful establishment of a cartel requires considerably more work than a flat statement of principles; so in subsequent years they drew up a series of further agreements, applicable to the cartel members that joined later, each one spelling out in more precise detail how the cartel would handle specific problems.[10] These accords were called the Memorandum for European Markets (1930), the Heads of Agreement for Distribution (1932), and the Draft Memorandum of Principles (1934). The strategy underlying all of them was that the international cartel should merely set policy, which should then be carried out by regulating the market in each country. This plan was most clearly stated in the Heads of Agreement for Distribution:

> The "Heads of Agreement" which follow have been drawn up with a view that they should be used as a guide to representatives on the field for

drawing up rules for local cartels or for local Agreements. It is the intention that all such local cartels or Agreements should be based on these "Heads."[11]

The agreements also set up procedures for dealing with the complex technical questions that confront any cartel: How to determine the correct sales quota for each member? How to discipline those who consistently over- or undersell their quota? How to set prices? How to combat outsiders? As stated in the original Achnacarry accord, the cartel was governed by the basic "as is" principle: members would not do anything to disturb the prevailing market division without consulting the other members. This was reflected in the pricing clause of the Memorandum for European Markets:

> It is agreed between the parties that they shall maintain at least the share of the total trade which they held during the basic period, and to this end prices and selling conditions shall be fully and frankly discussed and agreed between the local representatives. In the event of disagreement between the parties the matter shall be settled by a simple majority vote, each party having one vote for each complete one percent of quota.[12]

This system of voting, weighted according to market share, gave the biggest companies the biggest voice in cartel policies.

The companies agreed to punish any failure to meet established sales quotas — by selling either too much or too little — by a standard cartel device, a sliding scale of fines that would be levied on the oversellers and distributed to the undersellers. Firms that consistently undersold their quotas, however, would eventually have part of their market share allocated to another member. A quota could be enlarged, of course, if the company bought out an outsider. Otherwise, outsiders who seriously threatened market stability were to be fought by means of all-out price wars. Independent refiners and marketers could be supplied by cartel members in order to prevent them from dealing with independent producers of crude oil; for the cartel's greatest anxiety remained that independent producers would flood the world with oil from new fields, producing a glut and driving prices down. Finally, all these arrangements were to be policed by an international secretariat in London and two central working committees, one operating in London and governing distribution, the other in New York, governing supply.[13]

As always it is difficult to evaluate precisely what effect the petroleum cartel had on markets in the 1930s. The cartel never achieved absolute control over any market; there were always irritating independents to contend with, and during this period there was a steady flow of oil from fields in the Soviet Union which the cartel members could not control. But there is evidence that in many markets the cartel was effective. In Great

Britain, for example, prices remained stable throughout the decade — and this at a time, it must be recalled, when potential supplies were rising sharply because of new discoveries, while demand was declining because of the Depression. Shell, Exxon, and BP dominated the market and followed the "as is" principles in their dealings with each other. Independent distributors generally did not challenge the majors' pricing policies or market shares.[14]

In Sweden, detailed records of the local oil cartel were obtained by a parliamentary committee that completed an investigation in 1947. The market there was shared by Exxon, Shell, BP, Texaco, and two smaller companies. The frequent meetings held by these firms throughout the 1930s (for example, fifty-one in 1939 alone, at which 776 subjects were discussed)[15] illustrate the hard work necessary to keep a cartel functioning smoothly. The minutes of the meetings show that members agreed on price changes; they redistributed market quotas; they practiced price discrimination, consistently charging government agencies higher prices than private customers; they engaged in collusive bidding on contracts; and they successfully pressured independent importers and marketers to respect their pricing policies.[16]

Controlling the American Market

Ironically, the entire machinery of the international cartel depended upon control of the one market the cartel could not legally touch: the United States. In 1930 U.S. fields produced the vast bulk of the world's oil, and the United States consumed more petroleum products than any other country. Also, much of the oil that entered world markets still was exported from the United States, despite the discoveries that were increasingly concentrated in such areas as the Middle East, Venezuela, and the East Indies. The cartel had no chance of stabilizing world markets unless U.S. production could be absorbed in an orderly fashion; yet, because of U.S. antitrust laws, the American domestic market and exports of American oil had to be specifically excluded from the Achnacarry Agreement and its successors. In order for the cartel machinery to be complete, then, two essential pieces had to be forged in the country from which the industry had sprung: the basing-point system and prorationing.

The basing-point system had in fact been employed since the early days of the industry but was formally enshrined at Achnacarry. It was simply a method of maintaining prices at a level set by the strongest producing country. It was also known as the "Gulf-plus" system because it provided that oil delivered anywhere in the world, no matter where it originated, would be priced as though it had come from the U.S. ports on the Gulf of Mexico, from which most American oil was exported. In other words, if Shell delivered a cargo of its Iraqi oil to Greece, the price of the oil would be the posted price per barrel in the Gulf ports *plus* the cost of transport from the Gulf ports to Greece — even though the oil had actually come from Iraq. Shell thus made an extraordinary profit on two counts: Iraqi oil was cheaper to produce than American oil, yet sold for the same price; and Iraq was much nearer to Greece than the Gulf ports were, yet the company charged as though the oil had been transported from the Gulf. The companies obviously favored this rather irrational system because it eliminated price competition based on production costs and supply points; and the Americans liked it particularly because it protected their relatively expensive oil from being undersold. However, by the 1940s, when the Middle East had begun to supplant the United States as the leading export region, oil consumers began to protest the Gulf-plus system. The companies finally established another basing point in the Persian Gulf, thus eliminating "phantom freight" charges for Middle East oil; but the actual price of the oil was set as high as U.S. oil, even though it remained cheaper to produce.[17]

Even more important than the basing-point system was the control over U.S. production that was achieved under the "prorationing" system. By the 1920s the Rockefeller interests had lost their near perfect monopoly over American production. Gulf and Texaco were founded upon Texas oil, and that state soon proved to be fabulously rich — a fact that to the major companies was both a blessing and a curse. Texas, as one observer has called it, was "the wild edge of the industry," with hordes of mavericks and wildcatters prospecting for oil and thus keeping alive the awful specter of glut. In 1929 the industry's governing body, the American Petroleum Institute, announced a plan to limit U.S. production to the levels prevailing in 1928 — a plan, coincidentally enough, that was announced six months after the Achnacarry "as is" Agreements[18] and that would have complemented them handsomely. The attorney general soon declared this plan illegal, however, and in 1930 the worst fears of the major companies were realized. An old wildcatter known as "Dad" Joiner, drilling on land the majors had written off as worthless, discovered the vast East Texas field, and overnight the state was awash in oil. What was worse, most of it was in the hands of independents.[19] Export markets were soon glutted, the price began to drop, and it became impossible to enforce Achnacarry.[20]

In response the majors mounted a counterattack that finally achieved goals they had pursued for years. Ironically, they did so by shifting their position on a controversial policy they had hitherto resisted: the "conservation" of oil. Because of peculiarities in the American approach to mineral rights — notably the "rule of capture," under which oil belongs to whoever removes it from the ground, even if it is drained from fields underlying someone else's property — American oil fields had historically been exploited hurriedly and wastefully, using methods that left much of the oil irretrievably in the ground. By and large, the major companies had been hostile to calls for "conservation" that would grant some official or quasi-official body the power to regulate production. But by the late 1920s the noble public purpose expressed in the concept of conservation had come to fit the majors' desperate desire for production limits — limits that the antitrust laws prevented them from imposing on their own.[21] And East Texas gave them the perfect chance to turn apparent disaster into triumph. Independents might be strong in East Texas production, but the majors still controlled the transport, refining, and distribution. Like John D. Rockefeller before them, they realized the strength that control gave them in a buyer's market.

Between 1931 and 1933 the majors ruthlessly cut the price they would pay for East Texas oil, from a high of 98 cents a barrel to the absurd price of 10 cents a barrel in April 1933. Claiming that unrestrained production was forcing them to set such calamitous prices, they lobbied intensely at the Texas legislature for the creation of a body that could limit production to the level of market demand. As Karl Crowley, a Texas lawyer, put it in testimony before the Temporary National Economic Committee in 1939: "The majors said in effect, 'Cut production in East Texas to what we think it ought to be and we will pay you $1.00 a barrel for oil. If you do not, we will ruin you with low prices.' "[22] In November 1932, the legislature acceded, and ever since the Texas Railroad Commission has imposed prorationing on oil producers in the state, that is, demand for oil is rationed among the producers, with no production allowed over the level of demand.

With Texas disciplined, it was a relatively easy matter to extend production controls to the rest of the country. After a series of meetings of oil-state governors, Congress passed a measure that was signed into law by President Roosevelt in August 1935, establishing the Interstate Compact to Conserve Oil and Gas. Since then the compact has divided the estimated *national* demand among some thirty oil-producing states. The compact does not have the power to enforce the production quotas it suggests, but it has been a success nevertheless: since its creation, overproduction of domestic oil has almost never been so severe as to cause prices to drop.[23] And once the states had agreed to proration production amongst themselves, only one minor problem remained to be resolved: what to do about producers who secretly lifted more oil than their quota allowed and sold it in other states. The various state boards had no jurisdiction over such sales. But once again the federal government came to the rescue,

passing the Connally Act (known as the "hot oil" act) of 1935, which outlawed interstate sale of oil produced in excess of state quotas.

By 1935, in short, U.S. production of oil was determined by a mechanism which, in the words of a Senate Small Business Committee Report,
"operates as smoothly and effectively as the finest watch." The report
continued:

> The oil-control policies in effect in the United States consist of a series of
> State and Federal statutes, recommendations of committees made up of
> integrated-oil-company economists and recommendations as to market
> demand made by the Bureau of Mines of the Department of the Interior.
> No single item is in itself controlling; taken together they form a perfect
> pattern of monopolistic control over oil production, the distribution
> thereof among refiners and distributors, and ultimately the price paid by
> the public.[24]

With such tidy order imposed on the U.S. market — and the threat of
American overproduction removed — the Seven Sisters could and did
proceed with the more troublesome task of regulating commerce in oil
around the world.

The Middle East After World War II

For the oil companies, as for the firms controlling other major industries,
World War II was an interval during which cartel arrangements were
disrupted but not destroyed. In the United States, as noted in Chapter 1,
the war coincided with a brief period of more active official interest in antitrust prosecutions, spurred by the public outcry against cartels and given
particular impetus by the revelations about Exxon's deal with I. G. Farben
restricting the development of synthetic rubber. The antitrust case against
Exxon was settled with the company's plea of nolo contendere and a fine
of $50,000. More damage to the company's public image was done during
the hearings before the Senate Committee on National Defense, when
Senator Truman called the company treasonous. As if one charge of collaboration with the enemy were not enough, in 1940 it was revealed that
Texaco was underwriting a visit to New York by a German "commercial
counsellor" whose real job was to dissuade American businessmen from
selling arms to Great Britain.[25]

One might think that such bad publicity, particularly from the Exxon–
I. G. Farben case, would have made the companies leery of cartel arrangements that could prove so politically damaging. Exxon, in fact, stated that
the oil cartel was already defunct. The company claimed that the Draft
Memorandum of Principles, since 1934 the basic cartel agreement, had

been verbally terminated in 1938, and that "any activities that may have survived came to an end in September, 1939, as a result of the outbreak of the war."[26] But there is evidence to suggest that this was not true. The local cartels created under the master agreements remained in place, and a Swedish parliamentary inquiry showed that in that country, at least, the local cartel operated throughout the war years. Investigators later discovered that the oil companies had drawn up a Draft Memorandum of Emergency Arrangements shortly after the war began to apply to the neutral countries, such as Norway, Denmark, Sweden, Finland, Holland, Belgium, and Switzerland.[27] And a 1944 document from Exxon's own files, obtained by the government during another antitrust proceeding, indicated that the firm intended to maintain its cartel connections. Looking toward the end of the war, Exxon officials wrote, "The conclusion reached by all parties was that bygones would have to be bygones but that in equity each party should be entitled to resume his prewar supply position as soon as it was practical to do so and conditions permitted."[28]

* * *

Events after the war, however, soon made it obvious that simple resumption of "prewar positions" would not be possible. New circumstances required a reshuffling of shares in world production and markets. What is remarkable is how smoothly the cartel carried out the transition.

The new factor in the oil equation after the war was a country whose riches were proving to be unimaginably huge: Saudi Arabia. The story of Saudi oil actually begins in the 1930s, when a prospector named Frank Holmes won a concession in Bahrain, an island sheikdom twenty miles off the coast of Saudi Arabia in the Persian Gulf. None of the majors already involved in the Middle East was seriously interested in the Bahrain concession because under the terms of the Red Line Agreement none of the Iraq Petroleum Company participants could develop new fields in the area without the agreement and participation of the others. Holmes therefore sold his concession to Standard Oil (California), or Socal, which thus became the sixth of the Seven Sisters to enter the Middle East, in a move that was eventually to change the entire configuration of the cartel.

Socal struck oil in modest quantities in Bahrain in 1931, the main importance of the strike being that it led Socal to pursue a successful concession in Saudi Arabia. The company soon found oil there, but, not having markets for it, Socal in 1936 agreed to sell one-half of its Bahrain and Saudi interests to Texaco, another heretofore outsider to the Middle East which had substantial established markets but was short of crude. With Texaco's arrival, all the Seven Sisters were now operating in the Middle East, which was fast becoming, as the prescient geologist Everett de Golyer described it, "the center of gravity of the world of oil production."[29]

But after World War II the cartel's artful structure of control over Middle East production, allowing the oil to flow fast enough to meet demand but not fast enough to produce a glut, threatened to collapse because of Saudi Arabia. Not even the most enthusiastic geologists who visited the desert kingdom had guessed how much oil lay under the sands, and as early as 1941, according to the Federal Trade Commission, Saudi Arabia was capable of producing between 100,000 and 200,000 barrels of oil a day, whereas Socal's and Texaco's market position "east of Suez," where the oil was theoretically destined, could absorb only 12,000 a day.[30] The two companies therefore found themselves facing a decision of historic significance: whether to attempt to crash through the cartel's barriers by unleashing their oil on world markets and setting off a price war, or to cooperate with the cartel and attempt to "fit" Saudi oil into the prevailing pattern without disrupting it.

The choice took the form of whether or not to allow Exxon and Mobil, two companies linked to the cartel through the Red Line Agreement, the Draft Memorandum of Principles, and other accords, to join the Saudi Arabian consortium, which at that time was called Caltex. Within Socal a fierce dispute developed after the war between directors who favored Exxon's entry and those who opposed it. A leader of the latter faction was Ronald C. Stoner, whose memoranda documenting the battle were obtained by the Subcommittee on Multinational Corporations of the Senate Foreign Relations Committee. Stoner argued that Saudi Arabian oil was so cheap and abundant that Caltex could and should have a policy of unrestrained competition, which would soon place Socal and Texaco ahead of even Exxon and Shell as the world's leading oil companies. Stoner's memo is worth quoting at some length:

> We, the California-Texas, the only solely American group in the area . . . are in a position to expand rapidly; not because we already have the markets, but because we have cheap oil available right now; i.e., with relatively little investment we can put more oil into the Blue Line Area (East of Suez) and other areas, and by obtaining tankers we can put oil any place in the world until it seems advisable to lay the Trans Arabian pipeline. Our earnings in Arabia are tremendous and are going to be greater, deal or no deal with Standard-Vacuum [Mobil] for the simple reason that it will take such a small investment to put our crude from the oil fields of Arabia to the port of Ras Tanura and then to the world.[31]

In response to the contention that Exxon could provide Caltex with markets and capital, Stoner argued that Caltex was in a position to take over Exxon markets by providing oil more cheaply, and that additional capital could be raised from the smaller U.S. companies, which were eager for large supplies from a source other than the cartel.[32] This was what the majors feared above all — that the independents would gain access to cheap oil and force a major revision of market shares and control over production.

As things turned out, however, they need not have feared. Caltex was finally convinced, despite Stoner's pleas, to take the "responsible" course of action, that is, to join the cartel. By late 1946 Socal and Texaco had agreed to sell Exxon and Mobil 30 and 10 percent, respectively, of the Saudi concession (now known as the Arabian-American Oil Company, or Aramco), with the former two firms retaining 30 percent each. Saudi oil could now be absorbed in an "orderly" fashion, with the four companies collaborating instead of competing to develop markets. Also, Exxon and Mobil, by joining Aramco, could do their part to ward off the threat of glut by cutting back on production in their other fields to compensate for increased Saudi production.

That this was done on a large scale is illustrated by the case of Iraq. Having neatly tied up control over Iraq's production by the terms of the Iraq Petroleum Company and the Red Line Agreement, the IPC companies (which included Exxon, Mobil, Gulf, BP, and Shell) later adopted a policy of retarding production by a variety of means.[33] Areas with large proven reserves were developed slowly. Prospecting in new areas was carried out half-heartedly. The host countries naturally were eager for rapid development and high production so that their take from taxes and royalties would rise; the companies, fearful of losing their concessions to independent companies that might actually produce oil from them, had to take every possible measure to conceal their restrictive tactics. In Syria, where the IPC had a concession, numerous wells were dug, but only to shallow depths, as the company's managing director explained in a memo: "We have been steadily complying with the letter of the Mining Law by drilling shallow holes on locations where there was no danger of striking oil."[34] And during the investigation by the Senate Subcommittee on Multinational Corporations into the petroleum industry, Senator Edmund Muskie revealed a 1967 intelligence report on potential oil reserves in Iraq. The report stated, in part:

> The files yielded proof that IPC had drilled and found wildcat wells that would have produced 50,000 barrels of oil per day. The firm plugged these wells and did not classify them at all because the availability of such information would have made the companies' bargaining position with Iraq more troublesome.[35]

In fact, documents proving the IPC's consistent attempts to suppress Iraqi production were deemed so sensitive by the U.S. government that they were deleted from the 1952 FTC report on the grounds of national security and not released for twenty years.

With Socal and Texaco successfully absorbed into the network of cartel arrangements, there remained only one question to settle concerning Saudi oil: its price. The oil was extraordinarily cheap to produce, and neither Sheik Ibn Saud, the country's ruler, nor Socal and Texaco could see any reason for not placing the oil on the market at a price that would reflect its low production cost. One of Texaco's reasons for taking this position was described in a "personal and confidential" letter found in the company's files:

> If the crude price is determined by agreement among Aramco Directors and not on a cost-plus basis, there may be danger of violation of U.S. Anti-Trust laws . . . it may be contended that any agreement as to price arrived at by the Aramco Directors, who are also Directors of four large oil companies doing business in the United States, is in effect an agreement in restraint of trade with the United States.[36]

But Exxon insisted on protecting its other oil by setting an artificial price based on the old Gulf-plus system, and the Exxon position won the day: Aramco oil was posted at $1.43 a barrel, approximately the same as the posted price for other oil f.o.b. the Persian Gulf.[37] In 1947 a U.S. congressional committee headed by Senator Owen Brewster estimated that the total cost of production for a barrel of Saudi oil was about 19 cents, plus 21 cents royalty.[38]

❋ ❋ ❋

The next challenge to the oil cartel came in Iran. There BP had held an exclusive concession since 1933, but the company's high-handed attitude toward the locals, and Great Britain's meddling in Iranian politics after World War II, combined to produce tremendous resentment against the British. In the late 1940s, spurred by news of agreements that gave the governments of Saudi Arabia and Venezuela a larger stake in the profits from their countries' oil, the Iranian parliament, or Majlis, began to agitate for better terms from BP. The company offered concessions that fell far short of the Iranian demands, and soon the struggle over oil, fueled by the anti-British feeling, was the leading political issue in Iran. In early 1951, a nationalistic politician named Dr. Muhammad Mossadeq called for nationalization of BP's holdings. Not long afterward Mossadeq was elected prime minister of Iran, and the Majlis voted to seize the oil fields and refinery.

Although most of the other major oil companies, especially the Americans, felt that BP had stupidly provoked the upheaval by its haughty and uncompromising attitude, nationalization was an affront that could not be tolerated, lest other countries be tempted in that direction. Therefore the Seven Sisters, backed by their governments (who did their best to keep independent companies in line) instituted a world-wide boycott of Iranian oil. The fact that the boycott was extremely effective but caused hardly any disruption of world markets provides one of the most revealing clues to the cartel's power. Iran, one of the largest producing countries, saw its income from oil drop from over $400 million in 1950 to under $2 million in the two years between July 1951 and August 1953. Although the boycott cut Iran's sales of oil between 1951 and 1955 by a total of an estimated 900 million barrels (assuming 1950 production levels as a constant), that huge shortfall was almost entirely compensated for by rapid increases in production in other Middle East countries: some 300 million extra barrels in Kuwait, 200 million in Iraq, 300 million in Saudi Arabia, and the remaining 100 million from various smaller producers.[39] In other words, having themselves forced Iranian oil off the market, the Sisters had no trouble filling demand from their other sources — evidence of the tight command they held over the relationship between supply and demand.

Iran's economy was severely disrupted by the boycott, and in April 1953 the U.S. Central Intelligence Agency was able to organize a coup to topple Mossadeq and install the Shah, Reza Pahlavi, as absolute ruler. Under the circumstances the Shah, of course, was willing to restore Iran's oil industry to the control of the companies. But the power balance in the Middle East, and especially in Iran, had shifted. The United States was now the foremost power and had engineered Mossadeq's removal; the British were fading and were so widely hated in Iran that the reestablishment of an exclusive British concession was politically unthinkable. After prolonged negotiations involving the companies, the governments of their home states, and Iran, a new distribution was agreed upon in 1954.[40] An Iranian Consortium was formed that was the first joint venture in the Middle East to include all Seven Sisters. Each of the five American Sisters (Exxon, Mobil, Gulf, Socal, Texaco) was to receive 8 percent of the consortium. Shell was awarded 14 percent, and the Compagnie Française de Petrole got 6 percent. BP was left with a much reduced but still dominant 40 percent. The National Iranian Oil Company, Mossadeq's creation, would retain ownership of the fields but would pay BP the compensation that Mossadeq had refused. The consortium, by securing exclusive rights to buy and market Iranian oil, kept de facto control over production levels — the crucial issue, as always.

The only problem was the exclusive nature of the consortium. Only eight companies from only four countries would determine the speed and direction of the flow of oil from Iran, a fact which did not sit well with such excluded nations as Italy and Germany or with the smaller oil companies. Nor did the U.S. Justice Department like the arrangement. As one attorney there accurately remarked in a memo, it appeared to "manifest a continuation of the cartel pattern."[41] Unable to prevent the establishment of the consortium, antitrust officials in the Justice Department pressed for the inclusion of some American independent firms, which at least would loosen the Sisters' tight grip on Middle East oil supplies. After considerable resistance the cartel companies agreed, but the inclusion of the independents proved to be little more than "window dressing," as an Exxon official later called it.[42] In the first place, the State Department arranged for the accounting firm of Price, Waterhouse to evaluate the suitability of the independents to be included — and Price, Waterhouse was already well known as the firm that handled accounting for most of the cartel arrangements.* Once selected, the nine independents were not granted a substantial share of the consortium, as they and the Justice Department had wanted, but instead received only 5 percent to be shared among them. Again the cartel had effectively maintained intact its monopoly by redistributing shares.

The Iranian Consortium was also extremely important because it included a "participants' agreement" for limiting production in that country, and by extension in others. At the time this agreement was kept secret from the Iranian government, and it remained so for twenty years. The basis of the agreement was an unusual and complicated formula for determining the "average programmed quantity," or APQ. Each year, the eight companies in the consortium, plus the group of independents (known as Iricon), would put forward nominations for how much oil they felt the consortium should take from Iran that year. The nominations would be listed in order of descending magnitude, and, once companies whose share of the consortium totaled 70 percent had been listed, the last firm's nomination would be taken as the APQ, that is, its nomination would set the amount of crude to be produced, which would then be divided among the firms according to the size of their holdings. This system was first made public during the 1974 Senate hearings on multinationals and their effect on foreign policy. The record of the hearing included a table illustrating how the APQ for 1966 was determined.[43] The table shows that in 1966 it was the CFP nomination that became the APQ because it was the CFP's share of the consortium, when added to those companies that made higher bids, that brought the cumulative total to over 70 percent.

This curious method of determining production levels served several purposes. Most important, it allowed the firms that had abundant sources of crude in other countries — most obviously the three firms that held 30 percent shares in Aramco — to keep down production in Iran by making low bids. In fact, the pattern visible in the 1966 table held true for most years. Exxon's, Texaco's, and Socal's nominations were almost always below the APQ, whereas Shell and Iricon, both short of crude, nearly always made high nominations.[44] The APQ system also allowed the U.S. and European companies to check each others' influence; the combined share of neither group reached 70 percent so that neither could set the produc-

* See the report of the Subcommittee on Multinational Corporations of the Senate Foreign Relations Committee for its hearings on Multinational Petroleum Corporations and Foreign Policy. (93rd Cong., 2d sess., Part VII, pages 248–249.)

Example of APQ Procedure, 1966 APQ

Participation	Share (percent)	Cumulative (percent)	Nomination (thousand barrels per day)	Total Program (thousand barrels per day)
Iricon	5	5	101	2030
BP	40	45	811	2027
Shell	14	59	284	2027
Mobil	7	66	137	1964
CFP	6	72	117	1945
				...... APQ
Exxon	7	79	132	1890
Texaco	7	86	120	1712
Gulf	7	93	119	1700
Socal	7	100	117	1644

tion quota without the nomination of at least one firm in the other group affecting the figure. The APQ system was also self-enforcing, in that companies that lifted more than their quota of oil had to pay a sharply higher price for it.

Another significant feature of the Iranian Consortium is that the APQ system appears to have been used to determine production levels not only in Iran but also in Saudi Arabia. Following the Mossadeq upheaval, the Iranian government — that is, the Shah — found itself in a position to make certain demands on the consortium companies, which were now more sensitive than before to their political vulnerability. As a result, the growth of oil production in Iran was rapid, despite the secret restraints of the APQ, averaging about 12.5 percent between 1958 and 1972. As it turns out, Aramco also applied this growth rate in Saudi Arabia, where the richness of the concession forced the companies to respond to the government's wishes. However, if the same high growth rate had been followed throughout the Middle East, a glut would have ensued; so the companies cut back in countries where they were not so fearful of the rulers' wrath. Iraq, for example, saw its oil production rise by only 5.12 percent between 1958 and 1972 — and we have already seen how production was held back in that country. Kuwait, another country with large but not colossal deposits, appears to have been used as a sort of pressure valve; when more Middle East production was required, it came from Kuwait; when cutbacks were necessary, they were imposed there. Kuwait's growth during the period in question was 5.93 percent. A few of the oil-producing states — Nigeria and Indonesia, for example — expanded much faster, but it appears that the companies operating there were expected to reduce their Middle East take to compensate.[45]

The sum of these intricate arrangements and maneuvers has been an impressive degree of control by a very few companies over a commodity that one would expect to be one of the most volatile, in terms of production levels and price, on the world market. Evidence developed by John Blair shows that between 1950 and 1972 the expansion of oil production in eleven OPEC countries was astonishingly stable. Using OPEC statistics, Blair obtained the actual year-by-year aggregate increases in production, then computed the *average* annual growth, which was 9.55 percent. As shown in the chart, the actual annual increases are almost identical to the figures that would have resulted if production had been steadily increased by 9.55 percent per year. Yet this absolutely steady aggregate growth rate took place during a period when growth in some countries was extremely unstable, subject to sharp jumps or plunges from year to year, and when national growth rates varied enormously, from Venezuela's average of about 2 percent between 1958 and 1972, to Nigeria's 33 percent after 1968.[46]

*　*　*

But perhaps the single most important long-term result of the Iranian Consortium was one noticed by very few people at the time: it blocked any chance of effective prosecution of the major oil companies under U.S. antitrust law. The contest between the companies and the antitrust authorities already had a considerable history, with the laws, by and large, faring poorly: the case against Rockefeller's Standard Oil Company ended in 1911 with a symbolic but ineffective dissolution of the trust, and the case against Exxon and others in the early 1940s also generated much publicity but had little impact on the cartel's power. It was the next case, however, that brought a classic confrontation between the cartel and the American legal system, ending in near total victory for the cartel.

In 1952, in the midst of the Iranian crisis, the staff of the Federal Trade Commission published the report already referred to several times in this chapter: *The International Petroleum Cartel*. The product of two years' work by a team led by the economist John Blair, the report for the first time publicly described the Achnacarry accord and its successors, the significance of the Middle East joint ventures, and the major companies' control over technology and marketing outlets. Not long after its publication, President Truman ordered his attorney general to open antitrust proceedings against the oil companies. Blair says in his own account of the case:

> Its specific objectives . . . were to bring to an end: (a) the monopolistic control of foreign production; (b) the curtailment of domestic production

OPEC Crude Production:
Actual versus Estimated Growth
Rate, 1950–72

Billions of Bbl./Yr.   Millions of Bbl./Yr.

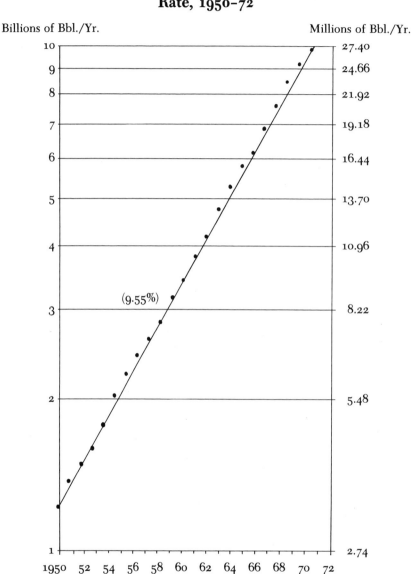

SOURCE: John M. Blair, *The Control of Oil* (New York: Pantheon, 1977), p. 100.

"to the extent necessary to maintain the level of domestic and world prices"; (c) the use of quotas to limit sales in foreign markets; (d) the limitation of U.S. imports and exports; and (e) the exclusion of American independents from foreign sources of supply.[47]

Almost as soon as the grand jury had been impaneled, though, the companies' counterattack, largely carried out through political channels, was having its effect. In January 1953, Truman ordered that the criminal case be substituted by a civil case, which made the acquisition of documents from the companies considerably more difficult. After the inauguration of President Eisenhower, the antitrust lawyers found themselves frustrated at every turn. Eisenhower and his secretary of state, John Foster Dulles, hoped to gain for American companies a substantial share of Iran's oil and were at that moment plotting the overthrow of Mossadeq. Understandably they were not enthusiastic about vigorously prosecuting the very companies they were hoping to push into Iran in order to make the United States' supply of oil more secure. The Justice Department first was informed that "national security" considerations would have to take priority over antitrust, and then jurisdiction over the case was removed from the Justice Department altogether and given to the State Department — an unprecedented move,[48] and one suggesting the importance Eisenhower and Dulles attached to the case.

Indictments were filed on April 21, 1953, against the five American Sisters. But Eisenhower's National Security Council continued to do everything in its power to hinder the prosecution, as Leonard J. Emmerglick, the Justice Department lawyer in charge of the case, later told a Senate subcommittee:

> The pressures were continuous from month to month, sometimes from week to week, to downgrade the importance of prosecution of the cartel case. We did not give up at the staff level in our purpose to achieve the aims which we set out to achieve, but we realized that new impediments were being thrown in our way as each one of these developments took place."[49]

First Emmerglick was ordered "not to challenge the legality of joint production, joint refining, joint storage, and joint transportation ventures among the seven international majors,"[50] even though these ventures constituted the essence of the cartel. When the Justice Department lawyers were shown the secret APQ for Iran and were told that the attorney general, Herbert Brownell, had exempted it from prosecution on national security grounds, they knew their case had been gutted — for what clearer and more egregious violation of antitrust principles could there be than the APQ, which allied American and European companies in a secret conspiracy to set prices and limit production?[51] Emmerglick was also informed that he should not seek dissolution and divestiture of the oil companies as a remedy.[52]

Nevertheless, the Justice Department lawyers plodded ahead, concentrating on the marketing arrangements set up by Achnacarry and the Draft Memorandum of Principles. Finally the case faded to an ignominious end. Exxon, Gulf, and Texaco signed consent decrees in 1960, which bound them not to engage in certain restrictive practices — but the decrees included loopholes that rendered them meaningless. Charges against Socal and Mobil, the two remaining defendants, were dismissed without prejudice in 1968. With the demise of the case ended the most promising opportunity ever to break the hold of the Seven Sisters on what may be the world's most important industry.

The Libyan Crisis and the Rise of OPEC

After Iran, and with a brief upheaval during the Suez crisis of 1956, the course of oil ran relatively smoothly through world markets until the late 1960s. Then the next crisis arose — this one in Libya, and this one foreshadowing the stunning events of 1973 that would permanently shift the control of oil from the companies to a cartel of sovereign states: OPEC.

Libya was a latecomer to the oil world and thus had the chance to learn from the mistakes of other producing countries. When the state began to grant concessions, King Idris cagily gave many of them to independent companies whose approach would not be influenced by their rich holdings elsewhere and the fear of excess oil on the market. The independents, thought the king, would actually look for oil, find it, and produce it, whereas past experience had shown that the majors might only make a show of doing so. The king's strategy proved wise: by 1970 Libya had become one of the world's five largest producers of oil, and independents were responsible for fully half the production — a situation unprecedented in the Middle East.

This development alarmed the majors, particularly since Libyan oil was of extraordinarily high quality and was located a very short distance from Europe, giving it important competitive advantages. As a result, the price of oil began to drop until, by the late 1960s, the posted price (that is, the official market price) stood at $1.80 per barrel while the real price was as low as $1.30.[53] Internal Exxon estimates from this period show that the rapid increases in Libyan production were preventing the Sisters from raising production elsewhere — which could conceivably lead to the loss of the all-important concessions in Saudi Arabia, Iran, Iraq, and Kuwait.[54] Yet almost overnight — between 1969 and 1971 — the problem was re-

solved. Most of the independents were eliminated from Libya, and production there dropped drastically. The story of how this came about is one
of the most mysterious in oil history.

On September 1, 1969, King Idris was overthrown by a group of radical
officers led by Captain (now Colonel) Muammar al-Qaddafi. The officers
were determined not only to extract better terms from the companies but
also to change the country's overall approach to its oil reserves. King Idris
had been content to let the companies pay a low price for their oil as long
as they lifted large quantities of it, and it was this strategy that had helped
to flood world markets; the independents were delighted to have a cheap
source of crude. Qaddafi, however, wanted to do the opposite: conserve
Libyan oil but earn the same (or higher) revenues by making the companies pay more for it. Just months after taking power, the new regime
made a number of demands, including a 40-cent increase in the posted
price. The companies adamantly refused, offering instead a token 5-cent
increase.

Qaddafi then took advantage of the king's original sagacity by splitting
the independents from the majors. In May and June of 1970, the government sharply reduced the output allowed Occidental Oil, which was
owned by Armand Hammer and was the biggest of the independents
operating in Libya. Occidental and the other independents were vulnerable to such cutbacks because they were dependent on Libyan oil for their
foreign markets, and their companies had prospered tremendously because of their foothold in international trade. The majors, on the other
hand, particularly Exxon, which was the largest single producer in Libya,
did not need Libyan oil, a fact crucial to an evaluation of ensuing events.
Following the clampdown on Occidental, Hammer pleaded with Exxon to
supply his company with oil from other sources, but Exxon refused. Occidental, desperate for crude, soon surrendered to Libyan demands for a
price increase — 30 cents immediately, rising to 40 in five years. With
their common front broken, the other companies in Libya were forced to
agree to similar terms.

However, the surrender left the companies in an even worse position
than before. The Persian Gulf states responded to news of the Libyan
price increases with demands for similar hikes on *their* oil, and the companies found themselves facing the dreaded "leapfrog" effect. That is,
Libya wanted a premium price because of the high quality and convenient
location of its oil and had proven its ability to win the premium, largely
because of the split between majors and independents. But the Persian
Gulf group was powerful enough to insist on parity with Libya. Thus,
every time Libya won an increase, the Persian Gulf would demand the
same, whereupon Libya would require still another increase to reattain its
premium, and so on. Unless the contest were halted, the prospect was for a
never-ending price spiral.

In early 1971, the oil companies — majors and independents — held a series of meetings in London and New York. The result was an agreement to adopt a "joint approach" to oil talks, that is, to negotiate as a unified group in order to arrive at a lasting "global" settlement and avoid the leapfrog effect. This accord was supplemented by another, the Libyan Producers Agreement, parts of which were kept secret for three years and which bound the companies in Libya to a united negotiating front.[55] Following a long tradition in the industry, the oil companies, which were now engaged in the vital task of negotiating the world price of an essential commodity with a group of increasingly combative Third World states, were given a tentative exemption from antitrust laws from the U.S. Justice Department, in effect legalizing their collusion.[56]

But the "joint approach" fell apart almost at once. The companies' proposal for global negotiations provoked bitter protest from Libya and the Middle Eastern states, which of course saw it as an attempt to limit their freedom of action. In the face of this resistance, the major oil companies and the U.S. government, which had been closely involved in preparing the joint approach, caved in. It was a historic moment, apparently the first time the companies had been resoundingly defeated by a force stronger than their cartel. On February 14, 1971, the companies signed the Teheran Agreement with the Middle Eastern producers, providing for an immediate 30-cent increase in the posted price. Libya, as expected, then demanded another increase and won it — a hefty 76-cent hike, raising the Libyan posted price to $3.30 per barrel.

But the evident rout of the companies did not end there. Qaddafi soon took up the cry voiced at an OPEC meeting in December 1970 for "participation," that is, for partial national ownership of oil production in the OPEC states. By 1973, fully 33 percent of Libya's concessions had been nationalized completely, and companies holding concessions to another 50 percent of the country's reserves had been forced to accept the government as majority partner.[57] But there was a curious pattern in the takeovers, namely, they affected the independents most severely. Bunker Hunt was nationalized. Occidental and Oasis (a consortium of three independents) lost majority ownership and suffered severe production cutbacks. Certain of the majors were also nationalized, but, interestingly enough, they were the firms known to be "crude-long," that is, with supplies of crude larger than they could easily market. BP, which along with Bunker Hunt held the concession to Libya's largest field, was nationalized. So were the holdings of Socal and Texaco, both members of Aramco and the Iranian Consortium, the mavericks among the Seven Sisters, with disquieting tendencies to sell crude to independent refiners and marketers. On the other hand, Mobil, a famously "crude-short" company, was not nationalized, nor was Exxon, although both lost majority ownership and were ordered to cut back production.[58]

To most of the world, and to not a few oil experts, the end of the Libyan crisis seemed to leave the oil companies in a state of disorderly defeat. Prices had risen sharply; concessions had been nationalized, and it was clear that other OPEC states would follow Libya's lead; and the companies' aura of invincibility had been shattered. But the actual state of the market after 1971 could not have pleased the majors more. Libyan production, which had threatened to get out of hand, had been cut from 3,318,000 barrels a day in 1970 to 2,100,000 in 1973.[59] The unruly independent companies in Libya had been nationalized or severely restricted. The losses of the majors in Libya were negligible as long as the world market was stable and the concessions in the Middle East were solid. Even the higher prices were of minor importance; sales of oil tended to drop only slightly in response to higher prices, and the companies simply passed on the increase to consumers. It appeared that Qaddafi, like so many magnates before him, had decided that the cartel's policy of restricted production and resulting high prices was the best. This was not to be the last case of the OPEC states learning crucial lessons from the Sisters.

The happy results of the uproar led some observers to question whether the major companies had not deliberately followed a policy that they knew would cripple the independents and reduce the supply of oil reaching world markets. The abandonment of the joint approach to negotiations with the OPEC states in particular has come into question. It happened so quickly as to be inexplicable, leading some observers to wonder whether the companies simply felt so vulnerable in the face of OPEC threats that they collapsed or whether the majors had secretly decided to submit to split negotiations, which they knew would hurt the independents more than themselves. At least one independent oil man favored the latter theory. During a policy meeting in London, when the majors made it clear they were planning to meet the demand for separate negotiations, Norman Rooney of Bunker Hunt protested: "You're selling us down the river!"[60]

*　*　*

The stage was now set for the triumph of the organization usually thought of as *the* cartel: the Organization of Petroleum Exporting Countries.

Ironically, OPEC not only is decades younger than the cartel of the Seven Sisters but was organized as a belated means of opposing it. In 1960, after an unusual bout of price competition had struck world markets, Exxon unilaterally imposed a cut in the Middle East posted price of 10 cents a barrel. The cut came on the heels of another, of 18 cents, the year before, and, because the major companies were so inextricably linked, the others soon followed Exxon's lead, in one stroke drastically reducing the income of the producing countries. At this, the outrage of the countries finally galvanized them into action, and in September 1960, five nations — Kuwait, Iraq, Iran, Saudi Arabia, and Venezuela — met in Baghdad and formed OPEC. In numerous interviews and articles, the participants remarked that the countries were simply copying the companies' tactics: "It was quite clear from the start that the price cuts might precipitate the establishment of what some delegates chose to call 'a cartel to confront the cartel.' It had precisely that effect!" wrote Fuad Itayim in the *Middle East Economic Survey*.[61]

However, OPEC found itself largely unable to exert any influence for the next ten years. The companies seemed too powerful — the example of Iran was still fresh — and they retained a virtual monopoly over knowledge and expertise. Also, during the 1960s there was a general oversupply of oil, which put the countries in a weak position; they all wanted to expand their sales and therefore were easy to divide and rule. But then came the Libyan crisis, and suddenly the countries realized they were in a position to do the dividing and ruling. Ten years had made a huge difference. Third World militance was on the rise, all nations were becoming progressively more dependent on oil, and the OPEC experts had learned much about the industry. Following the December 1970 meeting in Caracas, and accelerating after the Libyan nationalizations, the demands for "participation" swelled. At the end of 1972 Sheik Ahmed Zaki Yamani, Saudi Arabia's oil minister, reached agreement with Aramco on immediate 25 percent Saudi participation, rising to 51 percent in 1983. The Saudis also won an extremely high "buy-back" price, that is, the amount the companies would pay to purchase the Saudi share of the oil. This high price reflected a new and all-important factor, one which put the OPEC nations in an even stronger position: an apparently growing shortage of oil on world markets.

In October 1973 representatives of OPEC and the Seven Sisters met in Vienna in order to negotiate a new posted price for oil. The OPEC ministers were in a militant frame of mind, the steadily rising market price of oil having convinced them that a steep rise in the posted price was necessary. The companies, however, were equally determined to resist, having agreed just two years before to sharp increases that were meant to last until 1976. As if the impasse were not difficult enough, the talks were immensely complicated by the political situation in the Middle East: on October 6, 1973, Egypt and Syria attacked Israeli-occupied territory, and the Yom Kippur War was on. The Arab oil states were under pressure to use oil as a political weapon against Israel, whereas the governments of the countries where the Seven Sisters were headquartered — particularly the United States, of course — were sympathetic to the Israelis.

These circumstances led to a breakdown in negotiations and the culmination of the process that had begun in 1960: the oil-producing countries' drive to control their own resources. Sheik Zaki Yamani demanded an increase in the posted price to about $5. The companies' representatives were authorized to offer no more than a 25 percent hike and replied that before talking about larger increases they would have to consult with their governments because the price of oil was so clearly a matter of public concern. But OPEC, with war raging, would not wait. Three days after negotiations collapsed, OPEC unilaterally increased the posted price by about 70 percent — from $3.00 to $5.11. On the next day the Arab members met and then announced an embargo on their oil to states that supported Israel. The panic that ensued on world markets and the apparent shortage that resulted from Arab production cutbacks soon made possible another, even more stunning jump in the price, to $11.65 on January 1, 1974. In three months the price had nearly quadrupled. Never again would the OPEC nations haggle over price with anyone but each other. The "energy crisis" had arrived with a vengeance.

The companies now found themselves in an extremely awkward position. Theoretically toiling in the interests of the industrialized countries who consumed most of the world's oil, the companies were horrified at the astronomical price increase that was certain to damage the economies of those nations — not to mention the Third World countries dependent on imported oil, who were hurt far more seriously. OPEC had completely usurped the long-standing ability of the oil cartel to set the world market price, and gradually the companies' control over production levels — and their very ownership of the oil concessions — were being usurped as well. It would seem that OPEC and the companies would be implacable enemies. But the private cartel remained in firm control of most of the world's transport, marketing, and refining capacity. By opposing OPEC they would be risking their immense investments and their access to oil on terms more advantageous than the independents'. They therefore faced an unpleasant choice: either identify themselves with the consuming countries and do everything in their still considerable power to break OPEC, or cooperate with the producers' cartel.

The companies, of course, in keeping with the tradition of avoiding serious struggles at all cost, elected to cooperate with OPEC. During late 1973 and early 1974, the Seven Sisters in effect administered the embargo for the Arabs, using their marketing and transport expertise to cut back supplies to certain countries.[62] They repeatedly referred to the shortage of oil — which helped to justify the price increases — although statistics show that in 1973 OPEC oil production in fact expanded, and at a rate slightly *higher* than the stable growth rates that had prevailed in the past.[63] The companies made record profits in 1973, with Exxon's profit of $2.5 billion the highest for any corporation in history — news that greatly spurred public outrage directed at the companies in the United States and

Europe, where it was widely suspected that the so-called shortage was a sham.

The storm of indignation abated quickly, however, and the companies found they had weathered it in excellent shape. They might not be popular — indeed, they might be widely maligned and mistrusted — but their prosperity had proven to be unaffected by even the apparently most cataclysmic events.

In 1974 and 1975 came the final confirmation of the Sisters' loyalties. As a recession developed in the Western economies, partly as a result of the oil price increases, demand for oil began to drop and a surplus loomed. It was a moment many economists had been waiting for: the buyer's market that would inevitably cause OPEC's unity to collapse and the artificially high oil prices to fall. It was widely agreed that the organization could not survive a surplus. Yet survive it did, and handsomely, by using the technique long before perfected by the companies: cutting back production. In 1974, the year following the terrible "shortage," OPEC production was slightly *below* 1973; and in 1975 it fell sharply, although not for lack of capacity. As a result the price remained steady (in late 1975 the producers actually raised it by 10 percent) and OPEC strong.[64]

How was this possible? Twice before OPEC had attempted to ration production among its members and had failed. The states, all desperate for higher earnings, had never been able to agree on how production cuts should be shared or to discipline themselves to respect quotas. To be sure, OPEC had learned many lessons since 1960, in particular the value of unified action. Also, the price had risen to such levels that certain OPEC nations, such as Saudi Arabia and Kuwait, already were earning more money than they could spend. But the most important difference from OPEC's former attempts to cut production was that this time the countries were working with the companies and not against them.[65] The Sisters, as we have seen, were past masters at matching production to demand; the fact that they were serving the OPEC states by doing so did not make them any less eager than before for "orderly" markets. "Why abolish the oil companies," said Iran's oil minister, Dr. Amouzegar, to Anthony Sampson, "when they can find the markets for us, and regulate them? We can just sit back and let them do it for us."[66]

❋   ❋   ❋

The aftermath of the great oil upheaval, then, offered various ironies. The cartel that for so long had cavalierly toyed with the fates of the oil-producing nations now found itself serving them as a junior partner — although still a partner to be respected. The mechanisms that had been perfected over decades to ensure that the price the companies paid for their oil was low now worked impressively to keep the price high. Either way, the Seven Sisters reaped huge profits by making sure production did not outstrip demand. Even with ownership of the greatest fields increasingly in the hands of the OPEC countries, the companies' hold on the "downstream" end of the industry — refining and marketing — ensured a prosperous future for many years to come. OPEC might demand progressively better terms for their oil, but they could not afford to alienate or cut ties with the private cartel. In fact, it was to the countries' advantage to sell their oil on favorable terms to the majors in return for efficient marketing; and it was in the companies' interest to preserve their advantage. The two cartels needed each other.

4

Uranium:
Welcome to the "Club"

In recent years the cartel that has attracted the most attention in the United States *as a cartel* (the Seven Sisters, of course, are the subject of interminable writings, but they are rarely perceived as a cartel) has been the international organization of uranium producers that operated between 1972 and 1975. Although world trade in uranium is tiny in monetary terms when compared with major industries like petroleum or chemicals, the cartel was important for a number of reasons. Some of them have to do with its immediate impact and aftermath. Uranium is a crucial strategic material for any industrialized country, and the cartel presided over no less than a sixfold increase in its price in a very brief period. The membership of a Canadian subsidiary of a U.S. corporation, Gulf Oil, in the cartel raised tricky questions of antitrust law; and the way the Justice Department handled the case caused heated controversy over antitrust enforcement. Also, the uproar in the uranium market left behind it the largest group of civil lawsuits in American history, involving billions of dollars of possible damages hinging on the activities of the cartel.

It is not simply the monetary and legal fallout from the cartel that makes it significant; the presence of Gulf Oil is also noteworthy. The major oil companies, like most contemporary transnationals, have greatly diversified their holdings during the last twenty years. Mobil owns department stores. Atlantic Richfield owns copper mines and newspapers. Exxon makes office machinery, data-processing systems, and golf clubs. But the oil companies have not become heterogeneous conglomerates in the man-

ner of Gulf & Western, dealing in unrelated products ranging from sugar
to movies to insurance; rather, the thrust of their diversification has been
in related fields.[1] The Sisters and their smaller siblings have focused their
investments on the chemicals industry, many branches of which are inseparable from petroleum, and, more important, on other sources of energy.
Oil companies owned 25 percent of U.S. reserves of coal in 1978. They
have acquired large uranium deposits. And they have begun to devote
substantial research to the energy sources of the future: solar and geother-
mal power and the energy of the winds and the tides. The spread of oil
company control over all forms of commercial energy has caused alarm,
much of it based on the concern that the companies might delay the development of certain forms of energy in order to protect their investment in
others. But another suspicion arises: if the Seven Sisters have found cartelization such a boon to their petroleum enterprises, are they not likely to
practice it in other energy ventures? A 1979 report by the Tennessee Valley Authority noted that, as coal and uranium prices were shooting up, oil
companies were investing heavily, leading the authority to worry that
different sources of energy would not be "available on a competitive
basis." The TVA noted that at least a dozen "anticompetitive mergers"
had taken place in the energy field since the authority started studying
the problem in 1977. In addition, said the report, the uranium market
is "highly concentrated and is dominated by nine of the nation's largest oil companies, eight of which also have major coal interests."[2]
Thus it is no small matter to find Gulf playing a major part in the uranium
cartel.

The cartel is also intriguing because of its hybrid form. As with certain
raw materials cartels in the past, national governments helped to establish
the uranium cartel, and state-owned firms were members, so that it became an odd alliance of — and forum for negotiations among — individual transnational corporations, groups of firms urged to organize by their
governments, and the governments themselves. As we shall see, the degree
of state compulsion involved remains a controversial issue upon which
much of the litigation surrounding the cartel depended.

The Club

Uranium is employed mainly in nuclear weapons programs or as the fuel
for nuclear reactors, the latter consuming the overwhelming bulk of the
material. Both because of its military applications and the tremendous
amount of energy that can be gleaned from a tiny amount of uranium —
for example, one pound of the metal yields as much energy as 3 million
pounds of coal — it has for some time and in most countries been viewed

as a strategically crucial resource, the production and use of which must be ruled by national security policies. Governments, therefore, historically have played a large role in uranium commerce. Laws concerning the production (in the countries that possess reserves), import, export, processing, and use of uranium are on the books in every industrialized nation; in some, government agencies or companies hold a monopoly over some or all phases of the uranium cycle.

Five countries sell almost all the uranium now marketed in the non-Communist world: France (with "captive" reserves in the former French colonies of Africa, particularly Gabon and Niger), South Africa, Australia, Canada, and the United States. The metal, which is relatively scarce, is generally found in natural deposits with a low content of uranium. The deposits are mined and then milled, a process that yields uranium oxide, U_3O_8, colloquially known as "yellowcake." It is in this form that uranium usually enters international commerce.

Uranium is like many other raw materials in that its market is subject to violent shifts in supply and demand due to economic cycles, new discoveries, and political events. In the early 1970s, uranium producers found themselves the victims of such a market collapse. During previous years the price of yellowcake had been dropping steadily from about $8.00 per pound in 1967 to a low of about $4.50 in late 1971. The plunge was caused by a classic case of overcapacity, brought on in some countries by government policy. In the United States, the Atomic Energy Commission (AEC) had adopted an overly ambitious procurement policy in the late 1950s, and was forced to cut back its purchases in the 1960s so as not to be saddled with an immense stockpile. France, too, had overbuilt its uranium capacity, as had South Africa. Finally, the supply and demand equation was affected by large new deposits of uranium being developed in Australia and Canada, which were scheduled to begin producing in the early or mid-1970s.

The political factor that most directly affected international uranium commerce was that the American market, by far the largest in the West, was effectively closed to foreign producers. In 1954 the AEC, in order to encourage the domestic production of uranium, ruled that foreign uranium destined for use in American reactors could not be "enriched" in the United States. Enrichment is the process by which the concentration of the isotope uranium-235 found in yellowcake is artificially increased from about 0.7 percent to about 3 percent, the level necessary for nuclear reactor fuel. Enrichment requires extremely advanced technology, and in the United States the process has been maintained under a government monopoly. Since enrichment *outside* the United States is approximately twice as expensive, the AEC's ban on enrichment of foreign uranium had the effect of pricing it out of the American market. Foreign uranium could be purchased and stockpiled; but until the AEC changed its enrichment policy it could not be used. As a result of this insulation from foreign competition, yellowcake prices in the United States historically were somewhat higher than those abroad.

By late 1971, according to estimates of the eventual cartel members, major producers of uranium outside the United States had a capacity of at least 100,000 tons (and perhaps as many as 160,000) to sell between the years 1972 and 1977, whereas "uncommitted demand," that is, projected demand for uranium that had not already been covered by contracts for future delivery, stood at only 26,000 tons.[3] Even that figure seemed shaky, with rising construction costs, opposition from environmentalists, and other difficulties causing delays in completion of nuclear plants. Facing what they viewed as a disastrous continuation of a buyer's market, the producers did what came naturally to companies in their position: they organized a cartel.

It appears that several producers initiated movement toward a cartel more or less simultaneously in 1971. In Canada, representatives of a uranium-producing company called Rio Algom approached government officials with plans for an international quota system that would bring "order" to the market. Since Rio Algom was a subsidiary of the gigantic British-based transnational, Rio Tinto Zinc, which also had uranium interests in Africa, Australia, and the United States, the proposal carried weight; and, given market conditions, it met with government approval.[4] At the same time discussions were taking place among France, Germany, South Africa, and Japan on the subject of uranium. It was the French national firm, Uranex, that took the crucial next step: they invited the other producers to a meeting in Paris on February 1, 1972. Just three days later the basic structure of the cartel had been created.

The Paris meeting was attended by delegations from France, Canada, and Australia, as well as from Rio Tinto Zinc and the South African national firm, NUFCOR. Having reviewed the unhappy balance of supply and demand and noted that the U.S. embargo on foreign uranium was not likely to be lifted in the near future, the participants moved on to more intriguing matters: "future price trends" and especially "possible price stabilization mechanisms." Here again the French took the lead, suggesting essentially that producers agree not to sell yellowcake for less than $6.25 per pound for delivery in 1975, with the price rising about 3 percent per year after that. The French also proposed — and the others were agreeable — that the available market for uranium be parceled out on a quota basis. Most important, it was agreed that there should be some standing organization that could periodically review prices, quotas, market conditions, and other matters of interest. From the beginning this organization — the cartel, in effect — was known informally to its members as the "Club."[5]

Following the traditional cartel pattern, the uranium producers then proceeded to organize themselves on a national level. In France and South Africa, where uranium commerce was monopolized by a single company, the process was simple; but in Canada and Australia it was not. Between February and June, producers in those countries met repeatedly to try and answer various tricky questions: Which companies would take part? What would be their shares of the national quota? How big a share of the world market would they win in Club negotiations? What role would the governments play? The thorniest problem of all was posed in Canada, where a subsidiary of Gulf Oil was developing a large uranium deposit in partnership with a German firm. Both companies were deeply worried about violations of their home countries' antitrust laws, but their participation in the cartel was regarded as essential.

Further meetings of Club members were held in Paris in late February, March, and April of 1972, with each one producing further refinements in the cartel plans. The February parley produced a set of proposed understandings that were nearly identical to those finally adopted.[6] The March meetings drew up proposals for how to allocate the estimated uncommitted market among the producers. These were then reviewed by the various national groups, some of which were unsatisfied. The next meeting, therefore — in Paris on April 20 and 21, 1972 — was taken up by battles over market shares. Thanks to a memorandum written by one of the Canadians who attended, we have a detailed record of this meeting, which provides one of the most fascinating insights into this crucial aspect of cartel operations that has appeared in public to date.[7]

The April meeting opened with the French host inviting the national groups to report on their discussions of the proposed allocations. The Canadians stated that they had concluded they needed an increased share, but only a small increase, from 8100 to 9050 tons. The French and South Africans said their proposed shares were satisfactory. The Rio Tinto Zinc companies — Rossing, Parabola, and Mary Kathleen Uranium — also stood pat. But then John Proud, the spokesman for the Australian group, dropped a bombshell. The Australians, whom the Club members sometimes termed the "new producers" because several of them were just beginning to develop their deposits, would require a quota of 7550 tons instead of 3400. This requested increase, as well as the smaller Canadian one, meant that the demanded quotas surpassed the estimated total market by 5100 tons — nearly 20 percent.

So the haggling began, as the memo recounts. First the various producers expressed their dismay:

> Mr. Austin mentioned that he felt somewhat crushed by the turn of events.
> Mr. Albino said that he dreaded the situation developing where there

would be no agreement. If it did not happen, however, Rio Algom would compete in the marketplace.

Mr. Shilling felt that there was little more to say, since if new producers wanted to break into the market, it would not be possible to prevent their attempting to do so. He added that the situation could deteriorate rapidly into a price war.

Mr. Wright remarked that the meeting had reached the stage where it would gladden the hearts of all utility executives. Australia could see the possibility of sales at $4 per lb. and with a free enterprise country they would join the fray and suffer with the rest. It was a tragedy in his view.

The other Club members then began to importune the Australians to reduce their egregious demand. Veiled threats were made to unload government stockpiles at ruinous prices. At lunch the groups caucused, and during the Canadian caucus it was agreed to reduce their request slightly in order to appease the Australians. Mr. Proud was not much impressed but did raise the point that, if the agreement could be extended past 1977 — say, to 1980 — and the Australians were assured of a large quota in the later period, they might be willing to accept a smaller one now. The other groups were reluctant but not completely adverse to talk about extending the agreement and began to employ a sort of carrot-and-stick approach against the Australians: they discussed the post-1977 period with an eye to a large quota for the new producers, while insisting that Australia must yield at present because even the Australian companies, whose mines held rich and easily accessible deposits and therefore had some competitive advantage, could not win a price war against governments determined to unload huge stockpiles at any price in order to maintain a market share.

After another day of cajoling and threats, Mr. Proud agreed to take the Club proposals back to the Australian group for consideration. For the 1972–77 period every group scaled down its request, with the Australians taking the sharpest cut, from about 24 to 17 percent. But between 1977 and 1980 the Australians would be given fully one-fifth of the available market.[8] All the members must have breathed a sigh of relief: the cartel had been saved from collapse.

The next meeting of the Club convened in Johannesburg on May 29, 1972. There final agreement was reached on the form and functions of the cartel. It was to be temporarily headquartered in Paris, and, as is so often the case, it was given an innocuous name: the Société d'Études et de Recherches d'Uranium (known in English as the Uranium Market Research Organization), or SERU.[9] It consisted of a Secretariat, an Operating Committee, and a Policy Committee. Club members were to share administrative expenses on the basis of their share of the 1972–80 market. Final market allocations were determined, with the Australians apparently faring rather well:

Group	1972–77	1978–80
Canada	33.50%	23.22%
Nufcor	23.75	19.26
Uranex	21.75	19.26
Australia	17.00	24.44
Rio Tinto Zinc	4.00	13.82

The domestic markets of France, Australia, South Africa, and Canada were excluded from the agreements — an oblique recognition of home market protection — as was the United States, for antitrust reasons. Minimum per-pound prices were agreed upon:

Year	All Markets Except Japan, Taiwan, and Korea*
1972	U.S. $ 5.40
1973	5.75
1974	6.10
1975	6.45
1976	6.80
1977	7.15
1978	7.50

* For technical reasons, prices were slightly higher in these countries.

It will be noted that the prices were slightly higher than those proposed by the cartel just a few months earlier, although the increase was negligible compared with the hike soon to come.

Under the section "Working Mechanisms for Allocations" came the formulas by which it would be decided which group should get which sales contract. "The allocations would be initially based on contracted tonnages and as far as possible each group's quota would be filled at a uniform rate," read one clause. The secretary was to review all contracts to make sure they conformed to SERU rules. And the usual devious bidding procedure was devised to camouflage the cartel. The secretary designated the groups to be "leader" and "runner-up" for each particular order. The groups themselves then decided which firm within the group was to get the order (or serve as runner-up). The leader was allowed to bid as low as the cartel's minimum designated price at the time. The runner-up could bid no lower than 8 cents per pound above the minimum price; other bidders had to quote at least 15 cents higher than the minimum.[10]

The cartel also agreed upon three other measures of particular interest. The first was an attempt to squeeze out middlemen, that is, companies which bought uranium from the producers and then sold it to utilities. The Club members agreed that bypassing the middlemen would give the producers both greater control over the market and higher profits. The basic tactic against middlemen was to quote them a higher price than that quoted to utilities. Among the middlemen mentioned as targets were General Electric and Westinghouse, both manufacturers of nuclear reactors. In 1973, for example, the cartel's Operating Committee held a meeting that reaffirmed this principle, aimed particularly at the most important middleman: "It was agreed that nobody would enter into serious discussions with Westinghouse before coming back to the Club," read the minutes of the meeting.[11]

A second interesting feature was devised at the Cannes meeting of July 1972. This was an informal agreement, apparently never written into cartel rules, that producers would try to conceal the sources of the uranium they were selling. This would make it easier for the cartel members to subcontract among themselves for tonnages, thus making sure each producer got its correct quota of sales.[12] Finally, the cartel included the classic provision for penalizing members who went astray. Although some Gulf officials denied this was so, L. T. Gregg, one of Gulf's representatives to the cartel, admitted it during congressional hearings. Gregg said that the cartel several times imposed sanctions on member companies.[13] In one case, Rio Tinto Zinc used what Mr. Gregg called "a subterfuge to get a sale in Spain without telling the secretariat or any of the other club members what they were doing." Under the questioning of investigator William Haddad, Gregg amusingly recounted what happened when the trick was discovered — an illustration of the all-too-human conflicts that can bedevil a cartel:

> Mr. HADDAD: Mr. Mazel of RTZ [Rio Tinto Zinc] lied to the members in Johannesburg, or was evasive?
> Mr. GREGG: He was evasive.
> Mr. HADDAD: Did it come to a point where the tensions were so high that people nearly got into a physical battle?
> Mr. GREGG: It did.
> Mr. HADDAD: When you could not succeed with Mr. Mazel, what did you do? What did the cartel do?
> Mr. GREGG: The operating committee . . . went to Mr. Roy Wright, who was Mr. Mazel's boss . . . and asked Mr. Wright to censure Mr. Mazel for having done what he had done, and, further, for Mr. Wright to give assurances that Mr. Mazel's behavior and activities would be better controlled in future.
> Mr. HADDAD: And Mr. Mazel ended up in Brazil.
> Mr. GREGG: Well, I heard that he did go to Brazil.[14]

At the Cannes Operating Committee meeting in July 1972, the finishing touches were put to the cartel. Mr. André Petit, an official in the French

Commission d'Énergie Atomique, was designated secretary. The minutes
drily note: "From the security aspect it was thought convenient Petit
would be 'buried' in the large CEA HQ building."[15] The camouflage was
effective, and for the next two years the Club functioned smoothly, with
meetings held in such cities as London, Paris, Sydney, Toronto, and Las
Palmas. In 1974 the basic cartel rules were reworked during a gathering in
Johannesburg.[16] The rules changes refined the cartel's procedures to make
them more sensitive to varying circumstances. Market allocations were
altered slightly, and the cartel's period of operation was extended: the
market was provisionally parceled out among the members for the years
1981 to 1983.

But the most remarkable change was in the minimum price per pound.
Compare the price lists for 1972 and 1974:[17]

Year of Delivery	1972 price	1974 price
1974	U.S. $ 6.10	U.S. $ 8.50
1975	6.45	9.35
1976	6.80	10.30
1977	7.15	11.35
1978	7.50	12.50

For 1978 delivery the price had risen by about 70 percent, and it was not
to stop there. Rather, the upward trend accelerated rapidly. In 1974 U.S.
domestic prices (generally slightly higher than, but parallel to, foreign
prices) for immediate delivery of uranium rose from $7.70 in January to
$15.00 in December. The next year prices more than doubled again, from
$16.00 in January to $35.00 in December. By these lights the rise in 1976
was modest, to $41.00 by September.[18] Subsequently it rose to about
$44.00.[19]

This astonishing price eruption brought chaos to the uranium market
and phenomenal profits to the producers, both American and foreign.
How much it cost American consumers remains uncertain, but various
partial estimates have been made. In 1977 the California Public Utilities
Commission calculated that the higher prices for uranium would cost that
state's electricity buyers at least $1 billion in increased electricity bills
through 1990.[20] The New York State Assembly estimated similar costs to
New York's consumers.[21] And Aubrey J. Wagner, chairman of the Tennessee Valley Authority, noted that by the mid-1980s TVA would be using
7–8 million pounds of uranium per year.[22] Each increase of $1 per pound
in the price of uranium would thus cost TVA's customers $7–8 million per
year — and the price had *already* gone up by nearly $40 per pound be-
tween 1972 and 1977.

The cartel also left behind dilemmas for those who attempted to investigate it or judge the lawsuits it spawned. The questions it raised were by

no means easy to answer: To what extent was the cartel responsible for the increase? Did the cartel really cease to operate in 1975 because it was no longer necessary, as Club members claim? What was the actual relationship between private companies and governments within the cartel?

Gulf Mounts a Defense

The uranium crisis — for that is what it was, at least to those in the market — first became a matter of public concern on September 8, 1975, when Westinghouse "shocked the corporate world," as the *New York Times* put it,[23] with the announcement that it would not honor its contracts to sell nuclear fuel. Westinghouse is one of the country's leading manufacturers of nuclear reactors, and in order to assure their reactor buyers that fuel would be available during the reactors' working lives, Westinghouse often included in the deals a long-term commitment to supply uranium as well. The problem was that Westinghouse, in making such promises, did not have the uranium on hand; the company was not a producer but rather was "selling short," that is, selling what it did not own in hopes that when it *did* buy in order to make delivery the price would be attractive. Westinghouse made the catastrophic mistake — or bad gamble, depending on one's point of view — of pledging to provide some 65 million pounds of uranium over twenty years at a fixed price that averaged about $9.50 per pound. When, by 1975, the price had risen to $26.00, Westinghouse renounced contracts with twenty-seven electrical utilities, invoking a provision of the commercial law that permits the voiding of a contract if it is shown to be "commercially impracticable." Westinghouse argued that the uranium market was behaving strangely and that its losses on the uranium contracts could amount to $2 billion, which would wreck the company.

The utilities, of course, promptly sued Westinghouse to force the company to supply the uranium at the agreed price. Most of the cases were joined together and eventually came to trial in Richmond, Virginia. But meanwhile, in August 1976, a second bombshell was exploded in the uranium world, this one in Australia. An environmental organization called Friends of the Earth obtained — it is still not clear how — hundreds of pages of documents from the files of Mary Kathleen Uranium, the subsidiary of Rio Tinto Zinc. The documents included accounts of Club meetings and negotiations among the Australian producers' group, as well as a copy of the 1972 Johannesburg rules. The documents were immediately sent to the United States and passed on to the Justice Department, which had been gathering data on the uranium market since 1975. To most of the uranium industry the proof of the cartel's existence was not terribly surprising; the trade press had periodically reported the meetings of the Club. Although its inner workings were unknown, the existence of an international group that hoped to "stabilize" the market was more or less an open secret. However, the Australian documents provided Westinghouse with invaluable ammunition. On October 15, 1976, the company filed suit in a Chicago court against twenty-nine uranium-producing companies. One of them, of course, was Gulf Oil, whose Canadian subsidiary was unquestionably an active member of the cartel. Westinghouse argued that Gulf also was the link between the international cartel and other U.S. producers who cooperated and helped to drive up the price. Under antitrust laws, Gulf and the other companies faced the imposition of treble damages — which could have totaled a stunning $6 billion — if it were proved that they conspired to control the market. However, in 1978 Gulf responded with a countersuit charging that Westinghouse's offers to sell so much uranium were in fact an attempt to monopolize the entire nuclear market — reactors, fabricated fuel, and yellowcake — in the United States. The legal maneuvering in the early stages of the lawsuits was so astronomically expensive that one Gulf executive sardonically called the case the "Lawyers Full Employment Act." On December 31, 1980, Gulf and Westinghouse announced that they had reached a settlement out of court under which Gulf would pay Westinghouse $25 million and would supply 13 million pounds of uranium to Westinghouse customers. This settlement, however, did not affect Westinghouse's claims against the other cartel members.

In a final group of lawsuits, four U.S. uranium producers sued Gulf and an affiliated company, General Atomic, in an attempt to be freed from their contracts to provide General Atomic with large amounts of yellowcake at a fixed price. The producers said that with uranium priced at about $40.00 per pound, they stood to lose many millions if they were forced to sell at the much lower price in the contracts — and that they should be released because Gulf, as a member of the cartel, was directly involved in illegally driving up the price.

All told, the sums involved in this maze of claims amounted to nearly $10 billion. But the actual settlements, if they follow the pattern set thus far, will not approach that amount. Besides its compromise with Gulf in the cartel lawsuit, Westinghouse has settled out of court with all the utilities that sued the firm for breach of contract. The settlements have cost the firm an estimated total of nearly $1 billion, a relatively modest sum.

Most important, then, from the public's point of view are not the lawsuits, which still promise to plod through years with battalions of lawyers executing endless legal maneuvers. What actually allowed electricity consumers some knowledge of the cartel's operations were two official inquiries, one performed by the New York State Assembly Committee on Corporations, Authorities, and Commissions, and one by the Subcommit-

tee on Oversight and Investigations of the House Committee on Interstate
and Foreign Commerce, Ninety-fifth Congress. The records of those inquiries — and particularly the transcripts of the House hearings — offer
an instructive portrait of the cartel, especially because the evasive or self-
serving statements made by some of the cartel participants during the
hearings could be directly challenged by skeptical legislators or staff members.

The hearings focused on two basic questions: To what extent was Gulf
involved in the cartel? And, what effect did the cartel have on American
consumers? To these questions Gulf responded with two arguments that
documents showed had been in preparation almost since the moment Gulf
began its participation in the cartel.[24] The first was that Gulf was forced
to join by the Canadian government; the second, that the cartel had no effect on the American market and therefore Gulf's participation did not
violate antitrust laws.

It should be noted here that Gulf did not restrict its defense to these
points. The company also argued that the cartel had nothing to do with
the astronomical rise in uranium prices after 1973. In his introductory testimony before the subcommittee and in a prepared statement, Gulf chairman Jerry McAfee emphasized the reasons that, in his view, accounted for
the turbulent market:[25] (1) sharply higher costs for discovery and production of uranium; (2) the policies of foreign states, particularly the 1973 decision of the new Labour Party government in Australia to halt the development and export of uranium, a decision since reversed; (3) policies of the
U.S. government, including the embargo and certain technical changes in
the enrichment process and enrichment contracts; (4) the Arab oil embargo and the price hikes of that year, which "sharply increased the
pressure for acceleration of the development of nuclear power plants";
and (5) Westinghouse's massive short sales of uranium, which, when the
company revealed them in 1975, caused a scramble for available uranium. Whether for tactical reasons or not, Gulf publicly attached most
importance to the last factor, saying that Westinghouse's ruthless
attempt to monopolize the market by promising cheap, long-term fuel
supplies was the main reason for the supply squeeze. It seems likely that
all the above factors did have some influence on uranium prices. But the
question facing investigators was whether the cartel also had an impact,
either abroad or at home — and on this point Gulf's protestations were
unconvincing.

The company actually involved in the uranium cartel was Gulf Minerals
Canada Limited (GMCL), a wholly owned subsidiary of Gulf Oil. In the
early 1970s GMCL was developing a uranium mine at Rabbit Lake, Sas-
katchewan Province, in partnership with Uranerz, a subsidiary of a West
German firm. Although the project did not come on line until 1975, it was

clear that GMCL would be a major producer of uranium once production began.

When in 1972 the preliminary cartel discussions took place, the Canadian government made it clear to all Canadian uranium producers that it favored an international marketing arrangement and that it wanted all producers to participate. GMCL and Uranerz both expressed concern about violations of U.S. and German antitrust laws. Beyond these amply documented facts, however, the actual sequence and shape of events are extremely foggy and open to contradictory interpretations. In every forum available Gulf executives and lawyers have argued that GMCL was *forced*, or at least pressured very strongly, by the Canadian government, to such an extent that Gulf faced the choice of cooperating or abandoning a large investment. There is no question that the goverment was in a position to coerce if it so wished and needed. GMCL operated in Canada on the basis of permits that had to be reviewed every year. In a long series of statements dating to 1965, the government affirmed its supervision over marketing of uranium; and on April 21, 1972, nearly three months after the initial cartel meeting, the Canadian minister of energy, mines, and resources said publicly:

> The government of Canada has taken steps for the holding of discussions at an international level regarding the state of the uranium industry and of the development of nuclear programs. We firmly believe that the unduly depressed prices for uranium which are prevailing act as the major disincentive to the active exploration of a very considerable geological potential in Canada . . . In the absence of international market stability, the development of the reserves required for the nuclear power industry in the 1980s will not be ensured, with the possible consequence of a critical shortage of supply developing in that period. . . . We are determined to bring long-term stability to our resource communities and make sure their marketing difficulties are ironed out.[26]

The government invited GMCL representatives to early meetings of the Canadian producers and urged the company to attend the April 20, 1972, Paris meeting, which was, in fact, the first Club gathering that Gulf delegates attended. Gulf also received two telegrams from the government "requesting" that the company adhere to the cartel's "common terms." One of the telegrams stated that "the Canadian government endorses the principle of such an arrangement as in the national interest and will look to GMCL as a Canadian producer to take every reasonable step to ensure compliance."[27]

Citing these telegrams and statements, Gulf later contended that such pressures exempted the company from antitrust restrictions. To support its legal position the company referred to a Justice Department advisory

memorandum of January 1972, on the conflicts between U.S. antitrust
laws and the policies of foreign states:

> A foreign government may, because of its economic or national interest in
> "rationalizing" competition in certain industries, promote certain private
> cooperative agreements or understandings by companies within that in-
> dustry. It may, therefore, expect a U.S. company seeking to do business in
> its territory to abide by the governmentally desired — but not officially
> imposed — system of arrangements as a condition of securing, and keep-
> ing, the necessary permits and approvals.
>
> In general, restrictions such as these applying to commerce in the host
> country and imposed by the host government will create no antitrust haz-
> ards for the American company. In particular, price or capacity restric-
> tions in the foreign market and not involving exports to the United States
> should not violate U.S. antitrust laws.[28]

The investigators, however, were not so sure. They wondered whether
Gulf had in fact been compelled to join the cartel or whether the company
actually had been eager to join and had itself asked the Canadian government to make statements that would support the *appearance* of compulsion. Various pieces of evidence were obtained regarding this problem.
One letter from a Canadian government official to the vice-president of
GMCL asking that a Gulf representative sit on the Operating Committee
of the cartel (a position of some large responsibility) turned out to have
been drafted by GMCL itself *for* the government.[29] At a Canadian producers' meeting on February 16, 1972, shortly after the birth of the cartel,
a GMCL representative spoke to officials of the Energy Ministry about attendance at the next Paris meeting; according to a Gulf memo, "They specifically recommended against Gulf's seeking an invitation and it was
agreed that Gulf would not participate. However, [they] did agree to keep
us informed."[30] This does not appear to be the posture of a company being
dragged forcibly into the cartel. Nor does the fact that a Gulf executive
played a major part in drafting the 1974 "Johannesburg rules."[31] Nor does
a statement by the Canadian government representatives at the 1972 Johannesburg meeting that formalized the cartel. A memo summarizing the
meeting includes this passage: "Mr. Austin [a Ministry official] went on to
say there was a second tenet, namely that the Government had had as its
policy stance from the beginning that it would not force Canadian producers into an arrangement. This attitude had been clearly expressed in a
message sent to each of the producers by the Ministry of Energy, Mines
and Resources on April 14."[32]

Gulf officials, when asked about such evidence, responded that the government statement was merely a formality, as was the fact that Gulf had
drafted the above-mentioned letter; no doubt the ministry had requested
it, explained one executive. But considerable doubt remained as to

whether Gulf was not urging — demanding, even — the very compulsion it used as its excuse to join the cartel. At one point during the House sub-committee hearings, a New York State assemblyman who was present made a telling point when he suggested a posture Gulf could have adopted rather than its apparently enthusiastic participation in the cartel:

> Mr. KOPPELL: Would it have been possible for Gulf to have said to the Government of Canada, "We don't want to participate in this. We don't think we can. But if you tell us to charge a certain price or ship a certain amount, we will comply with such directives"? Would that not have been an alternative for you?

To which Roy D. Jackson, the Gulf lawyer who wrote the position paper arguing that Gulf had been forced to join, could only give the lame reply: "I don't know. It was not one that was presented."[33]

Another Jackson memo raised intriguing questions as to Gulf's professed desire not to engage in any egregiously anticompetitive activity. In anti-trust matters there are venial and mortal sins: fixing prices and market shares is regarded as serious, but far more serious is any conspiracy to drive a competitor out of business. Gulf executives, who worried that they might be exposed as members of a price-fixing cartel, were particularly concerned to dissociate themselves from the appearance of any predatory behavior. Imagine the consternation of Roy Jackson, then, when he received a copy of the minutes of a Canadian producers' meeting where a report on the cartel Operating Committee session at Cannes was presented. Among the topics covered at Cannes was the following item:

> There followed a general discussion of the impact of Westinghouse bidding in Europe. It was believed that the maximum amount of uranium available to Westinghouse at the moment was 3,000 tons of U_3O_8, considerably less than that required to fill the SSPB order, for example. Some members thought that Westinghouse should be approached directly, whereas other views were that it would be a dangerous move. The consensus finally reached was that if the club was to survive as a viable entity, it would be necessary to delineate where the competition was and the nature of its strength, as a prelude to eliminating it once and for all.[34]

Jackson granted that the language "bothered" him, and he soon wrote to Gulf with the following advice:

> My inclination is that Gulf representatives should always record their strong objection and total disagreement with any such predatory cartel action affecting or intended to affect American trade or commerce. I do not think that recorded expressions of this sort will seriously hurt Gulf as far as the Canadian government is concerned, because surely that Government will recognize the unique hazard presented as far as Gulf is concerned. There is the further practical consideration that Gulf's recorded objection and disagreement will in all likelihood just be noted and over-ridden by other cartel members.[35]

In this subtly worded passage the critical sentence is the last one. Jackson insisted that he meant it as a further warning, that no matter what protests Gulf made, if it was in a cartel it could not control what the cartel did and was therefore dangerously liable for any predatory action the other members might take. The logical and prudent step, as Assemblyman Koppell suggested, would be for Gulf to remove itself from the cartel in such circumstances. But we have seen that Gulf was not eager to do that. And the Jackson letter of course may be interpreted in quite a different manner. What he appears to be saying, in fact, is that Gulf could and should protect itself by putting on record some protest at the cartel's attempts to eliminate the competition; but that there was no danger of actually hampering the cartel in such attempts, since Gulf would surely be overridden in any case.

*   *   *

From the available record, then, it is difficult to judge whether Gulf unwillingly submitted to the Canadians' urgings, whether the firm cooperated eagerly, or whether it even initiated certain aspects of the Canadian arrangement. The Canadian government has sealed its records on the cartel (as has Australia) and prohibited its officials from testifying; so it appears unlikely the issue will be illuminated in the near future. However, it is possible to draw conclusions regarding the second fundamental prop of Gulf's defense: that the cartel had no effect on the U.S. market. Any credence that contention might have commanded was demolished during the House subcommittee hearings.

Gulf and other industry members who wished to minimize the cartel argued that it had little impact on the international market and thus could not have influenced price or supply in the United States. George White, president of the Nuclear Exchange Corporation (Nuexco), a private company that publishes an authoritative market report, testified that the Club was inefficient because the minimum prices it set consistently lagged behind the prevailing world prices, which were moving up rapidly for reasons that had nothing to do with the cartel. Because U.S. prices were always slightly higher than prices abroad, the cartel's laggard attempts to support the foreign market were meaningless as far as the United States was concerned. Foreign producers would not want to buy in the United States at a higher price; and American utilities were prevented from buying abroad by the embargo. The two markets were effectively isolated from one another. The same line of reasoning was followed in an "economic impact statement" written by a Gulf official to justify entry into the cartel.[36]

But this claim rested on a number of assumptions which on close inspection proved to be unwarranted: that the U.S. price was always higher;

that the cartel had little effect on prices abroad; and that the embargo kept foreign uranium off the U.S. market. It was an internal Gulf memo that suggested the fallacies in the company's official position. On March 28, 1974, W. D. Fowler, a Gulf expert on uranium supply and distribution, wrote to a colleague and described a pattern he perceived in the market:

> What appears to be happening is that the international producers are in effect setting the world price via
>
> (a) establishing a "floor" that is higher than the U.S. offers to buy
>
> (b) the U.S. producers refuse to sell at any price that doesn't give them a substantial margin above the "floor" being quoted by the non-U.S. producers.
>
> (c) thus, in essence, the international producers can stop any transactions by constantly nudging the floor upward.
>
> In the interim, the U.S. buyer becomes increasingly frustrated, offers a higher price in order to get some response and the cycle starts over again.[37]

In other words, a sort of "leapfrog" effect had developed, with the Club and American producers bidding the price up. In his testimony before the subcommittee, Fowler did his best to downplay the significance of his observations,[38] as did other officials. But there was evidence to corroborate the Fowler memo. Although George White of Nuexco had insisted that foreign prices lagged behind those in the United States, his own company's report for April 19, 1974, noted that American prices were "materially lower" than those in the world market, leading foreign buyers to bid aggressively for American uranium and thus drive up the domestic price.[39]

It appears that the reverse occurred as well: American utilities bought foreign uranium at prices set by the cartel. Gulf's position on this possibility was that the AEC embargo kept American utilities out of the foreign uranium market. But the investigation flatly contradicted that argument. A 1972 Gulf memorandum stated, "Price in the U.S. market will ultimately depend on what RTZ, Uranex and Nufcor are willing to quote for movement of non-U.S. material into U.S. if U.S. AEC ban is lifted."[40] In fact, it was widely expected within the industry that the AEC would gradually drop its refusal to enrich foreign uranium, beginning sometime in the late 1970s. In 1973 the AEC published notice of just such a change in regulations: the embargo would begin to be lifted in 1977 and would be completely lifted by 1984.

American buyers of uranium therefore knew that they would be able to enrich the foreign uranium they bought for delivery in the future, and, accordingly, during the 1970s they bought a great deal. The TVA bought about 20 million pounds of U_3O_8 from three foreign producers, including a 17 million–pound purchase in 1974 from Rio Algom, a cartel member, at a price pegged to the world market price.[41] Also in 1974, the Duke Power

Company of North Carolina contracted for 20 million pounds from Rio Algom for delivery between 1981 and 1990. The pricing provision was similar to the TVA contract.[42] Other American utilities had numerous contacts with foreign producers and were offered uranium at prices that exactly matched those set by the cartel; several of these utilities made major purchases.[43]

The weight of such evidence makes it difficult to credit Gulf's contention that the cartel had no effect on the international or domestic market. At the least there are strong indications that the cartel did contribute to the rise in the world market price; that foreign buyers did occasionally compete for American uranium, influencing the price; and that American buyers did acquire foreign yellowcake at terms set by the cartel. Even Gulf memoranda written in 1972 indicate the company knew that foreign and U.S. markets were inseparable.[44] Additional proof of this point can be found in the discussion regarding the cartel's duration. As we have seen, when the producers first came together they contemplated an accord lasting from 1972 to 1977, but the Australians soon demanded that it be extended to 1980. The date, from Gulf's point of view, was crucial for two reasons. First was the imminent end of the embargo. Gulf already suspected in 1972 that the U.S. embargo would be partially lifted during the late 1970s, making the American and foreign markets even more interpenetrated than they already were. Second, most experts agreed that the glut of uranium existing in 1972 would vanish by the late 1970s; that is, the supply and demand curves would cross[45] so that one of the justifications for the cartel — that it was merely an arrangement whereby producers would maintain the price at a "reasonable" level during a period of hardship caused by glut — would vanish. In short, Gulf expected that after 1977 there would be no economic rationale for the cartel to exist and increasingly less support for the claim that it did not affect the American market.

For this reason Gulf at first appeared extremely reluctant to extend the agreement beyond 1977. In May 1972, Mr. N. M. Ediger, an executive of GMCL, stated this sentiment unequivocally at a meeting of the Canadian producers: "Speaking for Gulf," the minutes state, "he said his company could not contemplate an arrangement that would extend beyond 1977."[46] At a later meeting Mr. Ediger observed: "However, so far as Gulf was concerned, their hazards with antitrust legislation would increase as the end of the decade was approached. . . . Gulf Minerals had agreed to take a business risk up until 1977 on the assumption that the U.S. embargo would not be lifted until 1978."[47] Yet, when the Australians insisted, the Canadian group, Gulf included, agreed to extend the agreement until 1980, in full knowledge of the fact that this greatly increased the likelihood of affecting the U.S. market. Nor did Gulf pull out of the cartel in 1974, when the producers' meeting in Johannesburg allocated market shares for the period 1981–83, a division spelled out in the "Johannesburg rules" that a Gulf delegate drafted.

But perhaps the most devastating blow to Gulf's defense that the cartel had no effect was the admission by one of its executives that it did. On June 16, 1977, during the subcommittee hearings, Mr. S. A. Zagnoli, who had been president of GMCL when the cartel was founded and who at the time of this testimony was executive vice-president of GMCL's parent company, Gulf Mineral Resources, could not escape the stubborn questioning of William F. Haddad, who headed the New York State investigation:

> Mr. HADDAD: Was the cartel successful overseas?
> Mr. ZAGNOLI: In my view it did raise the prices overseas. . . .
> Mr. HADDAD: My question is very simple, and I hope your answer is simple. Was the cartel effective in raising prices?
> Mr. ZAGNOLI: I would have to say it appeared to be effective.
> Mr. HADDAD: Was it effective in setting world quotas? You had 100,000 tons of supply and 26,000 tons of demand.
> Was it effective in setting world quotas? Was it controlling on Gulf's markets?
> Mr. ZAGNOLI: It was effective in allocating the market.
> Mr. HADDAD: Mr. Zagnoli, you are very vague. You were intimately involved in this. I have the records in front of me. You have read them. I have read them. Please, please don't insult our intelligence.
> Was it effective in setting world quotas; yes or no?
> Mr. ZAGNOLI: Yes.[48]

Another of the intriguing ambiguities the investigators did their best to elucidate was why Gulf neglected to inform the U.S. government of its participation in a cartel. This was an extremely important question; the answer would illustrate Gulf's attitude toward its own actions, that is, the degree to which the company demonstrated a guilt complex. Here again the sequence of events leaves considerable doubt that Gulf's motives were what the company later claimed they were.

In early 1972 GMCL undeniably found itself in a tricky position. The Canadian government and the other Canadian producers wanted to construct an international marketing agreement, and Gulf may well have shared that desire. The degree of official compulsion involved, as we have seen, is open to question. But there is no question that Gulf was worried about the *U.S.* government. At the very least the company knew it must create the appearance of compulsion, and the appearance that Gulf did not think it was doing anything illegal. But for precisely that reason its decision not to inform the U.S. Justice Department becomes suspect.

During the early talks in Canada about the cartel, Gulf officials repeat-

edly told the Canadians that the company would have to get clearance
from Washington. On April 10, 1972, at a meeting of the Canadian producers, executives of GMCL and its German partner "advised Mr. Austin
[an Energy Ministry official] that their participation would be dependent
upon a determination that it would not result in violations of United States
or German antitrust laws."[49] (Austin irascibly pointed out in response that
both companies were Canadian corporations and subject to Canadian law.
On another occasion he expressed "irritation" with the extraterritorial application of U.S. antitrust laws, a fact Gulf used to support its claim of
compulsion.) At a meeting in Canada a week later, R. K. Allen, then an
officer of Gulf Mineral Resources, took the following position:

> I agreed that the fact that the U.S. would be excluded from the arrange-
> ment and that foreign uranium is presently excluded from U.S. markets
> probably lessened the risk of a violation, but that in our opinion, it did not
> remove the possibility that Gulf's participation would be determined to
> be a violation. I further pointed out that Gulf management was unwilling
> to take such a risk, and, consequently, any participation by Gulf in the ar-
> rangement was conditioned upon receiving an expression from the U.S.
> Department of Justice satisfactory to Gulf.[50]

A memo from Roy Jackson on April 28 noted that Gulf was preparing a
"white paper" setting out its position, which would be presented not only
to the Justice Department but to various other government agencies, including the AEC and the Department of State.[51]

Just a month later, though, Gulf had decided not to seek government
clearance at all — from anyone. At a gathering of the Canadian producers
on May 28, the day before the crucial Johannesburg meeting convened,
"Mr. Allen said that the best advice Gulf had been able to obtain from
outside counsel was that they should not even file a white paper with the
Department of Justice."[52] What happened, in effect, was that Gulf unilaterally decided (with the advice, to be sure, of a prestigious Washington
antitrust firm, but there is no way of knowing what form that advice took)
that because it was being compelled by Canada, and because there would
be no impact on the U.S. market, there was no need to consult anyone in
the U.S. government. Gulf was not breaking the law — according to Gulf,
of course — so why tell the Justice Department about the cartel?

Investigators were understandably curious to know how and why such a
decision had been reached. But under close questioning neither Gulf's
chairman, Jerry McAfee, nor the quick-witted lawyer, Roy Jackson, was
very forthcoming. Both said that at some moment neither could pinpoint
it was decided to rely on an "opinion memorandum" prepared by Jackson
and delivered in September 1972. That lengthy document, itself relying in
part on a flimsy economic impact statement prepared by another Gulf em-

ployee — which not surprisingly concluded that there would be no impact on the United States — simply made the strongest case possible for the compulsion and no-impact arguments and reviewed antitrust cases supporting Jackson's position. Both McAfee and Jackson insisted that the reason Gulf decided not to consult the Justice Department was that it was so obvious Gulf was not violating the law. But we have already seen from internal documents that several high Gulf officials did not think it was all that obvious. The incredulous subcommittee counsel was moved to ask, "Isn't that all the more reason to seek the opinion — just to make it nice and neat? If it was so clear that Justice would have given you a favorable opinion, why on earth didn't you seek it?"[53]

The subcommittee hearings also explored an interesting tangent to the antitrust problems raised by Gulf's conduct. Not only did Gulf neglect to tell the U.S. government about the dubious goings-on in the uranium market; so did American utilities, which had good reason to suspect they were dealing with a cartel. In 1974 the TVA was negotiating for its large purchase of uranium — the largest it had ever made — with Rio Algom. In the process of the talks a TVA employee sent the following memo to A. T. Mullins, then chief of the Nuclear Raw Materials branch of TVA's Division of Resource Planning:

> George White, Jr., Energy Services Company, informed Erik Kvaven a few weeks ago that — according to a reliable source — the "unofficial club" of foreign uranium producers had met in Paris and had established the world uranium price for 1974 at $11.00 per pound.
> Mr. White reports now that he is aware of three different offers made by Canadian producers since the "club" met (in addition to Rio's offer to TVA). All three offers have a base price of $11.50 to $12.00 per pound plus escalation from 1974 as a minimum price. It would appear that Rio is a member of the "club" and our meeting with them tomorrow should provide some interesting insights.[54]

Mullins and higher TVA executives confirmed that they were aware, from the memo and reports they had seen in the trade press, that a uranium cartel of some sort was operating. Some of them said they viewed it as an OPEC-type cartel of foreign governments that could hardly be prevented; others claimed they felt the cartel's effectiveness was so minimal as to be not worth consideration. But the memo to Mullins indicates that there was at least some reason to suspect the cartel was affecting the price TVA would have to pay for its uranium. Yet none of the officers involved alerted the TVA Board of Directors, not to mention the Justice Department. Nor did they make any effort to bring a private antitrust suit. They apparently did not even broach the subject with Rio Algom.

During the discussion of this point, Representative Albert Gore, Jr., of Tennessee speculated as to why TVA had taken such a passive position.

Gore pointed out that the Authority, like most other utilities, simply passes along its fuel price increases to consumers, whether the increases result from inflation, the normal interplay of supply and demand, or the actions of a cartel. TVA therefore had no direct interest in battling the cartel; it was the consumer who paid. TVA Chairman Wagner angrily replied to such suggestions that "we have been as aggressive on protecting our consumers as anyone has been," which may well be the truth. But Mr. Gore used the example to make the point that, as a result of the Supreme Court's decision in the *Illinois Brick* case, only the immediate purchaser and not the ultimate consumer may bring an antitrust complaint against the seller.[55] In other words, TVA's electricity consumers cannot sue Rio Algom for fixing the price of uranium in such a way that TVA electricity bills rise; only TVA could. This fact, said Gore, made it especially imperative that utilities like TVA defend themselves against cartels instead of passing along the higher costs. In fact, as a result of the hearings — and, one might presume, the uncomfortable publicity — TVA eventually did file suit for $120 million against Gulf and twelve other domestic and foreign uranium producers.

Another Nolo Contendere

The uranium cartel case, then, is not yet closed. Powerful companies are still paying lawyers millions of dollars to wade through the swamp of civil suits, which might — at great length and cost — allow some more certain evaluation of how effective the cartel actually was. However, it is more likely that all the remaining cases will be negotiated to private settlements, with the public left none the wiser. And while the private suits have multiplied and dragged on, the controversy over the cartel has already provided another illustration of the weakness of public antitrust law enforcement.

The federal grand jury investigation of possible criminal actions by uranium producers and marketers was begun in 1975, a full year before even the Australian documents were leaked. Presumably the Justice Department had been alerted by the strange behavior of uranium prices and by the occasional reports of producers' meetings that appeared in the trade press. Yet, after eighteen months of inquiry, which assembled much of the same evidence that was later presented in the congressional and New York State hearings, the grand jury came to a rather anticlimactic end. (Of course, the jury was hampered on all sides in its attempt to gather evidence, both by national governments that deeply resented the U.S. investigation and lobbied against it at every opportunity and by private companies. Reports that Gulf had sent important documents to Canada, where they would be safe from subpoena, received some support from one executive during the subcommittee hearings when he vaguely recollected such papers being mailed, and were the subject of protracted proceedings in Westinghouse's civil antitrust suit.)

On May 9, 1978, the Justice Department filed charges against Gulf in Federal District Court in Pittsburgh, accusing the company of conspiracy to fix the price of uranium and refusal to sell to Westinghouse in order to eliminate a competitor. The alleged crime, at the time it was committed, was a misdemeanor with a maximum fine of $50,000 — although Congress has since changed the law to make such conspiracy a felony with a maximum fine of $1 million. Less than a month after charges were filed, Gulf employed the device so dear to companies facing antitrust action: the nolo contendere plea. By not contesting the case, Gulf was effectively admitting its guilt. But by pleading nolo contendere the company could continue to maintain its innocence, as it did, claiming that it made the plea only because "a successful defense would have been many times more costly than the maximum penalty provided by law."[56] That was true; but by avoiding a trial Gulf also accomplished the extremely important goal of not having details of the cartel discussed in open court. After the plea, Federal District Judge Gerald Weber fined Gulf only $40,000, explaining that he did not impose the maximum because Gulf's plea had saved the government time and money. This decision has permitted Gulf to claim its offense could not have been terribly serious because the maximum fine was not imposed.

The nolo contendere plea virtually closed the books on public action against Gulf and the uranium cartel. At the time the Justice Department filed charges, it was announced that the grand jury probably would not produce more criminal indictments, and that proved to be the case. But the matter did not quite end there. Under pressure from congressmen who felt that $40,000 was much too light a penalty for Gulf and from staff lawyers who were incensed that Gulf had been let off without any felony indictments, the Justice Department considered its options for some time. But the result was the same. On March 26, 1979, John H. Shenefield, then assistant attorney general in charge of the Antitrust Division of the Justice Department, testified before the antimonopoly subcommittee of the Senate Judiciary Committee. Shenefield told the senators that the department had not asked for indictments from the grand jury, saying "we could not win a felony prosecution" because it was difficult to show that any violations by Gulf continued after December 21, 1974, the date price fixing became a felony.[57]

Dissatisfied with this explanation, the subcommittee asked to see the Justice Department's papers relating to the case. Shenefield resisted, but after a court battle the department was ordered to turn over all papers except the grand jury records. Among the papers was a 1000-page "fact memorandum" prepared by the Justice Department investigating attorneys. It turned out that they had recommended *unanimously* that Gulf and other members of the cartel be prosecuted on felony charges.[58] The papers also made obvious, however, that the lawyers faced formidable opposition. The State Department was appalled at the prospect of a felony indictment, which would anger the friendly governments that had helped organize the cartel; and the Canadian government lobbied intensively in Washington against the indictments. Until the last moment, it appeared that the recommendations of the staff attorneys would prevail. Indictments were widely expected, and as late as April 10, 1978, Secretary of State Cyrus Vance sent a telegram indicating that on April 28 the Justice Department would inform Gulf and other firms that they had been indicted. But suddenly, for reasons that have yet to be elucidated publicly, the decision was reversed, and the misdemeanor charge was brought instead. Shenefield still maintains that political pressures had nothing to do with the outcome.

*　　*　　*

One final point remains unclear: what happened to the cartel? The final meetings of the Club were held in 1974, with the last formalities connected with it taking place in early 1975. Gulf claims that its connection to the cartel ended in 1974. But in that same year the producers agreed to set up an organization called the Uranium Institute whose "principal object," according to its constitution, is "to promote the production of uranium for peaceful purposes and to promote the coordination of production with the requirements for peaceful purposes, of processors, users or consumers of uranium."[59] As far as is known, the institute does not engage in the price fixing and bid rigging that characterized the cartel; but some Justice Department lawyers have been reported to suspect that, as with other cartels, formal arrangements have been succeeded by informal ones — and the institute certainly provides a convenient forum for producers to meet. Gulf and other industry members insist that the cartel lapsed because there was no need for it; the situation of oversupply had ended, and the price was high enough to ensure an adequate return. Certainly on the latter point there can be no disagreement. And it may well be that the cartel members, satisfied with a job well done, have in fact decided to leave their marketing agreements in abeyance until such time as they might be needed again.

5

Cartel Chemistry

SOME of the earliest international cartels, as we noted in Chapter 1, appeared in the chemicals industry. The Bismuth Syndicate was organized during the 1870s. Other early cartels covered borax, quinine, acetic acid, and carbide, and the great explosives cartel linking the du Pont and Nobel interests was formed in 1897. Ever since, the chemicals industry has remained one of the most heavily cartelized manufacturing fields. But there is a difference between chemicals and other industries we have examined. No single cartel — or even a few large cartels — could possibly hold sway over the myriad branches of the chemicals industry. There is no equivalent to the IEA in chemicals, or to the Achnacarry Agreement and Draft Memorandum of Principles that laid the foundations for world-wide control of oil. Rather, the chemicals industry is governed by thousands of mini-agreements which have proliferated haphazardly over the years. Very few of these accords would appear to be of great consequence when viewed individually; but in conjunction, they effectively bind together all the major chemicals firms (and many of the smaller ones) in a tangle of alliances which Stocking and Watkins have called "a seemingly amorphous yet actually integrated whole."[1]

There are various reasons why this particular cartel pattern arose in chemicals, the most important being the fantastic complexity of the industry and the multitude of its products. Indeed, the very term *chemicals industry* today embraces corporations and products so disparate that it has become difficult to define at all. The primary task of chemicals firms, of course, is to produce industrial chemicals, which number in the thousands and range from the most common, produced in great bulk, such as sulfuric acid, to exotic compounds for highly specialized uses. These chemicals are then sold to other industries for use in the manufacture of other goods. But basic chemicals make up only a part of the output of "chemicals" firms. They also turn out an enormous variety of finished products: soaps, cosmetics, fertilizers, insecticides, inks, dyes, drugs, vitamins, glues, paints, bleaches, polishes, lacquers, varnishes, refrigerants, detergents, solvents, synthetic rubber and fibers, explosives, petroleum additives such as antifreeze, and the countless forms of plastics. These products are far too multifarious to embrace in any one agreement; as a result, chemicals firms have long organized their cartels on a product-by-product basis.

Another factor accounting for the pattern of cartels in chemicals is technological change. More than most industries, this one is "science-based"; that is, scientific investigation is the direct source of its products and the processes by which they are manufactured. Competition in the industry, therefore, is also "science-based." The relative strength of the major chemicals firms rests to a large extent on their success in the perpetual race to develop new products and processes. They all maintain massive research departments. New discoveries are frequent, and important breakthroughs can create entirely new branches of the industry or wipe out established ones. As one writer put it, "A company which, because of a superior process, may today have other companies at its mercy, may find one of its own processes obsolete tomorrow and some part of its capital investment in jeopardy."[2] In short, the rapid and unpredictable flow of innovation makes for a high degree of risk, and the most effective way to reduce the risk may often be through agreements to trade technological discoveries.

These, then, are the salient traits of cartels in the chemicals industry as they have developed over the last century: a multitude of separate agreements cover separate products; and the agreements usually revolve around patents and licenses. Another interesting fact is that the vast majority of chemicals accords are bilateral, that is, they involve only two companies. When a number of major chemicals firms hope to control trade in a certain product, they generally do not join together in a formal cartel but instead negotiate bilateral agreements with each other that achieve the same effect. The advantage of this method, of course, is that it is much harder to detect. The chemicals firms favor other forms of oblique controls as well: joint ventures, for example, and cooperative research projects. Specialization of production is also notable in many branches, where — to use a simplified illustration — Company A will refrain from making a certain product of Company B's in return for Company B's allowing Company A to be the sole source of another product.

Riddled as it is with restrictive accords of all these types, the chemicals industry stands as the ne plus ultra of indirect cartelization. This fact should be qualified by two observations, however. First, as we have already noted, similar agreements are employed elsewhere, particularly in such "science-based" industries as electronics. It is the *extent* of indirect cartelization, the sheer number of accords woven into a dense fabric of interconnection, that makes the chemicals industry noteworthy. Second, the converse point: full-fledged classic cartels are hardly unknown to chemicals firms. On the contrary, at one time or another formal cartels have ruled numerous branches of the industry. As with other industries, the 1930s brought the heyday of classic cartels in chemicals; dozens operated during that decade. Even in the postwar era with its more stringent antitrust enforcement, formal chemicals cartels have not vanished. One indication of their prevalence came in 1960, when the EEC Commission demanded that all companies within the Common Market register any commercial accords that might violate the antitrust provisions of the Treaty of Rome. Of the nearly five hundred multipartite cartel agreements that had been registered by 1962, the chemicals industry accounted for seventy, more than any other sector except metals. Twenty-seven of the chemicals accords included plans to fix prices; twenty-five, multilateral licensing; and twenty-three, export and import arrangements. And the agreements that were actually reported were thought to be only a small percentage — estimates ranged from 5 to 50 percent — of the real number of restrictive pacts.[3]

Later in this chapter we will describe some of the formal cartels that have operated recently in chemicals. But here we stress again that they are the exception rather than the rule; and for that reason we will first examine a field known for its extensive use of indirect cartels and thus more typical of the industry as a whole.

The Pharmaceuticals Trade

The technological revolution that created the modern pharmaceuticals industry can be dated to 1935, when a chemist working for the Bayer division of I. G. Farben found that a certain red dye worked effectively as a drug against pneumonia, scarlet fever, and certain other bacterial diseases.[4] Other scientists soon discovered that the active ingredient in the dye was a substance known as sulfanilamide, which had first been isolated in 1908 but whose germ-killing properties had been overlooked. Further research quickly led to other "sulfa" drugs that were safer and more effective. With the first commercial manufacture of penicillin during World War II, the age of "wonder drugs" had arrived.

Until that time, the drug trade had been a relatively static business. Large numbers of drugs existed, most of them obtained from natural sources, but the pharmaceuticals firms engaged in little or no research, and therapeutic advances were rare. Also, few drugs could actually cure diseases. Their efficacy was limited to relieving pain or symptoms or inducing sleep. Of the few medicaments available that could cure diseases, almost none relied on the action of man-made chemical agents. (Paul Erlich, regarded as the father of modern chemotherapy, had discovered arsphenamine as a cure for syphilis in 1910, but twenty-five years passed before his breakthrough led to further advances.) The cures for such diseases as tetanus, smallpox, and typhoid were either vaccines — which stimulated the production of antibodies within the human body — or natural antitoxins, which used antibodies produced in animals inoculated for the purpose. What was different about the wonder drugs was that they did not rely on antibodies. Instead, they were chemical substances which *themselves* attacked specific diseases and which could be manufactured in quantity.

The pharmaceutical supply houses were quick to realize the potential of such drugs, and the trade was radically transformed. The search for new chemical agents that could cure or control disease became the driving force of the industry, and all the major companies developed large-scale research operations. Other chemicals firms that had never produced drugs learned that the chemistry of man-made pharmaceuticals was closely linked to areas of research they were already pursuing, and they entered the field — so that today such companies as American Cyanamid, Dow Chemical, ICI, and Hoechst are among the largest producers of prescription drugs.[5] The sudden increase in research efforts brought about an astonishing wave of major discoveries, which peaked in the 1950s, when the range of antibiotics was enormously expanded and tranquilizers, steroids, oral contraceptives, oral antidiabetic drugs, and cardiovascular drugs were developed. Since then the pace of research efforts has remained frenetic, although breakthroughs have come less frequently.

But this transformation of the drug trade created worrisome risks for the producers. Research is expensive; rewards for discovering an important new drug can be immense, but the cost of failure is high. There is always the danger that another firm pursuing an identical line of research will make a breakthrough first or that, once a promising drug is patented, a rival company will quickly produce an improvement supplanting it. Thus the pharmaceuticals firms were concerned to keep their competition within tolerable limits; and, as the wonder drugs were developed, so was a system of market regulation.

The basis of the system is simplicity itself: it involves trading patent licenses with territorial restrictions in a manner that neatly carves up the world market. And the transnational drug firms, which account for the great bulk of research and discoveries, have a strong preference for each other as licensees. For example, if a large German firm wins a valuable patent, it will sell rights for France (usually including traditional French "territory" in the former colonies) to a leading French firm, British rights to a major British firm, U.S. rights to one or two large American firms, and so on throughout all countries where drugs can be protected by patent. The result of this mutual courtesy is an orderly division of home and "captive" markets among the industry's dominant companies. Of course, the license terms vary widely from case to case. A license may grant full rights to manufacture and sell the drug, or — as is nearly always the case in less-developed countries — only to package and sell in dosage form, with the licensor supplying the drug in bulk form.[6] Or the patent-holding firm, if it already has an established position in a certain national market, may grant a local firm a license allowing it only a set share of that market. But no matter what the actual terms, the important fact is that in the industrialized countries, which offer by far the largest markets for pharmaceuticals, a few dozen firms are nearly always the participants in these licensing arrangements.

It is unfortunate that the last thorough investigation of international licensing in pharmaceuticals by a public authority with subpoena power took place twenty years ago, during the hearings on administered prices by the Senate Subcommittee on Antitrust and Monopoly, under the chairmanship of Senator Estes Kefauver.[7] As a result, the terms of recent licenses are virtually impossible to obtain. But the Kefauver committee material is still valuable because it dates from the years when the licensing system was being created. For example, among the contracts studied by the committee was one between Hoechst of Germany and the Upjohn Company, a major American firm. On August 30, 1949, the two companies signed an agreement giving Upjohn the right of first refusal on any "pharmaceutical chemical or pharmaceutical product or process inventions" that Hoechst might patent in the United States. In other words, should Hoechst develop a new drug and apply for a U.S. patent, Upjohn, should the company so request, would be granted an exclusive license to sell the drug in U.S. territory. The actual clause read, in part:

> In the field of the said inventions, HOECHST gives and grants to UP-JOHN the privilege and option to obtain the exclusive right to manufacture, use and sell throughout the United States of America and its possessions under any United States patent application and under any United States patent which issues on said application, or any extension or renewal thereof that HOECHST might secure during the life of this agreement.[8]

The import of this accord was effectively to foreclose all competition over the inventions of an extremely powerful entity in the pharmaceuticals world and effectively divide markets between Hoechst and Upjohn. It was to last for five years and in fact was renewed in 1954 and again in 1959. The latter renewal was interesting because it came with two amendments, one of which made the accord even more restrictive. The first provided that Hoechst or its subsidiaries would be permitted to sell the products in question in the United States, although only under the Hoechst trademark and in finished form, thus making Upjohn's license not absolutely exclusive. The second tied Upjohn to Hoechst as a supplier and even fixed a price for bulk supplies:

> 2. *Purchase of material*
> Upjohn agrees that when taking out a license or licenses for products covered by patent applications or patents under the Agreement, it will purchase at least 50 percent (50%) of their required bulk pharmaceuticals . . . from Hoechst or from a company appointed by Hoechst at a price determined by a mutually agreed upon "cost plus 20%" basis.[9]

As a prime example of how these patent and license agreements eliminated competition in drugs one might study Tolbutamide, an important oral antidiabetic medicine patented by Hoechst. In keeping with the basic agreement, Hoechst was to be the near-exclusive seller of this drug in Europe (with a licensee, Boehringer, holding rights in a few countries), and Upjohn was the only producer in the United States, a market from which even Hoechst was barred. In Canada the two firms formed a joint venture which held a monopoly in that market. The drug sold under different trademarks: Orinase in the United States; Rastinon in Europe. The effectiveness of the market division, which the patents and trademarks kept any party from disturbing, was illustrated by the fact that Tolbutamide sold for twice as much in North America as in Germany.[10]

In the report of the subcommittee majority on administered prices in the pharmaceuticals trade, the marketing of two other drugs was used to illustrate further interesting aspects of the industry. One such aspect is the high degree of concentration and specialization of production. Although at the time of the hearings there were some 1300 companies producing prescription drugs in the United States,[11] the largest twenty firms overwhelmingly dominated the manufacture and sale of most of the important patented pharmaceutical products. Of those twenty, usually only a few — and sometimes only one — sold any particular drug. In the words of the report:

> Thus, the nine principal hormone products are produced by only seven of the largest twenty companies. The diabetic drugs are produced by only five of the twenty, the tranquilizers by only six. In sulfas there are only three producers, in vitamins only six, in antibiotics other than penicillin eight, and in penicillin seven.[12]

One reason for this pattern, of course, can be found in agreements like the one between Hoechst and Upjohn. But even in the absence of such a binding accord, the large companies prefer to deal with each other. Any firm that has made a potentially lucrative discovery wants to grant licenses only to firms that have something to "trade," that is, that own valuable patent rights to discoveries of their own. Small firms, which cannot afford extensive research and which therefore have little or nothing to offer in the way of patents, tend to be shut out of the market. For example, when the Carter Products Company received its 1955 patent on the phenomenally successful tranquilizer meprobamate, the company was deluged with requests for licenses. By and large, requests from small firms were simply ignored. Carter licensed only one U.S. company, American Home Products Corp., to sell meprobamate in the United States, in part because that firm had the large contingent of salesmen that Carter lacked. American Home Products and one other major firm, American Cyanamid, were licensed for sales abroad. Investigators came across one case in which a small company asked Carter for a license to combine meprobamate with another drug; the combination had proved remarkably beneficial in the treatment of hypertension. Carter rejected the proposal. "Questioning by Senator Kefauver," noted the report, "disclosed that the second drug proposed was not a patent monopoly, and was sold by many companies under generic name. This fact in itself would, under Carter's policy, make the combination unacceptable — no matter how useful it might be to the medical profession."[13]

The construction of a network of protective patent agreements, and the means used to do so, were interestingly revealed through the tale of the antibiotic chloramphenicol (marketed as Chloromycetin). The patent on chloramphenicol was obtained by Parke, Davis in 1949, and remained in effect until 1966. Parke, Davis licensed no other producer in the United States. But this monopoly at home could not be duplicated abroad, at least in those countries which do not allow patents on drug products, as does the United States. Chloramphenicol was the only entirely synthetic antibiotic, produced by chemical means alone, and so was duplicated with relative ease by producers in several countries. Worried by such competition, Parke, Davis began an aggressive campaign to eliminate it.[14] According to the subcommittee report, the company used the State Department to bring diplomatic pressure to bear on countries whose firms were making chloramphenicol without a license from Parke, Davis. Patent infringement suits were filed in countries offering some degree of patent protection. To companies eager to escape such harassment, Parke, Davis offered licenses under highly restrictive terms. Several of the companies that accepted such licenses, and thereby recognized the Parke, Davis patent rights, had been producing the drug before entering into the agreement. The final result of the conflict over chloramphenicol was that Parke, Davis established near perfect control over where and how the drug would be sold around the world.

A good example of the terms Parke, Davis imposed comes from the firm's contract with its French licensee, the Laboratoire Française de Chimiothérapie. It was signed on January 25, 1950, and the basic provision was to limit the Laboratoire to sales in France and French territories. But it was the additional provisions — remarkable in themselves, but actually quite common in pharmaceutical licenses — that assured the isolation of the French market from all others. The Laboratoire pledged not to buy or sell chloramphenicol outside of its assigned territory and to ensure by every means at its disposal — including lawsuits — that none of the customers would resell the drug outside the territory. Also, the French firm agreed to "refrain from shipping in any parts of the territory quantities of chloramphenicol notoriously above its needs." This provision, which Parke, Davis imposed on other licensees as well, was intended to prevent any surplus chloramphenicol from escaping its assigned market. The French firm agreed not to sell the drug in bulk but only in finished dosage form. And the two firms pledged not to contest each others' patents, with the French making an additional commitment involving "grant-backs"; that is, if in future the Laboratoire achieved any discoveries in the field, it must share them with Parke, Davis.[15]

Such restrictions on patent licenses remain common practice, to judge from the few recent occasions when the terms of licenses have become public — usually because the firms have, for one reason or another, attracted the attention of official investigators. In 1968 the Justice Department filed a suit challenging the limits on patent licenses granted by two of Britain's largest pharmaceuticals producers, ICI and the Glaxo Group, Ltd., to three of the largest American drug companies: American Home Products, Schering Corp., and Johnson & Johnson. ICI and Glaxo had pooled their U.S. patents relating to griseofulvin, a drug used to treat fungus infections. They then licensed the patents on condition that the American firms agree to sell the drug only in finished dosage form. Sales in bulk to third parties were prohibited except with the express consent of ICI and Glaxo. The Justice Department argued that this system tied up the market as effectively as any formal cartel would have done. In 1973 the Supreme Court agreed, ruling that the American firms should be allowed to make and sell the drug in bulk and that more firms should be licensed.[16] A similar case in 1976 involved Beecham, another large British firm, and a license granted to Hoechst for the sale of ampicillin. Hoechst was permitted to sell the drug only in retail packs and only within Austria and West Germany.[17]

Many licenses of this type extend beyond the period of the patent grant, raising the question of why a company would agree to such restrictive terms — and to payment of royalties — after the date when the drug may be produced freely. Part of the answer is that the patent-holding firm may simply refuse to grant a license that does not bind the licensee for a lengthy period; and the high profits to be gained during the years of patent protection make it worthwhile for the licensee to sign a long-term contract. But perhaps more important is the fact that an exclusive license during the patent period allows the licensee to establish the drug under a trademark. For in today's pharmaceuticals industry, trademarks are of paramount importance. Once a drug has become popular under a certain name — for example, meprobamate as Equanil, chlorpromazine as Thorazine, or even aspirin as Bayer — it becomes extremely difficult for firms marketing the drug under other names after the patent has expired to win a large share of the market. This is true even if the other firms are selling the drug at a lower price, as is usually the case. Repeated studies have confirmed the apparently paradoxical fact that the most expensive brand of a certain drug is often the largest seller by far — and inevitably it is the brand that was introduced first.[18] Such trademark loyalty is achieved largely by massive advertising during the patent period. Because doctors do not actually pay for the drugs they prescribe, they tend to prefer brands they are familiar with, despite the fact that cheaper brands of equal quality may be on the market. Thus a firm that takes a license on a patented drug knows that, even after the patent expires, there is every likelihood that its brand will continue to be profitable until the drug itself is supplanted by a new discovery.

But if the terms of licenses granted by the major firms to each other tend to be restrictive, those granted to independent firms in less-developed countries are even more so. The reasons for this are obvious: the small companies have little to offer in return. Their markets are relatively small, and they cannot afford the research that would give them discoveries of their own to trade. They must approach the majors as supplicants, as the terms of their licenses reflect. Not only do the licenses usually prohibit all exports, they also withhold the essential technology involved. This is a crucial difference from license agreements between the majors, which generally grant full knowledge of the processes necessary to manufacture the drug and which thereby afford society an indirect benefit in terms of the spread of scientific knowledge. A 1975 OECD study of five semi-industrialized countries — Greece, Turkey, Yugoslavia, Spain, and Portugal — showed that, in the majority of cases, local drug companies accepting licenses were forced to import the active ingredients of the drugs from the licensing firms.[19] The local firms were limited to packaging and selling, so little transfer of technology took place. United Nations studies have indicated a similar situation in many Third World countries.[20] Thus the majors use licenses to establish their products in the LDCs without having to set up local production and distribution facilities, and they extend their system of market division to these countries without relinquishing any of their technological superiority.

Even given their preference for such indirect trade restrictions as these, however, pharmaceuticals producers are not above resorting to an old-fashioned cartel if circumstances warrant. An excellent example is the quinine cartel that operated in the early 1960s. Quinine is a medicine used primarily in the prevention and treatment of malaria. It is derived from a natural raw material, the bark of the cinchona tree, which is grown commercially in several tropical countries. There are relatively few producers of quinine in the world, and international trade is dominated by just two companies, one Dutch and one German. Commerce in quinine is therefore fairly easy to control, and in fact the producers have maintained cartel connections for the better part of a century. But the cartel's most recent incarnation (at least as far as is known) is particularly interesting because it is one of the rare cartels of which an extensive documentary record has become public, thanks to an investigation by the U.S. Senate Subcommittee on Antitrust and Monopoly.[21] The committee's curiosity was piqued by a series of abrupt price hikes that brought the price of quinine on world markets in 1966 to about five times the price just two years before. Because one of the companies involved was a subsidiary of the Rexall Drug & Chemical Company of the United States, the committee was able to subpoena and obtain detailed records of the so-called Quinine Convention.

The first recorded cartel agreement in quinine came in 1892, between the Dutch and German producers. In 1913 the Europeans entered into collaboration with the Javanese growers of cinchona trees and organized a classic cartel whose secretariat, called the Kina Bureau, was located in Amsterdam. In 1928 a U.S. grand jury indicted cartel members and American importers of quinine for illegal restraint of trade, but the usual consent decree settling the case had little impact on the cartel. The Kina Bureau was known to be still operating in 1951, and in 1967 John Blair (the same John Blair noted for his studies of the oil industry), who was then chief economist for the antitrust subcommittee, testified, "There is no indication that the [Kina Bureau] has ever been dissolved."[22]

During the 1950s the Kina Bureau's operations seem to have been restricted to the world's two leading producers, the Dutch firm N.V. Nederlandsche Combinatie voor Chemische Industrie (usually known as Nedchem), and the German firm C. F. Boehringer & Soehne G.m.b.H. They were struggling to cope with overcapacity resulting from massive expansion of production facilities during World War II, when demand for quinine mushroomed, and the sharp reduction in demand when the war ended. In 1959 Nedchem led the way in organizing a broader cartel, bringing French and British producers into a Quinine Convention that included all the world's manufacturers except one — a large factory at Bandung, Indonesia, formerly Dutch-owned, which the Indonesian government had nationalized in 1957, and which caused the convention no end of headaches. During numerous meetings over the course of three years, the convention members worked out four separate but interrelated accords; they were known as the stockpile agreement, the export agreement, the gentlemen's agreement, and the bark-pool agreement.

Together these four accords brought world trade in quinine under increasingly stringent control. The stockpile agreement was essentially a system of rigged bidding under which the members agreed not to compete with each other to acquire government stockpiles of quinine being sold on the open market — most notably the American stockpile, of which a huge amount was to be sold. By designating one member as bidder, the convention members were able to acquire stockpiled quinine at their price and then distribute it among themselves according to agreed percentages. The export agreement governed sales of quinine and quinidine (a drug derived from quinine and used in the treatment of heart ailments) everywhere in the world except the EEC countries, Great Britain, and the United States. All the usual provisions of an export cartel were employed: prices were fixed, sales quotas distributed among the members, and market territories assigned. It is interesting that this export agreement was presumed to be legal in Europe and was duly registered with the German Federal Cartel Office, thus offering another example of an illegal cartel operating under the cover of a legal one.[23]

The hidden side of the Quinine Convention was the "gentlemen's agreement," which extended the trade restrictions to those countries which the export agreement had specifically excluded in order to be palatable to the authorities. The gentlemen's agreement reserved home markets for all members except the British. It fixed prices for quinine and quinidine in the Common Market, Britain, and the United States, while granting special discounts to a few preferred buyers. Sales quotas were established for those countries as well, and it was agreed that members who exceeded their quotas would compensate those who fell short. The right to manufacture quinidine was assigned exclusively to the Dutch and Germans.

The only thing necessary to complete this system was some sort of control over the raw material for quinine, cinchona bark. The members wanted to ensure that just enough was produced to meet their requirements, thus avoiding surpluses that might fall into the hands of "outsiders"; and they wanted the price to be right. Therefore they created the "bark-pool agreement" in 1961, setting maximum prices that members could pay for bark from the various producing regions, thus preventing the members from bidding against each other and driving the price up. All purchases by members were then placed in a common pool, which was distributed according to prearranged shares.

By and large, the Quinine Convention was a magnificent success in keeping prices high. But it was not without its problems. The most troublesome was what one member called *"the* big outsider": the Bandung fac-tory.[24] The Indonesians were determined to win as much of the export trade as they could, and in 1961 they began cutting prices and taking busi-ness away from the cartel members. In response the convention adopted two measures: a total boycott of Indonesian quinine by the members; and a policy of fighting Bandung "whenever and wherever" by slashing prices in the markets where the Indonesians were trying to make sales. Even after granting a rebate of 20 percent off cartel prices, however, the Dutch still lost 75 percent of the Japanese market in 1961 to Bandung. This caused dissension within the cartel, the other members being concerned that the price wars would spread, and they began to urge that the Indone-sians be invited into the cartel. The Dutch argued, however, that the members could force Bandung to join on terms more favorable to the car-tel if the policy of all-out combat were pursued until the Indonesians sued for peace. This position prevailed, and the conflict continued until grow-ing shortages of quinine on the world market raised all prices and elimi-nated the problem.

The bark-pool agreement did not run smoothly either. The members could not agree on the best price levels, particularly for bark from the Congo. Some argued that higher prices would induce the Congo planters to produce more cinchona, but the Germans (who owned a large quinine factory in the Congo) adamantly opposed the idea. Finally the members decided that the bark pool caused more trouble than it was worth, and it was abandoned in October 1962.[25] A year later the convention members relaxed their other agreements somewhat, making compliance voluntary rather than compulsory. Part of the reason for this move was that market conditions, from the producers' point of view, were improving markedly; the glut of quinine of the late 1950s had dwindled, as was reflected in the cartel's prices. In 1964 the convention twice raised prices for finished qui-nine and quinidine, and in 1965–66, with the Vietnam War and other fac-tors causing demand to outreach supply, price increases became astro-nomical. These increases led the Quinine Convention, which had effectively "stabilized" the price during the difficult years, to dissolve in mid-1966; with prices going through the roof, there was little need for such an elaborate cartel.

Legal action was not long in following the exposure of the cartel. In the United States, a federal grand jury returned criminal indictments in 1968 against eight companies — including foreign manufacturers as well as American importers and dealers — and fifteen individuals, charging them with numerous violations of the antitrust laws. Most of the defendants eventually resorted to nolo contendere pleas, and fines were imposed amounting to several hundred thousand dollars.[26] In Europe, where the EEC Commission had been alerted by the U.S. inquiry, six Common Market firms — three French, two German (including Boehringer), and one Dutch (Nedchem) — were fined a total of $470,000.[27]

Industrial Chemicals

In the field of basic industrial chemicals, formal cartels are somewhat more common than they are in pharmaceuticals, largely because many of the products and processes involved are unpatentable or their patents have long since expired. In fact, there might be said to be two layers of cartels controlling industrial chemicals, roughly corresponding to the younger and older sectors of the industry. In the realms where research is intensive and knowledge is advancing rapidly, agreements based on patent licenses or joint research projects are prevalent. Whereas in the long-established, less dynamic sectors, companies hoping to minimize competition must rely on more direct cartel controls.

This pattern could already be discerned by the 1920s, when cartels covering some of the most important basic chemicals — including alkalies, dyestuffs, and nitrogen — were organized. The Depression saw the creation of other classic cartels in fertilizers, acetic acid, hydrogen peroxide, and sodium chlorate, to name just a few. But even during the prewar period, indirect agreements were probably more influential than formal cartels. The most important, certainly, was the Patents and Processes Agreement, or "Grand Alliance," between du Pont and ICI, signed in 1929. As we noted in Chapter 1, the accord covered almost every chemical product the two firms made — ranging from explosives, plastics, and paints to acids, alcohols, and synthetic ammonia — and committed them "to exchange technical information and exclusive licenses to make, use and sell under all their patents and secret inventions, present and future."[28] Although the breadth of this pact was extraordinary, its purpose and format were not. Both firms made their peace with the other member of the "big three," I. G. Farben, through a multitude of patent agreements covering specific products and with the other large chemicals firms as well. In 1939 ICI alone was a party to some *eight hundred* agreements covering its chemical business.[29]

The arrangements governing the manufacture and sale of nylon and terylene are good examples of the major firms' tendency, already remarked upon in pharmaceuticals, to license important discoveries only to each other. Du Pont discovered nylon in 1937. After negotiations with its partner in the Grand Alliance, du Pont gave ICI an exclusive license to manufacture nylon in the United Kingdom, the British empire excluding Canada, Eire, Egypt, Iran, and Iraq, with a nonexclusive license for Norway, Sweden, Finland, Poland, and Portugal. Both firms contracted not to make or sell nylon in each other's home country, nor could either export primary or semifinished nylon goods outside its designated territory. A few other large chemicals or textiles firms, including I. G. Farben, were given exclusive licenses for their home countries and for specific overseas territories that had not been granted to ICI or reserved by du Pont. A similar market division was achieved through patent licenses for the polyester fiber terylene, although in this case the patentee was a relatively small British firm, Calico Printers. Rather than produce the fiber itself, Calico Printers assigned sole manufacturing rights to ICI in most of the world and to du Pont in the United States. ICI then granted sublicenses to other firms, with the usual strict division of territories.

Naturally, many of these arrangements became unworkable after World War II broke out; but the participants apparently had no intention of allowing the war to disrupt their commercial alliances permanently. Instead, they merely suspended active collaboration and planned to resume it when hostilities ended. In the meantime they performed small courtesies to safeguard each other's interests. "In numerous cases American companies awaited permission from their cartel partners before shipping to markets which the latter could no longer supply," write Stocking and Watkins.

> They took over such markets only for the duration of the war. In some cases the American companies used the familiar German packages and trade-marks to preserve customer good will for the German products . . . Many American and German companies assigned to each other the patent rights which each owned in the other's country, in an attempt to carry out the spirit of the prewar agreements, and to avoid confiscation of the patents because of their ownership by enemy nationals.[30]

Despite the companies' good intentions, though, the war and attendant events did alter the pattern of cartels that had existed until 1939. In Germany, zealous U.S. occupation authorities were determined to break up the national cartels organized by the Nazis. I. G. Farben, with its notorious international connections (a 1943 report estimated the firm was involved in two thousand cartels)[31] was a prime target. The vast chemicals combine was divided into its component parts: the companies now known as Germany's "big three" — Bayer, Hoechst, and BASF — and nine smaller firms. (Several of the nine have since been reabsorbed by the utterly dominant big three.) In the United States, the flurry of antitrust prosecutions in the 1940s forced the dissolution of several major chemicals cartels. In a landmark case involving the world-wide cartel of alkali producers, the Supreme Court ruled in 1949 that it was illegal for U.S. firms to belong to international cartels.[32] The close ties between du Pont and ICI were broken in 1952, when a U.S. district court ruled that the Patents and Processes

Agreement violated the Sherman Act, largely because of the territorial division it imposed.[33] In the *National Lead* case, decided in 1945 and affirmed by the Supreme Court two years later, Judge Simon H. Rifkind observed in the district court ruling that a patent pool maintained by producers of titanium compounds amounted to an illegal cartel:

> When the story is seen as a whole, there is no blinking the fact that there is no free commerce in titanium. Every pound of it is trammelled by privately imposed regulation. The channels of this commerce have not been formed by the winds and currents of competition. They are, in large measure, artificial canals privately constructed. The borders of the private domain in titanium are guarded by hundreds of patents, procured without opposition, and maintained without litigation. The accumulated power of this private empire, at the outbreak of World War II, was tremendous . . . There was a complete absence of imports, and of exports except to the Western Hemisphere.[34]

Such decisions forced chemicals producers to become more circumspect. Most of the major cartels disbanded, or never resumed operations after the war. Those which remain on public register in countries such as England and Germany are pure export cartels (in theory, at least), with no effect on home markets. At the same time indirect agreements have multiplied, each one achieving some small degree of market control over a certain product and thereby contributing to the general atmosphere of cooperation among the transnational chemical firms.

Leafing through the trade press one encounters occasional brief reports of these accords. On July 3, 1978, for example, the *Financial Times* of London made note of a new arrangement between Dow Chemical and the German firm, Bayer. The pact concerned chlorinated polyethylene elastomers, used in rubber production. Dow had been marketing its own chlorinated polyethylene in Europe, but now, the two firms announced, Bayer would purchase Dow's production and market it under Bayer's trademark. Dow and Bayer also agreed to exchange technical information on the applications of chlorinated polyethylene. On its face this is a perfectly legitimate business deal; the motivation for it need not have involved restraint of trade at all. Dow may simply have decided that Bayer could market its product more efficiently, and the German firm was pleased to gain a larger share of the market for its trademark. Whatever the intent, though, the agreement restricts competition between the two. It eliminates the possiblity of price competition on the European market and limits technological rivalry as well. It also raises a series of questions: How many similar accords do these firms participate in? Which other companies are involved? Which products? What is the cumulative effect of such agreements, thousands of which are known to exist? We suspect that, for many products, the net result is a division of markets and fields following the patterns set up by the cartels of the prewar years. However, without a massive research effort backed by the subpoena power of various governments it is impossible to know for sure. The system is too diffuse; the whole is composed of too many fragmented parts. The actual terms of the vast majority of agreements — even those mentioned in the trade press — will never be publicly available because they are regarded as legitimate trade secrets to be protected by the companies involved.

Thus the anxiety and protest on the part of chemicals firms when the EEC demanded registration of all restrictive accords. At the time, one trade journal remarked that "specialists in international company law generally believe chemicals and drugs . . . are the fields which would be most directly hit by vigorous enforcement of the anti-cartel provisions."[35] But the vigorous enforcement has never occurred. Only when companies have grossly violated commercial propriety have they been investigated and chastised — and then only when their cartel efforts have somehow been exposed. Nevertheless, there have been a number of such instances since World War II, evidence that the longing for cartel security has not entirely waned. We will briefly describe some of these agreements in chemicals before going on to more detailed accounts of two fields, dyestuffs and fertilizers, known for their continuing devotion to cartels.

Red Phosphorus

The cartel governing world trade in red phosphorus — a chemical used primarily in the production of matches — was organized in 1959 and operated at least through the early 1960s.[36] Its members were based in five countries — Germany, France, England, Canada, and the United States — and included all the major producers except the Japanese and Soviets. Two of the world's largest chemicals firms were involved: Hoechst, which owned the German cartel member, a firm called Knapsack-Griesheim; and the French chemicals combine Kuhlmann, whose subsidiary Coignet was the French participant in the cartel. The other three members actually represented one common interest because the British firm Albright & Wilson owned the Canadian firm, the Electric Reduction Company, or Erco; and the Duff Chemical Co. of the United States was Erco's agent for international sales.

The accord signed by these companies was a simple market-division and price-fixing cartel called the Hunting Ground Agreement. It divided the world into four exclusive sales areas, generally along traditional lines: the British Commonwealth and Scandinavia for Albright; most of Europe for Knapsack; France, French territories, and some European nations for Coignet; and Central America, Colombia, the Caribbean, Mexico, and Venezuela for Duff (selling for Erco). A fifth area, mostly Asian countries and South America, was designated open territory, where all the members could bid freely for business. Prices were fixed at about 50 cents a pound, a price markedly higher than the prevailing level; Duff, for example, had been supplying its Latin American customers at prices under 35 cents. The division of territory apparently worked well, although the Japanese "outsiders" caused trouble by underselling the cartel.

White Lead

Prior to the war, white lead was widely employed as a pigment in paint manufacture.[37] Its commerce was controlled by a cartel organized in 1927 by British, German, Italian, Austrian, Dutch, and Belgian producers and reorganized in 1933 by members from sixteen countries. More recently, however, white lead has been supplanted to some degree as a pigment by other compounds. It is now used as an additive in protective paints and in plastics manufacture. And the number of producers has declined sharply; just three firms — one English, one German, one Dutch — now account for the EEC's entire white lead output, and most of the world's. In 1971 the three companies formed a cartel that fixed prices and market shares on all export markets, including those in Europe. They rewrote the agreement the following year, exempting EEC countries from all provisions except the exchange of information. But this attempt to make the cartel conform to antitrust laws did not convince the EEC Commission, which in 1978 voided the agreement. The Commission did not believe that the three dominant producers could eliminate competition among themselves throughout the world and leave it unaffected within the bounds of the Common Market.

Melamine

Melamine is a synthetic chemical substance whose qualities of hardness and resistance to heat make it important in the manufacture of various types of plastics, coatings, laminated panels, tiles, and other products. American consumers are most familiar with it in the form of hard plastic dishware; it is also a key ingredient of Formica. Melamine was subject to world-wide cartel control for many years. According to an antitrust indictment filed by the Justice Department in 1960, the American Cyanamid Company obtained a patent license in 1937 for a technological breakthrough in the production of the chemical. As is so often the case the patent license formed part of an international market-division scheme whereby Cyanamid was allotted the United States. The original patent eventually expired, but by that time Cyanamid had established its commanding position in the field. In 1958 the firm produced 86 percent of the unfinished melamine in the United States. The other 14 percent was made by Monsanto, which consumed its entire output, so that Cyanamid was the only seller of unfinished melamine on the U.S. market. The firm also produced 100 percent of the primary raw material for melamine, a chemical called dicyandiamide, or "dicy."[38]

To preserve this melamine monopoly, Cyanamid had to ward off both domestic and foreign competitors. Within the United States the firm did so by refusing to sell dicy to certain buyers or by offering it at such a high price that melamine manufacture would be rendered unprofitable. Cyanamid also refused to grant licenses for its discoveries in the field. The company bought two other firms that consumed large quantities of melamine, the Formica Company and the Panelyte Company, thus depriving potential melamine producers of two major customers.[39] Meanwhile, foreign competition was eliminated by cartel agreements for more than twenty years. The Justice Department complaint named four European companies — one Swiss, one French, and two British — as co-conspirators with Cyanamid. The Europeans apparently agreed not to export melamine to the United States in return for Cyanamid's limiting its exports to certain foreign markets. The net result was that Cyanamid's American monopoly was preserved, with prices markedly higher than they would have been in a competitive market. Cyanamid's policies also allegedly blocked development of new uses for melamine and retarded progress in finding raw materials other than dicy for its production.[40]

Cyanamid, of course, denied all these charges. But in 1964 the company accepted a settlement severe enough to indicate that the government must have had a very strong case.[41] Under the consent decree, Cyanamid agreed to sell the larger of its two melamine production plants in order to establish a competitive source of the product. The company pledged to limit its annual production of melamine, to buy a certain amount from competitors every year, and to sell dicy or melamine to anyone able to pay for it. The decree also provided that Cyanamid must grant royalty-free licenses on all its patents relating to dicy, melamine, and melamine resins and supply its know-how to any firm that wished to manufacture melamine products. Any discoveries during the next five years must also be licensed to all competent applicants, although Cyanamid could charge "reasonable" royalties. Finally, the firm was ordered to discontinue all of its agreements with foreign firms that allocated territories or customers and limited imports or exports.

Persulfates

Markedly similar to the melamine cartel is one that recently controlled trade in persulfates — chemicals used in the manufacture of plastics, hair bleach, and printed circuits.[42] According to a felony indictment filed in 1975 (later reduced to a misdemeanor), the FMC Corporation of Chicago conspired with foreign firms to seal off the U.S. market and fix prices. As usual, some of the world's largest chemicals firms were among the cartel members: the Solvay & Cie. of Belgium, a participant in many past cartels, and the Dutch giant AKZO. English and German companies were also involved. These firms apparently agreed, beginning at least as far back as 1971, to limit their exports of potassium, ammonium, and sodium persulfates to the United States. This left FMC, the only American producer, with about 90 percent of the U.S. market, worth about $7 million annually. Precisely what FMC may have pledged in return is unclear, but universal cartel practice would suggest it must have involved reciprocal protection for the Europeans' markets. The company pleaded no contest in 1977.

Dyestuffs and Fertilizers

To complete this chapter we will examine dyestuffs and fertilizers, two key branches of the chemicals industry with long histories of formal cartel activity. (A third branch known for its ongoing cartels, the synthetic fibers industry, will be discussed in Chapter 6.) In both these fields the elaborate cartels that existed during the Depression did not survive the war. But the memory apparently lingered, the impulse to restrain competition remained strong, and eventually the dyestuffs and fertilizer manufacturers reverted to their old habits. Cartels have reappeared, in Europe and in the United States, with the same firms using many of the same methods they perfected decades ago.

Until World War I, Germany thoroughly dominated the dyestuffs trade, as it did most other realms of the chemicals industry. However, during the hostilities other countries rushed to build up their capacities, and although I. G. Farben remained the industry leader in dyes between the wars, the other large chemicals firms became powers to be reckoned with. In 1927 the syndicate of French dyestuff makers, led by Établissements Kuhlmann (the company that produced over two-thirds of French dyes at the time), joined I. G. Farben in a cartel agreement that fixed prices, protected home markets, and set quotas for exports. Two years later the three Swiss manufacturers who dominated that country's dye industry — Ciba, Geigy, and Sandoz — entered the cartel. In 1931 ICI of Great Britain joined, followed by most of the remaining sizable European companies. During the Depression the European cartel controlled 60 to 70 percent of the world's output of dyestuffs, and its share of total exports was even higher.[43]

The U.S. market was equally cartelized, although perhaps not so formally. Five large companies — du Pont, Calco Chemical (of American Cyanamid), National Aniline (of Allied Chemical), General Dyestuff, and Cincinnati Chemical Works — held 90 percent (by value) of the dyestuffs market in 1939. The latter two were subsidiaries of I. G. Farben and the Swiss syndicate, respectively. All cooperated closely on prices, cross-licensing of technology, and other matters. Du Pont, it will be remembered, was ICI's partner in the Grand Alliance, which among other provisions established home market protection: du Pont withdrew from the British dyestuffs market, and ICI from the American. National Aniline respected that division.[44] In other words, through ownership ties, agreements, and a general policy of cooperation, American companies were so closely linked to the European cartel members that the cartel must be judged to have effectively included the United States.

We have discovered no information regarding dyestuffs cartels during the two decades immediately following World War II. This does not necessarily mean there were no such cartels, of course. Certainly many patent license agreements remained in effect among the major firms. The best that can be said for certain is that the next time a major investigation was conducted was in the mid-1960s, and it showed that the industry was thoroughly under cartel control.

In August 1967, ten of the largest European producers of dyestuffs gathered for a meeting in Basel, Switzerland — and two months later a general increase in prices for aniline dyes was put into effect. The circumstances of the increase intrigued German officials, and after an investigation several German firms were fined in 1968 for participating in an illegal scheme to fix prices within the EEC. (The fines were later quashed by a German court which ruled there was not enough hard evidence of price fixing to meet the standards of the country's cartel law.) As a result of these events the EEC Commission carried out a much more thorough inquiry. The EEC concentrated on the period between 1964 and 1967, and investigated the conduct of some sixty dyestuffs producers. It was decided, however, to concentrate on the ten largest firms, which together accounted for about four-fifths of European output, although the EEC observed that the smaller firms apparently followed the lead of the ten. Finally the EEC ruled — and the ruling was eventually upheld by the European High Court — that the ten companies had imposed "uniform and virtually simultaneous" price increases in Europe in January 1964, January 1965, and October 1967. After the 1964 increase, the EEC found, instructions from the companies to their subsidiaries or representatives ordering the price increase were couched in highly similar terms — occasionally in identical language.[45] The EEC also identified five distinct price markets within the Common Market and said the differences could not be accounted for by varying costs and charges to manufacturers. Each price increase was announced in advance so that others could follow. Taken together, these facts satisfied the Commission that "concerted action" in restraint of trade, as defined by Article 85 of the Treaty of Rome, had taken place, even though there was little documentary evidence of a conspiracy to fix prices. The ten firms — Bayer, Hoechst, BASF (the "big three" offspring of I. G. Farben), and Casella of Germany; Ciba, Geigy, and Sandoz of Switzerland; Société Française des Matières Colorantes (which includes the Kuhlmann interests) of France; ICI of Great Britain; and ACNA of Italy — were fined a total of $480,000 in 1969.[46] Virtually all the names were familiar as charter members of the old European dyestuffs cartel. In 1972 new uniform price rises took place, and after an inquiry the EEC stated that, although this time the hikes were not simultaneous, they still were identical within each member nation.[47]

In the United States, too, some of the usual names popped up again. After a seven-month grand jury investigation, nine U.S. dye producers (including subsidiaries of four European cartel members) were indicted in July 1974 for conspiring to fix dye prices. The investigation, like the one in Europe, resulted from a simultaneous price increase, in this case in March 1971. The nine companies were estimated to hold 60 percent of U.S. dye production. All nine — du Pont, American Cyanamid, Allied Chemical, Ciba-Geigy, BASF Wyandotte, GAF, the Verona Corporation (a subsidiary of Bayer), American Color and Chemical (a subsidiary of N.V. Philips of the Netherlands), and Compton & Knowles — eventually pleaded no contest and were fined $395,000.[48] In 1975 they agreed to pay $15 million in damages to settle a civil antitrust suit arising from the conspiracy.

*　　*　　*

Cartels in fertilizers possess a perennial quality similar to those in dyestuffs; after periods of dormancy, they inevitably flower again. (The similarity to dyestuffs is partly accounted for by the fact that some of the same firms are involved, notably such cartel stalwarts as Hoechst and ICI.) In fact, fertilizer manufacturers have been if anything even more tenacious in their cartel schemes than the dye makers. The first fertilizer accords took effect more than one hundred years ago, and the industry has harbored a fascinating assortment of cartels ever since. There is no indication that the penchant for cartels in fertilizers has abated in the slightest. One of the most important classic cartels known to be currently in operation is the Nitrex A.G., which has governed exports of nitrogenous fertilizers by European firms for the last eighteen years from its headquarters in Zurich.

The most important three elements that plants obtain from the soil are nitrogen, phosphorous, and potassium, and products based on those elements make up the bulk of the fertilizer trade. Nitrogen can be obtained or synthesized by a variety of methods; so there are numerous types of nitrogenous fertilizers. The primary source of phosphorous, on the other hand, is so-called phosphate rock, or mineral deposits that contain a high proportion of phosphorous compounds such as P_2O_5. Deposits in Florida and Tennessee were until the beginning of this century the fount of most of the world's supply of phosphate rock; since then the United States has been steadily supplanted by North African countries as the main supplier.

Potash fertilizers, containing potassium, are also derived from mineral deposits located in various countries, including Germany, France, Poland, Spain, Israel, the Soviet Union, and the United States. Compound fertilizers, made up of nitrates, phosphates, and potash in varying proportions, have greatly increased in popularity in recent years. Yet despite the widely differing sources and markets for the different kinds of fertilizers, all have repeatedly given rise to cartels.

Until World War I the huge deposits of natural sodium nitrate in northern Chile were the most important source of commercial nitrogen in the world. The Chilean producers organized their first cartel in 1884, and others followed during the years before the war. But the discovery of the Haber process of obtaining "synthetic nitrogen" from the air ended Chilean dominance. The industrial nations rushed to expand production of nitrogen, partly because it serves not only as a fertilizer but as an essential component of explosives and propellants. By the late 1920s massive overcapacity had developed. As often happens, overcapacity led to a cartel.[49] In 1929 I. G. Farben and ICI, the largest producers in their respective countries, joined in a one-year cartel agreement, which was replaced in 1930 by a more ambitious cartel known as the Convention Internationale de l'Azote (International Nitrogen Convention, or CIA). The CIA soon collapsed in a squabble over market shares, but it was reorganized in July 1932, and this time proved durable, lasting through various revisions of the basic agreement until the outbreak of World War II. The CIA was a classic cartel on the grand scale, complete with the usual paraphernalia: home market agreements, fixed export quotas with penalties for exceeding them, a joint sales agency, production cutbacks, and fixed prices. The members included producers from England, Germany, Norway, France, Italy, the Netherlands, Belgium, Switzerland, Poland, Czechoslovakia, Japan, and Chile. And although U.S. firms were not formally members of the cartel, there is strong evidence (including a consent decree that settled an antitrust case filed in 1939) that the Americans cooperated fully in the worldwide operations of the Nitrogen Convention by restricting American exports and imports, accepting market quotas in foreign countries, respecting agreed price levels, and so on.[50]

U.S. producers of "phosphate rock" were organized as an export cartel almost as soon as such organization was made legal by the Webb-Pomerene Act of 1918. The Phosphate Export Association was created in 1919, and later merged with the Florida Pebble Phosphate Export Association. These groups, in turn, collaborated with the Florida Hard Rock Phosphate Export Association. But as foreign — particularly North African — production grew to take a larger share of the world market, the Webb-Pomerene cartel did not suffice to control the trade. During the Depression the Americans joined with their foreign competitors in a cartel called the International Phosphate Rock Agreement, which "embraced practically the whole international market," as one writer put it.[51] The cartel was based on five "groups" of exporters: the Americans, the North Africans, the Dutch Curaçao group, the Egyptians, and the Pacific group, this last representing a French company that sold phosphate from southern Pacific islands. The cartel allocated sales territories and may have fixed prices.

The potash trade as well was governed before World War II by a powerful cartel that included U.S. firms. Germany accounted for most of the world's potash until World War I, and the German producers had collaborated as far back as 1879. But the tidy German control over the product was disturbed when the Treaty of Versailles ceded Alsace–Lorraine, containing some of the richest potash mines, to France. A period of sharp competition proved disagreeable to both countries, and in 1924 they agreed to fix prices and sales quotas for the U.S. and Swedish markets. This preliminary accord was followed two years later by a cartel agreement embracing the entire world, and that remained in effect through the 1930s.[52] However, as other countries expanded their potash production, brief price wars preceding the adherence of new members punctuated the cartel's history. The Polish, Spanish, and Palestinian producers joined at different times during the 1930s.[53] This left the Soviets — who reportedly did not formally join but respected cartel price levels out of fear of retaliation — and the Americans, whose rapidly growing potash output made their cooperation essential to the cartel. In 1935 the U.S. producers reached an "understanding" with the cartel that supposedly concerned research and advertising, but, as Plummer writes, "it is an open secret that it had a bearing on sales also."[54] In 1938 the Americans organized a Webb-Pomerene cartel, the Potash Export Association. The following year the three companies that comprised the association were indicted along with the international cartel's agency on criminal charges of rigging the world's potash markets. The case ended, like so many others, with the defendants accepting a consent decree. The criminal charges were dropped.[55]

*   *   *

Following the disruptions of World War II, the fertilizer cartels began to regroup. The members of the old nitrogen convention were not long in organizing a formal association that evolved into a full-fledged cartel. Evidence concerning potash and phosphates is more fragmentary; investigations have been infrequent, and the cartels themselves are mutable, appearing in one guise at a certain time, vanishing, and then reappearing years later in another. Also, the fertilizer producers seem to have adopted to some degree the postwar practice of other branches of the chemicals industry, that is, mini-agreements between two or three enterprises covering specific markets only. Even the fragments of evidence are enough, though, to indicate a pattern of periodic, and probably constant, cartelization of all three types of fertilizer.

In the case of potash, the small amount of data on cartels immediately following the war comes from a 1964 study by Corwin Edwards. He concluded there was a powerful group of European firms that worked to "exclude independent supplies of potash from the European market and to draw new suppliers into the sales organization."[56]

We do not know whether the cartel Edwards described is still operating, but EEC investigations in the 1970s revealed continuing restrictive agreements between certain firms. France's output of potash is marketed by a government-sanctioned monopoly called the Société Commerciale des Potasses et de l'Azote (SCPA), whereas Germany's producers are organized into a cartel that sells through a joint sales agency called Kali und Salz A.G. Until 1973, the SCPA and Kali und Salz maintained an agreement that fixed prices and quotas on all world export markets, including Common Market countries. The EEC Commission ordered the European joint marketing arrangements of the two agencies dissolved. In 1974 a similar action was taken regarding Kali und Salz and another potash firm operating in Germany but owned by the Belgian Solvay group. By coordinating their sales, the two enterprises had eliminated competition between them, both on domestic and export markets.[57]

Until recently, some of the leading U.S. potash producers continued to sell through a Webb-Pomerene cartel, the Potash Export Association, which was linked to the international cartel before the war; but there is no evidence of postwar connections between the American cartel and foreign producers.

As to the phosphates trade, information regarding Europe is scanty, whereas cartel patterns in the United States have been amply documented. Edwards reported in 1964 that European phosphate producers maintained territorial divisions and fixed prices, while conspiring to keep cheap sources of phosphates — such as a plant in Tunisia — out of export markets. One "significant buyer of phosphates" told Edwards, "Before the annual meeting of the associated producers . . . buyers cannot obtain quotations, whereas immediately after the meetings all producers quote a uniform price which prevails until the next meeting."[58]

While these practices were current in Europe, the U.S. phosphates industry was dominated by cartels influencing both domestic and export markets. The investigation that exposed the cartels was the result of an odd sequence of events. The industry's difficulties began in the early 1960s, when the United States was providing South Korea with large amounts of phosphate fertilizer through the foreign aid program, financed by the Agency for International Development (AID). When Japanese phosphate makers proposed to supply AID with fertilizer at lower prices, the American manufacturers insisted that AID continue its "buy American" policy. The protest backfired, however, for it led to a study of the supply of phosphates to Korea and thereby to an examination of the American industry.[59] A series of antitrust prosecutions followed in 1963 and 1964. In one case, two firms were charged with illegal conspiracy to fix prices of export sales of triple superphosphate fertilizer to Korea. A second indictment charged five firms with price fixing on markets around the world for almost all exports of Florida phosphate rock between the years 1959 and 1962. In both cases the firms pleaded nolo contendere and suffered light fines.[60] But a third case was somewhat more complicated, involving sales by five companies to AID for South Korea. The sales were made through a legally constituted Webb-Pomerene cartel, the Concentrated Phosphate Export Association (CPEA). The companies never denied that they had combined to fix prices; they simply contended that the cartel was legal because sales to foreign countries, even if financed by AID, were exports. After a trial and appeals, the Supreme Court disagreed, ruling in 1968 that sales to AID were *not* exports, and therefore the companies had violated the law.[61] AID, meanwhile, changed its policies and announced that it would no longer accept bids from Webb-Pomerene cartels but only from individual companies; as a result, the price AID (and, indirectly, the American taxpayer) had to pay for phosphate fertilizer soon dropped substantially.[62]

These cases were important to foreign buyers of American phosphates — particularly to the developing countries, which import large quantities of fertilizer — because they involved illegal price fixing on export markets. But of more direct concern to American consumers is the fact that the phosphate manufacturers did not restrict their collusion to foreign markets. As in so many other instances, the export cartels served to conceal schemes to regulate the domestic market as well. In February 1964, the Justice Department filed a civil suit against eight phosphate companies which together accounted for all the Florida production of phosphate rock, charging them with price fixing within the United States. The firms included those involved in the export cartels — W. R. Grace & Company; American Cyanamid; International Minerals & Chemical; and a subsidiary of Mobil Oil — as well as Swift & Co.; the Smith-Douglass Co.; Armour & Co.; and the American Agricultural Chemical Co.[63] Just three months later came a criminal indictment, this one in Los Angeles, charging five chemical companies with conspiracy to fix prices of phosphates in eleven western states. This time the array of firms was international: the California Chemical Co., a subsidiary of Standard Oil of California; the J. R. Simplot Co.; Balfour-Guthrie Co., a subsidiary of a British

firm; Cominco Products, a subsidiary of Consolidated Mining and Smelting of Canada; and Western Phosphates, Inc., a subsidiary of Stauffer
Chemical Co.[64] In the first case, charges against the Mobil subsidiary and
Smith-Douglass were dropped, and the rest accepted a consent judgment
forbidding price fixing.[65] In California, all five firms pleaded no contest
and were fined. In other words, eleven of the thirteen companies either
admitted guilt or agreed to refrain from the behavior they had been
charged with.[66]

The 1960s cases may or may not have put an end to illegal cartels in the
phosphate industry. Two Webb-Pomerene cartels in phosphates still operate, and one of them — the Phosphate Chemicals Export Association —
was recently under investigation by the Justice Department, which reportedly believes the cartel's foreign activities may have affected the
domestic market.[67]

But it is in the field of nitrogenous fertilizers that the prewar cartel system has been most nearly replicated. In 1953 a number of the most important companies in the old Nitrogen Convention founded a Geneva organization called the Centre d'Étude de l'Azote, or the Nitrogen Research
Center. Its ostensible purpose was to carry out studies and collect data on
the use of nitrogen. But in 1962 the members of the center organized the
Nitrex A.G. of Zurich, one of the most durable postwar formal cartels. At
that time, world capacity for nitrogenous fertilizer was some 14 million
tons per year, over 2.5 million tons more than the demand — and capacity
was expected to swell to 23 million tons before long.[68] During the 1950s
the European producers had been competing sharply with each other, and
for some years experts had expected the companies to create a formal cartel. Indeed, not long before the advent of Nitrex another round of price
cutting had taken place, as companies fought to gain a foothold in markets
they could then use in negotiating their share of sales under the cartel. The
companies themselves argued that, under the prevailing competitive conditions, the centralized state buying agencies of such countries as China
and India could play the fertilizer firms against one other by "dangling"
the prospect of large contracts before several firms, inducing each to bid
the price a little lower. This argument amounted to a plea of self-defense;
the cartel was necessary, said the companies, in order to present a united
front against such predatory buyers.

Nitrex's founding members included the German firms BASF, Hoechst,
and Ruhr-Stickstoff A.G.; the national cartels of producers in Belgium,
France, the Netherlands, and Italy; and manufacturers in Austria, Norway, and Sweden. Since then the membership has remained almost constant. The British firms Shell and Fisons reportedly maintain indirect links
to the cartel, and ICI, one of the largest producers of nitrogen, attends
meetings as an observer.[69] In 1964 the members of Nitrex accounted for

about 60 percent of the overseas trade in nitrogenous fertilizers, a substantial enough share, according to *The Economist,* to give the cartel "some market power to achieve its main objective of 'stabilizing' nitrogen prices."[70] Nitrex allegedly was (and still is) a "pure" export cartel, its policies applying only to trade in nonmember countries. The cartel office acts as a central sales office in dealing with state buying agencies; otherwise, companies are free to make sales on their own, but profits are pooled and distributed on the basis of pre-established quotas. This system has often allowed sales to developing nations at prices far higher than those prevailing in Europe.[71] But it has long been suspected that the members also respect each others' home markets, at least tacitly. In 1973 a report from the West German Ministry of the Economy angrily noted that German fertilizer prices were by far the highest in the Common Market — a mysterious disproportion, given the lack of tariff barriers.[72]

There have also been certain intriguing indications, but little hard evidence, that the cartel may embrace members other than the Europeans. A 1963 report in the *Oil, Paint and Drug Reporter* noted that representatives of the Japanese Ammonium Sulphate Industry Association "are just back from top-secret talks in Switzerland with Nitrex, West Europe's export cartel. Aim of the negotiations: to reach agreement on orderly fertilizer marketing in Asia and Latin America."[73] The article observed that the Japanese resented Nitrex's attempts to win markets in Asia, which the Japanese considered their preserve. From later reports in trade journals of battles between the Japanese and Europeans over sales, it would appear that agreement, if it was reached, was either short lived or did not include all markets. But in 1967 evidence presented before the Senate Subcommittee on Antitrust and Monopoly, during hearings reviewing the Webb-Pomerene Act, strongly suggested the existence of European–Japanese cartel ties. Robert O. Link, an official of the U.S. Agriculture Department, testified that he noted unusual patterns in the bidding for fertilizer contracts. His story is best recounted in the transcript of the hearings. (His interlocuter is Senator Philip A. Hart, Democrat of Michigan; the CCC is the Commodity Credit Corporation, the group that ran the barter program.)

> Mr. LINK: ... Prior to May 1967, CCC required from U.S. contracting firms only the usual certificate of independent price determination required by Federal procurement regulations ...
> However, late in March of this year [1967] when CCC received offers for delivery of 200,000 metric tons of urea for India we noted a striking similarity in the prices offered by the U.S. firms (acting as agents) for urea from European and Japanese producers, despite the geographical realities involved. About the same time several U.S. barter contractors who had previously supplied foreign-produced urea for (U.S.) AID programs, told

us that they were suspicious that urea prices offered by some European and Japanese suppliers were not being arrived at independently. CCC also considered the prices excessive. We, therefore, promptly rejected all offers and resolicited offers for one-half the tonnage, that is, 100,000 metric tons. At the same time we decided to require a special additional certificate of independent pricing to be furnished by named foreign suppliers . . .

While we succeeded, as a result of this readvertising, in reducing the prices by $2 to $3 per ton (that is, to about $82 per metric ton, f.o.b. port of loading) . . . there was still some question whether the prices offered from various sources reflected full and free competition.

....

Senator HART: You indicated, as I understand, that there was a similarity for both the Japanese and European procurements . . . What information or details can you give us on that? . . .

Mr. LINK: My recollection is that one firm offered a total of 158,000 metric tons to this invitation for 200,000. This was one indication to us that something might be amiss, and in addition this was the only firm —

Senator HART: For the record, explain why you would suggest something would be amiss?

Mr. LINK: Well, it suggested to us that this one . . . firm had some means by which it was completely controlling the sources of supply or was putting itself in a position to be not the sole offerer but the predominant offerer under the announcement.

In addition to that, this one firm was the only firm offering any Japanese material. It was the only one of two firms offering any European material. There was only one other firm offering Japanese or European material under this proposal. There were a number of other firms offering from areas like Taiwan and Kuwait, but they are not the major sources for this fertilizer. There was one other factor that I ought to mention and that is that we noticed that the cost on freight delivered prices per metric ton for fertilizer of Japan and Europe in some cases were offered at 10 cents per metric ton difference. Now, this appeared to be a peculiar circumstance. . . .

Senator HART: Will you explain to us how you initiated this supplier's certificate that asked assurances . . . that the quantity and prices have been determined separately and individually? . . .

Mr. LINK: We do not really know, Senator, how helpful this new certificate will be. We are conscious of the fact that when you are dealing with foreign suppliers it is difficult to insure individual price determination. They cannot be touched in the U.S. courts ordinarily.[74]

It was later noted in the hearings that the foreign concerns which carried out this apparently collusive pricing were a large "selling organization in Zurich, Switzerland" and the "Japanese Ammonium Sulfate Export

Co." There is no proof, however, of enduring links between the Japanese and the Europeans.

One final insight into the fertilizer industry — and the chemicals industry as a whole — comes from a case investigated by the EEC Commission and decided in 1978. The case concerned the Dutch market for nitrogenous fertilizers, which was dominated by two companies: the Unie van Kunstmestfabrieken (UKF), the largest producer of such fertilizers in Europe, and the Nederlandse Stikstof Maatschappij (NSM). (A third firm owned by Exxon held a minor share of the market.) Beginning not long after World War II, the corporate predecessors of UKF and NSM established a company called Central Stikstof Verkoopkantoor (CSV) to run their business jointly.[75] CSV, in effect, was a cartel that strictly controlled the Dutch nitrogenous fertilizer trade. Staffed by officers of the two parent firms, it made estimates of probable demand, "suggested" to the firms how much fertilizer of each type they should produce, allocated market shares, and at the end of each year arranged exchanges between the firms so that their quotas would be met exactly. Although CSV's near monopoly kept prices substantially higher in Holland than in some other EEC countries, there were almost no imports, apparently because of a tacit system of home market protection. Thus the Dutch market was "sealed off" from the rest of the EEC, and for that reason the Commission ruled CSV's operations illegal.[76] But one particularly interesting aspect of the case was that *NSM was not a Dutch-owned company.* Rather, 69 percent of its shares were held by the Italian chemicals giant Montedison, and 25 percent by ICI, both leading producers of fertilizer and participants in Nitrex.[77] In other words, the Dutch national cartel, which fixed prices and divided the market in Holland, was in fact an accord among Dutch, British, and Italian firms. This makes it easier to understand why the Dutch market was left undisturbed by producers from the rest of Europe. Intertwined in such joint ventures as they are, their interests frequently coincide rather than conflict; and mutual forbearance from competition is profitable for all.

❊   ❊   ❊

Thus, although the fertilizer trade probably remains more prone to classic cartels than do other branches of the chemicals industry in the postwar period, the Dutch mini-cartel provides an excellent example of the type of accord that today blankets the field. By the simplest means — a joint venture between two transnational giants and their agreement to collaborate with the leading Dutch producer — an entire national market was shielded from domestic or foreign competition. The only local "outsider," with its small share of the market, followed the price lead of the cartel. And foreign producers did not invade the Dutch market — first, because they would thereby invite retaliation, but also, undoubtedly, because they were themselves connected to ICI and Montedison in other ventures, in other countries, in other products. The reader will have remarked on the fact that the names of the same few firms surface again and again in a discussion of chemicals cartels. As Stocking and Watkins wrote in 1946, "The relationships of every chemical company with its rivals are necessarily conditioned and shaped by the entire range of external policies and commitments of all the others."[78] We have attempted to show in this chapter that the pattern today remains remarkably similar to the one they described thirty-five years ago.

6

Steel and Fibers: The "Troubled Industry" Solution

CARTELS are the offspring of ill fortune. Virtually every known cartel was organized at a time when its industry was in trouble — when competition had become "chaotic," "disorderly," "destructive," or whatever other term the competitors chose to signify "uncomfortably intense." In the electronics and petroleum industries, as we have seen, the basic cartels long outlived the initial moment of difficulty that gave rise to them; whereas the uranium cartel apparently disbanded once prices and profits had improved sufficiently. But what of industries that decline so severely that they are threatened with extinction? Aging productive facilities, or shifts in competitive advantage to other parts of the world, may transform a country's once powerful industries into ailing giants, marginally profitable only at the best of times. Yet if these industries are important enough, whether because of the nature of the goods they produce or simply because of the large number of people they employ, governments may choose to protect them long after they have ceased to be internationally competitive.

In recent years, the poor economic performance of the Western industrialized nations has intensified competition among them, causing great concern about the survival of weak national industries. Protectionism has again become a burning issue, perhaps more so than at any time since the Depression. Government attempts to protect industries may take a number of forms, such as high tariffs, subsidies, and nationalization; or governments may help the industries to reach cartel agreements with their com-

petitors abroad. Trade in many raw materials and commodities is openly
controlled by cartels of sovereign states. However, the cartel approach is
much more controversial when applied to manufacturing industries. Thus
far it has been largely the European nations that have experimented with
it.

This chapter, then, concerns the cartelization of two troubled manufacturing industries in Europe: steel and man-made fibers. In many ways the
histories and present circumstances of the two are oddly similar. They are
both basic industries of major importance to any industrialized nation, although steel, of course, is the more essential. Both have used cartels extensively for many years — steel since the 1880s, fibers since the early 1900s.
Both are subject to relatively lengthy cycles of boom and bust, so that
business may be depressed for stretches of years at a time. And recently
both have been critically weakened in Europe by shifting patterns of production. Since the 1960s, competition for international markets in steel
and fibers has traditionally been triangular — among Europe, the United
States, and the latecomer, Japan. But in the last decade Japan's steel industry has proven itself superior to all others, and its fibers producers are
highly competitive; and at the same time, a substantial number of modern
steel and fibers plants have been constructed in the more advanced Third
World nations. The older plants in Europe are now obsolete and, in a situation of severe world overcapacity, steel and fibers are generally thought
to be Europe's "sickest" major industries, as the trade journal *Chemical
Marketing Reporter* has called them. As a result, steel producers in Europe
have been organized into an EEC-sponsored cartel, and fibers producers
have pleaded for similar help, although they have been denied it thus far.
This is perhaps the most interesting similarity between the two European
industries: their reliance on private cartels when business is reasonably
good and their insistence on more far-reaching schemes, backed by government authority, when times are bad.

The Experience with Steel

Cartels in the steel industry date to the dawn of the cartel age. Among the
earliest of all was the International Rail Makers Association, which was
founded in 1883, and passed through various incarnations before disband-
ing in 1914. Several other steel product lines, including tubular products
and wire, were cartelized before World War I. But it was the war that led
indirectly to the creation of the first comprehensive steel cartel, in 1926.
And the problem caused by the war was to prove perennial for the industry: overcapacity. The world's steel manufacturers emerged from the war
with facilities that could produce far more steel than the world needed.
During the hostilities, plants had been constructed as fast as possible by

several of the warring powers; and the postwar period saw even more plant construction, as Germany, which had lost a large portion of its steel capacity as a result of the cession of Alsace–Lorraine to France and Luxembourg to the Belgian customs union, engaged in a massive, government-assisted investment and rationalization program. But in the early 1920s European demand for steel remained *below* the best prewar years.[1] European steel industries therefore operated far below capacity, and there was bitter competition for export markets.

Hoping to avoid a battle to the death among steel producers, the Europeans undertook negotiations that came to fruition in 1926 with the establishment of the Entente Internationale de l'Acier (EIA).[2] The members, who included producers from France, Germany, Belgium, Luxembourg, and the Saar, initially accounted for two-thirds of all world exports of steel. The cartel's basic technique was simply to estimate world demand for crude steel and then allocate to each member country an agreed share of the market — in effect, telling each member how much crude steel it was allowed to produce. Steelmakers from any one country who exceeded their quota were fined $4 for every excess metric ton, and countries that fell short were compensated at the rate of $2 per metric ton of deficit. But this attempt to restrict output of crude steel proved ineffective, and the cartel collapsed with the onset of the Great Depression, in 1931.

During the next eighteen months, with demand plummeting around the world, unrestrained competition was again the rule, and steel prices were at their lowest levels. The producers desperately desired a new accord, and finally, in 1933, they achieved it, this time creating a formidable cartel with an uncommonly straightforward name: the International Steel Cartel, or ISC.

The steel companies had learned an important lesson from their experience with the EIA: attempts to limit production of crude steel in various nations were too difficult to enforce. Therefore, when they formed the new cartel, they focused not on production levels but on export quotas. The agreement establishing the International Steel Cartel was signed on June 1, 1933, by producers from Germany, France, Belgium, and Luxembourg. It fixed overall export quotas for crude and semifinished steel for each national group. And it adopted a technique established by the early cartels in the industry, one which remains common today: the use of minicartels to control specific product groups. Six special agreements complemented the general accord by imposing specific quotas on exports of particular products such as bars, rods, and structural shapes. For each product a common sales agency was created to handle all export sales by the cartel members. The members could thus produce all the steel they wanted for domestic use — or even for stockpiling, if they felt it imperative to keep mills running at capacity — but the amount of steel entering world commerce would be strictly controlled.

The responsibility of each national group was primarily to keep its house in order, that is, to make sure the steel producers of that country, whether or not they were members of the cartel, did not exceed the country's export quota. As with most cartels, the International Steel Cartel provided for home market protection. But in return for such protection the cartel members — usually the dominant steel firms in each country — had to agree that exports by nonmember firms would be counted against the country's quota and therefore that members would cut their exports accordingly. Naturally, this gave members a strong incentive to absorb outsiders into the cartel or to destroy them — and, in fact, the ISC sponsored some brutal predatory battles.[3]

Even more important than the discipline imposed by the national groups, though, were the sales syndicates for specific products. The product-by-product approach to controlling exports proved highly effective, and soon the number of syndicates expanded from six to seventeen, as the ISC absorbed some independent cartels and created still others. The syndicates employed most of the classic cartel mechanisms: fines for groups that exceeded their quotas and bonuses for those which did not meet them; periodic meetings to review quotas and sales; fixed prices and sales conditions; and a combat fund for commercial wars against outsiders.

The cartel's work was so effective that new members were soon attracted. The original members were first joined by steel producers from Poland, Czechoslovakia, and Austria. Then, on July 1, 1935, the ISC gained enormous strength when the British steelmakers, under the aegis of the British Iron and Steel Federation, joined the cartel with the government's blessing. And in 1936 the Steel Export Association of America, a Webb-Pomerene export cartel founded by United States Steel and Bethlehem Steel, entered into negotiations with the ISC concerning U.S. participation. Previously the Americans had limited themselves to cooperation with certain of the sales syndicates; but when in 1938 the talks were completed and the American group became a full-fledged party to the agreements, the International Steel Cartel reached its apogee. It is estimated to have controlled 90 percent of all steel entering international trade in 1937, a figure which did not drop substantially until the outbreak of World War II.

As usual, it is difficult to measure the impact of the cartel, although it certainly affected the world price of steel. During the late 1930s prices were rising of their own accord because the business recovery from the trough of the Depression was sparking higher demand. But the cartel pushed prices even higher for products over which it maintained tight control; it kept prices relatively high in 1938, despite the recession that year; and thanks to its home market protection system it successfully maintained discriminatory prices so that steel costs were higher in the producers' home countries than on export markets.[4]*

In September 1939 the ISC formally ceased to function, but not all of its operations were suspended immediately. For example, German steelmakers who had been cut off from South American markets by the British naval blockade were able to buy steel in North America and sell it through their South American subsidiaries, thus preserving their allotted market share. But this American connection was eventually broken, and after 1941 world-wide hostilities momentarily prevailed over commercial friendships. In 1947 the authors of *Cartels in Action* could write: "The steel cartel is dead; but the cartel idea survives."[5] It was only six years later that the next comprehensive steel cartel took shape.

❁ ❁ ❁

The first step toward the new cartel was the 1952 treaty establishing the European Coal and Steel Community (ECSC). Known as the Paris Treaty, the accord ironically had as one of its aims the reduction of market controls over steel and coal in Europe. The war had destroyed the International Steel Cartel, but the industry was still riddled with anticompetitive agreements. One reason for this was the extensive government involvement that had already been the rule in steel for several decades; official oversight, restrictions, and outright government ownership tended to reduce the steel companies' freedom of action.[6] Nor did the private producers have any inclination to abandon the cartel practices that had proven so valuable for many years. Thus the ECSC had a contradictory mission and produced contradictory results. On the one hand, the treaty outlawed various forms of restrictive business practices, including several customarily used by cartels. Yet the ECSC aimed to centralize planning and control over Europe's steel industries, to rationalize them as much as possible, and to eliminate cutthroat competition among the major European states. To that end, the treaty established conditions under which the European steelmakers might agree to cooperate — which predictably led to an export cartel.

The cartel was founded by the experienced pioneers of the EIA and the ISC: France, Belgium, and Luxembourg. It came into effect in March 1953, and was soon joined by the Dutch, Germans, and Italians. It was

---

* One interesting aspect of the cartel was the Germans' use of it to finance their rearmament before World War II. In 1938 and 1939 so much of Germany's steel output was being used by the Nazi government to fabricate arms that the German group in the ISC rarely exported enough steel to meet its quotas. Under the cartel terms, this entitled the Germans to bonus payments from the other members, which the Germans demanded — and were paid. In effect, the German arms industry was subsidized by the Nazis' soon-to-be enemies, including the United States.

called the Entente de Bruxelles, or Brussels Export Convention, and its purpose was to regulate exports to countries ouside the ECSC.[7] Since production restrictions and market allocation were illegal under the terms of the Paris Treaty, the Brussels Convention members limited themselves to fixing prices for steel exports. Like the ISC, the Brussels Convention was a broad cartel covering various product groups. During the 1950s it successfully set obligatory minimum prices for exports to various markets — but this was during a period when steel sales were booming so that members often sold at prices *above* the agreed minimums. The real test of a cartel comes when times are bad, and in 1958, when the market for steel dropped off, the Brussels Convention proved ineffective. The cartel repeatedly reduced its minimum prices, but members secretly undersold each other. In subsequent years the members made attempts to reimpose the minimum pricing provisions, but without much success. As a substitute they simply exchanged pricing information or established *suggested* as opposed to obligatory minimum prices.

But the failure of the Brussels Convention, or any other broadly inclusive steel cartel, to replace the ISC after the war does not mean that steel ceased to be one of Europe's most thoroughly cartelized industries. Since the 1950s, the cartel idea in steel has taken two different forms: agreements governing specific products, some of which are direct descendants of the sales syndicates of the ISC; and repeated attempts, whether overt or covert, to achieve macro-agreements among national groups in order to regulate the entire disorderly market. The Eurofer cartel recently organized by the EEC is only the most ambitious of these attempts.

The best known of the product cartels, largely because of a major breach of cartel security, governs seamless and welded steel pipes. It was established in 1956 as the European Tube Cartel, which replaced the old International Tube Convention that had its headquarters in Düsseldorf in the 1930s and was part of the ISC.[8] British, French, Belgian, and German producers comprised the European tube group, but by 1966 its membership had expanded to include the Japanese producers,[9] reflecting the growing commercial power of that nation. Under the terms of the 1966 agreement, the Europeans and Japanese divided up export markets — that is, markets outside the members' home and "captive" territories — by establishing sales quotas and fixing prices.

The 1966 agreement was registered with the German Federal Cartel Office, in accordance with laws stating that German companies must register their membership in any international cartel that may have an effect on the German market. But in 1970 serious problems arose. The German cartel member, Mannesmann A.G. Roehrenwerke, the country's largest pipe maker, officially withdrew from the agreement in February of that year. However, negotiations over a new agreement apparently continued, with Mannesmann participating. Meetings were held in Tokyo in November, and in Düsseldorf in January 1971. The two-day secret gathering in Düsseldorf resulted in a draft agreement — which an anonymous informant then promptly mailed to the German Cartel Office and the magazine *Der Spiegel*. The story broke in the press to the dismay of the companies involved. Those who would comment claimed that the cartel limited itself to fixing prices and sales conditions on export markets, but most experts believed the Europeans were actually trying to get the Japanese to limit their sales on European markets, an act that would be clearly illegal under Germany's and other nations' laws. Indeed, there was speculation that the Japanese themselves had sabotaged the cartel by leaking the documents, in the conviction that they could profit more from competition than from the cartel arrangement.[10] The German Cartel Office fined Mannesmann 130,000 Deutsche marks for its involvement, although a legal technicality caused an appeals court to void the fine.

Two other cartelized product groups in European steel that have received brief mention in the London *Times* are sheet steel — the *Times* noted in 1968 that the publicly owned British Steel Corporation "is to join" with other European producers to fix export prices[11] — and tinplate. On October 11, 1966, the *Times* noted:

> Britain's big tinplate producers, the Steel Company of Wales and the state-owned Richard Thomas and Baldwins, meet other European tinplate producers round the table from time to time. There is no doubt that market sharing goes on. Customers for tinplate have complained that they have not been able to deal with the supplier of their choosing because of the marketing arrangement between the makers.

Much more is known about the cartel governing steel wheels and wheel sets, which was functioning in 1973 and may still be in operation.[12] In the early 1970s the cartel included producers from Germany, Japan, Great Britain, Belgium, Italy, and Sweden. It was a full-fledged classic cartel, which tightly controlled world-wide sales of steel wheels. Special combat measures kept outsiders — in this case, mainly Eastern European producers — from making inroads on the market. Home markets were protected, and there was the usual distribution of captive territories: Belgium received the former Congo, France its former colonies, Great Britain most of the Commonwealth, Japan certain countries in East Asia. The cartel was governed by a "London Committee," which determined market quotas, administered a complicated process of rigged bidding, and supervised the members to make sure they did not break ranks.

But these product cartels — and probably others that remain secret — have not afforded the world's major steel producers the security they desire; so there have been frequent efforts to organize the steel trade on a more comprehensive basis. The cause of all these efforts has been that perennial bugbear of steelmakers: overcapacity. Steel facilities burgeoned in

Europe and the United States after World War II, and the process was repeated somewhat later in Japan. In fact, it is the latter country that the
older steel firms blame for "disrupting" traditional market patterns.
Thanks to the low price of labor in Japan, the highly advanced technology
employed in their huge new plants, and perhaps unusually generous government backing, the Japanese have not only helped bring about an oversupply of steel but also have been able to compete successfully for almost
any market in the world, including Europe and North America. Japan's
impact began to be felt strongly in the mid-1960s. Since then, a triangular
struggle for supremacy has raged — a struggle in which the Europeans
and Americans have not fared well.

It is hardly coincidental, then, that in the mid-1960s the European steel
firms began to agitate once again for government-approved cartels that
would help them compete more effectively against the Japanese and
Americans. The trend was described in a major article on the world steel
industry published by *Business Week* in 1966, and headlined "Cartels
Fence in European Steel":

> Europe's cartels . . . are reappearing. They aren't quite the same as the
> prewar ones, but they have the same basic aim — limiting competi-
> tion . . . (T)he new trend toward cartelism involves the classic pattern of
> setting production quotas, fixing domestic and export prices, and imposing
> severe penalties on companies that violate the cartel agreements.[13]

French steelmakers, for example, had for some years been conducting
secret monthly meetings at which they agreed upon market divisions, production quotas, and prices. But now the French were going further. They
were lobbying within the ECSC for a program similar to the old Entente
Internationale de l'Acier, limiting the liquid steel production of the member states, with stiff fines for countries that failed to limit themselves.
Meanwhile, the Germans were also busy organizing *their* domestic industry: thirty-one steel companies were in the process of creating four marketing cartels based on geographical distribution of the nation's plants.
The Germans insisted that competition would continue among the four
groups, but there was considerable skepticism regarding that point.[14]
Business Week observed, "If thirty-one competing companies can unanimously, and simultaneously, agree to reduce the marketplace to four competitors, . . . there is little to prevent the four 'competitors' from reaching
additional agreement about the degree of competition."[15] It was widely
thought that the Germans secretly planned to restrict production and fix
prices. Nevertheless, the plan went forward.* And in 1967 another major
steel-producing nation, Great Britain, admitted that its private steel firms
could no longer compete and so nationalized the entire industry.

* In 1971, responding to pressure from the EEC Commission, the Germans agreed to
transform the four joint-sales agencies into bodies that would plan for "rationalization" of
the industry.

These national consolidations, of course, were meant to bolster the steel industries of the various individual countries. But they also strengthened the Europeans' collective position and must be viewed in the context of the global negotiations that began at about the same time. In late 1965, the top European steel executives met with their Japanese counterparts to negotiate the division of the world's steel markets. The basic agreement reached was that the Japanese would be granted the position of preeminent exporter to the U.S. market. The Europeans would continue to sell there as well but would not attempt to win a larger market share by sharp competition with the Japanese. In return, the Japanese producers would limit their exports to Europe. The two groups then entered into negotiations with the American steelmakers in order to arrive at "voluntary" restrictions on exports to the United States. After two years of secret talks, the Europeans and Japanese finally pledged to keep their exports below a certain tonnage during the years 1969 to 1971.[16] These arrangements worked for a time but collapsed in 1971 when President Nixon suddenly imposed a 10 percent surcharge on all goods imported into the United States.

Since that date the trilateral contest has intensified. Negotiations have been pursued and then abandoned; new "voluntary" agreements have been reached and proven insufficient; threats have been exchanged; protectionist measures have been considered and then dropped under diplomatic pressure; and scattered good years have failed to halt the general decline of the European and American industries. During most of the 1970s, in fact, steel was the cause of serious political strains among the three major Western powers.

U.S. markets continued to be flooded with Japanese steel. Imports from Europe generally were not as massive — perhaps as a result of the original agreement granting the Japanese predominance — but nevertheless were more than large enough to make the American producers unhappy. They protested with increasing vehemence that foreign steel was being "dumped" in the United States and demanded protection. Eventually, having failed in various attempts to develop a satisfactory program of "voluntary" restraints, the government in 1978 gave in to steelmaker pressure and imposed a system of "trigger prices," that is, federally determined prices below which foreign producers could not sell their steel in the United States without risking penalties for "dumping." But even the trigger prices proved insufficient to support the American industry; and in 1980, with employment in steel at its lowest level since the early years of the Depression, the Carter administration not only raised the trigger price by 12 percent but promised other quasi-subsidies for the industry, notably a relaxation of pollution control standards.

The condition of the European steel industry also sank from fair to critical during the 1970s. Cheap Japanese imports continued to be a problem despite repeated attempts to arrange "voluntary" limits. The Europeans therefore took the step that industry tradition might have led one to predict: they organized an EEC-wide cartel of steel producers under official auspices.

Germany, the largest steel-producing nation in Europe, led the way. In early 1976 the Germans founded an association of northern European steelmakers that included companies from Luxembourg and the Netherlands. The members accounted for about 45 percent of all EEC steel production. Although not a cartel in the full sense of the word, its main purpose being to coordinate and specialize production among the member firms, the association clearly had cartel potential. Other members of the Common Market apparently did not relish the idea of a German-led cartel, however; so the EEC, which had already been searching for ways to organize Europe's steelmakers in response to the Japanese onslaught, now hurried its work to completion. In October 1976 the European Commission of the EEC announced the formation of a new steel group called Eurofer. Using special powers granted under the treaty of the European Coal and Steel Community, Eurofer was expected to coordinate production and marketing of steel throughout the EEC. Its charter was carefully worded so as to fall within permissible limits of EEC antitrust law. The Commission called it a "trade association." Most observers called it a cartel.

Eurofer's immediate goal was to eliminate overproduction in Europe by estimating demand for steel and then allocating production among the various companies to meet that demand. In line with this approach, the EEC in December 1976 declared that the industry was in a state of crisis and ordered a general cutback in production, which Eurofer was to police. Compulsory minimum prices were imposed for certain products to end cutthroat competition in the export trade. But the cartel also had the long-term goal of "rationalizing" the entire steel industry of the EEC, that is, closing inefficient plants, trimming capacity, supervising investment, and specializing production. These efforts have been complicated by national rivalries and have proceeded slowly.[17] An example of the kind of problems that have arisen involves the cartel's treatment of the northern Italian steelmakers known as the Bresciani. The Bresciani plants, although small, are highly efficient manufacturers of certain steel products such as reinforcing rods. During the 1970s they greatly increased their share of European export trade. But Eurofer, responding to the complaints of the giant northern European members, sharply restricted the permissible exports of the Bresciani and set minimum prices that were much higher than those at which the Bresciani had been selling. Were the efficiency of the EEC's overall steel industry the main consideration, the Bresciani would have been allowed to take over the sectors in which they were the strongest. Instead, the politically powerful northern Europeans used the cartel to protect themselves against the Italians' efficiency.[18]

Eurofer, then, has not been an unqualified success. It clearly has not solved the problem of cheap imports; in January 1978 the EEC imposed a system of trigger prices similar to the American system but even more severe. And it has already demonstrated the common cartel tendency to coddle large but inefficient members. Nevertheless, its mere existence is significant. As we shall see in the following section on man-made fibers, Eurofer was created at a time when powerful figures in Europe were proposing a broad return to cartels as a cure for troubled industries. Steel was the perfect place to start, both because of the industry's cartel tradition and because the provisions of the ECSC offered a legal framework that made cartelization relatively noncontroversial. Eurofer thus should be viewed as an experiment, and one whose results industrialists in other fields will be watching closely.

Man-Made Fibers

The experience of the man-made fibers industry, on the other hand, suggests that the Europeans are not quite ready to approve full cartelization of industries less subject to public authority than steel. One thing that paved the way for Eurofer was the long history of close government oversight or direct ownership of steel plants. Most major fibers companies, however, are privately owned, and cartels in the industry have usually been private — and secret. Therefore, when the European fibers producers recently demanded the same sort of relief from antitrust laws that Eurofer accords to steel, the EEC Commission balked. It did, however, approve a compromise that amounts to a sort of camouflaged cartel, and the very bitterness of the controversy over fibers indicated that a major shift in competition policy could occur at any time.

The earliest cartels in man-made fibers came later than those in steel because the industry itself is younger. It was born in 1891, when a factory in Besançon, France, began producing artificial silk — which later came to be known by the generic term *rayon*. The basic material in rayon is cellulose, usually derived from some natural source such as wood pulp; the fiber is produced by extruding a cellulose solution through extremely fine holes in an apparatus called a spinnaret. Rayon and other man-made fibers can be manufactured either as filament yarn (long strands) or staple fiber (shorter fibers which can be spun into yarn in the same manner as cotton or wool). For nearly fifty years, rayon and a closely related cellulosic fiber known as acetate dominated the man-made fibers market. But beginning in the late 1930s the cellulosics were challenged by a new group of "true synthetic" fibers, whose long molecules (the basis of textile fibers) were not derived from a natural material such as cellulose but were produced entirely by artificial chemical processes. The first and still most famous of the synthetic group was nylon, a generic term for fibers made from polyamides. Other synthetic fibers important in the textile industry are made from acrylics (orlon, acrilan), polyesters (dacron), polyolefins, and polyurethanes.

During the early years of the rayon industry the most important producer in the world, and the largest exporter, was Samuel Courtauld & Co., Ltd., of Great Britain, now known as Courtaulds, Ltd. Courtaulds acquired rights to the viscose process of manufacturing rayon — which proved to be by far the most successful — in 1904, and began production of viscose textile yarn in 1905. In the following year, European rayon firms held their first joint conference in Paris. And in 1911 producers from England, Germany, France, Belgium, and Switzerland formed the first cartel of viscose yarn spinners, pooling markets and sharing technology.[19]

Between World War I and the Depression, links among the leading rayon manufacturers proliferated to such an extent that Alfred Plummer called the rayon trade "a remarkable example of a world-wide international combination of national units and combines. It is a good deal more than a gigantic international cartel. It is a vast and intricate network of interlacing interests, both financial and industrial."[20] As in other industries whose products derive from complex technology, most of the accords were based on exchange of patents and know-how. But the rayon firms also constructed a tangle of joint ventures and cross-investments so that all the major groups were linked by mutual ownership. Courtaulds, as the world's dominant producer, was the linchpin of the system. The firm worked with the French union of rayon makers.[21] In 1925, Courtaulds formed a joint venture as part of an overall alliance with the huge German rayon trust, the Vereinigte Glanzstoff Fabriken (VGF). In 1927 Courtaulds and VGF bought a controlling interest in the largest Italian producer, Snia Viscosa.* VGF, for its part, was directly linked to I. G. Farben through a joint venture and in 1929 effectively merged with the Dutch Enka group, forming a company called Algemeene Kunstztidje Unie (AKU). Courtaulds held a minority interest in AKU. The British, French, and Dutch–German combines all owned subsidiaries in Japan and the United States through which they collaborated with such local producers as du Pont.[22] And each of the major firms owned factories in smaller countries that were considered exclusive territory. The sum of these connections was a world market in

* Courtaulds sold its interest in Snia Viscosa gradually, beginning in 1962, but retained its share of their joint venture, Novaceta. Snia Viscosa is now owned by Montedison and Novaceta by Courtaulds.

which each major producer enjoyed its own sphere of influence and collaborated with the others to keep profits high everywhere.

Naturally the system extended to the United States, where the rayon market was dominated by two firms: the American Viscose Company, a subsidiary of Courtaulds, and the du Pont Rayon Company. Through the 1920s these firms nearly always charged the same prices for their products, thus providing "price leadership" for the smaller producers. As far as is known, the arrangement was entirely informal: a classic case of oligopolistic pricing. But the Depression cut deeply into rayon sales, and by 1931 only a formal agreement could ward off the threat of price wars. From October 1931 to May 1932, the U.S. rayon industry operated a price-fixing cartel; when it became obvious that even a cartel could not halt the decline in business, the companies simultaneously closed their plants and halted production for six months.[23] Evidence of the cartel scheme eventually found its way to the Federal Trade Commission, which filed a complaint in 1934, and in 1937, after years of hearings, ordered the companies to "cease and desist" from their conspiracy to eliminate price competition. Besides du Pont and American Viscose, the firms involved included subsidiaries of the major German, French, Swiss, and Dutch rayon interests.[24] But the FTC order had little effect on the practice of noncompetitive pricing. From December 1933 until January 1939, American Viscose and du Pont charged identical prices for the largest-selling grade of rayon. The two firms sometimes made price changes on the same day and often within a few days of each other. The smaller firms would then follow suit.[25] Lacking any evidence that the companies consulted with each other or explicitly agreed to charge the same prices, antitrust authorities were powerless to challenge the system.

In Europe, too, the Depression led rayon producers to join in a short-lived formal cartel. The network of patent exchange agreements and joint ventures could not prevent price wars during the downturn; so viscose yarn producers from England, Belgium, Italy, and Germany negotiated agreements in 1937 to regulate export trade. The cartel reportedly controlled the export of rayon to some twenty countries. In 1939 it was expanded to cover acetate fibers as well as viscose, and that year Swedish producers joined, extending the cartel's reach to Scandinavia.[26] Soon afterward the cartel had to be suspended because of war, but the war itself created the conditions for the more elaborate cartels of the 1950s.

As usual, overcapacity was the problem in the postwar period. Germany, Italy, Japan, and the Scandinavian countries had greatly enlarged their viscose staple fiber facilities between 1940 and 1945, and the expansion had nothing to do with any corresponding growth in the market; rather it was motivated purely by wartime imperatives. The market for viscose textile yarn was actually shrinking because of competition from natural fibers and the newer synthetics, such as nylon. Acetate yarn faced similar competitive pressures. By the late 1940s these difficulties caused cellulosic fibers producers to agree on the "urgent need for technical and commercial cooperation," as Courtaulds executives later described it.[27] The Europeans therefore organized three "associations" covering viscose staple, viscose yarn, and acetate yarn. Using data provided by the members, the cartel secretariats suggested minimum prices and conditions of sale to be imposed in each export market. However, according to Courtaulds the cartels were not particularly effective, and the company resigned from all three in 1953.

Four years later Courtaulds joined again, and this time the cartels attempted more ambitious measures. The viscose staple association adopted an export quota plan that assigned each member a recommended level of export sales based on the firm's production capacity. The members (not including Courtaulds, however) agreed not to increase their exports into each others' home countries and not to undercut prices in other members' home markets. They also pledged not to expand production capacity. A quota system — at first applying to all markets but later restricted to export sales — was also adopted by the viscose yarn association in 1959. All three associations continued to suggest minimum export prices.[28]

In 1962 Courtaulds again withdrew from the cartels, convinced that they could not be effective enough to be worth the effort. The other rayon producers apparently disagreed, however, because sometime in the early 1960s they organized a new cellulosic fibers cartel, headed by a company called Unicel A.G., with offices in Zurich. All the major European producers were members, with the exception of Courtaulds and the Scandinavians — and the latter group reportedly attended Unicel meetings as "observers." A similar organization of Japanese producers, called Konjestaple, worked closely with Unicel to establish sales quotas and fix export prices for viscose yarn and staple in virtually every country in the world.[29]

These powerful private cartels could not remain secret indefinitely, however, and in the late 1960s the EEC and the Federal Cartel Office of West Germany began inquiries into the man-made fibers industry. Eventually, in 1972, the full extent of its cartelization was revealed. In March of that year the Cartel Office fined nine German fibers producers 48 million Deutsche marks (about $15 million) for participating in agreements that illegally restricted trade on the German market. (High-level employees of the firms were also fined.) The essence of the charge was that the German companies had taken part in international cartels covering four product lines: staple fibers, viscose yarn, polyamides (perlon and nylon), and acetate. The cartels included members from Austria, Belgium, Finland, France, Italy, the Netherlands, Spain, Switzerland, and the United Kingdom. Documents seized by the Cartel Office also showed that the Europeans had negotiated deals with the Japanese establishing spheres of influence. Within Europe, home market protection was so effective that there was virtually no competition. Additionally, said the Cartel Office, the German producers had engaged in further collusion to eliminate competition within that country so that prices were maintained at an artificially high level. The German producers had in fact registered the existence of export and rebate cartels with the Cartel Office but had then used the legally approved cartels to pursue a variety of illegal restrictive practices.[30]

Perhaps embarrassed by the German revelations, officials of the Japanese Fair Trade Commission raided the offices of fourteen Japanese fibers producers on May 31, 1972, and less than a year later released important details about the European–Japanese collaboration.[31] The FTC's material showed that the cartels covered acrylic and polyester fibers as well as rayon, acetate, and nylon. The material also described crucial meetings of the European–Japanese cartels. The first important one took place in Milan in 1959, when three large Japanese rayon producers met with the European competitors, establishing home market protection and export curbs. In March 1972 this cartel convened in Rome and revised its export quotas.[32] Meetings between European and Japanese nylon producers took place in Zurich in 1968, Paris the same year, and Osaka in 1969. Eight Japanese polyester companies met with the Europeans in Tokyo in 1972 and agreed to restrict their exports of apparel-grade polyester to between 1000 and 1200 metric tons per month in seventeen European countries for the period from June 1972 to December 1973. In return the Europeans promised to curb exports to ten Asian countries. Rayon staple fibers producers gathered in 1967 to allocate territory: ten Asian countries were allotted exclusively to Japanese companies, thirty-eight European and Asian countries were given to the European group, and thirty-three countries were designated "common territory," where both groups received export quotas. Similar accords were reached for acrylics.[33] As a result of these revelations, the FTC prohibited Japanese participation in "any clandestine arrangement with European textile makers," the first such FTC order ever.[34]

The exposure of these private cartels aggravated the already serious structural difficulties of the fibers industry. Between 1963 and 1973 world demand for synthetic fibers grew by some 20 percent annually, an astronomic rate. Anticipating further rapid growth, the fibers producers expanded their capacity and did not hesitate to sell fibers plants to countries such as South Korea and Taiwan (in the case of Japan) or to Eastern European countries (in the case of the large Western European companies). But after 1973 the growth in demand suddenly dropped off, partly because of the deep world-wide recession of 1974–75, and partly because of changing consumer tastes. The result was a crisis for the industry from which it has not yet escaped. In 1975–76 the price of noncellulose fibers fell by 50 percent, and many firms suffered heavy losses. Plants around the world were operating below capacity; many were shut down altogether.[35] In the United States, textile and fibers manufacturers, like their counterparts in steel, angrily demanded protectionist measures against cheap imports, and the government negotiated import quotas with various Asian countries. In Europe, the fibers producers began to clamor for an EEC-sanctioned cartel.

In fact, the demand for an EEC cartel in synthetic fibers goes back as far as 1971, when a group of large producers petitioned the European Commission to let them form an association that would rationalize investment and regulate production and prices. The 1971 plan did not progress very far.[36] But by the late 1970s, with the fibers industry losing hundreds of millions of dollars per year, the idea was resurrected and put into practice. In May 1978 eleven of Europe's largest fibers companies, accounting for about two-thirds of all EEC fibers production, announced that they had formed a cartel. It was to have a life span of three years, and its work would be divided into two phases: first, a collective cutback of production capacity by about 15 percent; second, a market-sharing scheme that would take effect on January 1, 1979. In the latter phase the Italians, who were in the midst of expanding their fibers capacity, would be allowed to increase their sales from 17 to 21 percent of the EEC market, with the other producers holding constant.[37]

This market-sharing plan sparked a political furor within the EEC; for although collective cutbacks in production are regarded as a relatively innocuous form of collusion, division of markets by private companies is viewed as far more dangerous. The controversy raged within the European Commission itself, whose thirteen commissioners were split between two antagonistic positions on competition policy. The commissioner of industry, Etienne Davignon, was the primary architect of the fibers cartel and favored cartelization of other troubled industries. But the EEC antitrust authorities opposed the plan, as did other commissioners who felt that Europe would be inviting protectionist retaliation from other nations if the EEC was viewed as completely abandoning the principle of free trade.[38] The result was a political stalemate that lasted nearly two years. The Commission could not bring itself to approve the cartel — particularly the controversial market-sharing aspects — but could not decide to prohibit it either.

Throughout 1979 the fibers companies, the Commission, and the EEC governments held talks in an effort to find a form of cartel that would be effective and acceptable to all parties. The companies meanwhile argued that since the Commission had not explicitly outlawed the cartel, they could legally go ahead with their market-sharing plan — and so they did.[39]

Finally, in December 1979, the Commission abolished the cartel. The decision was seen as a victory for antitrust advocates and free-traders. But the fibers producers soon returned with a new plan. Formal market sharing was canceled and replaced with "gentlemen's agreements" under which the northern European producers would voluntarily buy the Italians' surplus fibers as that country's capacity expanded. A price war could thus be avoided, and the market would remain "orderly." But the purchasing arrangements would be conducted informally, on a company-to-company basis, rather than being spelled out in a cartel accord.[40]

*   *   *

The fibers compromise, of course, did not settle the question of "troubled industries" cartels in Europe. Quite the contrary: the long stalemate within the EEC Commission illustrated the degree to which Europe's competitive philosophy is in doubt. This makes it difficult to predict how the EEC will react the next time an industry in crisis asks leave to suspend competition. But that is almost certain to happen soon. The shipbuilding, plastics, and aircraft industries have already been mentioned as cartel candidates. The fate of the steel and fibers cartels, therefore, will have an influence extending well beyond the two industries themselves. If the cartels help restore profitability to the giant firms that organized them, and if they strengthen Europe's hand in the intensifying commercial struggle with Japan, the United States, and the Third World, the temptation to extend the experiment to other industries would be overwhelming. And if Europe openly flouts the principles of competition that have been generally accepted in the West since World War II, weakened industries elsewhere will almost certainly demand the same latitude. In these days of dismal economic performance and rising protectionist pressures, a return to the open cartelization of the 1930s is far from impossible.

7

Cartels on the High Seas

ON June 8, 1979, an international cartel of maritime shipping companies was ordered to pay the largest fine ever imposed in a U.S. criminal antitrust case. Judge June L. Green of U.S. District Court for the District of Columbia fined the seven companies and thirteen executives $6.1 million for price fixing on the lucrative North Atlantic freight routes between 1971 and 1975. The case was an anomaly of sorts because the shipping industry has long been run by cartels — with the knowledge, approval, and often aid of national governments. What, then, led to such an immense fine? The answer is rooted in century-old cartel patterns, the strains caused by the changing shape of modern shipping, and the highly controversial trend toward deregulation of the transport industries.

In the United States, as in all other major maritime nations, ocean shipping is a regulated trade. This means that the shipping lines are exempt from many provisions of the antitrust law and are permitted to govern their business through cartels, known as conferences, that do most of the things unregulated cartels do: fix prices, allocate markets, limit production, standardize terms, and battle "outsiders." To counterbalance these privileges, however, the conference agreements are subject to government approval and supervision. The system is not unique, of course; other modes of commercial transport are regulated by similar rules. The U.S. trucking, airline, and railroad industries all operate under some degree of regulation that affects rates, routes, terms, and schedules and in some cases limits the entry of newcomers into the business. The rationale for such reg-

166

ulation is that its absence would quickly lead to chaotic and cutthroat competition, which in turn would mean less reliable transport service, quite possibly at a higher cost in the long run. In the specific case of shipping, the conference members and their supporters say that unrestricted competition would soon force freight charges down to ruinous levels, driving many firms out of business, wreaking havoc with schedules and finally leaving fewer ships that would provide less frequent service at higher rates than before. Conference members also argue that, in return for offering scheduled services, with ships that sail on time no matter how much cargo they are carrying, they should be protected against loss by being allowed to fix rates jointly at profitable levels. Over the years, U.S. legislators have generally agreed, judging that the public has a vital interest in an orderly commercial transport network and that a combination of private and public controls is the only way to get it.[1]

Recently, however, that consensus has been challenged, if not altogether destroyed. Deregulation has become the watchword for a new attitude toward the transport industries that has taken hold in Washington. The reason is that regulation, as practiced until recently by such government agencies as the Interstate Commerce Commission or the Civil Aeronautics Board, left much to be desired. All too often the regulators proved subservient to the desires of the regulated so that the transport industries were able to perpetrate many of the abuses associated with monopoly while remaining free of vigorous official oversight. The result of this enviable status was that, like most monopolies, the transport industries grew flabby. Wasteful practices abounded; management was often slipshod. The bureaucracy inherent in regulatory agencies further contributed to inefficiency. The price for this kind of "regulation" was paid by the public, of course, and eventually the public reacted against it.[2] Increasing numbers of legislators argued that what the transport industries needed was a bracing dose of competition. In 1978 and 1980, over the anguished protests of trucking and airline companies, Congress passed bills partially deregulating those industries, that is, imposing somewhat more competitive conditions; and in 1980 came a railroad deregulation bill that rescinded the lines' right to fix rates collectively but made it easier for individual lines to raise rates and abandon unprofitable routes.

There has been no similar attempt to deregulate U.S. ocean shipping, however. And not because the industry is faring well as is. Quite the contrary; it is beset with problems, many of them identical to those which have plagued the other transport industries. The problems have caused bitter controversy in recent years between those who believe that shipping cartels should be strengthened and those who think they should be scrapped. But the result of the fight thus far has been a stalemate. This chapter, then, will describe the controversy and its origins in the functioning (and malfunctioning) of the conferences. Admittedly, shipping cartels lie somewhat outside the main focus of this book, being government-sanctioned. But the topic, like that of "troubled-industry" agreements, is crucial to any discussion of cartels; for the questions at the heart of the "deregulation" battle are the same raised by all restrictive agreements: Just *how much* competition is ideal? And if there are to be controls to reduce instability, who should run the controls?

The Conference Rationale

Broadly speaking, there are three types of cargo ships: private carriers, tramps, and liners. Private carriers transport cargo owned by the company that owns the ship. Tramp steamers are independent ships that usually do not adhere to fixed routes or schedules. Tramps are distinguished also in that they usually carry only the "bulk" cargoes, such as mineral ores, grain, and petroleum. Because of their large number, the irregularity of their service, and the fact that each charter is negotiated separately, tramps make up the unregulated, highly competitive sector of maritime shipping. Liners, on the other hand, sail according to fixed schedules and are equipped to carry many different kinds of freight, including mail and small lots (and sometimes passengers). They tend to be newer, larger, and faster ships and to carry more lucrative cargo. A 1977 study estimated that liners carried less than 10 percent of American ocean-borne foreign commerce by tonnage but more than 50 percent when measured by dollar value.[3] Liner operations around the world are controlled almost completely by conferences.

A conference is a cartel formed by shipping lines to regulate business on a certain trade route or between certain ports. The conferences generally have names that define their scope, and often they apply to trade in only one direction; thus, on the North Atlantic, two important conferences are the North Atlantic United Kingdom Freight Conference (which handles eastbound trade) and the North Atlantic Westbound Freight Association. Hundreds of such conferences exist world-wide; in 1967 the Federal Maritime Commission reported that some 140 conferences were involved in U.S. trade with foreign nations,[4] and the number today is thought to be about 100.[5] In theory, the conferences are completely independent of each other so that, although a shipping line may belong to various conferences, its agreements on one trade route may be quite different from those on another.

In the United States the open restraint of trade practiced by the conferences has always been cause for a certain degree of ambivalence among authorities concerned with shipping. Most American studies of the industry (with one exception, which we shall mention later) have concluded that the conference system is a "necessary evil" and that unrestrained competition in the shipping lanes would be traumatic.[6] The "evil," of course, stems from the fact that it is all too easy, as shipping history suggests, for a cartel created in the public interest to cross over the vague line that separates its beneficial activities from abuses of monopoly power. Once companies are permitted to subdue competition among themselves, they may be tempted to eliminate it altogether — by jointly destroying outsiders, for example — and then charge exorbitant rates. A disturbing difference between shipping conferences and regulatory systems in other transport industries is that conference agreements are secret. International airline ticket prices are a matter of public record, as are the prices for hauling most freight by truck or rail within the United States; but the conferences have long claimed the right to establish their rates in secret, with no public justification, and reveal them only to interested customers. (In recent years, as we shall see, conferences involving U.S. trade have been an exception to this rule.) For this reason, U.S. antitrust officials have never been comfortable with the notion of shipping conferences. As *The Economist* put it in a 1964 article, "The Americans are suspicious, and rightly, of cartels that have a whole superstructure of verbal agreements too secret even to be committed to paper, balanced on top of written agreements that are closely guarded secrets."[7] Despite the conferences' periodic collisions with U.S. law, though, they have maintained their domination of the liner trade.

The first of the modern shipping cartels was the Calcutta Conference, organized in 1875 to fix rates from United Kingdom ports to Calcutta. British ships dominated the first and subsequent conferences; but, as European and American merchant fleets grew and began competing fiercely with the British, international shipping conferences were born.[8] By 1912 conferences were already so prevalent that the U.S. House of Representatives passed a resolution creating the Committee on Merchant Marine and Fisheries, one of whose express duties was to investigate the conferences and determine "their significance in foreign trade and national defense."[9] The House investigators found that the conferences were making widespread use of the same unsavory methods that the great trusts had made notorious.[10] In order to drive out competitors, conferences designated "fighting ships" to operate at extremely low rates. Once a monopoly was established on a particular route, the conference members could grant discounts to favored customers, while charging others discriminatory high rates. But the favorite conference device — one that remains controversial — was the "dual rate" system, often enforced by "deferred loyalty rebates."

Under the dual rate system, exporters who are "loyal" to the conference, that is, who ship their goods only in ships belonging to conference members, are granted a discount, usually 15 percent, off the rates charged "disloyal" customers. Often the discount is not paid immediately but rather in the form of a deferred rebate, which has the effect of further tying the customer to the conference. For example, a customer who ships $10,000 worth of freight during a six-month period, all on conference ships, may be entitled to a $1500 rebate. But the rebate will not be paid unless the customer uses conference ships exclusively during the *next* six months. With the cartel thus constantly owing him money that will be paid only if he remains loyal, the customer obviously has a powerful incentive to do so — and the cartel has a powerful method of keeping business from competitors. Nonconference lines, of course, might offer the same system of rebates. But if the conference members own most of the ships plying a certain route, as is usually the case, the "outsiders" can rarely offer the same frequency of sailings as the conference. The common situation is that an exporter might wish to send an occasional load on a nonconference ship, but the dual rate system prevents him from doing so.

All these practices, to the extent that they affected American commerce, were clearly illegal under the Sherman Act. But Congress, in considering what to do about the conferences, proved sympathetic to the argument that unrestricted competition would harm rather than help the shipping industry. The result was the Shipping Act of 1916, which amounted to a trade-off: the shipping lines were granted the legal right to combine in ways that would otherwise be forbidden by the antitrust laws, but in return the government reserved the power to regulate the conferences closely. All conferences involving U.S. trade were ordered to report their agreements to the U.S. Shipping Board (the first of a series of agencies set up to regulate shipping), which had the power to disallow agreements it considered unlawful, unjustly discriminatory, or detrimental to U.S. trade.[11] The Shipping Act also called for government control over such common shipping cartel practices as division of territory, allocation of sales quotas, and pooling of revenues.

Between the wars the conferences proliferated, in keeping with the general trend toward cartelization of world trade. From the American point of view, the shipping conference system operated free of any substantial problems until after World War II. In the early 1950s, however, trouble arose when an extraordinarily determined "outsider," Isbrandtsen Lines, challenged the bulwark of conference power: the dual rate system. Isbrandtsen had entered the Japan, Okinawa, and Korea–U.S. Atlantic and Gulf ports trade after the war as the only independent. When the line began to take a hefty share of the market from the conference, the latter applied to the Federal Maritime Board for permission to institute a dual rate system. Over Isbrandtsen's protests the board approved the system, and after a bitter rate war Isbrandtsen lost most of its market share and eventually was forced to raise its rates to conference levels. The conference's predatory pricing thus was successful; but Isbrandtsen's legal challenge to the dual rate system slowly proceeded through the courts, and in 1958 the Supreme Court ruled that the form of dual rate contract used by the conference — and by most other conferences — was illegal.[12] This case not only threw the basis of conference power into limbo; the publicity it generated also led Congress to begin its second in-depth investigation of the ocean shipping industry.

What the investigation uncovered is indicated by a key paragraph from a 1962 report of the Antitrust Subcommittee of the House Committee on the Judiciary (often called the "Celler Committee" after its redoubtable chairman, Representative Emanuel Celler [D.–N.Y.]):

> After a careful study this subcommittee has concluded that our national shipping policy is basically sound. However, the administration of the Shipping Act and the enforcement of laws regulating ocean shipping have been woefully deficient. Alert and diligent administration and enforcement of applicable laws could have held the conduct of the shipping industry to an ethical plane and would be beneficial to U.S. foreign commerce. This could have been achieved through imposition of exacting competitive standards and close supervision; exactly the contrary has occurred. American trade routes are permeated by abuses of all sorts — unfiled anticompetitive agreements, discriminatory rebating, fighting committees in lieu of fighting ships, predatory practices, discrimination against ports and against shippers, fictitious classifications of cargo and excessive rates, to expound but a few. Some indications of the degree of saturation of our international sealanes with malpractices may be gained from the fact that with no more than three investigators, the Antitrust Subcommittee has, in the relatively short period of its investigation, unearthed some 240 cases involving possible violations of Federal statutes or conference agreements.[13]

These revelations provoked a brief panicky uproar in the industry, but it soon became obvious there was no cause for fear of sweeping reform. In 1961 Congress passed the Bonner Act, amending the Shipping Act of 1916. The Bonner Act ordered all liners operating in the foreign trade of the United States, and all conferences in that trade, to file their rates for approval by the Federal Maritime Commission (newly created as an independent regulatory authority) and abide by those rates. Previously the conferences had been required to file only their general agreements, not their rates; the new measure was meant to stop the widespread use of secret rebates. Another provision gave the FMC limited power to disapprove rates it deemed "unjustly discriminatory" or "unreasonably high or low." The Bonner Act also strengthened the conference system by legalizing the dual rate contract, although with certain controls; the most important of these was that the shipping companies could not grant a discount larger than 15 percent to shippers willing to sign a contract promising to use conference ships exclusively.[14] This approval of dual rate

contracts was supported by those arguing that conferences were necessary
to the stability of international shipping and that conferences required the
dual rate system in order to be effective. It is worth noting that several
stiff antitrust provisions of the Bonner Act were removed in the
House–Senate conference that drew up the final version of the bill and
that Senator Estes Kefauver, one of the most vigorous defenders of antitrust principles ever to serve in Congress, fought the bill bitterly, pointing
out during the debate that "the net effect of the whole piece of legislation
is to legalize cartels" in the trade.[15]

So the conferences survived the flap, and little if anything changed. Although the Celler Committee had amassed evidence indicating numerous
violations of the law by the shipping companies, the grand jury appointed
to investigate them was dismissed, and no criminal charges were ever
filed. The Federal Maritime Commission at first proved worthy of its
predecessors in its lackadaisical approach to regulation. By 1963, two
years after its creation with a mandate to impose effective public control
over the conferences, the FMC had not even attempted a serious study of
how freight rates were determined and had rarely vetoed a major conference agreement.[16] That year President Kennedy appointed a new FMC
chairman, Rear Admiral John Harllee, who succeeded to some degree in
shaking up the moribund agency. But in 1965 another congressional report
on ocean shipping noted that the industry continued to suffer from the
same monopolistic practices that had caused such a scandal just a few
years before. Secret rebates were still common. So were market-division
schemes, which operated, for example, by granting certain lines exclusive
rights to certain ports. So were arrangements for pooling freight or revenues among conference members — although the FMC had developed a
more healthy skepticism as to the public benefits of such accords and was
subjecting them to more vigorous scrutiny.[17] In short, the cartels were still
acting like cartels, attempting to stifle competition as thoroughly as possible. Indeed, there were indications — but no proof — that many conferences did not operate altogether independently of each other but rather
were woven together in "a complicated structure affecting the entire
ocean freight market."[18]

Fixing Rates Against America?

The cartel practice that provoked the most outrage in the mid-1960s (and
remains a problem today) was rate fixing that discriminated against
American exporters. Repeated studies confirmed that shipping conferences often charged much more for outbound freight, that is, freight

shipped from the United States to other countries, than for equivalent in-bound freight. In 1965, for example, it cost $38.25 to ship one long ton of iron and steel pipe from New York to Germany but only $20.75 to ship a ton of German pipe to New York.[19] This gross disparity held true for commodities of all sorts, as illustrated by the following table:

U.S. Pacific Coast–Far East Trade Route
[Freight rate per ton weight or 40 cubic feet]

Commodity	Outbound	Inbound
Canned goods	$47.50	$22.75
Cameras	54.50	32.25
Radios	57.25	33.25
Sporting equipment: ski, tennis rackets, and fishing equipment	66.25	17.50
Motors, electric	52.50	33.25
Toys	52.75	17.50
Frozen fish	97.50	78.75

SOURCE: U.S., Congress, Joint Economic Committee, *Discriminatory Ocean Freight Rates and the Balance of Payments*, 89th Cong., 1st sess., 1965, p. 14.

A similar disparity existed between rates for U.S. freight shipped to countries in Africa, Asia, and Latin America and rates for freight shipped from Europe or Japan to those countries. One study showed that, for a sample of forty export commodities, the average freight rate from the United States was $9.85 per 1000 miles. The average rate from Japan for the same commodities to the same ports was $4.14 per 1000 miles; and from London the average rate was $5.30.[20]

Naturally, such disparate rates had an ill effect on the U.S. balance of trade. Not only did the rate differences generally reduce the cost of U.S. imports as compared with U.S. exports; they also put U.S. manufacturers at a disadvantage when competing for export markets with companies from Europe or Japan. Investigators found several cases in which American exporters had lost markets abroad because the higher freight charges from U.S. ports made their goods more expensive to foreign buyers than comparable goods produced and shipped elsewhere.[21]

Nor was there any economic reason why the same ship would charge twice as much for carrying a ton of steel pipe from New York to Hamburg as it would for carrying it from Hamburg to New York. The conference members argued that the discriminatory rates resulted from the fact that the United States exports more than it imports; therefore the number of ships required to carry the outbound trade is larger, leaving a surplus of ships competing for the limited inbound shipments and thus driving the price down.[22] But this hardly accounted for the same pattern of discriminatory rates for shipping between the various industrialized countries and the Third World, that is, the fact that it cost nearly twice as much per ton-mile to ship many commodities from New York to Rio de Janeiro, for example, as it did to ship them from London to Rio. Rather, the Joint Economic Committee concluded that the reason behind the discriminatory rates was simply that American lines were outvoted in the shipping conferences. In all but seven of the more than one hundred active conferences handling U.S. foreign trade in 1965, U.S.-flag lines were in the minority.[23] This meant that the foreign lines, some of which were government-owned, could use the technique of bloc voting to set rates, rules, schedules, and market shares to the detriment of the U.S. economy. And since the FMC normally did not examine the voting procedures used to determine the conference agreements, there was no way to know whether the American lines protested, simply acquiesced, or willingly participated in the discriminatory rate systems.

But the investigations and protests from exporters finally jolted the agency out of its lethargy. Under the new leadership appointed in 1963, the FMC studied discriminatory shipping rates for several commodities, including books, whiskey, and lumber, and succeeded in forcing one conference to abandon a surcharge it had levied on shipments from U.S. ports that had caused some American exporters to lose sales.[24] And, presumably stung by the Joint Economic Committee's urging that it move "further, faster" in enforcing the law, the FMC carried out other inquiries in the mid-1960s, which at least put the conferences on warning that their cartel activities would not go wholly unexamined in future.

The most important effort by the FMC concerned rates on the rich North Atlantic trade routes. The North Atlantic inquiry was one of the first undertaken by the revised agency, and from its early moments it encountered an obstacle common to international cartel cases: foreign opposition. When the FMC opened the investigation, it requested data on shipping rates and costs from numerous lines in an effort to decide whether the rates were economically justifiable.[25] The response from other countries was overwhelmingly hostile. Eleven nations filed formal objections to the FMC's request, and the British government went so far as to pass legislation in 1964 forbidding its steamship lines to obey U.S. laws. After difficult talks, the fourteen nations in the Organization for Economic

Cooperation and Development (OECD) agreed in December 1964 to urge their shipowners to turn over the data the FMC had requested.[26] But for the next two years the commission still skirmished with reluctant companies and countries, winning several court tests and obtaining some material by voluntary agreement. Finally, in January 1968, after a year-long study of rates for certain goods, the FMC staff recommended that the commission disallow the rates for ten commodities because they were "so unreasonably high as to be detrimental to the commerce of the United States."[27] In August the commission accepted the recommendation, ordering the North Atlantic–United Kingdom Freight Conference to lower certain eastbound rates. It was the first time since the Shipping Act of 1916 was passed that such action had been taken,[28] and it established an important precedent for American control over the conferences.

In another case fought out in the courts at about the same time, the FMC was not ultimately successful; but this case, too, gave notice that the commission was willing to go further than ever before in enforcing the law. In 1965 the seven shipping lines in the Calcutta, East Coast of India and Pakistan–U.S.A. Conference raised their freight rates for jute. A jute processor in Pakistan complained to the FMC that the rates were too high, and the commission opened an inquiry. The four foreign lines, sailing under the flags of India, Great Britain, and the Netherlands, refused to comply with the FMC's subpoena for documents, claiming their governments had ordered them to do so. The FMC then took them to court, and the impasse was apparently resolved when the Supreme Court ruled in late 1966 that the companies must comply. But they defied the order, and as a result the FMC ordered in September 1967 — again for the first time in the history of U.S. maritime regulation — that the conference be dissolved.[29] The order was made "without prejudice" to the American companies, which had honored the subpoena; the FMC invited them to form another conference, if they wished, but the four recalcitrant foreign firms would be barred from participation. On appeal, however, the FMC's order was reversed by a U.S. court of appeals, which ruled that the commission had not had "sufficient provocation" to abolish the conference.[30] The case was returned to the FMC, and the conference was allowed to keep operating.

During the late 1960s and early 1970s the FMC pursued a variety of other cases involving rates, questionable practices, and the rights of non-conference lines to compete with the conferences. There was further political skirmishing with European maritime powers over the question of "closed" conferences — conferences that refuse to admit new members — which are forbidden under U.S. law. The Europeans, always more openly sympathetic to cartels, protested that, by forcing conferences involved in American trade to remain "open" to new members, the United States had fostered a surplus of shipping capacity on the North Atlantic, with result-ing rate wars and predatory practices.[31] But through all the wrangling over the proper amount of competition the basic cartel system was not seriously challenged. It took the severe recession of 1974–75, with the corresponding fall-off in trade and glut of ships on most ocean routes, to bring out the worst in the conferences and to make them once again the focus of political battles in the United States.

The worst difficulties were to be found on the Pacific trade routes, where rate wars in 1975 caused *The Economist* to say, "The pattern of shipping established for the last 100 years is now under threat."[32] Compe-tition sparked by overcapacity of ships on the Pacific was exacerbated by the fast growth of a powerful "outsider" — the merchant fleet of the So-viet Union, which on these routes uses the name Far East Shipping Com-pany, or FESCO. Just who originated the rate war is unclear; members of the Pacific conferences accused the Soviets of cutting rates by up to 40 percent in order to grab business and earn much-needed hard currency; the Soviets, on the other hand, protested that they were forced to cut rates because the conference members were all granting large secret rebates. Whichever party struck first, though, there is no doubt that large rebates were a nearly universal practice in the Pacific conferences and that FESCO was quoting rates far below the official conference tariffs.[33] The war grew so fierce that in June 1975 the eastbound Trans-Pacific Freight Conference of Hong Kong and Taiwan collapsed altogether, with fifteen of eighteen members resigning, including the Americans and Japanese. The collapse sent shock waves through other conferences around the world; it was feared that overcapacity and Eastern bloc competition (which affected many trade routes, although it was not as intense on most as in the Pacific) might destroy other cartels. "It's like an avalanche. One rock starts to go and they all go," remarked Donovan D. Day, then chair-man of the Pacific Westbound Conference.[34]

As it happened, the avalanche was contained, in large part through the labors of the FMC — although at substantial political cost. Highly alarmed at the disintegration of the Trans-Pacific Freight Conference and worried about the spread of illegal practices, especially rebates, FMC Chairman Karl E. Bakke undertook prolonged negotiations with the con-ference members and the Soviets. In May 1976, Bakke obtained pledges from the Pacific route shipowners that they would curb rebates by im-proving their "self-policing" techniques. With this promise in hand, Bakke was able to negotiate the so-called Leningrad Agreement in November 1976, which provided for gradual Soviet entry into key conferences.[35]

The Leningrad Agreement was a rescue operation that saved the con-ferences and eliminated an important "outsider," but the collapse of the eastbound Hong Kong conference had thoroughly frightened the established interests of the ocean shipping industry. The Pacific rate war was not the only ominous signal. In the spring of 1976, Sea-Land Service, Inc., one of the largest American shipping firms and the pioneer of containerized shipping — Sea-Land is a subsidiary of R. J. Reynolds Industries, Inc. — voluntarily approached the FMC and revealed that a company audit had found evidence of massive rebate payments, probably totaling around $20 million, between 1972 and 1976. After an investigation the agency and the company signed a settlement agreement under which Sea-Land agreed to pay a penalty of $4 million but did not admit to any illegal practices. (This was the equivalent of a nolo contendere plea.[36]) The Sea-Land case was important not only because of the massive violations by an American company but also because the details provided by Sea-Land for the first time gave the FMC a data base for a thorough study of hard-to-prove rebating practices in the industry.

The study made it obvious that malpractices, as they were delicately called, were perhaps even more pervasive than in the bad old days before the Celler Committee. The 1961 amendments to the Shipping Act, and the various FMC and court rulings since then, simply had not worked. But the question of *why* they had not worked raised anew the controversy over regulation versus deregulation. Some observers felt that the failure of the Bonner Act to curb abuses was proof that the conference system was too powerful, could not be regulated effectively, and should either be abolished or opened to substantially more competition. The Justice Department, for example, opposed the Leningrad Agreement on the grounds that independent competitors were necessary to keep the conferences from charging exorbitant rates.[37] To others, however, the lesson of the Pacific rate war and the Sea-Land case was that the conferences were not powerful *enough* and therefore were compelled to break the law in order to survive.

The procartel forces found a forum during 1977 hearings before the Senate Subcommittee on Merchant Marine and Tourism of the Committee on Commerce, Science, and Transportation. There, FMC Chairman Bakke testified that there was "a pervasive pattern of rebating in virtually all significant U.S. liner trades."[38] The yearly amount of rebating in the U.S. foreign trade was estimated at $70 million.[39] There was also general agreement that the reason for malpractices on the U.S. trade routes was the cartel-crippling U.S. laws. Chairman Bakke set the tone in a March 8, 1977, speech, which he requested be inserted into the record of the hearings:

> There is no question that our current antitrust and related shipping policies have brought the United States into conflict with most of the rest of the world. Our antitrust exemption for conference members is predicated basically on the preservation of an "open" conference system which af-

fords ocean carriers of all nations the right to join or leave conferences.
Yet, closed conferences are the norm in virtually all other ocean trades of
the world. Also, carriers in the ocean trades of the United States may not
provide transportation services at rates below their published tariffs, notwithstanding that rebating is a legal and common competitive practice
throughout virtually the rest of the world. Finally, we are committed to
assuring open access to ships of all nations in the inbound and outbound
ocean trades of the United States, whereas there is a rising trend throughout the world, particularly on the part of the developing nations, towards
reserving substantial portions of their inbound or outbound cargo to their
own national lines or favored foreign flag "affiliates."

I believe that the challenge we face is whether to harmonize our maritime laws and practices with those of the rest of the world, or to continue
to "go it alone."[40]

Although Bakke's sympathies clearly lay with the former alternative, he
did not take a public position; but other witnesses felt no need to be diplo-
matically reticent. Among the more outspoken was Karl-Heinz Sager,
deputy chairman of Hapag-Lloyd A.G., a large German shipping firm.[41]
Sager argued that the problems in ocean shipping stemmed largely from
overcapacity and "weak" conferences — in short, too much competition.
His advice, echoed by most other industry witnesses, amounted to a recommendation that the world's liner shipping trade be placed entirely in
the hands of the cartels. He urged that U.S. laws be amended to allow
closed conferences, flexible tariffs in order to meet outside competition,
and "effective tying devices or contract systems," that is, deferred rebates.
He also insisted conferences should be given more leeway to form cargo
and revenue pools and to merge small cartels into large ones. These measures, he said, would "rationalize" the industry and eliminate illegal rebates (in part by the simple method of legalizing them). Cartels would be
kept from abusing their power by "self-policing" mechanisms and government oversight.

The foremost champion of the opposing point of view was the Justice
Department, which under President Ford carried out a series of studies
arguing powerfully for deregulation of the transport industries.[42] In January 1977 the department released a report entitled *The Regulated Ocean
Shipping Industry*, which contained a stinging attack on the conference
system. Among its conclusions were the following statements, infuriating
to those with a stake in the status quo:

Examination of the premises underlying regulation has revealed that a
competitive shipping industry could yield the same benefits thought to be
achievable only under the conference system ... At the root of the congressional preference for the regulated conference system over a competitive market is the assumption that a competitive system would produce

ruinous competition and monopoly. The Report has shown this assumption to be doubtful. A competitive system would tend toward an equilibrium point as supply adjusted to meet demand. Congress sought to forestall monopoly by sanctioning a limited monopoly. The result has often been, instead, the creation of a monopoly possessing all of the attributes Congress sought to avoid. Government regulation seems to have abandoned a balancing of interests in favor of promoting "stability" and increased cartelization of the industry.[43]

The bulk of the report was a detailed critique of the rationale for regulated monopoly. First it noted that "assumed constraints on conference power are absent,"[44] those constraints being competition and regulation. A basic tenet of the theory behind shipping conferences is that there will always be a degree of independent competition to keep the cartel honest, but in fact such competition is often ineffective. Independent lines in the U.S. trades are permitted by the FMC to enter into "rate agreements" with the conferences; although such agreements preserve the right to change rates on short notice and often set the independents' rates slightly below the conference's, they tie the supposed independents very closely to the cartel. (On the North Atlantic in the first quarter of 1975, four-fifths of the nonconference container capacity and three-fourths of the nonconference dead weight tonnage were carried by independent lines belonging to rate agreements.[45]) Truly independent lines tend to lack the financial backing to withstand bruising and prolonged battles with a conference; those that do survive usually hold only a tiny share of the market. More powerful outsiders often follow a "compete-and-join" strategy, challenging a conference only in order to obtain a substantial market share and then become an "insider." This was the case with some of the better-known independents, such as Isbrandtsen, Sea-Land, and the Soviet fleet. Even competition *between* conferences (which might rival each other for freight originating inland that could travel through one or another port) is largely vitiated by FMC-approved accords under which the conferences agree not to compete.[46]

The Justice Department also challenged accepted dogma on the question of entry barriers. Ships are mobile and relatively cheap to acquire, and the ease with which newcomers can enter the industry is often cited to support the contention that lack of conferences would soon lead to ruinous competition. But new entry in fact is not as easy as it might appear. In the first place, the capital requirements for establishing a modern shipping operation have increased immensely since the mid-1960s, when Sea-Land began a revolution in the industry by introducing the first successful container-ship service. Containerization — shipping freight in containers of standard size that are easily transported to and from port by truck or rail and need not be opened until they reach their destination —

greatly reduces the cost of shipping because it cuts the time for loading and unloading to a fraction of what it was formerly. However, it also requires expensive new ships, port facilities, special cranes, containers, and other equipment. Thus only newcomers with the most solid financial backing could hope to challenge the advanced established companies, all of which already have large container fleets. Dual rate contracts are another obvious barrier to new entrants. There are others as well, the most important being predatory pricing — the age-old cartel device of cutting rates in order to force the competitor to cease and desist or join the cartel. Predatory pricing, of course, is illegal under the shipping laws, but by the time the FMC can complete a proceeding against a conference the damage almost always is done. In four out of five predatory pricing cases handled by the FMC from the 1950s to the mid-1970s, the "outsider" was either forced out of the trade altogether (three times) or became a member of the conference (once).[47]

Thus independent competition can hardly be relied upon to discipline the conferences. Evidence stretching back many years indicates that government regulation cannot do the job either. The Justice Department, for example, after reviewing FMC actions concerning protection of independent lines against unfair attack, concluded that the agency had defined "predatory pricing" so narrowly as to effectively gut the statute that prohibits it.[48] Despite the agency's somewhat more vigilant stance since the 1960s, it has still manifested a dangerous tendency to approve virtually all agreements proposed by the conferences — including pools, dual rates, and interconference accords — without serious review. In 1968 the agency ruled in a crucial case, *Aktiebolaget Svenska Amerika Linien* v. *FMC*, that anticompetitive agreements were presumed to be against the public interest and that conferences must bear the burden of proving that their agreements met such a serious need that they would serve the public *better* than competition would. But the *Svenska* "public interest" standard has never really taken hold; rather, the FMC has tended to approve agreements simply because they would promote "stability" in the shipping trades. "In effect, the *Svenska* burden may be met by demonstrating potential or existing instability (vigorous competition, malpractices, or overtonnaging) and that the competitive restraint will alleviate the instability ... Thus, the presumption against the restraint of competition is overcome by showing the existence of competition," drily observed the Justice Department report.[49]

Not only has the FMC approved most agreements in the interests of "stability," but it has also ignored glaring evidence of secret, illegal accords. The best illustration of this point is the recent history of the North Atlantic trade routes. In 1968, the seven largest container ship companies on the North Atlantic proposed a "superconference" to cover "trade between the U.S. North Atlantic and all of Europe, from the Baltic to the Mediterranean, including the Scandinavian countries, the United Kingdom, and Eire."[50] The new group would have absorbed seventeen existing conferences. The idea provoked heated opposition, however, and in the midst of FMC hearings in 1971 the seven companies dropped it. Nevertheless, later that year the same firms proposed a revenue pool and sailing schedule agreement covering almost the same territory, which, had it been approved, would have amounted to a superconference under another name. The initial FMC decision was favorable; however, when one firm dropped out because it was unhappy with the proposed division of the market, the pool proposal collapsed, too.

Instead, what took place was the secret development of a superconference while the FMC apparently turned a blind eye. To a great extent the superconference grew out of the massive shift to containers. In 1968 the seven major containerized shipping companies dominated only one of the six conferences covering trade between U.S. and European North Atlantic ports. By 1972, however, they constituted almost the sole membership of all six conferences (along with a seventh they formed that year) and have continued to do so since then.[51] Data gleaned from publicly available material on file with the FMC show that the six conferences had a common administration, common policing authority, uniform price increases from 1971 to at least 1975, little competition from nonconference lines, and no competition among the six conferences themselves. Yet the FTC did not even investigate.[52]

It was left to the antitrust authorities to take action; and it was this cartel of seven companies — Sea-Land Service, Atlantic Container Line, United States Lines, Hapag-Lloyd, Dart Containerline Company, Seatrain Lines, and American Export Lines (merged in 1978 into Farrell Lines) — that in 1979 achieved the dubious distinction of agreeing to pay the largest fine ever in a U.S. criminal antitrust case. (Of the lines, four are American; Atlantic Container is a group headquartered in England; Dart is a consortium based in Bermuda; and Hapag-Lloyd is German.) After a four-year grand jury investigation, the firms and thirteen executives were charged with numerous violations of the Sherman Act. The broad scope of the superconference's activities is best described by quoting from the indictment, to which the companies and executives pleaded nolo contendere. The indictment alleges that the shipping lines:

(a) Established, without the approval of the Commission, committees, including a Senior Management Committee (SMC), which reported to the heads of the lines . . . and a Pricing Policy Committee (PPC), each composed solely of the seven lines, to fix rates, charges, and other factors directly affecting price levels . . .

(b) Set and implemented through these committees, without approval of the Commission, revenue targets for the operations of the seven lines in the United States/Europe trade. These targets were known as the "Revenue Plans."

(c) Set rates, charges and other factors directly affecting price levels, without the approval of the Commission, for the ocean transport of freight in the South Atlantic trade, by, among other methods, agreeing that rates in the South Atlantic trade would be equalized with rates in the North Atlantic trade . . .

(d) Set rates . . . for the shipment of cargo in the United States/Europe trade via Canada when there was no approved Section 15 agreement permitting such activity.

(e) Established several related agreements between the seven lines and various independents, without the approval of the Commission, to fix rates . . .

(f) Filed with the Commission tariffs and tariff revisions that were the product of the combination and conspiracy.[53]

Clearly, then, one must seriously question whether the monopolistic power of shipping conferences is checked either by independent competition or government regulation. In the absence of either, one would expect certain market distortions associated with monopoly — and these, in fact, do occur. The market shares held by the conferences on the routes studied by the Justice Department were consistently high, usually between 75 and 90 percent. The conferences showed the ability to charge different buyers different prices for essentially the same service — which is impossible in a competitive market. And the real cost (adjusted for inflation) of shipping increased on *all* the routes studied between 1965 and 1975, with the hikes ranging from 34 to 149 percent. Such increases might stem from higher costs to the shipping lines, or from their growing monopoly power, or both. It is certainly interesting that the sharpest increases were on the North Atlantic routes covered by the superconference.[54]

What of the benefits claimed for the conference system? Here, too, there is at least cause for skepticism. The system's defenders argue that it ensures regular and frequent liner service. But even were the cartels dissolved, shipping companies would still strive to offer services as frequent and dependable as warranted by the amount of freight to be shipped. In a more competitive environment, some cutbacks on routes by major lines would be expected, as has occurred in the deregulated trucking and airlines industries.[55] But smaller independent firms could be expected to pick up some of the routes, and the overall deterioration in service would probably be minor. As for the famous price "stability" enforced by the conferences, it may be questioned whether such stability is desirable. In any case, studies suggest that conference prices are not particularly stable but rather tend to rise.[56] Finally, far from being a solution to overcapacity, the conference system encourages it. Like all cartels, the conferences tend to reduce the need for innovation and thus protect inefficient companies, keeping them in the trade when competition might winnow them out.

For all these reasons, the Justice Department report concluded, "Society would benefit from a restoration of a more competitive environment in ocean shipping markets."[57] One possibility is simply to repeal the provisions of the Shipping Act that allow the lines to enter restrictive agreements. Another approach would be through more piecemeal reform, outlawing certain kinds of restraint that afford the cartels too much power to repress competition. Dual rate contracts could be banned. Conferences could be forced to demonstrate beyond a reasonable doubt that the public would gain more than it would lose from an anticompetitive accord. Rate agreements and pooling arrangements between the conferences and independent lines could be prohibited. And the cartels could be given more flexibility to change rates in response to changing conditions, as has been done with the airlines and railroads.

* * *

The Congress, however, appears to be moving in the opposite direction. After extensive hearings from 1977 to 1980, and after an Interagency Task Force study ordered by President Carter, Congressman John Murphy's Committee on Merchant Marine and Fisheries reported out a bill that undertook the much needed complete overhaul of U.S. shipping policy. The bill — the Omnibus Maritime Regulatory Reform, Revitalization, and Reorganization Act of 1980 — was a massive, complex document dealing with a range of issues, including subsidies to U.S.-flag carriers and incentives for U.S. shipbuilding. But in its approach to the cartel question, the bill amounted to a total defeat for the idea that the shipping industry and the public would profit from more competition. Instead, the Murphy committee accepted virtually all the arguments of the major conference lines, and the bill acceded to the conferences' most fervent pleas. It flatly exempted most conference activity from the antitrust laws, stating that violations of the act would only be prosecuted under the terms of the act itself. It legalized closed conferences. To counterbalance conference power, it permitted shippers to form councils to bargain with the shipping cartels. Perhaps most important, it greatly weakened the regulatory authority of the Federal Maritime Commission. Under previous law, anticompetitive agreements were presumed to be contrary to the public interest, and conferences were required to prove that their accords were beneficial. The omnibus bill reversed the burden of proof, requiring the FMC to show that cartel agreements were *not* in the public interest. Otherwise the accords would automatically take effect sixty days after filing.

The omnibus maritime bill was never brought up for a vote before the full House during the Ninety-sixth Congress. Representative Murphy, its chief sponsor, was defeated for reelection in 1980.* But even without Murphy's sponsorship, the omnibus bill will serve as a model for legislation that may well pass during the Ninety-seventh Congress. In short, the United States may soon join other nations in adopting a shipping policy that was best described by a dissenting witness during the hearings as "cartels with a vengeance."[58]

* Shortly after the election, Murphy was convicted of accepting a bribe in the so-called Abscam scandal. The conviction is now on appeal. Throughout his career, Murphy has received large contributions from shipping industry and maritime union interests.

8

The Cartel Threat

THE preceding chapters have shown that cartels are much more prevalent and powerful than either the public or most economists believe. International cartels are now operating — or have recently operated — in manufacturing industries (steel, chemicals, electrical equipment), raw materials (petroleum, uranium), and service industries (shipping). In addition to the cartels that we have been able to document extensively, there are hundreds more on register in England, Germany, and Japan, as well as an unknown but unquestionably large number that have escaped detection.[1] Their members include many of the world's largest and best-known transnational corporations; and although their schemes to control trade assume a multitude of forms, they all share one simple purpose: to reduce competition and thereby increase profit. It is now time to assess their impact.

We believe this task of evaluation is particularly important today because cartels are likely to spread even further during the coming decade. The reasons have to do with the strange new economic epoch the Western world has embarked upon, an epoch which might best be called the Age of Stagflation.

In the early 1970s, the economies of the advanced capitalist nations underwent a profound change. The era of unprecedented growth that followed World War II came to an end, and another, more gloomy era began. What caused the change remains a matter of bitter debate, but there is general agreement as to its attributes. The most worrisome of these is the condition known as "stagflation," a combination of slow growth, high unemployment, and high inflation — a grim trio that was not supposed to appear in the same place at the same time.[2] According to the tenets of orthodox economics as practiced by the Western nations

185

since 1945, inflation and unemployment were presumed to offset each other and to rise and fall in opposition, like the ends of a seesaw. When an economy was highly "heated" and growing fast, unemployment dropped but inflation tended to rise; whereas when growth "cooled off," joblessness rose but inflation abated. Governments were able to adjust the temperature of the economy by administering fiscal and monetary medicine, that is, manipulating the sum of taxes collected, the size of budget deficits, and the growth in the money supply.

But lately the trusty formulas have lost their old healing magic. Economic growth throughout the West slowed sharply in the 1970s as compared with the previous two decades. Unemployment, as a predictable consequence, has risen almost everywhere. But so has inflation — and a troubling inflation this one is. It appears relatively insensitive to its opposite number, the jobless rate. Yet it is morbidly sensitive to the growth rate, which means that it takes much less growth than before to send prices spurting upward. Another unpleasant attribute of the new age is that recessions are more severe and last longer, while recoveries are shorter and less complete. Also, the business cycles of the major capitalist countries are more synchronized so that recessions occur simultaneously, aggravating each other.[3] Finally, shifts in the alignment of international economic power — most notably the rise of multinational firms and OPEC — have had an ill effect on the trade balances of many industrialized nations, especially the United States, further weakening them.

In short, economic prospects in the Age of Stagflation do not look bright. Widespread frustration with government inaction reflects the simple but often unrecognized fact that officials are often powerless in the face of the weird symptoms their economies are exhibiting. The Western governments, advised by bewildered economists and led by politicians pinioned between the equally unpalatable choices of deep recession or inflationary growth, can do little more than tinker with the business cycle in hopes of smoothing its extremes.[4] This leaves the world in a constant semirecession, which may last a long time. Growth lags and unemployment fluctuates between high and very high. Companies, industries, and entire countries that greatly expanded their productive capacity during the latter phase of the boom now face shrinking markets and bitter competition. Naturally the result is protectionist sentiment, which is rising everywhere and promises to become even stronger. There is considerable apprehension that if stagflation persists it may bring such severe strains to some economies that a general trade war might erupt, similar to the one that was a major factor in deepening and prolonging the Depression.

What effect is world-wide economic stagnation likely to have on cartels? The answer is suggested by two facts. First, cartels, as we have seen, are most often organized in periods of a declining market, when industry is suffering from overcapacity. Second, the heyday of formal cartels to date was the Great Depression.

In fact, there are already hints that the Age of Stagflation may become, as it were, the Second Age of Cartels. The most obvious sign is the ongoing controversy in Europe over the extent to which the EEC's troubled industries should be allowed to cartelize. European steelmakers and fibers producers, as we have seen, participate in officially approved cartels. In 1978 Viscount Etienne Davignon, then the EEC commissioner for industrial affairs, prepared and vigorously promoted a plan that would have encouraged cartels in any EEC industries the Commission decided were "in crisis."[5] Shipbuilding, plastics,[6] and even the auto industry were mentioned as possible candidates. Davignon's plan was expected to win approval but surprisingly was voted down by other commissioners. Nevertheless, the support it evoked has not vanished, as indicated by the long battle within the Commission over the fibers cartel proposal. At least some of Davignon's backing came from experts who were convinced that EEC-sponsored cartels would serve to ward off something worse. Kurt Stockmann, chief of the International Division of the Federal Cartel Office in Germany, remarked at the time that, if Davignon's plan failed, "the vehicle for cartelization will be voluntary agreements between private industries with the support of their governments."[7]

Even in the United States, where antitrust philosophy is more deeply rooted than in Europe, the current tendency to try to escape the hazards of competition can be discerned. As yet there have been few public advocates of cartels. But in industries that have recently been threatened by competition from abroad — steel and textiles, for example — the government has heeded American producers' cries of anguish by forcefully persuading foreign companies to restrict their exports to this country and by creating the trigger price system to prevent imports of cheap foreign steel. Similar protection is currently being considered for the auto industry. From such steps it is not far to the notion that American steelmakers, for example, should be allowed to talk over their troubles with their foreign competitors and reach agreements, perhaps to forbear in each others' markets — particularly when the European industry is already cartelized so that the Americans can claim they should be permitted to present an equally united front. This argument already is being used by U.S. ocean shipping lines, whose representatives say their inability to form effective cartels puts them at a disadvantage (see Chapter 7).

Thus cartel history (particularly from the Depression), current events, and the dynamic of competition all suggest that as the international economy sinks into the doldrums, cartels and their defenders are certain to multiply. At such a time it is crucial to understand the claims made for cartels and the warnings advanced against them. We therefore devote the first part of this chapter to a critical look at the benefits cartels theoretically might provide, and the second to a study of the specific effects of cartels on the West — in both the less-developed nations and the industrialized powers where the cartels have their headquarters.

The Case for Cartels

We know of no more succinct or fervent statement of what the world stands to gain from cartels than a speech by Lord Harry Duncan McGowan during a debate before the British House of Lords in 1944. Lord McGowan was the ideal spokesman for this point of view, being one of the founders of Imperial Chemical Industries, the giant combine famous for its extensive cartel connections; and he was speaking at a time when important segments of the British business community (including the Federation of British Industries) viewed wholesale cartelization as the solution to the world's trade problems once the war ended.

McGowan said, in part:

> In this country, many manufacturers have ceased to believe in the inherent superiority of *free* or *extreme* competition . . .
>
> The purpose of [cartel] agreements is, in the main, to regulate but not to abolish competition. Such agreements can lead to a more ordered organization of production and can check wasteful and excessive competition. They can help to stabilize prices at a *reasonable* level . . . They can lead to a rapid improvement in technique and a reduction in costs, which in turn, with enlightened administration of industry, can provide the basis of lower prices to consumers. They can spread the benefits of inventions from one country to another by exchanging research results, by the cross-licensing of patents, and by the provision of the important "know-how" in the working of these patents. They can provide a medium for the *orderly* expansion of world trade.[8]

Running through McGowan's eulogy of cartels is an implied tension between the two key concepts, stability and competition. Although he tries to occupy a middle ground ("to regulate but not to abolish competition"), he knows that basically the two elements stand in opposition: the more competition in a capitalist economy, the less stability, and vice versa. Cartels are the offspring of this tension. They represent an attempt to elude the very force that drives a market economy. At the heart of any controversy over cartels, then, lies an essential question: To what extent can the process of competition be restrained without sacrificing the benefits it is supposed to bring society?

A competitive market is best understood as a system of deciding what a society shall produce and how it shall be distributed among the populace. Resources in a capitalist society are allocated not according to plan but rather by the unpredictable ebb and flow of supply and demand. A good that is in demand but relatively scarce will fetch high prices. Investors searching for the most profitable outlet for their capital will be drawn to produce that good. The resulting increased output, making the good relatively more abundant, will cause the price to drop — causing investors to look for more attractive fields. "Thus by a process of continual adaptation, competitive markets promote economic equilibrium," write Stocking and Watkins.[9] And it is this "process of continual adaptation," the enormous *flexibility* of the ideal competitive system, that is its greatest virtue. On that flexibility rests the claim that a free market economy is the most efficient method of allocating production and distribution. In theory, the market responds so sensitively to changes in supply and demand that in the long run most people can buy what they need at a price they can afford. Another theoretical advantage of competition is that it fosters rapid technological change. Each producer, hoping to gain an advantage over his competitors, is eager to discover and adopt new technology which will enable him to produce faster, or more cheaply, or with higher quality, or all three. Because of this incessant impulse to improve, the productive capacity of society grows and the standard of living rises.

But this means that competition is inherently *destabilizing*. Products, companies, entire industries suddenly materialize and transform the shape of modern life; others decline and disappear. Investment and consumption rise and fall in a rhythm, known as the business cycle, that remains largely unfathomable. As bountiful as change may be for the society over time, in the short run it exacts a heavy toll from the unfortunate: capital losses, plant closings, mergers, bankruptcies, unemployment. Competition destroys as it constructs; and the destruction can be so severe — witness the Depression — that few societies rely exclusively on the functioning of the market to right what it has put wrong. Instead, numerous devices are used to offset the market's tendency to wreak social havoc. Governments use Keynesian macroeconomic tools, social welfare programs, and loan guarantees to failing companies (viz., Lockheed and Chrysler), to name just a few examples, in order to soften the impact of economic shifts. And private companies may resort to cartels.

Indeed, as Lord McGowan's speech demonstrates, cartel members have long been prone to find fault with the free market, vociferously reminding the public that competition rarely works as it should. There is more than a little irony here, of course. Most great corporations, at some point in their history, have triumphed in fierce bouts of "chaotic," "wasteful," or "destructive" competition during which they ruthlessly eliminated local

rivals. Yet when the field of battle becomes the world and the other contenders are firms of equal size and power, the perils of competition are
loudly proclaimed, and the virtues of cooperation extolled.

Nevertheless, the fact that many cartel members have profited from
"chaotic" competition in the past does not necessarily invalidate their argument that it should be avoided in the present. It is certainly conceivable
that in some industries all-out competition would provoke violent booms
and busts, with the attendant disruptions in the economy — rampant
overproduction one moment, widespread shutdowns and unemployment
the next — and needless failures of weaker firms. The question, then, is
what the cartels have to offer in return for robbing the free market of its
flexibility and sensitivity to changing conditions. The claims that cartels
can "stabilize" markets, create "orderly" trading conditions, and maintain
"reasonable" prices must be evaluated on their merits. We will therefore
examine the effects cartels may have in four different realms: prices, production, efficiency, and technological progress.

Private cartels today are in such disrepute that few businessmen publicly defend them, as Lord McGowan did, on the grounds that they keep
prices pegged at "reasonable" levels. Yet that is a common rationale for
cooperation among competing enterprises, one still employed openly by
executives of regulated industries like shipping. In a 1977 speech, the deputy chairman of Hapag-Lloyd, Karl-Heinz Sager (who was later fined
$50,000 in the North Atlantic shipping cartel case) stated in the course of
praising closed conferences:

> The positive effect of such a joint approach has been that over-tonnaging
> is generally avoided, but that there is sufficient space to cover the re-
> quirements of the trade to and from all ports. Freight rates are contained,
> because the optimal utilization of ships and equipment has been achieved.
> Last but not least this also allows shipowners to make a reasonable return
> on their investment.[10]

The Eurofer steel cartel, established by the EEC in 1976, sets minimum
prices for various products and penalizes members for price cutting. The
uranium producers, upon founding the "Club" in 1972 talked constantly
among themselves of the need for an "orderly" market in which prices
would be "reasonable" and "sufficient to provide an incentive for further
exploration."[11]

There are problems, though, with the notion that cartels stabilize prices
at "reasonable" levels. The most obvious concerns the question of who is
to determine what is reasonable. What may seem a fair and/or desirable
return to the cartel members may not seem so to someone else; yet generally no one but the companies themselves has access to the data on unit
production costs that might allow a consensus on what prices should be.

Very few cartels — the exceptions being those in which governments play a large part — consult the public in any manner on pricing policy. And although it is impossible to arrive at a definitive conclusion given the complexities involved, there is evidence that while cartels always make strong efforts to keep prices from falling, they do little to prevent them from *rising*. Price stability, in other words, tends to be a one-way street.[12]

The best recent example of this tendency to exploit rising prices is the uranium cartel. Although serious overcapacity first brought the producers together in the "Club," and although cartel documents show that the desired "stability" could have been achieved with only modest price increases, from $6.10 per pound in 1972 to $7.50 per pound in 1978, the members were ecstatic when yellowcake rocketed to $42.00 in 1975. Certainly they did not attempt to brake the price increase by releasing quantities of yellowcake from their large stockpiles. The Quinine Convention, too, began as an effort to stabilize prices and only disbanded after the price had quintupled between 1964 and 1966.

Naturally, there are cases of cartels that have maintained stable prices over long periods of time. We have seen that the Seven Sisters kept the price of oil on the world market remarkably steady during the 1940s through the 1960s. Upon reflection, however, one may doubt the value of this stability. The underlying market situation was one of severe overcapacity; the companies could have pumped much more oil than they did. The Sisters held tight control over the relation of supply to demand, particularly through their intertwined joint ventures in the Middle East. By concealing discoveries of new fields, by intentionally developing discoveries at a snail's pace, and by inducing each other not to overproduce, the companies for many years were able to increase the supply of oil on the market only as fast as demand increased (see Chaper 3). In short, by clamping limits on production, the cartel prevented prices from falling. This deprived consumers of the benefits of cheaper energy and in some cases — notably Iraq — robbed producing states of taxes and royalties. Of course, in 1973 the record of price stability came to a stunning halt, as the price of oil quadrupled in a year, and the companies tacitly supported the OPEC cartel — which otherwise might have collapsed — by lending their administrative and marketing expertise.

Hand in hand with the problem of prices goes that of production. If the most fundamental cartel impulse is to push prices higher, its most basic technique is to cut back production. Virtually every cartel mentioned so far has attempted to reduce the supply of its product in one way or another. The reduction may apply to specific geographical areas, as in home market protection clauses (which keep out foreign goods) and agreements to divide export territories; or it may involve simply setting limits on output, as in the Iranian Consortium agreement between the Seven Sisters, with its complex formula for arriving at production quotas. Indeed, some cartels rely exclusively on production cutbacks. Most, however, combine cutbacks with other agreements on pricing, rigged bids, combat clauses, and the like.

Debate over production limits imposed by cartels closely parallels that over price agreements, especially in regard to distressed industries. For example, if the European synthetic fibers industry suffers from massive overcapacity (as it does), would it not be "reasonable" for the companies to meet together, assess their prospects, and then limit themselves to producing only what the market requires? In Japan, national manufacturers can do just that by means of legal "depression cartels"; and Viscount Davignon's cartel plan for the EEC would have permitted production controls along with other measures in order to rationalize Europe's ailing industries. On its face the idea seems good, making even better sense than the cartel pledge to keep prices from sinking too low or rising too high. Why, after all, should companies produce more goods than the public needs? But, on the other hand, if the companies alone are to gauge the market and allocate production, who is to police against abuses? Once practiced in the art of cooperatively regulating production, supposed competitors can just as easily create artificial shortages as guard against gluts. Here again the policies of the oil companies in the Middle East illustrate the point. Were the jointly managed production controls there beneficial to the public, or did they keep prices artificially high?

Cartels also may have an effect on the overall efficiency of the industries they control. Efficiency is a crucial factor in any society's productive system; it means the ability to produce the goods needed by that society in the largest quantity, of the best quality, and at the lowest cost possible. In theory, the competitive struggle promotes efficiency through survival of the fittest: the efficient inevitably prosper, and the inefficient — companies that are poorly managed or organized or that do not keep up with changes in technology or public tastes — inevitably are destroyed. As with prices and production, however, the procartel position on efficiency is that an industry whose productive patterns are planned cooperatively can work better than one left to the vagaries of competition. Theoretically a cartel can plan how much production is needed and then apportion out the work among its members in the most efficient manner. "Rationalization" cartels may even decide that old, outmoded, or unfavorably located plants should be closed to reduce capacity and concentrate production in the most efficient plants.

In fact, though, stability is often achieved by protecting high-cost, inefficient producers. Far from phasing out the laggards of an industry, cartels frequently set their prices high enough so that even the least efficient members can make a profit — which allows the healthier firms, of course, to reap extraordinary returns. Why should cartels adopt such a policy?

Because, insofar as possible, companies prefer to eliminate elements of risk. We have observed that international cartels usually are the products of monopolies or oligopolies on the national level, and even the weakest members are formidable enough that they could inflict heavy losses should full-scale competitive war break out. The most efficient firms may suspect they would win in the long run, but the cost of victory would be high. Thus they judge it more prudent to reach cartel agreements reserving for themselves a hefty share of the market and preserving high prices for all producers.

Finally, there is the matter of technology. Lord McGowan said in his speech,

> [Cartels] can lead to a rapid improvement in technique and a reduction in costs, which in turn, with enlightened administration of industry, can provide the basis of lower prices to consumers. They can spread the benefits of inventions from one country to another by exchanging research results, by the cross-licensing of patents, and by the provision of the important "know-how" in the working of these patents.

This is the crux of another procartel argument: agreements between companies, particularly companies from different nations, can speed up the spread of technology and thus improve the quality of life everywhere. This claim is difficult to evaluate conclusively because almost all the agreements are secret. In general, however, one can say that, although cartels may help certain firms gain access to each others' inventions, the members usually are at least as interested in restricting access to technology as they are in spreading it.

"Technology is the key to economic power in the modern world," note Barnet and Muller in *Global Reach*, continuing: "Global corporations . . . are for the most part oligopolies. Their enviable position usually rests on some piece of exclusive technology which they are not anxious to make available to actual or potential competitors."[13] The usual means by which technology becomes "exclusive," of course, is the attainment of a patent. We have seen how great corporations can be founded on a single patent of transcendental significance and how these firms, particularly in the "science-based" industries such as electrical equipment or chemicals, trade patents among themselves. Such trading may come about for largely defensive reasons, as in the case of firms from different nations that have made similar discoveries and wish to avoid competition between them; or the exchange may have a more "aggressive" quality, as when a firm with a unique invention trades it to a foreign company for a different discovery, giving each a monopoly on both inventions in its home market. In both of these cases, technology is indeed spread from one enterprise to another and from one country to another. Presumably, the public benefits.

But as numerous examples in preceding chapters illustrate, there is a very thin line between agreements to exchange technology and those to establish market control. A patent pool that allows the major firms in a particular field to use each others' inventions, such as the pool that covered radio and television receivers (see Chapter 2), can be an extremely powerful means of *withholding* access to technology from any potential challengers. Patent licenses often accomplish the same thing by the imposition of restrictive terms. Several types of restrictive clauses appear over and over again in licensing agreements. Probably the most important involve territorial limitations; the licensee is permitted to use the patented invention only within a circumscribed area. Often the licensee is also barred from exporting products made under license and from importing similar products. License agreements may dictate the price to be charged for the products, although certain forms of such price fixing are illegal under U.S. law. Or the license may fix limits on the quantities that may be produced. Another important clause frequently encountered binds the licensee to turn over any improvements on the original patent that might be discovered during the life of the agreement.[14] Such clauses clearly lead to a concentration of technological power in the hands of the firm holding the patent.

We return, then, to our query. Do cartel members, by exchanging their secrets, spread the benefits of breakthroughs and thus help raise the standard of living? For the reasons outlined above, we believe that to be the case only to a very limited extent. Because cartel members tend to be the largest firms operating on an international scale in their respective industries, the trading of technological capability among them only increases concentration in a very few hands. This is not at all the same as making the technology widely available, and we would argue that it may have the opposite effect. In the first place, the major firms sometimes exchange discoveries for the precise purpose of preventing each other from licensing them to smaller, more aggressive firms that might not be amenable to the usual patterns of market division and mutual forbearance from competition. Second, companies in a monopoly or oligopoly position may have an interest in suppressing or holding back new technology. If the increase in profit from introducing a new product or technique is not significantly larger than the costs of developing the product or remodeling the production apparatus, there is little reason for the company to undertake the innovation.[15] It can make almost as much profit simply by ignoring the invention. But the only reason such a firm can afford to hold back is that it has little fear of competition. Ironically, then, by agreeing to share all patents they develop in a certain field — which cartel members often do — the firms may actually *retard* progress because each firm, shielded from the threat of competition, need not be so vigorous in its pursuit of invention. Finally, although the exchange of licenses may contribute to the spread of technology, the restrictive terms imposed often enormously increase the price of its benefits to the public.

Another aspect of the relationship between cartels and technology is the growing tendency for cartel members to engage in joint research and development projects. Such efforts have proliferated since World War II, and their returns, both to the companies and the public, would seem to be obvious. By pooling knowledge, funding, and facilities, the firms avoid wasteful duplication of research efforts and benefit from each others' unique expertise. But joint research ventures, much like joint production ventures, can easily lead to what Kronstein calls the "technological cartel."[16] In most major industries the number of firms that can afford a full-fledged research program is minimal, and they are the same firms that belong to cartels. When two or more of them combine to carry out research, they attain an overwhelming advantage — in resources and accumulated expertise — over any potential rivals. The discoveries they make are likely to dominate the field; and, through judicious employment of patents and licensing agreements, the companies are likely to carve up the market in classic cartel fashion. Whether the public gains more from the economies of joint research than it loses from the uses to which the research is put is debatable. There is no question, however, that such technological cartels have a chilling effect on independent research. The simple knowledge that two huge firms have embarked on a joint research project is enough to make any smaller firm think twice before beginning a project along similar lines.

On every major point, then, the claims made in favor of cartels must be questioned. Cartel members inevitably announce that their only desire is to maintain "reasonable" prices; all too often, they work to keep prices as high as possible. They pledge to keep production in balance with demand; in fact, they are not above engineering shortages. They advertise their ability to enhance industrial efficiency; but frequently they shelter the inefficient. They boast of disseminating technology; but to whom, and on what terms? In the years to come, as such blandishments are proffered more openly — and we are convinced they will be — they should be greeted with the skepticism they merit.

Government Cartels

We now wish to digress again from the main subject of this book, private international cartels, and briefly evaluate cartels in which governments are involved. For the economic squeeze of the Age of Stagflation does not affect private corporations alone; governments, too, will increasingly feel the pressures to resort to cartels, as has been obvious most recently in Europe.

Broadly speaking, there are two types of cartel in which governments usually play a major role: marketing agreements meant to stabilize trade in some raw material and programs to rescue industries in crisis. Agreements of the former type proliferated in the 1930s, when the commodities covered by international conventions included coffee, beef, rubber, tea, timber, wheat, sugar, and tin.[17] Today, of course, the most famous raw material cartel of sovereign states is the Organization of Petroleum Exporting Countries. But OPEC is unique. It consists entirely of countries that produce and sell the commodity, and it resembles a classic private cartel in that its goal is less to stabilize the market than to make sure its members get the price they want for oil. No other group of commodity producers has been able to copy the OPEC success formula, although several have tried. More common agreements are those between producing and consuming countries. These typically arise from chronic, severe imbalances in supply and demand — and their purpose is to shelter producers and consumers alike from devastating price swings and shortages.

Because raw materials markets are notoriously unstable, the method most often used to regulate them is to try to balance supply with demand by limiting production and/or sales. Since World War II, agreements of substantial duration have affected trade in wheat, sugar, rubber, olive oil, cotton, tin, and cocoa,[18] and there have been many short-lived attempts to regulate other commodities. Perhaps the best example of an effective commodity cartel is the International Coffee Agreement, or ICA.[19] Organized in 1962 by the main producing and consuming nations (including the United States, the largest consumer of all), the ICA fixed a sales quota for each producer based on past share of the market. Producers could sell their quota at any price. However, if the price of coffee sank below a "trigger price," quotas would be reduced.

The idea behind the ICA was that prices would remain high because production was restricted. But for the first years of the agreement the ICA functioned poorly; some producers were unhappy with their quotas so they cheated by overselling. A compromise was reached that granted the group larger quotas but also made the enforcement apparatus more effective. Between 1968 and 1972 the ICA ran smoothly. By then, accumulated stocks had been reduced and consumption had caught up with production; so the agreement seemed unnecessary and its main regulatory provisions were scrapped. But from 1973 until 1976 coffee prices suffered a series of sharp boosts and collapses that once again convinced ICA members that close cooperation had its virtues. The latest edition of the agreement, ratified in 1976, restores the market-regulating provisions. But this time the scheme is better planned. Producers are free to sell as much as they can as long as prices remain satisfactory. Export quotas are put into effect only if prices drop below a certain level, and they are suspended once prices rise again. This scheme largely eliminates the temptation to cheat. The United States and other consumer signatories also insisted that the agreement offer various incentives for coffee-growing nations to expand production.

In Chapter 6 we described two examples of the other common type of government-sponsored cartel: the rescue operation for "troubled" industries. These cartels tend to be considerably more controversial than international commodity agreements. Of course, few people would question the right of governments to assist their beleaguered industries on the national level, although the actual terms of assistance may be angrily debated. In the United States such aid ranges from Chrysler loan guarantees to price supports for American agriculture. In Europe and the Third World, where antitrust and laissez-faire ideals are not as deeply rooted, governments may take a hand in the administration of privately owned industries and sometimes take the ultimate step of nationalization. In Japan, industries suffering from "extreme disequilibrium of supply and demand" may form "depression cartels," which permit the firms to make agreements that would otherwise be prohibited. But what is regarded as proper within the boundaries of a nation-state becomes problematic when extended beyond its borders. It is one thing for the French government to play a strong role in the restructuring of France's steel industry; it is quite another for France to join with other countries in an effort to regulate the market for steel in the entire Common Market.

One reason for suspicion of international "rescue" cartels is that they use techniques identical to those of private cartels. Price fixing is the most obvious; the Eurofer cartel, for example, sets minimum prices for many steel products. Market division is accomplished by estimating demand and then allocating production among the member countries. Both Eurofer and the EEC fibers cartel stress rationalization, the goal being to cut back capacity by phasing out inefficient plants and to encourage specialization in different product lines. Rescue cartels often include additional measures to shield the industry from outside competition, such as protective tariffs.[20] Perhaps the only mechanism often found in private cartels and absent from public ones is the combat fund for destroying outsiders; but governments have means of achieving a similar effect. When U.S. steelmakers complain that Europeans are dumping their steel on American markets at prices below the cost of production, they claim that such dumping is possible because the Europeans receive covert support from their governments in the form of tax concessions and subsidies. These claims are hard to prove because of the financial intricacies involved; however, to the extent they are valid, it means that the governments are using their national treasuries as a sort of combat fund to give their steelmakers an unfair advantage in international trade.

How, then, to evaluate government-sponsored cartels? First, it would seem that the justification for them is more consistently valid than for private accords. Commodity agreements and rescue cartels are always organized when the trades affected are severely troubled, whereas private firms sometimes form cartels not because there is a pressing need but in order to achieve the highest possible profits on new inventions. Nevertheless, it is clear that public cartels are prone to enough abuses that the argument for them is hardly conclusive. In the case of commodity plans, the desired balance between supply and demand can be achieved by means that in the long run are either destructive or beneficial. When the producers and consumers of a certain commodity simply decide to restrict output and set inflexible sales quotas in order to drive up the price — as in the 1962 coffee accord — it is hard to see what the world gains as a whole. The producers may earn more, and sharp cycles of boom and bust may be averted for a time; but the net effect is that less of the good is produced, while everyone has to pay a higher price for it. Such a scheme creates a constant temptation to drive supply down below demand so that astronomical profits can be earned. On the other hand, the 1976 coffee agreement seems better gauged to maintain equilibrium while encouraging high output and fair prices. It includes production incentives and imposes sales quotas only if the price dips drastically. This allows the various producing nations the maximum of freedom to compete for a larger share of the market, while offering them some security against overproduction and price collapse.

Rescue cartels, by the same token, are at best problematic enterprises. If the sole effect of the cartel is to protect antiquated or inefficient producers by forcing up prices and fixing strict market divisions, no adjustment is accomplished; on the contrary, the normal workings of competition are thwarted, distortions in the market become more pronounced, and the stage is set for a more painful collapse at some later point. Here again the Eurofer cartel may serve as an example. To the extent that it cushions European steelmakers while they gradually make the changes necessary to succeed in a fast-evolving world steel market, then it is praiseworthy. But Eurofer has already evinced worrisome tendencies, illustrated by its coddling of the North European steel companies at the expense of the highly efficient Italian plants known as the Bresciani (see Chapter 6).

One final point should be made in differentiating public from private cartels: government-sponsored cartels are subject to some degree of public influence. A private corporation has no obligation to anyone but its stockholders. When it enters a cartel (assuming it remains within the boundaries of the law), it need not reveal or justify that decision to the public at large. It need not release the data or analysis upon which it based the decision; it need not respond to any protest. When a government supports a cartel, on the other hand, the action — at least in theory — is taken because officials believe it to be in the best interests of the populace. Most important, the officials can be held accountable. Their decisions are subject to public scrutiny and political pressure. Of course, governments vary in their degree of responsiveness. Even in a democracy, the public's direct impact on government policies, particularly those regarding complex matters of international trade, is minimal. But one may still feel more comfortable with cartels that in some measure must answer to the people whose lives they affect.

The Third World and Cartels

Having reviewed the arguments generally advanced in favor of cartels, we now wish to assess their impact more specifically, first on the countries of the Third World, and then on the industrialized West.

The most obvious effect of cartel activity in the Third World is the destruction or takeover of locally owned industry. Prior to World War II, this usually took the form of preventing the establishment of factories in the underdeveloped countries, either by tight control over manufacturing technology[21] or by selective price cutting to scare off potential competitors. In 1941 the California Alkali Export Association explained a price reduction as follows:

> The main factor was the apparent need for some temporary price action in the face of unusual pressure for the erection of local industries, particularly in Mexico, Brazil and the Argentine, and with special references to caustic soda and soda ash — and where government assistance was being sought . . . In the Argentine ash prices were also reduced as a temporary measure, first because of interest of government in the entire alkali picture, and second, owing to considerable interest by local groups in such a venture. Ample capital seemed available.[22]

Thus these important South American nations were kept from developing production of alkalies, one of the most basic industrial chemicals.

But the Depression and World War II made it more difficult for the major firms to block industrialization of the LDCs. International trade declined sharply during the 1930s, and the war thoroughly disrupted previous patterns of commerce. The hostilities hamstrung the cartels. In these circumstances, some developing countries were able to expand their own industry — usually ill-financed and on a small scale, but nevertheless locally owned. After the war these countries hoped to protect and nurture their home-grown plant, and many adopted a policy of "import substitution," favoring domestically produced goods over foreign ones, often by erecting tariff barriers against imports. Transnational corporations wanting a share of these markets were increasingly forced to build or acquire facilities within the Third World countries.

But import substitution policies have been less than a complete success, largely because they have failed to deal adequately with a crucial question: import substitution *by whom?* It is one thing for growing production by domestic firms to replace imports; it is quite another for huge, foreign-based corporations, the same ones that formerly supplied the imports, to set up factories and drive their local competitors out of business. The latter process is called denationalization, and all too often it has gone hand in hand with attempts at import substitution. We have already detailed, in Chapter 3, the sweeping denationalization that has taken place in the Brazilian electrical industry.[23] Similar shifts have taken place in other Brazilian industries, including chemicals, pharmaceuticals, and machinery. In Mexico, foreign ownership of the transportation, electrical machinery, and rubber industries had already reached 100 percent as early as 1962; and between that year and 1970 the foreign-owned sector of the metal industry rose from 42 to 68 percent, and of the tobacco industry from 17 to 100 percent.[24] Various studies have shown the same pattern in other Latin American countries.[25]

Foreign investment, of course, is supposed to contribute to Third World development by providing capital, new production facilities, and employment. Undoubtedly it does so, but the extent of its contribution may be considerably less than commonly supposed. Much of the capital — in the range of 80 percent, according to several studies of U.S. investment in Latin America during the 1960s — employed by TNCs actually comes from local sources, such as banks and private investors.[26] Critics have charged the global corporations with favoring capital-intensive projects that create relatively few jobs; the mechanization of agriculture on huge farms often *decreases* employment opportunities in rural areas, for example. The establishment of a TNC subsidiary in a developing country does not necessarily mean an addition to the country's productive resources because TNCs often break into the market *by buying out a preexisting local firm.* A report published by the magazine *Business Latin America* in 1970 showed that nearly half of the 817 manufacturing subsidiaries set up by U.S. TNCs in Latin America between 1958 and 1967 were founded upon purchases of companies; the researchers also observed that declining rates of acquisition in some industries were probably due to the "scarcity of local firms" left to buy.[27] Newfarmer confirms this trend in his study of the electrical industry. His data on acquisitions by American electrical TNCs show that the tendency to acquire rather than found a new firm is increasing.[28] He also points out that in the advanced developing countries, such as Brazil and Mexico, the pattern is most pronounced. Over 90 percent of the growth in the foreign share of Brazil's electrical industry between 1960 and 1974 came about through acquisitions of local firms.[29]

Transnational corporations have a propensity to displace firms in the Third World whether or not the TNCs belong to cartels, but there is no question that when cartels are involved the prospect of denationalization is even greater. Local firms in developing countries do not always agree willingly to acquisitions or mergers. Sometimes they are destroyed — or forced to sell out, which amounts to the same thing — by predatory competition or the threat of it. Many of the cartel contracts that have come to light — including contracts for the International Electrical Association, the International Cable Development Corporation, and IBEMEP, the Brazilian branch of the electrical cartel — provide for a combat fund. Here we might recall Article 24 of the IBEMEP accord: "The final sales price agreed upon during the meeting will include 2 percent payable by the winning member to a 'reserve for combat purposes.' "

Cartels have various other ways of increasing the already substantial advantage that TNCs hold over firms in the developing world. One is the concerted refusal to sell, resulting in a cutoff of supplies to local firms that depend on transnationals for essential components. As related in Chapter 3, the refusal of IBEMEP members to sell copper wire in 1969 and 1970 appears to have hastened the failure or takeover of Brazilian firms. And, when bidding against local competitors for major orders, cartel companies achieve important advantages by consulting with each other in advance, deciding what the low bid should be, and selecting the firm to submit it.

Another major factor in the process of denationalization is the enormous technological superiority of the global firms over their Third World competitors. The TNCs claim, of course, that they spur development by providing otherwise unavailable technology and know-how. There is little question that the claim has some validity. But the true value of such "technology transfer," as it is carried out by the TNCs, is a matter of considerable doubt. Transnational firms investing in the Third World tend to offer technology that is either incomplete or outdated or both.[30] Frequently the developing nations get technology for only one phase of production of a certain commodity — the phase, naturally, that best fits the interests of the global firms. Copper-producing countries such as Chile and Zaire, for example, may be provided the most modern mining equipment, but to a large extent the smelting, refining, and particularly the fabricating of the metal is carried out in the home countries of the transnational mining firms. Or an electronics company may build an ultramodern assembly plant in Mexico but still manufacture key components in the United States. In either case the worth of the technology transferred is sharply circumscribed. Equally often the technology or know-how received by developing countries is already obsolete, but nevertheless they are overcharged for it. In one case, the subsidiary of a transnational paper company was found to be importing *used* machinery from its parent firm at a cost twice the going price of comparable *new* machinery on the international market.[31]

The global firms have numerous ways to make sure that the transfer of technology does not go too far: Cartel agreements are vitally important to this strategy; by eliminating competition among the major firms, they also eliminate the incentive for *preemptive* transfers of technology. To explain this concept, let us imagine two transnational chemical firms, one American and one German, engaged in identical lines of research. As occurs not infrequently, they might make similar valuable discoveries at about the same time. Each would then be strongly tempted to license the discovery in as many markets as possible as a preemptive move against the other. That is, the American firm might hurriedly grant a license to a Peruvian company on favorable terms for fear the German firm would do so first and thereby grab the Peruvian market. A cartel accord, however, removes this element of uncertainty. By exchanging exclusive licenses to each other's discoveries, and by agreeing to divide the world's markets between them, the two firms are freed from any competitive pressure to reveal the technology to third parties. Each is now free to exploit the discovery in its assigned territories as it sees fit, whether by exporting from the home country or by establishing subsidiaries abroad. Either way, the technology remains firmly in the hands of the transnationals.

Two recent examples illustrate the negative effect of cartels on the technological development of the Third World. The first resembles the hypothetical situation described above. It involves an agreement between two of the world's largest producers of cans and other metal containers, the Continental Can Company of the United States and the Metal Box Company of Great Britain. In 1966 these firms granted to each other exclusive, nonassignable licenses to all their patents or patent applications governing cans and can-making machinery. Each agreed that it would use the other's patents only within a certain specified territory. Metal Box's territory was defined as the British Isles, Italy, and a number of Commonwealth countries in Africa, Asia, and the West Indies. Thus, in all these nations, access by other firms to the technology developed by Continental Can was effectively blocked, and Metal Box was spared the danger of serious competition. The converse naturally was true in Continental Can's territory.[32]

The other example concerns the electrical lamp cartel organized in India by three British firms and the Dutch firm, Philips. As we described in Chapter 2, the firms produced lamps through a joint venture called the Electric Lamp Manufacturers (India) Private Ltd., or ELM. They also agreed to buy virtually all machinery, equipment, and parts for ELM from Philips. This effectively deprived India of the chance to develop its own technology because the firms that dominated the market were pledged to buy all their capital goods from Philips, and Philips, under the agreement, had the right to match any competitor's bid. Under these conditions it would be foolhardy for any Indian company to invest in electric lamp technology because there would be no market for it in the country.[33]

*   *   *

We believe, then, that the major result of cartel activity in the Third World is the loss of local control over available capital, productive facilities, and technological resources. But from the point of view of the developing world, what exactly is wrong with foreign economic penetration? Why do most Third World countries struggle so vigorously against denationalization, even those most hospitable to the TNCs?

The basic reason is that the interests of the global corporations are not those of the developing countries. The raison d'être of a TNC is to produce profit. How and where the profit is made is a matter of relative indifference. And the very transnational nature of the TNC means that its loyalties to any one country — even its home country — are tenuous. If capital must be drained from Peru, say, in order to invest it in Italy, then it will be drained, and Peru's "development" be damned. Thus the deep anxiety about denationalization on the part of poor countries. They fear the process leaves critical decisions about investment and production in the hands of foreign-based firms that do not have local interests at heart. They know that TNCs have a thousand more or less subtle methods of bleeding financial and natural resources from countries in which they have invested.

For example, there is the problem of imports. For obvious reasons, most developing countries are eager to substitute locally produced goods for imports. As noted above, TNCs in recent years have been moving more of their plants into the Third World to take advantage of cheap labor or to bypass the high tariff barriers erected as part of "import substitution" policies. But in a great many cases the TNCs still hope to preserve the developing countries as export markets for surplus production from home-country plants. In fact, studies have shown that subsidiaries of TNCs in the developing countries have a tendency to import more than their local competitors. In a study of Peru in 1973, Constantine Vaitsos found that, in nearly every industry examined, foreign-owned manufacturing firms used more imported intermediate products than did Peruvian-owned firms.[34]

This tendency is almost certainly aggravated when cartels are involved. Again we might recall the lamp cartel in India, whose members agreed to import *nearly all* their equipment, machinery, and parts from Philips. A less clear-cut but in some ways even more suggestive example involves the production of heavy electrical equipment in Brazil. In 1964 the subsidiaries of several transnational electrical firms — which, it will be remembered, organized the Brazilian branch of the IEA that same year — requested and eventually received permission to import *duty-free* hydroelectrical plant, including equipment of a size that had been produced previously in the country. Between 1965 and 1975 two-thirds of all hydroelectric plant installed in Brazil was imported.[35] It may be argued that it was to Brazil's advantage to import the equipment given that generally it could be produced in the industrialized countries at a lower cost than in Brazil. But it is most interesting to note that some of the same firms that were importing hydroplant into Brazil had large factories in Europe that were heavily dependent on Third World markets for their production, Europe's hydroelectric potential having been fully realized long before.[36]

Exacerbating the adverse effects of this tendency to import is the fact that imports by subsidiaries of TNCs are notoriously overpriced. Most export cartels exist precisely so that members will not engage in price competition with each other; through prior consultation and/or collusive bidding they raise the cost of their products to the Third World. That overpricing of imports by subsidiaries of TNCs is a standard practice has been confirmed in numerous countries. Vaitsos's study of Colombia in the 1960s compared the prices of imports by TNC subsidiaries with world market prices and found overcharges of the following magnitudes: in electronics, from 16 to 60 percent; in pharmaceuticals, 155 percent; in rubber, 40 percent. Other investigations show that during the same period overpricing in Peru ranged from 50 to 300 percent; in Chile, from 30 to 700 percent; in Ecuador, from 75 to 200 percent.[37] UNCTAD reports similar figures for nations in Asia.[38]

Of course, the overpricing of imports is not the only way that TNC subsidiaries drain resources from developing countries, although it may be the most important.[39] Besides the capture by TNCs of available local investment capital, there is the ever controversial problem described by the term *repatriation of profits*. Third World countries naturally would prefer that profits earned by subsidiaries be reinvested locally; the TNCs often want to "repatriate" the profits, or shift them to some other sector of their far-flung networks. This conflict gives rise to an endless cat-and-mouse game in which developing countries devise new laws to limit and regulate the profit drain and TNCs devise new ways to evade the regulations. All the tricks that the accounting trade can apply to international dealings — tricks involving royalty payments, licensing fees, taxes, phony exports, understatement or overstatement of assets, and dozens of others — are used to conceal the true amount of profit being removed from the country.

The simplest but most significant of these devices is called transfer pricing. It occurs when a firm trades with itself — usually a subsidiary with the parent firm or with another subsidiary — so that the transaction is not carried out at "arm's length" and the prices can be set at whatever level the firm wishes. When the parent firm grossly overprices the products it sells to a subsidiary and grossly underpays for the products it buys from that subsidiary, the profits recorded by the subsidiary are thereby greatly reduced, although in fact they are simply flowing to the parent in another guise. Studies suggest that nearly every TNC takes advantage of transfer pricing to some extent, and some firms have clearly used the technique both to camouflage astronomical profits being made by their subsidiaries and to extract those profits from the countries of origin.[40] (It should be said, however, that in the last decade the developing countries as a body have grown more sophisticated in matters of intracorporate finance and have achieved a greater degree of control over repatriation of profits.)

All the byproducts of denationalization have a disastrous effect on the balance of payments of the typical developing nation. To the extent that imports are increased and overpriced, the country loses precious foreign exchange. And the chance to recoup by increasing exports is often stifled by restrictions placed on patent licenses. Global corporations are hardly inclined to create subsidiaries that will compete with them for export markets, and they are even less likely to support locally owned firms that might do so.[41] One study of the Andean Pact nations (Colombia, Ecuador, Peru, Chile, Bolivia) found clauses banning exports in 92 *percent* of the licenses granted by TNCs to locally owned firms.[42] We have described cartels in the radio, television, and pharmaceuticals industries that follow this practice; and UNCTAD has reported similar restrictive clauses in licenses for technology relating to such varied products as automobile clutches and batteries, cigarette filters, and plate glass.[43]

The facts lead to only one conclusion: cartels contribute to the *under*development of the Third World. Their drive for market control intensifies the process of denationalization that increasingly afflicts the developing nations, and their methods aggravate every one of its unfortunate effects. Cartels block the growth of locally owned business enterprises. They do everything in their power to maintain the technological backwardness and dependency of poor countries. They siphon off scarce resources by forcing the Third World to rely on exorbitant imports and by hindering the development of potential exports. In so doing, the cartels affect more than the abstract measures of an economy's health, such as inflation, the balance of payments, or the growth of the GNP. For a nation's burden of debt and the strength of its industry and agriculture have a direct impact on all the human problems associated with the term *underdevelopment* — hunger, disease, illiteracy, unemployment, political instability, and repression. The depredations performed by cartels on the economies of Third World nations exacerbate the crushing poverty of much of the human race.

Cartels and the West

For the rich nations of the West the impact of cartels is more ambiguous, even contradictory. On the one hand, these nations reap the benefits of cartel penetration of the Third World; at the same time, though, cartels cause problems for them that strikingly resemble those of the developing countries.

We have shown that one of the most important functions of international cartels is to preserve the hegemony of the firms belonging to them. The firms in most cases have been dominant in their respective industries for decades and have their headquarters in the advanced capitalist states. Their cartel ties help them to seize the lion's share of world markets and to extract large returns from the Third World countries where they operate. Cartels thus play a major role in the transfer of resources from the countries of the so-called South to the coffers of the transnationals of the North, and, in theory, the fuller those coffers, the more the firms are able to invest and thereby raise standards of living at home. Many transnationals report much higher rates of profit on capital invested in low-wage areas abroad than on investments at home.[44] Were these extraordinary foreign profits not available, the corporations would have to increase profit levels at home — which can only be done by reducing production costs, including wages, or by raising prices, or both. Workers and consumers in the home countries are thus being indirectly subsidized by the more intense exploitation of the Third World. There is considerable truth in the widespread perception that the luxuries we enjoy in the United States are paid for by the impoverished peoples of Asia, Africa, and Latin America.

From this point of view cartels would seem to be highly advantageous to both the global firms and the populations of the industrialized countries. But the matter is not that simple, for cartels do not restrict their endeavors at market control to the Third World. The United States is victimized by many of the same cartel machinations as is Brazil and is affected by them no less profoundly. Here it is useful to raise the notion of the "Latin-Americanization of the United States." In his brief formulation of the concept in an essay published in 1972, the economist Carlos F. Diaz-Alejandro said:

> But if ten years of [the Alliance for Progress] have not made much of a dent on Latin American problems, there is some evidence that the U.S.

has become Latin-Americanized during that period. Note the 1969–70 U.S. inflationary recession, so familiar to Argentines, and the U.S. campus disorders. Frequent power shortages, creaky and bankrupt railroads, erratic mails, and bitter ideological debates are experiences increasingly shared by Americans, North and South. Alas, even import substituting protectionism . . . has been picked up in the North.[45]

Barnet and Muller then examined the idea more thoroughly in *Global Reach*,[46] pointing out that TNCs have much to do with chronic social and economic problems — notably increasing inequalities of wealth and government inability to regulate the economy adequately — that make the United States resemble an underdeveloped country.

The most obvious way cartels contribute to this "Latin-Americanization" is by forcing prices higher. We have shown that consumers in the advanced countries pay inflated prices for the finished goods of several basic industries — electronics, steel, chemicals, textiles, petroleum — as well as numerous smaller ones because of cartel action. The sine qua non of most cartel systems is home market protection, which allows the leading national producers in Europe, Japan, and the United States to set prices at whatever level they see fit without fear of being undercut by foreign competitors. As we have seen in the cases of the uranium cartel, the cable cartel, the quinine cartel, and others, corporations are by no means above price gouging if they can engineer a corner on the market and maintain tight cartel discipline. Naturally this price gouging exacerbates price inflation in the industrialized countries. Also, many economists have noted the relationship on the national level between the rise of monopoly (or oligopoly) capitalism and inflation, observing that companies in a monopoly position are relatively insulated from the pressures of the market and therefore can raise their prices almost at will in order to meet profit goals. In effect, international cartels extend these systems of "administered prices" across national boundaries.

Cartels, then, spur inflation in both the developed and developing countries. But there is an even more significant similarity between the two realms. In the Third World cartels contribute to the process of denationalization; in the advanced West, they intensify the parallel process of *international economic concentration* — the trend that many experts view as the salient economic event of the postwar years. Just as the great trusts were formed in the late nineteenth century in order to fortify and extend their member firms' hold on their respective national industries, so a few hundred transnational corporations today are extending their sway over all world markets.[47] We have already detailed the methods cartels employ to destroy established competitors and prevent the rise of new ones, methods that include predatory competition financed by combat funds and the withholding of technology from "outsiders." Each time a potential competitor is absorbed, scared off, or driven out of business by a cartel member, world trade becomes a degree more concentrated.

For the consumers and governments of the industrialized states, the problem posed by this trend is that economic concentration inevitably leads to concentration of political power — both in the narrow sense of influence over which individuals are elected to office and in the broad sense of influence over the production and distribution of goods in society. Attendant upon the Watergate scandal came revelations of massive illegal interference by giant corporations — mostly by means of secret campaign contributions — in the U.S. electoral process. There is nothing new about money buying elections or businessmen providing it. Watergate was striking only because it demonstrated beyond a doubt the huge scale and pervasiveness of the meddling. Since then, election law reforms are supposed to have eliminated the worst abuses. But the trend that gave rise to them — the growing economic concentration that has given each transnational corporation vast resources to spend, infinite methods of concealing the spending, and immense interests hanging on the outcome of elections — has proceeded apace.

It is not merely through direct electoral influence, though, that transnational corporations leave their imprint on our society. With their armies of well-paid executives, lobbyists, and experts, all wise in the ways of government, they pressure and cajole the legislators and bureaucrats whose countless daily decisions comprise the country's economic policy. Such decisions usually are reported, if at all, only on the business pages of newspapers and often go ignored or poorly understood by the general public. But they shape every aspect of our lives, from where we work and the prices we pay for staples to the quality of the air and the landscaping of our towns and cities. The TNCs exercise power over tax policy — how much of the gross national product will be absorbed by the government and who shall pay what portion. They naturally work to shift the tax burden from the corporate sector to private individuals, and they consistently seek and receive favored treatment for foreign-earned income.[48] They have power over tariffs, which determine the prices we pay for imported goods, and thus for similar domestic goods.[49] Their tremendous financial reserves give them power over the entire international monetary system; in fact, that system's vulnerability has been shown in repeated crises when TNC holdings in such unregulated havens as the Eurodollar market have been used for speculative purposes, to drive currency values sharply up or down.[50] Large corporations are currently leading a relentless campaign in the United States against government regulation, particularly those regulations having to do with environmental protection or occupational health and safety. The mobility afforded them by their global scope gives the giant firms great power over production and employment patterns;

it is the simplest thing for a TNC to close a factory in Pennsylvania and open its equivalent in Taiwan if the saving in labor costs warrants the move.[51]

Such are the varieties of political power that accrue to transnational corporations as they expand their control over the world economy. The dangers inherent in such power can best be understood by reflecting on the Seven Sisters and their stranglehold on a critical sector of the U.S. economy. Aside from their collusive and profiteering propensities, the companies are famous for their capacity to wring favorable treatment from legislatures, both federal and state. Their power in Washington is especially legendary, usually channeled through such oil-state congressional power brokers as former Representative Sam Rayburn, former Senator Lyndon Johnson, or, at present, Senator Russell Long of Louisiana.[52] Aided by these and other satraps, the oil companies have won tax concessions worth many billions of dollars over the years, notably the oil depletion allowance (finally done away with for the majors, and reduced for small producers, in 1975) and the right to credit foreign royalty payments against U.S. taxes. The most recent example of congressional adherence to the oil industry's cause was the whittling down of the "windfall profits" tax proposed by President Carter when he decontrolled domestic oil prices (itself a multibillion-dollar concession).

But the basic impact of the oil companies on our society does not stem from their power over prices or their ability to win tax favors. Still more fundamental is the political influence the companies have long wielded in two crucial arenas: foreign policy and, of course, energy policy. From the fall of 1978 until January 1979, fifty-two hostages were held in the U.S. embassy in Teheran. Their plight can be traced directly back to 1951, when the Seven Sisters began a boycott of Iranian oil in response to the Mossadeq regime's nationalization program. The companies' implacable opposition led to Mossadeq's overthrow in a CIA-led coup that reinstalled the Shah in 1953. For the next twenty-five years the U.S. government and the oil companies that profited so handsomely from Mossadeq's downfall enthusiastically backed one of the world's worst tyrants; thus, the anti-American feeling that exploded upon the Shah's ouster was hardly surprising. The result today is sharply increased tension and the markedly greater threat of war. And Iran is only the most egregious single case of the oil companies adversely affecting U.S. interests in the Middle East. Indeed, OPEC was originally formed in reaction to the companies' cavalier treatment of the then weak oil-producing states. For decades U.S. policy toward those states *was* the policy of the oil companies, a situation that remained largely unchanged until 1973, when OPEC realized its potential and rudely quadrupled oil prices. After that the United States was left to reap the ill will the companies had sown — while the Seven Sisters merely

changed sides and continued to earn huge profits, now as OPEC's hand-
maidens.

The American "energy crisis," too, has everything to do with the fact
that the country's energy policy has been inseparable from oil company
policy. Oil import quotas, first imposed in 1959 and not lifted until 1973,
kept cheap foreign oil out of the country — and thus allowed the companies to use up America's own oil, leaving us today staggered by the burden of exorbitant imports.[53] The exclusion of foreign oil protected the
sales price of domestic oil, but the companies were not satisfied with that
measure; we have already described how the Texas "prorationing" system,
at the center of an intricate web of other federal and state laws, allowed
the oil industry to decide collectively how much oil was needed and then
to produce no more — a unique degree of exemption from antitrust principles in a "nonregulated" industry. The major oil companies are
thoroughly integrated, that is, they perform every phase of the oil business, from initial exploration to retail marketing, and thus are in a position
to make crucial decisions at each step: how much exploration will be
done, how the crude will be distributed around the world, how much
crude will be refined into what final products, and so on. Congressional
attempts to break up the majors into their constituent parts in order to reduce the degree of centralized control have failed abjectly. The oil companies do not simply control oil; they have huge investments in competing
sources of energy, including coal, uranium, natural gas, and the various
forms of solar energy technology. John Blair argues that oil shale could
have provided large quantities of energy by now had the oil companies not
scuttled important experimental projects years ago.[54] At present, proposals for serious conservation of energy, such as a sharply higher federal tax
on gasoline to discourage driving, are bitterly (and, thus far, effectively)
fought by the companies.

These are only a few examples of how the oil industry has been and still
is the overwhelming power behind U.S. energy policy. And the companies
could not have accumulated such power without their cartel connections.
Beginning as far back as the 1920s, accords such as the Achnacarry Agreement, the Red Line Agreement, and the Iranian Consortium made possible the enormous profits that helped the companies to grow into the giants
they are today. Cartel agreements allowed the Sisters to fend off independent competitors and to negotiate from a position of strength with the
governments of oil-producing states. By the 1950s, U.S. interests in the
Middle East had already become so intertwined with the oil companies'
cartel agreements that the Justice Department's attempt to prosecute the
Sisters for antitrust violations was quietly quashed.

The oil industry also offers a good illustration of another dilemma that
the advanced Western nations increasingly share with the Third World:

governments lack the information and techniques to adequately monitor the TNCs and thus have lost control, to a frightening extent, over their national economies. Barnet and Muller argue that this is a major factor in the "Latin-Americanization" process:

> Large corporations plan centrally and act globally, and nation-states do not. It is this difference that puts government at a disadvantage in trying to keep up with and control the activities of global corporations. As individual business units become more powerful and more mobile, as their balance sheets become less and less accurate reflections of real economic activity, government finds itself handicapped, administratively and politically, in regulating the economy with traditional Keynesian methods. The ease with which global corporations can conceal or distort information vital for the management of the economy is creating the same sort of administrative nightmare for the advanced industrial state that underdeveloped countries have lived with for years.[55]

It is now notorious that the U.S. government, in its attempts to comprehend the oil industry and thus devise a coherent energy plan, is dependent on data supplied by the oil companies themselves, data which for obvious reasons are suspect and which have repeatedly proven erroneous.[56] It is not simply information concerning energy discoveries and reserves that is lacking. The problem is pervasive. Take the realm of foreign trade, for example. An estimated 50 percent of U.S. exports are made by companies selling to their own subsidiaries and affiliates abroad.[57] The prices of these goods are not determined by the market but by the intricacies of transfer pricing, which makes it unlikely that the official balance-of-payments figures reflect the real value of goods leaving and entering the country. Also, thanks to the wizardry of today's accounting firms, profit figures — which are a major factor in determining how much tax a company must pay and the price of its stock on public markets — are equally unreal. It is difficult for any of the advanced nations to be sure of meeting their targets for domestic money supply because they simply cannot control the flow of the hundred *billion* dollars' worth of highly mobile funds in the Eurodollar market.[58]

Not only are the global firms sophisticated enough to withhold or falsify essential information; they are also strong enough to distort the market itself. This returns us to the central factor responsible for "Latin-Americanization": concentrated wealth and power. Current economic theory presumes that, apart from minor and temporary "imperfections," the market still works well as a distributor of resources and a guide to government intervention in the economy. But growing economic concentration has severely damaged the market mechanism by the imposition of permanent "imperfections." Among these are cartel agreements whose very purpose is to subvert the free market. Such built-in distortions mean

that governments cannot get the expected results from manipulations of
fiscal and monetary policy. The virulent strain of inflation infecting Western economies is resistant to cure by the usual treatments, partly because
the oligopolistic position and cartel agreements of many TNCs allow them
to raise prices even in periods of declining demand. Thus cartels are both a
cause of stagflation and a major reason why governments are powerless to
solve it.

*   *   *

When it comes to cartels, then, the rich countries have more in common
with the poor than might be readily apparent. Although cartel profits
generally flow from South to North, the superprofits extracted from the
home countries, too, are substantial; and, as we have shown, the process of
economic concentration in the North mirrors that of denationalization in
the South, robbing nation-states of power over their own affairs. There is
one strictly political byproduct of cartels that should be mentioned here:
their impact on *relations between the developed and developing worlds.*
The fact that those relations become daily more important is repeated so
often in the press that it has become a cliché, but we believe its full meaning has yet to strike the peoples of the United States, Europe, and Japan,
who still regard the developing nations as ill-mannered beggars. The
North depends more and more on the South as a source of natural resources. The TNCs are also reaping larger percentages of their profits
there. Never before have the rich countries been so dependent on the
poor, and the poor know it.

They also know, however, that the countries and corporations of the
North remain powerful and unscrupulous. Little by little the Third World
is learning to force better terms from the transnational firms that operate
there. But resentment against the TNCs continues to build, as anyone who
has traveled recently in Africa or Latin America will have remarked; and
the predatory activities of cartels can only heighten it. In numerous countries, pent-up anger against the West and its corporations fuels social unrest. The overwhelming reception that greeted the first edition of this
book in Brazil is one indication of public sentiment in a country where
TNCs have played a major role for the last twenty years. When the unrest
explodes, as in Chile in the early 1970s or Iran in 1979, the results can be
grave, ranging from embassy seizures to oil boycotts to nationalizations —
all the way to complete suppression of private enterprise. Given the rapidly shifting currents of international affairs, we believe it would behoove
the advanced countries to consider whether the unsavory business practices that bring rich returns today are worth the political price that inevitably will be paid tomorrow.

example, a group of corporations from the United States, England, France, Germany, and Japan might gather in Holland and formulate a cartel agreement dividing up markets in Latin America. They might then agree that any disputes arising from the agreement would be arbitrated by a Swiss court. This would mean that the cartel's conflicts, which might often involve the enforcement of restrictive cartel provisions, would be adjudicated in a country basically friendly to the cartel's designs. The importance of this system to international commerce can hardly be overstated.

In the face of such problems, we believe the cause of freely competitive world trade would be well served by blanket prohibition of export cartels of any sort. Within the United States there is some movement in that direction: several private and official reports have proposed that the Webb-Pomerene Act be repealed, either because it tends to foster domestic monopoly, or because it has not served its alleged purpose of nurturing exports by smaller firms, or simply because Webb-Pomerene cartels have been ineffective in all but a few cases.[4] Should the United States repeal the act, it would then be in a good position to pressure its trading partners to at least ban *international* export cartels, which are the most prone to abuses. But even if other nations feel there is more to be gained from permitting "pure" export cartels than there is to be lost from their frequent impurities, such cartels should certainly be obligated to register with the authorities — which is not now the case in various countries, most notably Germany and the United Kingdom. The registration lists, with accompanying data on the cartels' activities, should be open to the public; to allow "pure" export cartels to completely escape official or public scrutiny evinces an attitude of trust that is hardly justified by experience.

Not only law regarding export cartels should be brought into harmony, though. One obvious gap in the West's defenses is the fact that Switzerland offers a haven where cartels are largely protected against unwelcome attention, whether from reporters or prosecutors; as long as Swiss law remains so lax it will be impossible to regulate the cartels effectively. Also, the legal doctrine of "party autonomy" should be reconsidered — at least insofar as it is applied to cartel contracts — in light of the extraordinary power it bestows on cartel members to conduct their affairs by their own rules, shielded from the oversight of countries whose interests may be strongly affected by the proceedings.

What are the chances of achieving such reforms? There are favorable signs: the strong antitrust legislation adopted by the EEC and its vigorous attacks on certain important cartels; the guidelines for multinational corporations passed by the OECD in 1976,[5] and the recent accord between the United States and Germany establishing formal consultations on antitrust matters, as well as the negotiations aimed at similar agreements between the United States and other advanced countries.[6] Such bilateral ef-

forts strike us as a particularly promising approach toward reducing dis-
agreements between the United States and other nations, at least for the
short term. As to the prospects for broader, longer-lasting agreements,
however, we are not optimistic. Too many states still believe that permis-
siveness toward restrictive practices on the part of *their* corporations will
work to their national benefit; to quote a Brookings Institution study,
"What all nations want, of course, is for others to eliminate restrictive
practices, unilaterally."[7] Although the United States has had some success
in exporting its antitrust philosophy[8] and may yet have more if it sets the
right example, countries are notoriously sensitive to assaults on their sovereignty in the form of pressures to adopt legislation that does not appear
to reflect their interests. It should be remembered that from the end of
World War II until the 1960s, American firms accounted for the overwhelming bulk of direct foreign investment by the advanced countries,
whereas today Germany and Japan hold a substantial and fast-increasing
share. Those countries therefore have much more at stake than before in
the matter of international antitrust and can be expected to resist any
American blandishments that are perceived as harming their position.

❂   ❂   ❂

What if the task of policing anticompetitive behavior by TNCs and cartels
were placed in the hands of some neutral international agency? This approach could be more effective than the attempt to harmonize antitrust
policies through bilateral negotiations. In fact, since World War II there
have been repeated proposals for an international antitrust apparatus,
none of which has met with much success. The first was the most important: the abortive attempt to found an International Trade Organization
under the auspices of the United Nations. After long years of work involving negotiations among some fifty countries, the Draft Charter of the ITO
was approved at the Havana Conference in 1948. The provisions included
weak measures for control of cartels. The United States, however, which
had been the strongest force behind the ITO proposal, eventually scuttled
the agreement. The Congress refused to ratify the treaty, and other nations consequently lost interest.[9] Among the reasons for congressional hostility was the concern that U.S. corporations would be subject to antitrust
proceedings by an international body, which was regarded as an incursion
on national sovereignty.

   The United States then proceeded to undermine another, similar effort
it had originally sponsored. In 1951, at the behest of the U.S. government,
the United Nations Economic and Social Council set up an Ad Hoc Committee on Restrictive Business Practices and ordered it to evaluate the possibility of multilateral oversight and enforcement. The committee's report, delivered in 1953, advanced a plan similar to that in the Draft

Charter of the ITO, but by this time the United States had changed presidents, and the Eisenhower response to the plan came in 1955: a rejection on the grounds that "national policies and practices" were so divergent that an international agency would be inadequate to the task; what was needed, said the United States, was further work to develop "effective national programs" in order to achieve "a greater degree of comparability."[10] A subsequent proposal for international consultations under the auspices of the General Agreement on Tariffs and Trade also came to naught.

Such failures notwithstanding, various experts and organizations have continued to pursue the grail of an international antitrust agency possessing real authority. One source of inspiration for these visionaries has been the unexpected success of the EEC Commission in its enforcement of the antitrust provisions of the Treaty of Rome, which are among the most strict in the world. Few expected the provisions to amount to much more than rhetoric, but the aggressiveness of the Commission's Competition Department and the legal doctrines developed by the European Court of Justice in landmark cartel cases have in fact made the EEC the best existing model of a multinational antitrust body. Of course there are other factions within the EEC, led by the commissioner of industry, Viscount Davignon, who are firm believers in cartels. It must be remembered, too, that the power of the EEC to enforce its antitrust laws rests on the theory that its members are moving toward economic, monetary, and eventually political union. It is much more difficult to create an enforcement body operating across national lines when the nations involved have no plans to unite.

Nevertheless, there has been no shortage of proposals by economists and other experts for an international agency to oversee transnational corporations. Most of these proposals are exceedingly modest, reflecting their authors' belief that nothing more substantial would be accepted by sovereignty-minded nations. Bergsten, Horst, and Moran, in their book *American Multinationals and American Interests*, suggest that, as part of a "new international regime for multinational enterprises," there should be an agency whose first tasks should include collection of data on the enterprises themselves and on government policies toward them.[11] In 1973 Robert E. Smith advocated an "international cartel office" to be called "Intertel," whose purpose would be to gather and disseminate facts about restrictive practices.[12] Goldberg's and Kindleberger's proposal is somewhat more ambitious: they argue for a full-fledged treaty, tentatively named the General Agreement for the International Corporation, that would establish accepted norms of conduct for TNCs. The treaty's administrative agency could investigate complaints about "oppressive policies" and recommend measures whose implementation would be completely voluntary.[13] Finally, George Ball argues in a famous 1967 article, "Cosmocorp: The Importance of Being Stateless," that the world community should draw up a set of supranational laws to govern the behavior of TNCs. Ball goes so far as to suggest that TNCs be incorporated, or chartered, under the auspices of a world agency, making them literally "stateless." His basic rationale for this plan is that it would make the world a less problematic place for TNCs because they would be subject to only one set of rules and thus would be freed from the vicissitudes of differing national legal systems.[14]

Much more to our liking is the agency proposed by the economist Sigmund Timberg, which differs from most of the others in that it would focus specifically on antitrust questions (rather than the entire realm of TNC investment abroad) and would possess one all-important attribute: enforcement power.[15] Timberg is convinced that effective harmonization of national approaches to antitrust is impossible and that consultation between nations is of limited use. Instead he proposes an international convention, or treaty, which would be designed and dominated by the major nations of the West (as is the United Nations), which control the bulk of world trade and would hardly consign real power to an agency in which the Third World plays a major role. The agency created under the treaty would have strong subpoena power in the signatory nations so that it could acquire all the data it needs for inquiries. The agency would also make the determination as to whether accepted global antitrust standards have been violated and *must have the authority to enforce its decisions* (although national governments might be legally bound under the treaty to carry out enforcement themselves). An international high court would be the final judge of all appeals.

This is an ambitious program indeed. But the simple fact is that anything less would have slight impact on cartels. Any information-gathering agency would be shackled without the power to force countries or companies to turn over germane data. There would be some value in a treaty whereby nations agreed upon general principles to guide investment by TNCs and the policies governments should follow toward them; but in the realm of antitrust, as long as the treaty agency is limited to suggestions for voluntary reforms, it would have as much chance of stamping out cartelization as the United Nations does of stamping out war. As for George Ball's advocacy of an international commercial legal code, complete with world incorporation of TNCs, we agree with Barnet and Muller when they call it an attempt "to legitimize most of what global corporations are now doing by establishing minimal and largely unenforceable limits on their power to penetrate all national borders in the process of private global planning."[16]

Thus the only problem with Timberg's plan is that it cannot be implemented. Political realities make it utopian, at least in the near future. The moment one raises the notion of an international body with the power to force its members to obey specific laws, one must confront some very difficult questions: Who will choose the officers of the agency who will exercise such power? How will they be shielded from political pressure? (One obvious way would be to appoint the authorities — and especially the judges of the last court of appeal — to very long terms; but this only sharpens the tension surrounding the previous question.) How could the agency punish a country that blatantly refused to accede to its dictates? Such dilemmas, of course, account for the impotence of the United Nations. No doubt they could be solved, given the requisite political will; but a great many years are likely to pass before the industrial nations develop such a will.

In the meantime, something probably would be better than nothing. Even an agency devoted solely to collecting and evaluating publicly available material on international antitrust matters would be useful, and even one empowered to study specific cases and make unenforceable rulings might serve as a forum to put political pressure on miscreants. Publicity is what cartels abhor above all else, and such an agency would generate publicity. Also, bodies that *do* have effective power, such as the U.S. Justice Department or the EEC Commission, tend to follow up each other's actions, as in the dyestuffs cartel case, which was first investigated in Europe and then in the United States, or the quinine case, which proceeded in the reverse manner. Similarly, an international body might feed its material to interested parties who would make use of it.

In general, however, we believe that the idea of an international agency offers little hope for real regulation of cartels, at least in the short term. Much more effective will be antitrust activity on the part of individual nations, or bilateral agreements to work together in the exchange of information and the prosecution of cases. Therefore, we will now evaluate the anticartel efforts of the nation famous for having the most fearsome antitrust apparatus in the world: the United States.

Antitrust in the United States

At first glance, U.S. antitrust law would seem to provide an adequate weapon to combat international cartels, at least insofar as they directly affect this country. The fundamental legislation, the Sherman Act of 1890 and the Clayton Act of 1914, both cover foreign trade; in the words of the former, "Every contract, combination in the form of trust or otherwise, or conspiracy, in restraint of trade or commerce among the several States, *or with foreign nations* is declared to be illegal" (italics added). And through a series of court decisions, the most significant (as regards international cartels) coming in the *American Tobacco* (1911), *Alcoa* (1945), and *Alkasso* (1949) cases, the law acquired effective "extraterritorial reach."[17] Very few U.S. corporations today would be so foolhardy as to sign a formal cartel agreement with foreign firms. The agreements registered in the various European countries usually contain a standard clause exempting the U.S. market from their provisions. Yet, as we have shown, despite the fact that American and foreign companies demonstrate a healthy fear of the Sherman Act and the Department of Justice, cartels abound. The law is not entirely toothless; merely, some teeth are missing.

First is the prosaic problem that cripples so many agencies charged with protecting the public's interest: acute lack of manpower and money. In 1980 the entire budget of the Antitrust Division of the Justice Department was $44 million, less than many single TNCs spend for legal services annually. The Foreign Commerce Section of the division consisted of only twenty-two lawyers. Even with other attorneys from the division helping with trial work, this small band is hardly equipped to investigate the range of antitrust matters involving foreign trade. As a result, the number of "foreign" cases filed is low, despite the burgeoning importance of the TNCs and the increasing amount of their business that is conducted overseas. The Federal Trade Commission, the other agency responsible for enforcing the competition laws, pursues very few international antitrust cases.

Short-handed in general, the Justice Department's Antitrust Division chooses to stress "domestic" rather than "foreign" violations, partly because of the official conviction that the American public benefits more "per dollar of litigation" from domestic cases.[18] Certainly another factor, though, is the sheer difficulty of bringing international cartel cases. We have observed that U.S. authorities, when investigating foreign firms, often meet resistance from the firms' home countries; indeed, some countries have made it a crime to turn over commercial information in response to judicial orders from abroad (see Chapters 4 and 7). Even if sufficient data could be obtained to win a conviction, the remedies or penalities often cannot be imposed on a recalcitrant foreign firm backed by its government.[19] The high sensitivity to American "bullying" often displayed by nations with different antitrust attitudes must always be taken into account, making antitrust pursuits a matter of extreme delicacy.[20] The State Department must be consulted as to the foreign policy implications of every case brought by the Foreign Commerce Section; and, although the former chief of the section, Wilbur L. Fugate, has stated that State Department objections never quashed a case, he has also admitted that when necessary the division "looks a bit harder at the facts of the case."[21]

The results of "looking a bit harder" can be disturbing, as illustrated by the uranium cartel case. In Chapter 5 we described how Gulf Oil was allowed to plead nolo contendere to a misdemeanor and was fined the laughable sum of $40,000 for its Canadian subsidiary's part in the cartel. The investigating attorneys in the Antitrust Division had unanimously recommended a felony prosecution, but the forces arrayed against such a move were formidable. In the course of the investigation, both Canada and Australia passed laws denying the Justice Department access to documents. The Canadians also intervened directly at the highest levels: Secretary of State Henry Kissinger apparently met with the Canadian minister of external affairs, and President Carter and Prime Minister Pierre Elliot Trudeau reportedly discussed the case at two meetings. Canada attempted to keep the issue on a purely political plane, representing the case as a violation of its sovereign right to conduct trade as it wished rather than a legitimate inquiry under U.S. law into the possibly criminal behavior of a U.S. company. The State Department, too, was known to be horrified by the investigation. Justice Department lawyers knew very well what they were up against. In April 1978, the deputy assistant attorney general, Joe Sims, wrote, "To decide to bring a prosecution creates a possibility that we will have an interagency confrontation with other parts of our Government, including State." He added, "Given the merits here, that is a fight we might very well lose. In either event, the division's position as a relative 'untouchable' might be damaged and that could in the long run impair future enforcement efforts."[22]

Foreign opposition is not the only imposing obstacle the Antitrust Division faces in bringing a cartel case. *Domestic* political factors are often as important, especially when the cartel involves huge U.S. corporations whose support or hostility can make or break careers of government officials at home. The outstanding example, of course, is the oil industry. Ever since the first Standard Oil decision in 1911, the industry has compiled an amazing record of surviving antitrust cases, both domestic and international, practically unscathed. The dismal story of the only major oil cartel case filed in this country* has already been recounted in Chapter 4. It is necessary to add only that, to complement their financial power over elections, their hold on key senators and representatives, and their immense propaganda resources, the oil companies in the cartel case availed themselves of a special protective armor that has proved most useful ever

---

* An earlier case against twenty-two major oil firms, involving mostly domestic abuses, was settled in 1941 by meaningless consent decrees. And a 1973 complaint against eight majors, including all the Seven Sisters except BP, is apparently headed for a similar fate. The FTC staff originally argued that breakup of the firms was the best remedy for their pattern of "collusive actions." In 1980 the FTC backed away from that stand and proposed "conduct remedies" that would theoretically force the majors to operate more competitively. We find it improbable that the Reagan administration will prosecute the case vigorously.

since: the "national security" argument. Pointing out that they produced and controlled the nation's industrial lifeblood, the companies argued that to disclose any inconvenient information — about their secret arrangements in the Middle East, for example — would get them in trouble with host countries, which would be bad for the United States. The argument was devastatingly effective. "How can you try a case when your adversary keeps claiming that to reveal what you seek would violate the national security, especially when the court and the executive branch go along?" complained one lawyer who worked on the case.[23]

Even if a cartel case makes its way through the mine fields of domestic and foreign resistance and ends in a conviction, is it likely to have a substantial and lasting impact? In too many cases the answer is no. The penalties applied to violations of U.S. antitrust laws are usually so petty that the crime pays off whether or not the criminal is caught. Until 1974 the maximum fine for violating the Sherman Act was $50,000; in that year it was raised to $1 million, but even that figure often represents a tiny percentage of the extra profits earned through illegal practices. Only on the rarest occasions are executives convicted of felony violations; and, although the law provides for prison terms, they are almost never imposed.[24] The treble-damage provisions of the Sherman Act, under which plaintiffs in private antitrust suits may collect three times what they have lost because of illegal business practices, have proven innocuous because of the high cost and difficulty of proving the exact amount of losses. Even in the most open-and-shut cases the parties usually settle out of court for a fraction of the claim.

The light fines and rarity of prison sentences handed down in antitrust cases stem from the fact that the courts, like most other institutions in the United States, do not take white-collar crimes seriously. Many judges have shown open hostility to antitrust prosecutions, regarding them as stupid harassment of businessmen by means of antiquated and unrealistic laws.[25] The courts are largely responsible for the overwhelming recourse by defendants to nolo contendere pleas as a painless way of settling criminal cases. This greatly weakens the deterrent effect of antitrust laws because of various crucial differences between such a plea and a guilty plea or conviction. The first is that judges mete out milder penalties to defendants who plead nolo and thus do not require protracted trials. The second is that a nolo plea keeps evidence out of the court and thus out of the press. But perhaps most important is that a guilty plea constitutes prima facie evidence in any civil treble-damage suit that might arise, whereas a nolo contendere plea does not. In other words, the plaintiffs in a private suit against a company that has pleaded nolo contendere to antitrust offenses *must prove guilt all over again,* which is often very hard to do; the plaintiffs do not always have access to the evidence presented to the grand jury that brought the criminal indictment, nor do they have the government's broad subpoena and investigatory powers to develop the evidence. Justice Department prosecutors, well aware of these facts, often protect against nolo pleas and demand a full trial; but they are almost always overruled by judges.[26]

Finally, antitrust cases are often gutted by the Justice Department itself, usually by means of the consent decree. The great majority of cases brought by the Antitrust Division are civil suits seeking "to prevent and restrain" violations of the law, and they are ended by consent decrees in which the defendants, without admitting any past violations, agree not to commit any further breaches of the laws under which they were charged. This dubious exercise was lampooned by antitrust economist Richard Posner in a 1970 article:

> It is extremely common for the Department in price-fixing cases to obtain a decree that, stripped of the redundancies that are dear to lawyers, merely forbids further price fixing. Since the illegality of price fixing under the Sherman Act is well established, and directly punishable as a crime, the purpose of such an injunction is not immediately obvious.[27]

The Justice Department insists that consent decrees achieve the same effect as a conviction after trial but without the immense expenditures of time and money a trial requires. This claim can be challenged on a number of grounds. Consent decrees afford guilty firms the same advantages as nolo contendere pleas, including the fact that consent decrees cannot be used as prima facie evidence in private suits. And consent decrees tend to be unenforceable. The department at present cannot hope to keep track of whether companies are complying. There are more than a thousand operative consent decrees on file, whereas the Antitrust Division has only a handful of attorneys to monitor them.[28] Lacking any strict program to ensure that terms of the decree are met, the department and the public find themselves back where they started.

Laws do not hold back history, and the history of capitalist economies is the gradual self-destruction of competition and spread of market control. Small wonder, then, that the government legally entrusted with maintaining competition is divided against itself. Virtually all U.S. officials, elected and otherwise, praise the bracing virtues of competition and the benefits it has brought the country; yet those whose paeans to the competitive system are most passionate are also the greatest champions of the multinationals that have smothered it forever. And we cannot expect this political fact to change. As long as the great oligopolies dominate the American economy, the government will not wholeheartedly devote energy and resources to antitrust. To be sure, there does remain an antitrust constituency, enough resentment against overgrown corporate power to keep the

Antitrust Division in business — underfunded, understaffed, and under-standably timid, but still struggling. Today, however, the political tides are flowing against antitrust — witness the 1980 law sharply restricting the scope of FTC inquiries and subjecting its decisions to congressional review. In the foreseeable future, barring some cataclysmic transforming of public opinion, antitrust enforcement will continue to be what it has long been: a holding action against irreversible economic forces.

It is thus unlikely that the U.S. government will go far in pressuring other nations to halt cartelization, simply because it lacks the political will to do so. The TNCs and their divisions of world commerce are too well established and have too many powerful backers. Certainly the Justice Department is to be congratulated for reaching a few bilateral agreements on antitrust matters, which at least extend its holding action to the international arena. But the political weakness of antitrust within the United States is exacerbated when foreign affairs become involved. For similar reasons, we do not foresee the Justice Department turning more of its attention to restrictive practices in foreign commerce, as we believe it should. The connection between international cartels and American standards of living has not yet been widely grasped; so there is little political impulse for the Antitrust Division to begin the extremely difficult, costly, and lengthy work needed just to understand the subtler methods of cartels.

Yet, short of major new initiatives involving foreign commerce, there still is much that could be done at home. The antitrust laws need to be reformed and enforcement needs to be tightened. The Antitrust Procedures and Penalties Act of 1974 made some good changes, notably the increases in maximum fines, the increase in maximum jail sentences from one year to three, and the upgrading of a Sherman Act violation from a misdemeanor to a felony. (It is worth pausing to reflect on the fact that, until 1974, a burglar who stole a TV set had committed a felony, whereas an executive who directed a conspiracy whereby consumers were robbed of millions had committed a misdemeanor.) But many experts feel the 1974 law did not improve matters substantially. In fact, there is such dissatisfaction with the present state of affairs that further antitrust reforms are not a political pipedream.

What should the reforms be? Among the most pressing needs is to increase financial penalties for violations of the antitrust laws and to *make the fines vary to fit the crime.* The $1-million maximum fine now in effect may seem large, but it is hardly a compelling deterrent. In the North Atlantic shipping case, for example, seven firms were fined $5,450,000, the highest criminal antitrust penalty ever imposed. Yet the cartel had controlled a 60 percent share of the North Atlantic trade for five years, and every year the total freight billings on those routes amounted to $1 billion.[29] Even if the companies' collusion increased their take by only 1 percent, a ridiculously conservative estimate, the cartel scheme netted them

$30 million in extra profits, more than five times the fine. In such cases, the penalties should be linked to the firms' earnings. Elzinga and Breit, whose *The Antitrust Penalties* is one of the most comprehensive studies of the subject, recommend "antitrust violations be penalized by a mandatory fine of 25 percent of the firm's pretax profits for every year of anticompetitive activity."[30] Stiffer penalties for recidivists could also be instituted.

The question of prison sentences seems clear-cut as well: they should be serious and, more to the point, mandatory in some cases. Some experts argue that society does not benefit from incarcerating highly skilled businessmen whose productive capabilities are thereby wasted.[31] Others point out that it is hard to pinpoint responsibility for corporate crime; middle-level henchmen tend to be jailed while their bosses go free,[32] and prison terms in reality have no deterrent effect because of judges' notorious reluctance to jail upstanding members of the business community.[33] However, the latter objection would be disposed of were prison terms mandatory in cases when individuals had committed willful violations. The terms need not be so long that juries would hesitate to convict; the certainty of having to enter prison would be enough. This threat of the special disgrace that a stay in jail brings would have such a deterrent effect that society would reap benefits far outweighing the occasional social costs of incarcerating the criminals. As for the objection that high corporate officers remain invulnerable, the Ralph Nader Study Group on Antitrust Enforcement has suggested that a strong law be passed imposing criminal liability on individuals who know (or, we would add, should have known) about antitrust crimes but fail to stop or report them.[34]

The government's methods of settling most criminal and civil antitrust cases is also badly in need of reform. The law should be changed so that nolo contendere pleas would be prima facie evidence in private treble-damage suits. The entire consent decree process must be reexamined. The 1974 antitrust act takes a step toward making consent decrees less arbitrary; the Justice Department may no longer simply hand them down like an oracle, but must file a "public impact statement" describing the basic facts of the case, the reasons for which the particular remedy was chosen, and the alternative remedies considered. But the statements offer few details; so the public remains largely in the dark. More important, the decrees still are negotiated in secret, as part of a purely *administrative* process, shielded from public influence. Since consent decrees can shape the future of entire industries, this lack of public review means that the Justice Department is single-handedly making economic policy for the country.[35] Mark Green, in *The Closed Enterprise System,* advocates that all proposed consent decrees be subject to an adversary hearing under the auspices of the Federal Trade Commission. Interested parties could challenge any flaws they detected, after which "the consent decree, together with an FTC report suggesting modifications, would then be forwarded to the court."[36] Along with this valuable reform, defendants should be made to pay the costs of monitoring consent decrees and should submit periodic detailed reports on their compliance. In addition, the Justice Department should insist on clauses in most consent decrees allowing them to be used as prima facie evidence in private treble-damage suits.

On the other hand, more than a few experts think that private suits should be discarded altogether as an antitrust remedy. They argue that such suits clog the courts — more than 1000 per year were being filed in the early 1970s — and are so costly and cumbersome as to be a highly wasteful enforcement method.[37] Also, critics warn that many of the private suits are filed on purely spurious grounds by lawyers working on contingency fees. These lawyers, it is said, can force innocent firms to settle out of court because the firms, although convinced of the suit's spurious nature, cannot take even the slim chance that they would be convicted by a jury and slapped with stupendous treble damages.

We are not convinced, however, that the failings of private suits outweigh the benefits. Admittedly, the treble-damage figure is arbitrary (why not four times the amount? or ten?); granted, too, spurious suits are a real problem, and the upsurge of cases clogs the courts and makes the Antitrust Division's task more complicated. But deterrence is again our main concern. When Congress included the treble-damage provision in the Sherman Act, its goal was to give the private sector an incentive to enforce the antitrust laws so that both public and private energies would be engaged in maintaining competition. This remains a sound idea. Many more violations are likely to be detected if private parties have an interest in doing so than if government agencies, with their meager budgets, shoulder the burden alone. The treble-damage system will continue to be untidy and somewhat wasteful of time and money and will even produce the occasional bad decision, but we believe its deterrent effect to be strong and worth preserving. Certain reforms could at least mitigate its problems. For example, if plaintiffs were liable for hefty court costs in cases they lost, the number of spurious suits would certainly decline. Then, too, methods can be found to streamline antitrust cases. One proposal is to grant the opposing parties a fixed period before trial to agree upon a narrative of the basic facts of the case. The trial could then concentrate on the points in genuine dispute rather than lingering for weeks or months, as is now often done, over the presentation of facts that both sides agree to be true. The Nader study group suggests that, in cases in which the government has already proved a violation, triple damages immediately be assessed and placed in a special fund; private claimants would then simply have to show that they had been damaged rather than prove the violation all over again in a lengthy trial.[38]

Most of the reforms detailed above would have their main impact on purely domestic violations, of course. Cartel activity affecting the U.S.

market will not be eliminated until the Antitrust Division makes the decision and obtains the resources to pursue the international aspects of antitrust much more vigorously. But, insofar as enforcement of the antitrust laws within the United States becomes swifter, surer, and severer, the possible penalties for cartel activity might begin to offset the potential gains. The reforms, in short, would make the United States a much more risky place for cartels to operate.

The Patent System

The United States' defenses against cartels would also be strengthened by reform of another set of laws: the patent system. As long ago as 1931, William Meinhardt, who, as the founder of the Phoebus light bulb cartel, presumably knew whereof he spoke, wrote that carefully knit webs of patents and licenses formed the "cornerstone" of many international cartels.[39] The wave of anticartel reformers active in the years following World War II recognized this fact, and all felt that the patent system demanded revisions. But the postwar spread of antitrust legislation was not accompanied by any substantial changes in the West's approach to patent law; and the result, as we have shown, was that cartels resorted more and more to the camouflage provided by restrictive patent and license agreements.

In the United States, the government's power to issue patents and thereby grant inventors a legal monopoly for a fixed period of time (now seventeen years) is established by the Constitution. But neither that document nor the patent laws (the basic code was enacted in 1870 and revised in 1952) spell out the extent of the patentee's power under his patent rights. Therefore, since the passage of the Sherman Act in 1890, there has been constant tension between the patent and antitrust laws. On the one hand, patent laws grant the patent holder ill-defined rights to restrain trade — to dictate who can produce, use, and/or sell the invention and under what conditions. On the other hand, the antitrust laws, in equally vague language, prohibit virtually all restraints of trade. The result of this conflict has been endless legal skirmishing over what kinds of conditions patentees may impose when they grant licenses. Questionable conditions include a panoply of favorite cartel devices: minimum price resale provisions; territorial restrictions; import or export prohibitions; "grant-back" clauses (licensees must turn all improvements on the patent over to the patentee); "tie-in" clauses (licensees, as part of the agreement, pledge to buy goods not covered by the patent from the patentee); package licensing (licensees are forced to buy an entire block of patents rather than the specific ones they want); field-of-use restrictions (which limit the ways the licensee may use the patent); and certain forms of patent pools.

In the absence of legislation specifically governing these practices, the dilemmas they raise have had to be resolved by the courts. Over the years, U.S. court decisions have established that certain license restrictions, for example, minimum price resale, tie-in, and grant-back clauses, are nearly always illegal. But each case presents a new and often extremely complicated set of facts open to interpretation; courts can disagree, and the Supreme Court has been known to reverse itself. As long as the case-by-case approach is maintained, the limits of patent power will remain in flux.

They will also remain the subject of political controversy. There have been many attempts to pass laws stating more exactly what rights a patent entitles its holder to exercise, but all have failed because disagreement is so bitter and so much is at stake. Some experts, who might be called the "laissez-faire" group, argue for the legalization of most restrictions that patentees might include in licenses. In this view, tie-in clauses, territorial restrictions, grant-backs, field-of-use limits, resale price maintenance, and the like are perfectly legitimate means for patent holders to garner the maximum profit possible. Ward S. Bowman, Jr., in his book *Patent and Antitrust Law*, claims these restrictions even enhance society's economic efficiency because they increase the patentee's flexibility; with so many devices to choose from, he is free to grant a license on terms that perfectly fit the circumstances.[40] Thus most of the Justice Department's enforcement efforts in the patent field make little economic sense because they shackle patent holders and deprive society of the benefits of inventiveness.

We could not disagree more thoroughly. It is doubtful that strict antitrust enforcement would greatly weaken the patent incentive to invent, simply because the returns to the patentee would remain so substantial. To legalize the whole range of restrictive licenses is to invite wholesale cartelization by means of patent agreements.[41] Certain of the more extreme restrictions, such as resale price maintenance and output limitations, should be flatly banned by law. Companies should be barred from acquiring patents or exclusive licenses from another party when the acquisition would tend to give the firm a monopoly in the field. Field-of-use and territorial restrictions might be permitted, but only on condition that after one applicant has been granted a license, all further qualified applicants must be licensed on terms no more restrictive — this to prevent market division by granting only one license for each field or territory.[42]

But the single reform that we believe would be most effective in breaking the hold of cartels on technology is the general compulsory licensing of patents. Requiring a patent holder to grant licenses in certain circumstances is already common practice abroad; in fact, the United States is one of the few industrialized nations whose patent code does not provide for compulsory licensing when patent holders have not "worked" a patent for a certain number of years after it was granted. Compulsory licensing is not altogether a foreign concept; U.S. courts have often imposed it as part of the relief ordered in antitrust or patent misuse cases. But should the practice be greatly extended? Once a patentee has granted a license to anyone, should he be legally bound to grant one to other qualified applicants on equal or better terms? The notion is radical but not new; Stocking and Watkins advanced it in 1948.[43] More recently, Martin Adelman has argued that compulsory licensing should be required after *two* licenses have been granted voluntarily; this requirement would give patentees more flexibility, allowing them, for example, to choose to grant one exclusive license in cases when they were not equipped to work the patent but did not want it licensed widely.[44]

Not surprisingly, compulsory licensing is unpopular among members of the laissez-faire school. Some attack it as an unconstitutional violation of property rights,[45] others as an unwarranted and misguided scaling down of the rewards society must pay to spur invention. Bowman easily dismisses proposals for compulsory licensing of all patents because they have never found favor in Congress and focuses his attack on the only extensive use made of the device in this country: as relief in antitrust cases. He claims that in most cases such relief is inappropriate and poorly administered. Noting that companies convicted of antitrust violations are often ordered to license their patents at "reasonable" royalties, he observes that what is "reasonable" is often hard for the companies themselves to determine, let alone for government administrators who know little about the industry involved.[46]

None of these arguments withstands close examination. A patent is not exactly like any other piece of property; it is a special privilege granted by society — acting through Congress — to fulfill a specific social goal. The Constitution does not grant Americans the right to hold patents; it grants Congress the power to bestow the patent privilege, and therefore Congress has every right to define it, including the right to mandate licensing or to permit compulsory licensing as a remedy for abuse.[47] As for the claim that compulsory licensing would reduce the incentive to invent, it is mere conjecture, because the system has never been tried. There is no reason why it should shrink rewards to the inventor; licensees would still pay royalties. It may be true that the use of compulsory licenses as relief in antitrust cases has been ineffective and ill administered. But the same can be said about the entire antitrust apparatus. Should it be abandoned for that reason? The problem, as we noted earlier in this chapter, lies in a *political* stalemate: those who favor active antitrust efforts (including compulsory licensing) are strong enough politically to keep the idea alive; but those who detest antitrust are strong enough to keep it from working. It seems to us that compulsory licensing could be a first-rate antitrust remedy were more money and staff available for oversight; however, such increased support will have to await a shift in political tides.

The same point can be made concerning the only objection to compulsory licensing that strikes us as substantial: the difficulty of determining "reasonable" royalties and "qualified" licensees. Any sort of compulsory licensing system would be meaningless were patent holders free to demand prohibitive royalties or to reject applicants they considered unworthy. To prevent such sabotage, an arbitration system would be needed, and, given the requisite political support, one could certainly be created. In cases when the patent holder and applicant for a license could not agree on a royalty, or when the patentee felt the applicant was unqualified to work the patent, an arbitrator would be called in to settle the matter. Such arbitration should be performed by a specialized body set up to administer the patent system, similar in function to the National Labor Relations Board. Because of the complexities involved, some arbitrations would be time consuming, and the system as a whole would impose certain costs on society. These costs would be more than offset by the benefits from freer competition and broader access to technological advance. Compulsory licensing would also reduce the enormous waste of resources now expended on "inventing around" patents that already exist.

In the Third World, patent reforms are even more desperately needed than in the industrialized West. In fact, the patent system is such an important element in preserving the dominance of foreign enterprise that many development experts ask whether it would not be best to abolish it in the LDCs altogether.[48] In 1972, just 16 percent of the patents registered in LDCs were held by nationals of those countries; and an unknown number of those "nationals" were actually local corporations controlled by foreigners.[49] Even more significant, according to Surendra Patel, more than 90 percent of the foreign-owned patents in LDCs are "never used in production processes in those countries."[50] The purpose of the typical patent registered by a transnational firm abroad is to preempt the local market for imports. Even when the patents expire and theoretically enter the public domain, they are usually worthless, both because they have been superseded by more recent (foreign-owned) patents and because their descriptions of the patented inventions are often incomplete.

The laws of many Third World countries provide for compulsory licensing upon failure to work a patent, but these provisions are usually modeled on the Paris Union Convention for the protection of industrial property, the basic international agreement governing patents. The Paris Convention provides that:

> An application for a compulsory license may not be made on the ground of failure to work or insufficient working before the expiration of a period of four years from the date of filing of the patent application or three years from the date of the grant of the patent, whichever period last expires; it shall be refused if the patentee justifies his inaction by legitimate reasons.[51]

In practical terms, this provision means that the grant of compulsory licenses is usually delayed so long that the patent is useless by the time the grant is made. For that reason, says Constantine Vaitsos, compulsory licensing as a means for transfer of technology to the Third World is a "myth."[52] We have already seen how the same licensing restrictions that are usually ruled illegal in the United States are frequently employed by transnationals in Third World countries.[53]

One way to turn the patent system more to the Third World's advantage would be for LDCs to reject the "principle of equality of treatment" under which foreigners are granted the same patent rights as nationals. Peter O'Brien and others believe that LDCs, if they choose to have a patent system at all, should place strict limits on the patent power granted to foreigners, while allowing nationals greater rights and rewards in order to encourage local invention.[54] Another step, already taken by India, would be to establish that patents are not meant to grant a monopoly for *imports* but only for local production; this provision, however, to be meaningful must be supplemented by an effective program of compulsory licensing for nonworked patents. Brazil and the countries of the Andean Common Market, among others, have begun to review international licensing agreements with an eye to vetos of onerous restrictive provisions.[55] Still another measure would be to subject *all* patents in the Third World to immediate compulsory licensing from the date of the grant. But these measures would require renunciation of the Paris Union Convention; and, although that agreement probably causes more harm than good to the developing countries, most are not prepared for so radical a move.[56]

The Tyranny of Information

"If knowledge is power, ignorance is impotence," write Barnet and Muller.[57] The controversy over patent reform, when reduced to its essence, is a battle over information — and the same can be said of many other reforms discussed in this chapter. In fact, for several reasons we believe that the single most important element in any program to control or eliminate private cartels will be *increased access to information in all its forms*. First, information itself, in the shape of technology, know-how, and knowledge of markets and resources, is increasingly becoming the basic product of modern industry. As boundaries between markets break down and the world evolves toward an integrated commercial system, the *processing* of information — the ability to acquire accurate data and transfer them quickly from one corner of the globe to another — becomes ever more critical to business success. On the global level nations should cooperate to gather and release data on business practices that affect trade between them — and chief among such practices are cartel schemes. Earlier in this chapter we noted the lamentable fact that most developed countries do not even require registration of "pure" export cartels, those which theoretically have no effect on the home market. This stance involves an absurd double standard, of course. It amounts to saying that it is permissible, even laudable, for firms to commit business depredations abroad that would be illegal at home; thus it invites retaliation in kind from trading partners. The same sort of beggar-thy-neighbor policy is evident when nations refuse to supply commercial information requested by another nation in the course of an investigation. There is simply no legitimate reason why countries and firms whose economic health is affected by cartels should not be privy to all the facts about them. If export cartels are to be permitted — and we believe they should not be — they should *all* be required to register, and the registers should be open to the public, along with full details of the cartels' business.

The UNCTAD Secretariat suggested in a 1975 report that not only cartel agreements but certain practices of "dominant firms" should be disclosed to the public.[58] The report observes that TNCs sometimes do not need cartel connections to restrict competition unfairly, particularly in the Third World; they can do so single-handedly, and therefore the public ought to know whenever dominant firms employ methods that invite abuses, such as rebates, tied sales, price leadership, exclusive dealerships, ownership or control of distributors, retailers, or competitors, and mergers or takeovers in foreign countries. Registration of such practices could take place on the national or international level, the important thing being that the public have access to the data. The UNCTAD proposal is valuable, although it omits one crucial matter: agreements covering transfer of technology. Given the central role of patent and know-how licenses in modern schemes of market control, all licensing agreements between two or more firms of different nationalities should be recorded by an international agency and should be open to inspection. A central, computerized file of this nature would make it easy to find patterns of patent licensing that suggest cartelization.

Consumers in the developed countries undoubtedly would benefit from these reforms, but it is in the Third World that they would make an enormous difference. Poor countries today, when negotiating with TNCs over the terms of investment, are crippled by ignorance of how the corporations operate the deals they may have struck with other nations. During the last decade the LDCs have become aware of this disadvantage and have worked to change it, but progress has been slow and will remain slow until at least some of the developed Western nations — and the United States in particular — take the courageous step of demanding disclosure within their national borders.

From modest beginnings, the sovereign corporation in the United States has become a legal Frankenstein monster, seizing rights indiscriminately, among them the "right" to keep corporate information secret from shareholders, competitors, the government, and the public. But this "right" is utterly spurious.[59] Since the creator of corporations is the public, corporate privacy is the public's to give and the public's to take away. There may have been a period, 150 years ago perhaps, when private corporations controlled a small enough part of the nation's economy that corporate secrecy could be tolerated as a reasonable price to pay for encouraging investment. But today, when the 200 largest industrial firms account for three-fifths of the country's industrial assets, the price is much too high.[60] Firms of such size and power can hardly be regarded as private; they are subsidized by the state in dozens of ways, and their decisions have profound social impact — on employment, pollution, use of resources, race and sex relations, foreign affairs, and so on. For this reason some reformers advocate the public election of officers and directors of huge firms. Even without going that far, though, society at least should be able to *evaluate* the inherently social decisions made by the corporations it has created. To that end, the public must have access to the information corporations guard so jealously.

The corporations, besides claiming a "right" to secrecy, also resist disclosures with panicky protestations that it would expose them to mortal harm from competitors. It is hard to see why this would be so. Disclosure laws obviously would apply to *all* corporations above a certain size so that none would gain an unfair advantage; certainly the conditions and probably the methods of competition would change, but they would change in the same way for all. In fact, competition would probably intensify (which may be precisely what the great firms fear) were companies able to find out more quickly what their opponents were doing.[61] Also, corporations expend considerable energy in spying on each other to steal the very data we are suggesting should be made public. As economist Robert Heilbroner puts it, "I suspect that most of the great firms know much more about each other than the public knows, either as consumer or as government."[62] Thus the reason for corporate horror at proposals for more disclosure may not be so much because of what *competitors* might learn, but what the *public* might find out — and what an informed public might do.

Perhaps the most important information that needs to be made public would be data on ownership. One of the most astounding aspects of today's United States is that no one, not even the government, can obtain the information necessary to answer the most basic of economic questions: Who owns and controls the nation's industrial and financial assets? The true shape of the economy remains a mystery, and fundamental economic policies — in particular, the tax structure and antitrust policy — are based on crude guesses and misunderstandings. Yet repeated attempts, both public and private, to learn more about who owns what have been stymied, largely because of inadequate disclosure laws and the multitude of means to conceal stock ownership. True, the SEC did tighten its disclosure requirements somewhat in 1979. A publicly held corporation must now reveal if any of its officers, directors, or shareholders own 5 percent or more of any class of stock. (A holding of 5 percent of a large corporation whose stock is widely dispersed is often enough to control the firm.)[63] Major institutional investors — banks, insurance companies, mutual funds, and the like — have to report all holdings of securities of public companies registered in the United States. Institutions must also reveal the extent of their power to trade and vote the stock they hold, thus indicating whether they are simply acting as agents for someone else. And individual investors must report when they acquire 5 percent or more of any class of stock in a publicly traded company and reveal any changes in their holdings above that amount.

These provisions are an improvement upon lax rules of a few years ago, but they are still so riddled with loopholes that it is impossible to learn who really owns the great firms. The most obvious way to conceal a large interest, of course, is to disperse the stock among various "owners of record" so that no one person appears to surpass the 5 percent limit and therefore no disclosure is necessary. A single family might own 30 percent of a firm's stock, but if the holdings are divided among a dozen individuals, none with 5 percent or more, the family's entire interest may remain secret. And investors may still hide behind a bewildering array of front organizations, "nominee owners," and legal representatives — often four or five layers of such camouflage are employed — who report stock ownership in their names, shielding the true owner.

The recent SEC reforms, then, do not go far enough. The 5 percent disclosure threshold is much too high; it should be reduced to 1 percent for all classes of investors. The Nader report urges that corporations also name the one hundred largest stockholders of each type of security.[64] The SEC, along with the other federal agencies that demand some degree of disclosure from the firms in the industries they regulate — that is, the Interstate Commerce Commission (ground transport), the Federal Communications Commission (broadcasting), and the Civil Aeronautics Board (commercial aviation) — should adopt far more stringent measures to discover who stands behind "owners of record." At each level of corporate camouflage, the apparent owner of stock should be required to state whether he or she has full powers to trade and vote the holdings and, if not, who does. Even with the likelihood that ingenious corporate lawyers and accountants would devise new methods of concealment, such reforms would greatly expand the public's knowledge of who owns America.

Along with information on ownership must also come revelations of what goes on *within* firms. Several kinds of internal corporate data now regarded as privileged should be placed in the public domain. Among them are the books and tax returns of transnational corporations. Most TNCs keep various sets of books, each presenting a different picture of reality and each designed for a different audience.[65] In the United States, firms may report one set of profit figures to the IRS and a different one to stockholders, an absurd practice. Public access to all sets of accounts would eliminate this important source of corporate mystification. And access to tax returns would allow the public to know much more about the resources corporations own, what they paid for them, how they raised the money, and how the resources are being used. Finally, the government should receive much more complete information on financial dealings between parent firms and their subsidiaries in foreign countries. We have already indicated how transfer pricing can obscure the true flow of funds within a transnational corporation, with serious effects on the U.S. balance of payments and on the amount of tax collected from TNCs. Laws and regulations now exist theoretically enabling the IRS to ferret out cases of transfer pricing, but the agency has never had enough trained staff to tackle the forbidding complexities involved.[66]

Another vital area of corporate disclosure, one that has long been pursued by the FTC and is directly relevant to the exposure of cartels is "line of business" reporting. An ever larger share of the nation's commerce is in the hands of conglomerate firms, each one composed of hundreds of subsidiaries selling hundreds of disparate products. The classic example of a conglomerate, ITT, in 1980 owned some 250 principal divisions and subsidiaries. The firm was a major marketer of such varied products as telecommunications equipment, baked goods, insurance, car rentals, manmade fibers, and defense and space technology — to name just a few. The meager financial information that firms such as ITT do disclose today is virtually indecipherable; revenues from utterly different products are lumped together to conceal which of the firm's lines of business are profitable and which are not. Such knowledge is of vital interest not only to investors but also to labor unions, economists, and public policy makers. As it is, these groups have only the vaguest idea of what revenues are being generated and what profits made in specific product lines of the economy — facts that would be immensely important to antitrust investigators, for example, who might be alerted to the existence of cartels if extraordinarily high profits were being earned in similar product lines by a number of supposedly competing companies.

Since the 1950s the FTC has tried to persuade Congress of the need for a meaningful line-of-business reporting system.[67] Congress has resisted, however, largely because of ferocious lobbying from the corporate community, which advances the predictable objections: divulging financial details of product lines would aid competitors; the paperwork would be onerous; the companies themselves don't compile the information; such data are "proprietary." In the mid-1970s the FTC finally did win approval

for a modest line-of-business reporting system for the 500 largest manufacturing corporations, and the proposed system survived years of court
challenges from recalcitrant firms. But the annual reports are inadequate.
First, they should cover more firms, at least the 1000 largest. Second the
FTC should not treat the data as strictly confidential. So sensitive is the
commission to the corporate penchant for privacy that at present the
public still cannot learn the details of any one firm's performance in any
particular line of business, or even the aggregate for all firms in that line.
Finally, as the Nader group pointed out in 1976 — and their point is even
more apt today — the FTC's definitions of "lines of business" are based on
the outdated Standard Industrial Classification (SIC) system used by the
Census Bureau.[68] The SIC categories are so broad and antiquated that a
reporting system based on them becomes more misleading every year. The
SIC should be reformulated.

One final note. No program of corporate disclosure, regardless how
modest or ambitious, will be of any use unless it is accompanied by major
reforms of accounting practices. Despite a series of scandals in the early
1970s and two highly critical congressional reports, the accounting profession remains largely self-regulating — which in practice means very
loosely regulated indeed.[69] Statements of a corporation's financial condition are not supposed to be approved by an accountant unless they conform to "generally accepted accounting principles," a phrase that has
been described as being "about as restrictive as jello."[70] Because a firm's
accountants and accounting techniques are selected by management and
because notions of "generally accepted" practice seem to expand inexora-
bly, firms today use accounting as financial sleight-of-hand to produce
whatever results they want. The main goal of this practice, of course, is to
mislead stockholders and tax collectors. But it also renders worthless any
data the public may pry from corporations simply because the accounting
techniques used by different corporations vary so widely that their data
cannot be compared. To remedy this situation, the authority to set "generally accepted accounting principles" should be taken away from the Financial Accounting Standards Board, a private group dominated by members of the "big eight" accounting firms and financially supported by the
same large companies whose accounting practices must be approved by
the board, and returned to the SEC, which abrogated its statutory authority over accounting in the 1930s. Also, the United States should adopt
an accounting code that would specify which practices are permissible
and would require all firms to adhere to them so that financial statements
would be comparable. Various European countries enjoy such a code, the
French one being probably the most effective.[71] That such an obvious reform was not adopted long ago is further testimony to the overwhelming
power of the corporate lobby in the United States.

Epilogue:
Transnational Politics

Is there in America a political constituency strong enough to break the cartels' power with a program of reforms such as we have proposed? The obvious answer is no — at least not for the moment. No effective safeguards against cartel practices will be put into place by the international community in the foreseeable future; and reforms on the national level will come step by step, haltingly, at a different pace in each country. The latter circumstance allows businessmen to argue against every proposed reform, be it a ban on export cartels, a requirement for more financial disclosure, or a mandate for better antitrust enforcement, by angrily claiming that the main beneficiaries would be competing foreign firms that do not labor under such draconian regulations. We have noted instances when this argument has been used to great effect in the United States, and legislators abroad are equally sensitive to it (see Chapters 4 and 7). Nor would we deny that in occasional cases the claim has substance. A country that moves ahead of others in demanding socially responsible behavior from its corporations may sacrifice some competitive edge in the process. Witness the current cries of woe from American businessmen who are forbidden by the 1977 Foreign Corrupt Practices Act to be as free with bribes to foreign officials as their European or Japanese counterparts. Clandestine aspects of the issue make it impossible to learn how much business the Americans have really lost, but Justice Department waivers granted to businesses that wish to bribe have already gutted the law.[1]

Tensions between the need for greater control over huge firms and the fear of abetting foreign competitors will never entirely lift, but the fear is certainly exaggerated. We believe that one nation's ability to take advantage of another's stricter regulations will steadily be reduced by a subtle change now taking place around the world, a process that mirrors the rise of the transnationals themselves: the transnationalization of politics.

As the TNCs gradually transform the world into one integrated market, they are also bringing into being a single, world-wide political arena. The process is in its early stages, and as usual the political transformation lags behind the economic; thus far, the EEC is the only case in which the intertwining of national economies has been reflected to an impressive degree by formal political links. But, as the global firms tie more economic sectors of more countries into an ever denser web of commerce, political connections naturally multiply as well, so that political tremors are quickly transmitted from one place to another. Upheavals, movements, mere ideas rarely occur in isolation today; rather, they win adherents or produce imitators elsewhere almost immediately. Appropriately enough, there is no better evidence of this trend than the development of attitudes toward the global corporations that contributed so much to it. Fear and mistrust of the transnationals is a transnational phenomenon. In rich and poor countries alike, people are coming to understand that the TNCs powerfully affect their lives, whereas they have little power over the TNCs. In response, networks of opposition stretching across continents are being formed. We have already observed how new information about TNCs and new approaches to negotiating with them spread rapidly. Particularly in the Third World, innovative controls on TNC investment are soon passed on from one country to another. Even in the advanced countries this sort of interchange takes place. American antitrust principles have spread to Europe and Japan, especially influencing the laws of the EEC; and nations have changed their approach to specific restrictive business practices in response to studies by such groups as the OECD.

But reforms spring from political pressure, and pressure is generated by groups that feel their vital interests are at stake. Potentially, the constituency for the reforms we suggest is enormous. A number of groups have a direct interest in them: the millions of people who work for TNCs, or whose livelihoods otherwise depend on them; consumers of TNC products, which, in the developed countries, means virtually everyone; small and medium-sized businesses threatened by predatory competition; and even government officials, to the extent they are truly dedicated to public and not private ends. These interest groups transcend national boundaries. Americans, Italians, Japanese, Peruvians, Senegalese, and Malaysians all have similar interests in taming the TNCs, especially when it comes to cartel practices. True, there is some genuine divergence of interest between inhabitants of advanced countries and those in the Third World, the former often gaining from the exploitation of the latter. But there is also a basic transnational community of interest, of which this book, written by a Brazilian and an American, is one small expression.

The petroleum industry offers an excellent example of transnational politics at work. World trade in oil has been controlled by a cartel of TNCs for over fifty years, and international resentment of the Seven Sisters has been building for nearly as long. Probably no firms are so deeply hated in so many remote corners of the globe as the oil companies; it is commonly accepted everywhere that something is desperately wrong with the way the industry works and that part of the problem is that private companies cannot be trusted to look after the world's interests. Recently, of course — and happily for the oil companies — much opprobrium has shifted to the OPEC nations. But Anthony Sampson makes the fascinating point that *a major factor in OPEC's birth, survival, and later success was the battle against the Seven Sisters by citizens of their home countries:*

> It would be quite wrong, I think, for the Western nations to regard the change in the balance of oil power as a sudden new external threat to the essential Western civilization. For it is clear from the history of oil that much of the opposition to the companies, and the formation of OPEC, was the result of liberal tendencies within the United States and Europe, as much as the emergent nationalism in the Middle East and Latin America. The 1952 report by the Federal Trade Commission was the textbook for Arab technocrats to understand the Oil Cartel: the Labour Government's nationalizations in Britain were the cue for Dr. Mossadeq to nationalize Iranian oil, and thus increase the Middle East militancy. The anti-trust movement, which was both magnificent and muddled, effectively prevented long-term co-ordination between the companies and Washington . . . Thus OPEC, from the beginning, was armed with ammunition from liberals and trust-busters.[2]

Successful agitation for reform of the TNCs, heterogeneous as the "movement" is, will certainly be transnational in scope and results. Some writers, responding to the self-serving claims of the global firms to have grown beyond the outmoded confines of the nation-state, call for an aggressive assertion of national "sovereignty," but what they mean is that national governments should be the main *vehicles* for reform, which must actually take place globally.[3] And so, we are convinced, it will. Groups demanding change in one country will be echoed abroad; reforms achieved in one locale will be mirrored elsewhere. Again we stress that the process will be choppy and painfully slow. But we believe that, over time, this transnationalization of politics will render increasingly empty the complaint that reform in one nation will cripple its corporations and strengthen unfettered foreign competitors.

In the course of this struggle over the transnationals, reformers will have to evaluate two fundamentally different approaches to the organization of the world economy. One posits a reversal of the trend toward conglomeration and concentration. The huge firms that rule world trade today base their claim to social legitimacy on the efficiencies that stem from size: economies of scale, global division of labor, and highly centralized management of far-flung operations. But many experts, arguing that the pernicious effects of immense enterprises more than offset their vaunted efficiency, believe the best use of social and natural resources can only be made by scaling down economic units and decentralizing economic power. This argument might be broadly characterized as the "small is beautiful" approach; it takes many forms, but among its basic proposals are the following: breakup of transnational corporations; smaller units of production; local control (and perhaps ownership) of local industry; preservation of the family farm; more emphasis on self-sufficiency; and less emphasis on trade.[4] In the Third World, one expression of this outlook is the demand that local firms be shielded by protective tariffs so that domestic production and technology will flourish, even if the cost of producing something locally may often be much higher than importing it. In short, this view has it that the world economy should not be turned over to an ever smaller number of gigantic corporations, which will produce and distribute the goods we all desire cheaply and efficiently; rather, the economic apparatus should become more intimate, comprehensible, and democratic.

Other reformers see transnational enterprises as useful but would subject them to greater social control. Size, in this view, is not the problem; the global firms' claims of efficiency are accepted. The problem is accumulation of vast economic power in private hands — and very few hands at that — and its use for harmful ends. The task, then, is not to do away with TNCs but to democratize them. This might be done by turning them into full-fledged public enterprises, owned and operated by governments or international agencies, or by choosing top management by popular vote, or by creating some other mechanism for public review of TNC decisions. Short of such radical measures, many of the reforms urged in this book would allow the TNCs to retain their global reach but would prevent them from committing the more egregious abuses to which they are prone.

These two approaches do not exclude each other but rather offer alternatives that must be weighed. It seems likely that decentralization and small-scale enterprise will fit some economic sectors, whereas others will be served best by a new incarnation of the TNC. We recognize, of course, that the fate of global firms will be affected by debate over issues that are not in the purview of this book, including national economic planning, the proper balance between public and private enterprise, and the priority accorded such goals as full employment, the quality of the environment, and safety in the workplace.

Given the atmosphere that prevails in the early 1980s, it may be difficult to imagine major reforms of corporate practices ever taking place, at
least in the United States. The terms of political debate are being set by
the corporate community and its spokesmen in government. The country,
notoriously, is "moving to the right." Even politicians regarded as liberal
voice their enthusiasm for quashing or postponing reform and returning to
the invigorating ways of laissez faire. In part this trend seems a reaction to
the anticorporate sentiment that exploded during the 1960s and early
1970s, and the significant steps toward public oversight of private enterprise that were taken during that period. But, more deeply, the current
mood is one response to the increasingly obvious bankruptcy of Keynesian
economic policies in the face of stagflation. Corporate propagandists, taking excellent advantage of their opportunity, have gone far toward
convincing the country that the blame for stagflation lies largely with
those infamous "government regulations" on entrepreneurs who would
soon restore prosperity to the land if only they were freed from their
shackles.

We would not for a moment deny the importance of the fact that big
business has seized the political initiative in this manner; the United States
may have to suffer its effects for years to come. But we expect that when
the weakening of public regulation is followed, as it inevitably will be, by
the recrudescence of all the corporate outrages that provoked the controls
in the first place, the political pendulum will begin once more to swing in
the other direction. At that point, public opinion may heed the economists
who think that the basic cause of stagflation lies not in government controls but in the corporate structure, that is, in grotesquely concentrated
economic power, and the wholesale waste of resources that oligopoly capitalism encourages, particularly through massive spending on armaments.
In short, we believe that, when the falsity of the "government regulations"
bugaboo is exposed, serious discussion of controlling the giant corporations
will begin again.

When it does, the subject of cartels must be confronted. Cartels, of
course, are not *the* problem. They are a symptom of an underlying malady:
the progressive takeover of the capitalist world's economy by corporations
for whom oligopolistic practices are second nature. But that takeover
cannot be understood without understanding cartels; and it cannot be
halted, or even slowed, without dismantling the cartels. For it is collusion
among the great firms that enables them, if not to avoid competition
among themselves altogether, then at least to *manage* it, to keep it within
comfortable limits, so that their advantage over unprotected outsiders becomes overwhelming and the social benefits of a competitive system are
lost.

If the free market is a historical relic, it is imperative that we understand its passing and act accordingly. Our hope is that this book will aid the effort, not only by destroying the illusion that cartels vanished after World War II but also by suggesting that their private hold on the world economy need not be tolerated any longer.

Appendixes
Notes
Index

I. The IEA: Anatomy of a Cartel

Among the papers recently leaked from the cartel are its current Articles of Association.* The version dates from 1973, when the IEA, concerned that Great Britain's impending entry into the Common Market would cause the cartel problems because of the EEC's antitrust legislation, vacated its London offices. (The new location was a mystery until a reporter from *Le Monde* discovered the Lausanne headquarters in 1976.) Aside from new provisions for financing the organization, the 1973 articles hardly differ from those filed in 1945. Article 2 establishes the "object" of the IEA:

> To provide for and be a central medium for the acquisition of, and to circulate among its Members, information on all subjects and matters, and particularly such as related to the electrical manufacturing and contracting industries associated therewith, as may be calculated to interest or benefit or be to the advantage of the Association or its Members or any one or more of them or to further or promote their interests in exports.

In fact this description is strictly correct. It merely neglects to mention some rather important matters: precisely what type of information is exchanged, and what the members do with it.

In 1977 the IEA was made up of fifty-five members from twelve countries, each member belonging to one or more of ten product sections. The cartel also embraces, according to its basic agreement covering exports, each member's "associated companies and licensees insofar as it can control" them. The sections are as follows. (It should be noted that most of them are designated by the same letters as originally used in 1934.)

Section A	Steam Turbines
Section B	Steam Turbine Driven Generators
Section E	Water Turbine Driven Generators
Section F	Synchronous Condensers
Section G	Switchgear
Section H	Transformers
Section K	Rectifiers
Section P	Rolling Mill Equipment
Section T	Gas Turbine Generating Plant
Section W	Water Turbines

* All documents cited in this appendix are reprinted in U.S., Congress, House, Committee on Interstate and Foreign Commerce, Subcommittee on Oversight and Investigations, *International Electrical Association: A Continuing Cartel*, prepared by Barbara Epstein and Richard Newfarmer, 96th Cong., 2d sess., 1980.

The drop in the number of sections from at least sixteen in 1956 to ten in 1977 seems to have come about because the members of those sections resigned, although it is not clear why.

Certainly the most important new member in the cartel has been the Japanese. Until the mid-1960s Japanese exports of heavy electrical equipment were negligible. After that time, however, Japanese competition for world markets increased: between 1968 and 1970, for example, average annual Japanese exports of steam turbines were ten times what they had been during the period 1960–67. Similar growth took place for generators and steam hydraulic turbines, and, as the competition intensified, so did the European companies' desire to bring the Japanese into the IEA. They appear to have succeeded, although to an unknown degree, by 1968, which is the earliest date to which Japanese participation can be traced from the available documents. By 1970, Japanese firms were involved in six product sections, at least to the extent of keeping the IEA informed of inquiries and orders. In two sections, W and E (Water Turbines and Generators) they were also taking part in the program for dividing up orders among member firms.

According to IEA membership lists from 1977, six Japanese firms belong to the cartel: Hitachi Limited, Mitsubishi Electric Corp., Toshiba Shibaura Electric Co., Mitsubishi Heavy Industries, Fuji Electric Co., and Meidensha Electric Manufacturing Co. But Japanese membership is treated differently from that of the European firms. The Japanese members are designated in IEA communications by code letters rather than the numbers used for all other firms: Hitachi is "A," Mitsubishi Electric "B," and so on. The Japanese apparently do not attend annual general meetings. They have always paid membership and administrative fees on a different basis from the Europeans; at first the Japanese were billed at about half the European rate, but as their activity within the IEA has increased they have agreed (as of 1976, documents show) to contribute a flat 25 percent of the cartel's total budget. The purpose of this special treatment seems to be to promote the fiction that the Japanese do not really belong to the IEA. In a 1978 letter to the Japanese group, the secretary-general of the IEA, Derek Rose, remarked that the special dues arrangement "has the merit of establishing that you are not Members of the Association." The intended targets of this ploy, of course, are antitrust authorities. Japan's Antimonopoly Act of 1947 makes it illegal for firms to enter "into an international agreement or international arrangement which contain such matters as constitute unreasonable restraint of trade or unfair business practices."

Laws to the contrary notwithstanding, the members and especially the officers of the IEA seem to be highly solicitous of greater Japanese involvement in the cartel. Informed sources say that by the mid-1970s the secretary-general was making frequent trips to the Far East for discussions. The sources report that meetings took place in Manila, Singapore, and Tokyo; in the latter city talks lasted a full fifteen days during May 1978. In IEA code the representative of the Japanese group is always referred to as "Mr. Japan," who in 1973 is known to have been Dr. S. Matsuda, executive managing director of Mitsubishi Electric, and in 1978 was Mr. Katsuzo Nagai, senior executive managing director of Toshiba.

Aside from the somewhat equivocal status accorded the Japanese group, the administrative structure of the IEA is straightforward. Full powers are held by the association convened in general meeting, which happens once a year. Only the general meeting is empowered to alter the Articles of Association and make other fundamental decisions. The meeting elects the members of the Council, the IEA's governing body. The Council is responsible for important administrative matters, such as changes in the bylaws of the cartel or approval of new product sections. The Council also issues reports on market conditions in specific countries or regions and on threats from outsiders, such as the report on "competition from American Manufacturers" that was proposed at a Council meeting in 1973. Only "directors or other officers" of IEA firms may be elected to the Council, and in fact Council members tend to be from the highest levels of management, including presidents and board chairmen. This fact belies the IEA claim of being nothing more than a research organization. Top executives of large transnational corporations would hardly find it necessary to preside personally over the administration of such an agency.

Besides the general meeting and the Council, the IEA also conducts business through committees appointed by either body. Little is known about these committees, however, since available documents include no committee records. To an unknown extent the IEA seems to operate under a sort of federal system, that is, through national groups of manufacturers who thrash out their own arrangements and then send designated representatives to IEA forums to negotiate with other national groups. In some cases these groups set up trade associations that serve to cartelize the home market and also form national export cartels that provide the actual link to the IEA.

The day-to-day business of the IEA is carried on by headquarters personnel in Lausanne, consisting of the secretary-general (at present an Englishman, Mr. Derek Rose), an assistant secretary, various engineers specializing in specific product sections, and clerical staff. The cartel's financial dealings are transacted through a complicated system of accounts in Swiss banks. Fees levied on members fund the cartel administration. As of 1977, members paid an annual subscription fee of 2000 Swiss francs for each product section they belonged to; but this did not fully cover the cartel's budget. The remaining portion was financed by billing members on a pro rata basis, according to their share of IEA business during the preceding three years. From 1975 through 1977, for example, Brown Boveri's share of the orders handled by all the IEA sections to which the firm belonged was 22.44 percent; Brown Boveri thus was billed for 22.44 percent of the cartel's 1978 budget, net of subscription fees. Other European members' shares for the same period are as follows:

Kraftwerk Union	15.55%
Alsthom	8.47
General Electric (British)	7.60
Siemens	5.80
AEG	4.36
ASEA	4.19
4 firms	2–3
8 firms	1–2
30 firms	under 1

The Japanese group, as noted above, was billed on a different basis, paying a flat 25 percent of the cartel's budget.

*   *   *

The framework of the IEA is contained in two binding contractual agreements to which all members subscribe: the Export Notification Agreement (code name "Agreement X") and the Tendering and Contracting Agreement, or TCA (see Appendix IV). These accords set out the basic procedures by which the cartel operates, and they rarely change. To this framework is attached a superstructure that is constantly being remodeled: the agreements covering specific product sections. Because the market for each product presents unique problems, and because each section has a different set of member firms, the members themselves hammer out the section accords and revise them as changing circumstances dictate. The three elements most commonly found in the section contracts are price fixing, allocation of orders (usually based on a system of rigged bidding), and compensation payments, but each section uses a different mix.

The original dates of the agreements are difficult to determine; in most cases available documents offer only the most recent versions. But the documents do show that most of them have been in force for at least fifteen to twenty years and that some probably date back further. For example, the earliest date that can be established for the existence of Agreement X, the Export Notification Agreement, is October 1962. But a comparison of the "definitions" contained in the 1962 accord with the original INCA agreements of 1930 reveals close similarities (see Appendix III). The current version of the TCA is the "Fourth Issue," and is known to have been in effect in 1970; an earlier version was operative in 1963, but when the TCA was first drawn up is not known. Some of the annex agreements can be dated to the late 1950s, and the 1957 British Monopolies Commission report suggests that they existed prior to that date, although perhaps in different form. Generally speaking, IEA agreements seem to remain in force indefinitely, until changing market conditions, shifts in cartel membership, or new cartel strategies cause them to be revised. The latest versions were in effect in 1979, and there is every reason to presume that they remain operative today.

The essence of the IEA is contained in Agreement X, which prescribes the very measure that IEA officials publicly assert is the sole function of the cartel: the exchange of information. It might seem unimportant that competing companies should notify each other of bids solicited and orders accepted, but in fact such notification revolutionizes the trade in question. It allows all firms to know what the others are doing and to gauge the precise level of demand, thus sharply reducing the pressures to compete vigorously; and it often serves as the foundation for more complicated collusions. For that reason notification was the basic principle of the INCA in 1930, and it remains so for the cartel today.

Clause 9 of Agreement X provides that the IEA secretary must be informed "if a member receives an enquiry or forms an intention to submit a tender." Upon notification, the "Secretary shall immediately advise all Members who have notified of that enquiry." Thus only members who have been invited to bid are advised of the others in contention. To comply with Clause 9, the member fills out a "notification card" and sends it to IEA headquarters, which reportedly receives some 2000 cards annually. Members are also required to inform the secretary of the orders they receive, and notice of the orders is passed on to "every notifying member." Whenever members learn of orders won by nonmembers, they are also required to report. The secretary compiles all this information and sends each member of each section a quarterly list of orders received by members and nonmembers.

The purpose of the IEA notification program, of course, is to enable members to meet before tenders are submitted and decide how to handle the order. The goal is to arrive at what the cartel calls an "arrangement" — an agreement on who is to get the order, and at what price. The contract that sets out the basic procedures for arriving at "arrangements" is the Tendering and Contracting Agreement. Under the heading "General Rules," the TCA describes how meetings are to be organized, negotiations conducted, and disputes resolved. It also establishes what pressures may be brought to bear on recalcitrant members and what penalties imposed if cartel etiquette is seriously violated. Under a section titled "Commercial Rules," the TCA commits the members to reach agreement concerning the complex terms of trade involved in the sale of heavy electrical equipment, thus avoiding competition in the realms of guarantees, service, replacement of defective parts, payment schedules, liability, arbitration, and other matters.

Having agreed to abide by these general procedures, the members of each section detail in the annexes (and sometimes in additional Special Agreements) exactly what products will be covered, and what techniques will best suit the market for those products. Pricing agreements are used by almost every section. The most common approach is to establish a reference price list that fixes the minimum price at which the members agree a specific product *should* be sold, in normal circumstances. For example, the Price Memorandum governing Sections A and B (steam turbines and steam turbine generators) reads: "Any party . . . shall . . . quote not lower than the price determined from and in accordance with the Price and Heat Consumption Manual multiplied by the factor stated in Appendix 1 hereto." Members who wish to bid lower than the agreed price must inform the secretary, who in turn tells the other firms bidding on the order. Reductions of more than 10 percent below the reference price are forbidden except by unanimous consent. Naturally, the basic price schedules must be recalculated frequently to keep up with changing conditions in the industry. Documents show that between May 1973 and May 1977, at least six meetings of a special committee of Section A and B members were held to discuss the price manual and reference price lists. Four of these meetings, in late 1976 and early 1977, involved negotiations between the European and Japanese groups in the sections.

Of course, whenever possible the members of the cartel prefer to sell at prices *above* the minimum, and to that end they negotiate "arrangements." Each section has its own system for doing so, but they do not differ greatly. In a typical case, after all the firms concerned with a certain order have been notified of the other prospective bidders, the secretary himself may suggest an "arrangement," that is, the price level he thinks appropriate. If all the bidders agree, no further work is necessary. If there are complications, the secretary calls a meeting at which the details of the "arrangement" are hammered out. The purpose of the meeting is to set prices as high as possible but not so high that cartel members will lose the order. Certain circumstances, however, may justify prices even lower than the reference price; the agreement covering Section E, for example, allows for cases "where an arrangement is concluded . . . and the tendering parties unanimously agree that [lower] prices . . . may be offered due to outside competition."

But pricing agreements would frequently break down if some members felt others were getting an unfair share of orders; thus the need for allocation schemes. Half of the ten IEA product sections are known to have formal programs for allocation of orders, but available documents only give full details for two, E and P. The two are similar, but the former being slightly less complicated, it may serve as an example.

On July 1, 1970, the members of Section E entered into Agreement A(E)-70, "A" meaning allocation, "(E)" referrring to the section, and "70" to the year of the accord. The agreement determined what share of the total business would go to each member and also the sequence in which they would initially allocate orders, as follows:

	Percent of Business	Initial Allocation Sequence
AEG–Telefunken	8.00	8
Brown Boveri	13.50	9
GEC–English Electric	9.00	7
Siemens	21.25	2
ASEA	21.25	5
Alsthom	13.00	4
Elin–Union	4.77	6
ASGEN	3.63	3
Marelli	2.74	10
Jeumont–Schneider	2.86	1

Thus, when members of the section are invited to tender for an order, they meet to determine which shall be designated the "winner" — the member selected to receive the order. For the first series of allocations, the selection simply follows the predetermined sequence listed above. The "winner" is granted the right to make the lowest bid, and, once that firm has announced what the bid will be, the others must bid higher: "Basic prices for all other parties shall be at such percentage or percentages in excess of the allotee's basic price as may be agreed but in no case shall this excess be less than 7.5 percent."

However, after the initial allocation sequence has been run through, the selection of winners becomes more tricky. At that point, the secretary must calculate which member is due to receive the next order by means of a formula that involves both the total value of orders accumulated to that date by each member as well as the share of the total business allotted to each. For example, the secretary might find that Marelli had the lowest total value of orders accumulated, but, Marelli's agreed share of the business being small, the next order might still be awarded to Siemens, whose share is much larger.

Obviously, the market shares allotted to each firm are a matter of paramount importance, and one can surmise that they are the subject of heated and periodic negotiations. Unfortunately, IEA documents reveal very little about the process whereby shares are fixed. Probably the central factor is the market share each firm *already* possesses when it joins the cartel and whether it expects to grow substantially or not. A firm that develops new technology, giving its product a strong competitive advantage, would be expected to demand a larger share on that basis. Other factors that might upset the balance of power are levels of investment by each firm for particular products, and slumps or booms in each firm's general economic strength. Underlying all negotiations over market share is the threat that dissatisfied members will quit the cartel; so any firm's bargaining position, to some degree, rests on the damage it could do as an "outsider." And, of course, the entry of new firms into the cartel requires a redistribution of shares. A hint of such conflict comes from the minutes of an IEA Council meeting in Switzerland on October 19, 1973. Apparently the European members had begun negotiations with the Japanese over market shares for hydroplant in 1971, but by 1973 there was discord over the allocation agreements in Sections E and W (water turbines and generators):

> The Japanese had been pleased. However, amongst the Europeans there was not such satisfaction. There had been discussions over the previous six months regarding a replacement for the Allocation Agreements. In the case of Section E, support had been nearly achieved for a further Allocation Agreement. In Section W, the Europeans wanted an automatic pool scheme, which the Japanese had accepted on principle. There was to be a meeting in Lausanne in the next week of a committee from Section W.

Precisely how the problems were resolved is not known, but documents mention two new price and allocation agreements for Sections E and W that were finally concluded in 1973 or 1974.

Rounding out the melange of restrictive practices used by most IEA sections are compensation arrangements. Seven of the ten sections use some form of compensation, whose purpose is to offset the costs of preparing bids. The complexity of heavy electrical equipment is such that simply to draw up designs and estimates in response to an invitation to bid can be a very expensive process, ranging from $20,000 to $80,000, depending on the product and size of the order. Cartel members, having themselves already selected the "winning" firm, naturally would be reluctant to spend such sums on bids they knew to be futile; yet the appearance of competition must be maintained for the cartel to operate successfully. Therefore, the winning member usually pays a fee, based on the price of the order, which is distributed equally among the other bidding members to reimburse them. In Section E, 2 percent of the order price must be paid as compensation. (Interestingly, before the entry of the Japanese, Section E compensation payments were suspended whenever Japanese firms were known to be bidding, in order to make the cartel members' bids more competitive.) The compensation fee for Section H was formerly fixed at 7 percent of the reference price, although whether that level still pertains is not known; in Section P it is only 1 percent.

As might be imagined, the task of accounting for the cross-currents of compensation payments among members is sizable. A "Balancing and Settlement Scheme," in effect since 1958 (it had another name until revision in 1977), spells out the procedure in great detail. During the course of the year, each time a member wins an order, the IEA secretary informs that member of whatever amount may be due under compensation and pooling provisions. The member pays that amount into a special account maintained for the purpose. Then, at the end of the year, the secretary determines how much each member owes to every other member, and payments are shuffled among the accounts until all debts are settled. The sums involved in these transactions are, as the secretary remarked in a letter, "very substantial." It is not uncommon for payments of 50 million Swiss francs (about $30 million) to pass through the IEA's coffers in a year — and that figure includes only *international* settlements, calculated after accounts have already been settled among members of the same country.

One final fact should be noted about the IEA agreements: they have a tendency to become more restrictive as time passes. Agreements are elaborated in ever greater detail, and attempts are made to extend cartel control over more and more aspects of the trade. This can be observed through the history of certain IEA sections for which relatively complete documentation is available. For example, Section H, transformers, resembles other sections in that it flourished during the 1930s, went into decline after the war, and then regained strength in the 1950s. In 1959 its members signed Agreement P(H), which established a method for calculating reference prices and committed the members to pay 7 percent of each order into a pool to compensate others for the costs of bidding (except when outside competition threatened, in which case the fee was reduced to 2 percent). By 1965, P(H) had been replaced by Agreement P(H)C, which added to the above measures a system of stiff fines upon members who took orders below the reference price. By the early 1970s, according to sources within the cartel, P(H)C had been supplemented by an allocation scheme complete with fixed market quotas. Yet even these agreements apparently were not sufficient, for in the mid-1970s came the so-called H Procedure, governing the sale of particularly large transformers. This accord spells out the protocol for convening a meeting of prospective bidders, polling the members as to whether they would accept an arrangement, and then applying pressure on any who appear reluctant. The fact that Section H found it necessary to institute a special procedure for large transformers suggests that there may have been sharp disagreement over these lucrative orders — disagreement that could only be contained by tighter controls.

II. Membership in the IEA, by Country, 1936/38 and 1977

Company Name	IEA Code	1936/38	1977
Germany			
AEG	1	X	X
Siemens	8	X	X
J. M. Voith–Heidenheim & St. Poelten	41	X	
J. M. Voith–Heidenheim	41		X
Maschinenfabrik Augsburg–Nurnberg (MAN)	18	X	X
Kraftwerk Union	9		X
Transformatoren Union	7		X
Demag	27	X	
Gutehoffnungshutte Oberhausen	28	X	
Switzerland			
Brown Boveri & Co.	3	X	X
Maschinenfabrik Oerlikon	15	X	(into 3)°
Escher Wyss Engineering	19	X	X
Bell Maschinenfabrik	35		X
Ateliers de Secheron	34		X
Sprecher & Schuh	33		X
Ateliers des Chamielle	42	X	
United Kingdom			
General Electric Co. Ltd.	5	X	X
English Electric Co.	4	X	(into 5)°
British Thomson–Houston	2	X	(into 5)°
Metropolitan–Vickers	7	X	(into 5)°
Hackbridge Electric Construction Co.	21	X	(into 5)°
Hewittic Electric Co.	24	X	(into 5)°
C. A. Parsons Co.	11	X	X
Bruce Peebles & Co. Ltd.	22	X	
Parsons–Peebles	22		X
A. Reyrolle & Co.	13	X	X
Ferranti	10	X	X
Ferguson Parlin	12	X	

Company Name	IEA Code	1936/38	1977
British Electric Transformer Co.	20	X	
Compton Parkinson	29	X	
British Electric Engineering	30	X	
Johnson & Phillips	49	X	
Foster Engineering Co. Ltd.	50	X	
Electric Furnace Co. Ltd.	51	X	
Boving–Karlstads	40	X	X
Walmsleys (Bury) Limited	53	X	
Vickers–Armstrong Limited	54	X	
Worthington Simpson Limited	55	X	
Bryce Limited	56	X	
The Mirrlees Watson Co. Ltd.	57	X	
Hick, Hargreaves & Co. Ltd.	58	X	
Hawker Siddeley	28		X
Bonar Long	89		X
Steatite & Porcelain Products	33	X	
John Brown Engineering	94		X
Sweden			
ASEA	14	X	X
Karlstads Mekaniska Werkstad	39		X
Nohab	64		X
Stal–Laval Turbin	23		X
France			
Société Générale d'Applications Electro–Thermique	52	X	
Société Générale de Constructions Électriques et Mécaniques (Alsthom)	16		X
Alsthom–Savoisienne	17		X
Compagnie Générale d'Électricité (Delle–Alsthom)	24		X
Creusot–Loire	44		X
Jeumont–Schneider	70		X
Merlin Gerin	26		X
Neyrpic	43		X
SOGET (Société Rateau)	25		X

Company Name	IEA Code	1936/38	1977
Italy			
AMN Impianti Termici et Nucleari	53		X
ANSALDO Societa Generale Elettromeccanica	47		X
Fiat Termomeccanica e Turbogas	95		X
Riva Calzoni	45		X
Franco Tosi	46		X
Turbotechnica	98		X
GIE	97		X
Italtrafo	88		X
Industrie Elettriche di Legnano	32		X
Magrini Galileo	82		X
Ercole Marelli	67		X
Austria			
Elin–Union AG für Elektrische Industrie	31		X
J. M. Voith (St. Poelten)	49	(see 41)	X
Netherlands			
Smit Transformatoren	83		X
Smit Slikkerveer	n.a.		X
Norway			
National Industri	81		X
Kvaerner Brug	48		X
Finland			
Oy Tampella	65		X
Canada			
Canadian Porcelain	31	X	
United States			
International General Electric	6	X	
Westinghouse Electric International	9	X	
Ingersoll Rand Co.	25	X	
Ohio Brass Co.	32	X	

Company Name	IEA Code	1936/38	1977
Country Unknown			
Erste Bruner Machinen Fabrika	17	X	
Japan			
Hitachi Limited	A		X
Mitsubishi Electric Corporation	B		X
Toshiba Shibaura Electric Co.			
Ltd.	C		X
Mitsubishi Heavy Industries Ltd.	D		X
Fuji Electric Co., Ltd.	E		X
Meidensha Electric Mfg. Com-			
pany Ltd.	F		X

* "Into" refers to merger with another member whose code number is indicated.
SOURCE: U.S., Congress, House, Committee on Interstate and Foreign Commerce, Subcommittee on Oversight and Investigation, *International Electrical Association: A Continuing Cartel,* prepared by Barbara Epstein and Richard Newfarmer, 96th Cong., 2d sess., 1980.

III. Agreement X

AN AGREEMENT made the 22nd day of October 1962 (which may be referred to as "the Export Notification Agreement" or "Agreement X") WHEREBY for itself, and for its associated companies and licensees in so far as it can control the same, each and every company whose name appears as a subscribing company in any annex hereto AGREES with all other companies whose names appear as subscribing companies in the same annex (referred to herein as "the said Annex") that it shall from the date hereof observe and be bound by the following provisions and such further provisions as may be contained in the said Annex.

1. DEFINITIONS.

   In this Agreement, which, where the context so requires, shall be construed as including the said Annex,

   (a) "Member" means any company whose name appears in the said Annex as a subscribing company;

   (b) "plant" means any machinery or apparatus stated in the said Annex to be subject matter of the Agreement;

   (c) "purchaser" means any person, other than a Member, who issues to a Member any enquiry or order for plant;

   (d) "enquiry" means any invitation, whether oral or written, issued by a purchaser to a Member to submit a tender for plant;

   (e) "notification" means submission to the Secretary of a notification card or other document in such form as may be prescribed from time to time by the Secretary, and "notify" shall be construed accordingly;

   (f) "notifying Member" means a Member who has notified an enquiry in accordance with this Agreement;

   (g) "tender" means any offer, whether submitted in any prescribed form or not, to supply plant;

   (h) "tendering Member" means a notifying Member who submits a tender which is not subsequently withdrawn;

   (j) "order" means a written notice of acceptance of a tender, written instructions to put work on plant in hand, or instructions in consequence of which work on plant is put in hand;

October 1962

258

(k) "the Secretary" means Mr. J. Skene Brown or such other person as the Members may appoint.

2. WITHDRAWAL.

A Member may withdraw from this Agreement on the thirty-first day of March, the thirtieth day of June, the thirtieth day of September or the thirty-first day of December in any year provided he shall have given to the Secretary at least twelve months' notice in writing of his intention. Upon receipt of any such notice the Secretary shall immediately advise the remaining Members and if, within thirty days of the date of such advice, any Member gives to the Secretary written notice of intention to withdraw such withdrawal may take place upon the same date as that of the Member first giving notice.

3. EXPULSION.

If any Member wilfully commits any breach of this Agreement or if, in the expressed opinion of all the other Members, his remaining a Member would be prejudicial to the successful operation of the Agreement the membership of that Member may by the unanimous decision of all the other Members be terminated at any time.

4. LIABILITY AFTER TERMINATION OF MEMBERSHIP.

Liabilities incurred or obligations assumed by a Member during membership of this Agreement, whether in respect of orders received or otherwise, shall continue thereafter until they are fully discharged or performed.

5. NEW MEMBERS.

Membership of this Agreement shall be confined to those who, being members of the section of the International Electrical Association Limited concerned with plant of the type stated in the said Annex to be subject matter of the Agreement, are admitted as Members, whether conditionally or unconditionally, by a resolution of not less than seventy-five per cent of the Members for the time being.

6. AMENDMENT OF THE AGREEMENT.

The Agreement may, on the application of any Member, be amended by the unanimous resolution of all the Members at any time provided the Secretary shall have given not less than thirty days' written notice of the proposed amendment.

October 1962

7. SUBJECT MATTER.

The machinery or apparatus forming the subject matter of the Agreement shall be that set out in Part I of the said Annex.

8. TERRITORY.

Th Agreement shall apply, subject to any provisions from time to time contained in the said Annex, to plant for use in the territories set out in Part II of the said Annex, and it shall be the duty of every Member, before submitting any tender, to take all reasonable steps to ascertain with certainty the territory in which the plant is intended to be used.

9. NOTIFICATION OF ENQUIRIES.

(a) If a Member receives an enquiry or forms an intention to submit a tender he shall immediately notify the Secretary thereof by means of a notification card provided for the purpose, and the Secretary shall immediately advise all Members who have notified that enquiry.

(b) The information given on the notification card shall be in accordance with the enquiry. If the required information is not stated in the enquiry or if the Member is free to decide the particulars of the plant to be offered, the information given on the notification card shall be the particulars of the plans to be offered. Any subsequent modification of the information given on any notification card shall immediately be notified to the Secretary.

(c) If, in the case of any particular transaction, a notifying Member requests the Secretary to inform him of the dates upon which each of the other notifying Members first submitted a notification the Secretary shall provide all notifying Members with such information.

(d) After there has elapsed from the date of the first notification of an enquiry such period as is specified in Part III of the said Annex the Secretary shall advise all Members that the notifications of that enquiry for the purpose of the Agreement are cancelled, and such advice shall be issued from time to time as Members may agree. After the receipt of such advice Members shall notify each enquiry with which they are then still actively concerned or with which they become actively concerned, and such enquiries shall for the purpose of the Agreement be treated as new enquiries.

October 1962

(e) If a Member decides either not to tender or to withdraw the tender or tenders submitted by him he shall immediately inform the Secretary of his decision and the Secretary shall advise all notifying Members accordingly.

(f) When an enquiry relates to machinery or apparatus below the limits set out in Part I of the said Annex but a Member nevertheless intends to tender for plant within those limits he shall, in accordance with this clause, notify the plant he intends to offer.

(g) When an enquiry relates to plant within the limits set out in Part I of the said Annex but a Member nevertheless intends to tender for machinery or apparatus below those limits he shall, in accordance with this clause, notify the machinery or apparatus he intends to offer.

10. REPORT OF ORDER.

(a) Immediately he receives an order a Member shall report the fact to the Secretary, giving such particulars as will enable the Secretary to complete the advice of order form as set out in Part IV of the said Annex and send a copy thereof to every notifying Member. A Member who has reported an order shall report to the Secretary any subsequent modification of the order which is material to the Agreement, and the Secretary shall advise all notifying Members accordingly.

(b) Should a Member receive information that an order has been placed with a non-Member he shall report the fact to the Secretary with such particulars as are in his possession, and, after receiving reasonable confirmation that the order has been so placed, the Secretary shall complete and despatch to every notifying Member an advice of order form such as is referred to in sub-clause 10(a) hereof.

11. MEETINGS.

For the purpose of considering matters of a general character arising out of the operation of this Agreement, a meeting of Members may be held at any time at the request of two or more Members or at the Secretary's discretion provided the Secretary shall have given reasonable notice of the time, date, place and subject for discussion.

October 1962

12. MEMBERS' DECISIONS

When, under the provisions of this Agreement, a Member is required to cast any vote or make any decision on any matter, the vote may be cast or the decision may be made either at a meeting of Members or by means of a postal communication addressed to the Secretary. In all such cases each Member shall have one vote and may vote by proxy.

13. ADMINISTRATION EXPENSES.

In order to provide for the expenses of administering the Agreement each Member shall pay to the International Electrical Association Limited the amounts set out in Part V of the said Annex.

14. ACCOUNTS AND REPORT.

The Secretary shall keep proper accounts regarding income and expenditure arising under the Agreement. The Secretary shall present to the Members, in the form set out in Part VI of the said Annex, quarterly reports of all business transacted under the Agreement.

15. INFORMATION.

The Agreement and all information, whether oral or written, coming to the knowledge of any Member or the Secretary with respect to any matter arising out of the operation of the Agreement shall be treated at all times as having been communicated in strict confidence and shall not be disclosed except so far as may properly be required by law.

16. ACCREDITED REPRESENTATIVES.

Every Member shall communicate to the Secretary the name of a person to act as that Member's accredited representative. Each such accredited representative or, in his absence, his duly appointed substitute, shall be empowered to bind his company at all meetings.

17. PERFORMANCE OF OBLIGATIONS.

(a) Should any Member or the Secretary be in doubt as to whether a Member has performed any of his obligations under the Agreement the Secretary shall be given all such documents and information as he may require for the purpose of resolving the doubt.

(b) If, after resolving the doubt as aforesaid, the Secretary considers that any Member has failed to perform any obligation

October 1962

under the Agreement he shall immediately direct the Member concerned to do whatever may be necessary to rectify the fault.

(c) If, within a reasonable time after the direction aforesaid, the Secretary is not satisfied that the Member concerned has performed the obligation the Secretary shall report the name of the Member and such facts as he may consider relevant,

(i) if the obligation relates to a particular enquiry, to all the tendering Members and subsequently to the next ensuing meeting of Members;

(ii) if the obligation does not relate to a particular enquiry, to the next ensuing meeting of Members.

18. INTERPRETATION.

In the interpretation of the Agreement the Secretary's decision, which he shall in all cases communicate to all Members without divulging particulars of any enquiry in relation to which the point may have been raised, shall, subject to the Conciliation Rules of the International Electrical Association Limited (which Rules shall be deemed to be incorporated in this Agreement), be binding.

October 1962

IV. The TCA

AN AGREEMENT dated the first day of July One thousand nine hundred and seventy (which may be referred to as "the Tendering and Contracting Agreement" or "T.C.A.") WHEREBY, for itself and for such other companies in so far as it has declared that it will exercise control over them in respect of tendering and contracting, each and every signatory (referred to herein as "Member") of any annex hereto AGREES with all other signatories of the same annex (referred to herein as "the said Annex") that it SHALL (and the word "shall" is used in this context and throughout this agreement as imposing a binding obligation) —

   (I) subject to its right to withdraw from this agreement after eighteen months from the date hereof provided it shall have given to the Secretary General of the International Electrical Association Limited (referred to herein as "the Secretary") not less than six months' previous notice in writing, maintain all the terms of this agreement;

  (II) observe and be bound by the rules in the schedule hereto in the case of all enquiries, tenders and contracts to which the said Annex applies;

(III) admit as valid and binding, at the expiration of ninety days from the despatch by the Secretary of written notice of the proposal therefor, any amendment of the rules which may within the said ninety days have been agreed to by every Member which, being a signatory of any annex hereto, has replied to the said proposal therefor;

(IV) in the case of all enquiries, tenders and contracts to which the said Annex applies, observe and be bound by such technical rules and such other matters as may be set out in the said Annex from time to time by agreement of the signatories of the said Annex;

  (V) issue to all persons or bodies, physical or legal, acting on a signatory's behalf or in his name, such instructions as will ensure that, without its previous consent, no tender is modified in such a way as to be contrary to the rules or to the technical rules or other matters which may be set out in the said Annex: and

1st July 1970

(VI) subject to its rights under the Conciliation Rules of the International Electrical Association Limited (which Rules shall be deemed to be incorporated in this agreement), abide by the Secretary's decision in respect of the interpretation of this agreement, the rules, the technical rules and any matter which may be set out in the said Annex.

THE SCHEDULE

A. GENERAL RULES

A.1. RELAXATION OF RULES BEFORE TENDERS ARE SUBMITTED.

If, in the case of any specific enquiry, a relaxation of any rule is requested by any Member before tenders are submitted, the request may be agreed to, through the Secretary, by a majority of the Members concerned in that enquiry, and such agreement shall not be unreasonably withheld. Members not originally concerned in the enquiry but subsequently becoming so concerned shall be informed by the Secretary of any relaxation agreed.

A.2. RELAXATION OF RULES AFTER TENDERS HAVE BEEN SUBMITTED.

(a) In the case of any specific enquiry in respect of which tenders have been submitted, any tendering Member (that is, a Member who is concerned in the enquiry and who can satisfy the Secretary, if called upon to do so, that he has submitted a bona fide tender) may, stating the reasons therefor, request a relaxation of any rule or technical rule. The Secretary shall then inform all the other tendering Members of the relaxation requested, and the relaxation shall be made, provided always that a breach of a rule or technical rule shall not be considered a sufficient reason for making a relaxation, if —

(i) in any case in which there are three or less tendering Members, those tendering Members unanimously agree; or if,

(ii) in any case in which there are more than three tendering Members, not less than 75 per cent of those tendering Members agree.

1st July 1970

(b) If no reply to the Secretary's communication of a request for a relaxation has been received from a tendering Member within such time limit as may be specified by the Secretary but in no case less than four working days from the despatch of that communication, that tendering Member shall be deemed to agree to the relaxation.

A.3. ATTEMPT TO OBTAIN UNANIMOUS AGREEMENT.

If, in the case of any specific enquiry, one or two or not more than 25 percent of the Members concerned disagree with a proposal circulated by the Secretary, then the Secretary shall attempt to obtain unanimous agreement. Should he fail to do so, he shall inform those Members who have agreed to the proposal of the names of those who have not agreed so that the former may endeavour, by direct contact with the latter, to obtain unanimous agreement.

A.4. INFORMATION REGARDING COMPANIES WITH WHOM MEMBERS ARE COLLABORATING ON SPECIFIC ENQUIRIES.

Members shall inform the Secretary of the names of the companies, whether Members or not, with whom they intend to collaborate on any specific enquiry so that if any arrangement is made by the Members concerned in that enquiry they may be informed by the Secretary of the competition, so far as it is known, to be encountered. The name of a non-Member made known to the Secretary under this rule shall not be disclosed to Members except with the permission of the Member who has communicated it.

A.5. OBLIGATIONS OF MEMBERS WHOSE CONCERN IN AN ENQUIRY BECOMES KNOWN AFTER AN ARRANGEMENT HAS BEEN MADE.

(a) Whilst the Secretary shall at all times use his best endeavours to inform Members of the existence of an arrangement applying to a transaction, it shall nevertheless be the duty of every Member to have ascertained whether or not an arrangement exists in respect of each enquiry against which he proposes to tender.
(b) If any Member becomes concerned in an enquiry after an arrangement has been made but fourteen days or more before tenders are due from the parties to that arrangement, that Member shall endeavour to maintain the arrangement and be a party to it.

1st July 1970

(c) If any Member becomes concerned in an enquiry after an arrangement has been made but later than the fourteenth day before tenders are due from the parties to that arrangement, that Member shall maintain the arrangement and be a party to it.

A.6. ACTION ON INVITATION TO RE-TENDER.

When prices in tenders have become known and the purchaser, with or without minor modification to the previous invitation, invites Members to re-tender, tendering Members shall, at the request of any one of them, meet and discuss what action is to be taken.

A.7. ACTION ON CHANGES TO LOCAL FISCAL LEGISLATION.

Members shall ensure that if after the date of tender an increase or reduction in the contract value occurs by reason of an addition to, repeal of, or amendment to the internal laws or regulations of the purchaser's country, or the taxes or dues prevailing therein, the amount of such increase or reduction shall be for the purchaser's account.

A.8. BREACHES.

8.1 If any Member of this Agreement or if any party to an arrangement knows, suspects or alleges that another Member is in breach or is about to commit a breach of this Agreement or of the arrangement, as the case may be, he shall immediately inform the Secretary of all the facts, suspicions or allegation.

8.2 The Secretary shall thereupon raise the matter with the Member or Members known or suspected or alleged to be in breach, or, if no such Members are identified, with all the Members.

8.3 If, in the opinion of the Secretary, there is no prima facie evidence of either an actual or a contemplated breach, the Secretary shall immediately report the fact to the Member or Members raising the matter.

8.4 If, in the opinion of the Secretary, there is prima facie evidence of either an actual or a contemplated breach, the Secretary shall forthwith require the Member whose actions are in question to rectify matters to the Secretary's satisfaction.

8.5 Any refusal, neglect or inability so to rectify to the Secretary's satisfaction shall be reported by the Secretary to the Members concerned in the transaction and the following shall then apply —

Reissued 23rd May 1972 (superseding page dated 1st July 1970)

8.5.1 In the case of an admitted breach of the provisions of this Agreement or of an arrangement, the other Members concerned in the transaction, or, as the case may be, the other parties to the arrangement shall be entitled to accept the same terms or conditions as those accepted by the Member who admitted the breach notwithstanding any provision to the contrary either in this Agreement or in the arrangement EXCEPT THAT if an arrangement on a non-composite transaction prescribes a price preference, only the party or parties entitled to the preference shall be free to modify their offer so as to maintain the original preference.

8.5.2 In any case where the breach, be it of this Agreement or of an arrangement, is not admitted, the other Members concerned in the transaction, or, as the case may be, the other parties to the arrangement shall be entitled to decide, upon a majority of two-thirds of their number (excluding therefrom the Member or Members allegedly in breach), to accept the same conditions or terms offered by the Member allegedly in breach or, where an arrangement has been infringed, to decide upon any modification or termination of the arrangement notwithstanding any provision to the contrary either in this Agreement or in the arrangement: EXCEPT THAT in the case of a price preference arrangement such decision to modify or to terminate shall not be valid without agreement of the party or parties entitled to preference.

8.5.3 The operation of any provision in rule 8.5.1 or 8.5.2 shall not in any way affect or be deemed a condonation of a breach whether admitted by or alleged against a Member, nor shall the other Members concerned in a transaction be prejudiced regarding any rights they may wish to pursue in relation to any form of redress from the Member or Members admittedly or allegedly in breach.

8.6 The provisions of this rule shall be applied and shall operate independently of any action taken under any provisions which may be agreed from time to time regarding the setting up of any panels of enquiry.

Reissued 23rd May 1972 (superseding page dated 1st July 1970)

B. COMMERCIAL RULES

B.1. DELIVERY GUARANTEE

(a) Rate of Liquidated Damages.

No rate of liquidated damages exceeding ½ per cent of the contract value of each unit supplied per full week of delay shall be offered, unless otherwise specified by the purchaser. In no case shall a rate higher than 1 per cent be offered or accepted in any contract.

(b) Limit of Liquidated Damages.

No limit of liquidated damages higher than 5 per cent of the contract value of each unit supplied shall be offered unless a higher limit is specified by the purchaser. In no case shall a limit higher than 10 per cent be offered or accepted in any contract.

(c) Limitation of Liability for Delay.

It shall be stated in every tender and in every contract that liquidated damages shall be payable only if late delivery of the material contracted for results in delay in putting plant into operation. It shall also be stated that the payment of liquidated damages shall be in full satisfaction of the Member's liability for delay.

(d) Rejection Limit.

Members shall ensure that purchasers shall only have the right to reject plant under a clause such as the following, which is based upon sub-clause 7.5 of U.N.E.C.E. Conditions ME/188, and provided that a suitable force majeure clause is also included in the contract.

If any portion of the plant in respect of which the purchaser has become entitled to the maximum reduction by way of liquidated damages provided for by the contract remains undelivered, the purchaser may by notice in writing to the vendor require him to deliver and by such last-mentioned notice fix a final time for delivery which shall be reasonable taking into account such delay as has already occurred. If for any reason whatever the vendor fails within such time to do everything that he must do to effect delivery, the purchaser shall be entitled by notice in writing to the vendor, and without requiring the consent of any court, to terminate the contract in respect of such portion of the plant and thereupon to recover from the vendor any loss suffered by the purchaser by reason of the failure of the vendor as aforesaid up to an amount which rep-

1st July 1970

resents that part of the price payable under the contract which is properly attributable to such portion of the plant as could not in consequence of the vendor's failure be put to the use intended.

B.2. GUARANTEE PERIOD WITHIN WHICH DEFECTIVE PARTS SHALL BE REPLACED

(a) Members shall ensure that any guarantee period indicated in a tender for the repair or replacement of defective parts shall be limited

EITHER to 12 months after the satisfactory putting into operation of the plant
OR to 18 months from the time of notification of readiness for despatch of the plant
UNLESS the purchaser specifically asks for a longer period of guarantee in which case such period shall be limited
EITHER to not more than 18 months after the satisfactory putting into operation of the plant
OR to not more than 24 months from the time of notification of readiness for despatch of the plant.

(b) Members shall ensure that the period for which any repaired or replacement part may be guaranteed shall be limited wherever possible to 12 months from the date upon which the plant is first satisfactorily put into operation after the repair or replacement of the part, but in no case shall this period exceed 18 months.

(c) In any case where, by reason of any defect developing, plant or any portion thereof is put out of operation during the subsistence of a guarantee period permitted by any sub-rule of this rule, it shall be permissible for the supplier of the plant or portion thereof affected to grant such extension to the original guarantee period as may be required for the remedying of the defect.

B.3. CONTRACT PRICE ADJUSTMENT

(a) Subject to the following provisions, Members shall ensure that escalator clauses, based upon the supplementary clause in U.N.E.C.E. Conditions ME/188 without tolerances, are used in all tenders and contracts.

(b) Except where the delivery period for plant is within twelve months, Members shall not offer, unless expressly requested to do so by the purchaser (in which case the Member shall inform the Secretary if he intends to accede to the purchaser's request), any of the following conditions:

1st July 1970

(i) a firm price

(ii) a fixed portion which is greater than 20 percent of the price

(iii) an escalator clause with a ceiling which is less than an amount calculated at the rate of 4 percent per year of the delivery period (or average delivery period if more than one machine is offered) where the delivery period (or average delivery period) is at least 12 months but not more than 30 months,

(iv) an escalator clause with a ceiling lower than 10 percent where the delivery period (or average delivery period if more than one machine is offered) exceeds 30 months, or

(v) any tolerance referred to in the supplementary clause in U.N.E.C.E. conditions series ME/188.

(c) Whenever any Member so informs the Secretary that he proposes to grant any of the conditions mentioned in (b) above, the Secretary shall advise the other tendering Members accordingly, without disclosing the name of the Member concerned, so that they may likewise offer or accept any of those conditions.

B.4. DELAY IN PAYMENT

Every Member shall take steps to provide that if, due to no fault of his own, he is unable to ship, erect or commission any plant, payments due against shipping documents and all subsequent payments (except shipping costs and the cost of erection) shall be paid not later than three months after the due dates.

B.5. TERMS OF PAYMENT

(a) Subject to the provisions of sub-rule (b) of this rule, every tender and contract shall provide that at least 15 percent of the contract price of any portion of the plant shall be paid at or before the date of despatch ex works, or of delivery of shipping documents, or of the placing of the plant f.o.b. or f.o.r. in the country of origin, and that the balance shall be paid by equal instalments over a period not exceeding five years thereafter: EXCEPT THAT where a request is contained in a tender document from the purchaser so to do, a Member may grant terms of payment under which not less than 85 percent of the contract price of that portion of the plant shipped shall be paid upon landing of the same at the port of destination or upon delivery of the same to site.

1st July 1970

(b) Notwithstanding the provisions of sub-rule (a) of this rule, terms of payment more favourable to a purchaser than those specified in sub-rule (a) of this rule may be granted by a Member for a particular transaction provided that Member can obtain from the credit insurance organisation in his own country normal insurance cover for the more favourable terms of payment which he intends to grant and proves to the satisfaction of the Secretary, who shall inform the other tendering Members accordingly, that he can obtain such insurance.

(c) This Rule B.5 shall not be subject to relaxation under rules A.1 or A.2 notwithstanding anything therein contained.

B.6. FORCE MAJEURE CLAUSES.

Members shall ensure that a force majeure clause, effectively taking account of all events beyond the reasonable control of the Member, is included in every tender. In tenders in which the cases of force majeure are stated in detail it shall be provided that, if there are important castings or forgings, their rejection shall be treated by the purchaser as a case of force majeure giving the right to an extension of the delivery time.

B.7. VALIDITY PERIOD.

(a) No longer period than three months for validity shall be given in tenders unless otherwise specified by the purchaser in his enquiry, in which case the period shall not exceed six months.

(b) No period of extension shall exceed three months and the maximum period of validity from the original date of tender shall not exceed nine months.

B.8. BID BOND.

(a) A bid bond, when insisted upon by the purchaser, shall not exceed 5% of the total contract value of the plant.

(b) Members shall ensure wherever possible that

   (i) the maximum life of the bond shall be limited in time to the validity period of the tender;

  (ii) automatic cancellation of the bond shall be provided for simultaneously with the ending of the validity of the bond;

 (iii) liability under the bond shall be provided for only in the case where the supplier will not accept the order under the conditions of his tender;

1st July 1970

(iv) it shall be provided that the place of jurisdiction shall be that of the domicile of the supplier.

B.9. PERFORMANCE BOND.

(a) A performance bond, when insisted upon by the purchaser, shall not exceed 10% of the total contract value of the plant to be supplied and, wherever possible, progressive reductions shall be provided for in line with the progress of the execution of the contract.

(b) Members shall ensure wherever possible that

   (i) the wording of the bond should be definitively agreed not later than the date of confirmation of the order;

   (ii) the life of the bond shall be clearly limited especially in the case where delivery cannot be made for reasons for which the supplier is not responsible;

   (iii) liability under the bond shall be expressed not to arise on simple demand or without reasons, but only when the customer can justify accusations of non-compliance with the contractual conditions;

   (iv) it shall be provided that the place of jurisdiction shall be that of the domicile of the supplier;

   (v) it shall be provided that the bond certificate must be surrendered immediately after its termination.

B.10. U.N.E.C.E. CONDITIONS OF CONTRACT.

Members shall endeavour to ensure that they neither offer nor accept conditions of contract less favourable to themselves than those embodied in U.N.E.C.E. General Conditions of Contract Series ME/188 and 574 (as appropriate).

In cases where U.N.E.C.E. Conditions ME/188 or 574 are used by a Member, the appendix to those conditions shall be completed in a manner not less favourable to the Member than the following:

(A) Percentage to be deducted for weeks delay: In accordance with rule B.1(a)

(B) Maximum percentage which the deductions above may not exceed: In accordance with rule B.1(b)

1st July 1970

(C) Maximum amount recoverable for non-delivery:	Leave blank, but free to enter some figure if desired.
(D) Maximum amount recoverable on termination by vendor for failure to take delivery or make payment:	Leave blank, but free to enter some figure if desired.
(E) Rate of interest on overdue payment:	Each Member free to state his own percentage with a minimum of 6%.
(F) Period of delay in payment authorising termination by vendor:	Maximum of six months.
(G) Guarantee period for original plant and parts replaced or renewed:	In accordance with rule B.2.
(H) Maximum extension of guaranteed period:	In accordance with rule B.2.
(I) 1. Daily use of plant:	Leave blank, but free to enter some figure if desired.
2. Reduction of guarantee period for more intensive use:	Leave blank, but free to enter some figure if desired.

In cases where other conditions, such as national conditions or recognised sets of conditions published under the auspices of engineering institutions or other similar bodies are used instead of the aforementioned U.N.E.C.E. conditions, Members shall ensure that conditions less favourable to the Member than those itemised from (A) to (I) above shall not be offered or accepted.

B.11. LIMITATION OF LIABILITY.

Every contract shall contain a clause to the effect that the Member shall not be liable to the purchaser for —

(a) any loss of profit or of contracts suffered by the purchaser,

(b) any claim made against the purchaser, except as provided in the contract (regardless of whether the contract is terminated or not),

1st July 1970

(c) any damage or injury caused by or arising from the acts or omissions of the purchaser or of others (not being the Member's servants or sub-contractors),

(d) any loss or damage in circumstances over which the Member has no control (except loss or damage caused by any such risk as is required in the contract to be covered by insurance).

Furthermore, every contract shall provide for the inclusion of a clause to the effect that, except in respect of personal injury or damage to property conferring on a person other than the purchaser a good cause of action against the Member, the liability of the Member to the purchaser for any one act or default shall not exceed the contract price.

B.12. ARBITRATION.

Except in those cases in which the contract with the purchaser contains provisions to the effect that arbitration is to be in accordance with the arbitration laws of any of the Members' countries, or with arbitration laws based upon or derived from such laws, it shall so far as possible be provided in every contract that arbitration shall be carried out by or arranged through the International Chamber of Commerce.

1st July 1970.

V. Agreement P(H)C

Orders Reported from May 19, 1965, up to December 31, 1967

Territory	No. of Tend.	Price Levels %	Ø	Hz	DW or AW	MVA	KV	Tap Changer	Pool
AUSTRALIA	15	104.6	3	50	D	40/40/5	330/132/11	Off-circuit	
	12	98.5	3	50	D	72	140.8/11.8	OLTC	
	16	91.0	3	50	D	180/180/60	275/66/11	OLTC	PC
	15	119.0	3	50	A	150	220/115	OLTC	PC
	14	108.5	3	50	D	80	138.6/11	Off-circuit	
	17	78.9	3	50	D	144	275/13.8	OLTC	PC
	10	98.1	3	50	A	196/190/6	330/132	OLTC	PC
	1	113.0	3	50	A	150/150/5	330/138.6/11	OLTC	OT
	16	91.8	3	50	D	144	142/13.8	OLTC	SA
	12		3	50	D	145	195/13.8	Off-circuit	PC
NEW ZEALAND	11	66.6	3	50	D	55.5	110/11	OLTC	PC
	11	62.6	1	50	D	16.667	220/19.053	Off-circuit	PC
	11	66.1	1	50	D	16.667	220/19.053	Off-circuit	PC
	16	108.0	3	50	D	60	110/22	OLTC	PC
	11	76.7	3	50	D	55.5	110/11	OLTC	PC
	13	86.5	1	50	A	66.6/66.6/20	127/63.5/11	OLTC	PC
	11	84.6	1	50	D	16.6	110/33	Off-circuit	PC
	14	103.5	1	50	A	33.3/33.3/20	220/110/11	OLTC	PC
	15		1	50	D	16.667	220/19.05		PC
	18	72.2	1	50	D	66.6/66.6/20	127/38.1/11	OLTC	PC

Country	No.		Ph.	Freq.	A/D				
INDIA	1	147.0	1	50	A	33.3/33.3/5	220/128/11	OLTC	OT
	1	120.4	3	50	D	30/30/10	110/33/11	OLTC	OT
PAKISTAN	15	91.3	1	50	A	33.3/33.3/5	220/132/11	OLTC	PC
	1	146.0	3	50	D	60	132/11	Off-circuit	OT/PC
	13	102.0	3	50	D	172	132/18	Off-circuit	
SOUTH AFRICA	17	67.0	3	50	D	220	420/15.75	Off-circuit	PC
	13	117.3	3	50	D	72	141.6/11	Off-circuit	
	22	63.3	3	50	D	120/120/25	400/88/22	OLTC	PC
	21	76.9	3	50	D	90	132/33	OLTC	PC
	13	105.0	3	50	D	45	132/33	OLTC	PC
	10	99.7	3	50	D	72	88/11.8	Off-circuit	PC
	7	113.0	3	50	D	45/45/15	80/11/10	OLTC	PC
	1	121.0	3	50	A	75/75/12.5	275/132/22	OLTC	OT
	1	101.0	3	50	D	90	130/42		OT
	17		3	50	D	35	275/11	OLTC	PC
	17	95.2	3	50	D	30	275/22	OLTC	PC
	19	149.7	3	50	A	400	400/275	OLTC	PC
	14	194.4	3	50	D	37.5/37.5/12.5	88/33.3/11	OLTC	PC
	14		3	50	D	30/30/0.1	66/33/11	OLTC	PC
RHODESIA ZAMBIA	3 {	118.0	3	50	D	74/60/20	220/88/11	GLTC	OT
	{	116.9	3	50	D	74/60/20	220/33/11	OLTC	
	1	182.0	3	50	D	65/65/32.5	220/72.6/10.6	OLTC	OT
	3	118.0	3	50	D	74/60/20	220/88/11	OLTC	
	1	151.3	3	50	D	45	88/33	Off-circuit	OT
	1		3	50	D	65/65/32.5	220/72.6/10.6	OLTC	OT
	1	151.3	3	50	D	45	88/33	Off-circuit	OT
	3		3	50	D	50	220/11	Off-circuit	OT

Territory	No. of Tend.	Price Levels %	Ø	Hz	DW or AW	MVA	KV	Tap Changer	Pool
NIGERIA	17	85.7	3	50	D	80/60/30	330/132/13.8	OLTC	SA
IVORY COAST	2	214.0	3	50	D	40	100/12	Off-circuit	OT
HONG KONG	1	213.7	3	50	D	75	66/11	Off-circuit	OT
	1	232.2	3	50	D	35	33/11	OLTC	OT
	1	189.6	3	50	D	80	132/33	Off-circuit	OT
	1	221.6	3	50	D	40	66/33	OLTC	OT
	1	221.0	3	50	D	40	66/33	OLTC	OT
	1	199.0	3	50	D	80	132/33	Off-circuit	OT
	1	196.8	3	50	D	80	132/66	OLTC	OT
	1	223.4	3	50	D	60	66/33	OLTC	OT
MALAYSIA	17	87.4				68	132/11	Off-circuit	PC
		99.6				30	132/11	OLTC	PC
		104.1	3	50	D	30/30/10	132/60/11	OLTC	PC
		110.6				36	66/11	Off-circuit	PC
		113.3				30/30/10	66/22/–	OLTC	PC
JAMAICA	10	91.75	3	50	D	37.5	72/13.8	Off-circuit	
IRELAND	10	97.6	3	50	D	31.5	110/40/10.5	OLTC	
	11	83.4	3	50	D	125/125/42	225/110/–	OLTC	
CYPRUS	9		3	50	D	37.5	66/11.8	Off-circuit	
BRAZIL	13	78.8	1	60	D	61.333	345/13.8	Off-circuit	SA

PARAGUAY	1	73.8	1	50	D	19	230/13.8	Off-circuit	OT
CHILE	17	94.1	3	50	D	45/45/32.5	154/69/13.2	OLTC	PC
	19	84.7	3	50	D	85	230/13.8	Off-circuit	PC
	15	107.5	3	50	D	147	161/13.8	Off-circuit	
	3	109.5	3	60	D	36	88/13.8	Off-circuit	
COLOMBIA	18	84.6	1	60	A	60/60/20	220/110/46	OLTC	
	11	103.5	1	60	D	20	115/33	Off-circuit	
VENEZUELA	10	111.0	1	60	A	33.3/33.3/6.6	230/115/34.5	OLTC	
	10	97.7	3	60	D	30	115/34.5	Off-circuit	
	7	137.0	3	50/60	D	75/79.6/25	67/30/11	Off-circuit	
	9	100.5	1	60	A	100/100/25	400/230/34.5	OLTC	PC
	9	96.7	1	60	A	150/150/35	400/230/34.5	OLTC	PC
	7	238.0	3	50/60	D	75/79/25	67/30/11	Off-circuit	
	4	144.0	3	50/60	D	37.5/37.5/9.62	66/30/11.47	Off-circuit	
	9	101.7	1	60	A	150/150/35	400/230/34.5	OLTC	PC
	9	101.3	3	60	D	255	400/18	None	PC
	5		3	50/60	D	86			
PANAMA	4	111.0	3	60	D	45	115/13.8	Off-circuit	
FORMOSA	1	120.0	3	60	D	34	154/13.8	Off-circuit	OT
CHINA	2	147.0	3	50	A	80/80/40	220/110/35	OLTC	
KOREA	2	110.0	3	60	D	125	154/16.5	Off-circuit	
	1	108.0	3	60	D	125	154/16.5	Off-circuit	
	1	106.6	3	50	D	137.5	242/16.5	Off-circuit	
IRAN	2	166.01	1	50	A	36.6/36.6/6	230/132/6	OLTC	OT
	7	127.5	3	50	D	44.75	63/13.2	Off-circuit	OT

Territory	No. of Tend.	Price Levels %	∅	Hz	DW or AW	MVA	KV	Tap Changer	Pool
	9	114.8	3	50	D	30	63/11	Off-circuit	PC
	1	108.5	3	50	D	40/40/15	230/63/15	OLTC	OT
	13	86.8	3	50	D	84	230/13.2	Off-circuit	
KUWAIT	11	118.0	3	50	D	30	132/33	OLTC	PC
	1	127.0	3	50	D	45	132/33	OLTC	OT
	4	126.5	3	50	D	87.5	140.6/13	OLTC	
	4	126.5	3	50	D	87.5	140.6/13	OLTC	
	7	129.0	3	50	D	34.4	140.6/13	OLTC	
IRAQ	6 {	118.7	3	50	D	50/50/25	132/69.3/11.55	OLTC	OT
		118.5					132/34.5/11.55		
SPAIN	1	114.0	1	50	A	56.6/56.6/16.6	210/132/13.2	Off-circuit	OT
	2	151.0	3	50	A	100/100/30	220/140/15	OLTC	
	11	105.5	1	50	A	200/200/66.7	420/240/24	Off-circuit	
	1	126	3	50	A	100/100/20	230/138/25	OLTC	OT
	11	94.6	3	50	A	400/400/120	400/232/24	OLTC	SA
DENMARK	5	89.5	3	50	D	150	152.5/66	OLTC	
	1	125.7	3	50	D	290	132/18	None	OT
	1	125.7	3	50	D	290	132/18	None	OT
	4	96.3	3	50	D	125	165/67	OLTC	
	1	101.6	3	50	D	80	157.5/66	OLTC	OT
	4	89.6	3	50	D	125	165/67	OLTC	

	1	—	3	50	D	290	175/18	OLTC	OT
	3	94.7	3	50	D	100	132/55	OLTC	OT
	1	98.8	3	50	D	100	124/52	None	PC
	5	112.0	3	50	D	120	71.2/13.5	Off-circuit	
	5	99.4	3	50	D	160	132/13.8	Off-circuit	
GREECE	9	140.0	3	50	D	180	150/15.75	OLTC	PC
	18	87.5	3	50	D	66	150/23	Off-circuit	PC
	10	101.6	3	50	D	190	150/15.75	OLTC	
	17	100.3	3	50	D	90/45/45	150/21/21	OLTC	
	11	103.5	3	50	D	55	150/15.75/21	OLTC	
ROMANIA	6	111.2	3	50	D	75/37.5/37.5	220/15.75/15.75	OLTC	PC
YUGOSLAVIA	2	118.0	3	50	D	41.3	110/20.2	OLTC	
	4	98.4	3	50	A	150/150/50	220/115/6.3	OLTC	PC
	6 {	95.6	3	50	A	150/150/50	220/115/10.5	OLTC	PC
		97.1				320	242/15.75		
	7	100+	3	50	D {	32/16/16	110/6.3/6.3		
						32/16/16	15.75/6.3/6.3		
TURKEY	16	116.0	3	50	D	47.3	169/6.6		PC
PHILIPPINES	3	109.0	3	60	D	232	115/14.4	Off-circuit	
	1	216.0	3	60	D	232	115/14.4	Off-circuit	
INDONESIA	1	112.3	3	50	D	30	63/20/11.55	OLTC	OT
ISRAEL	4	150.0	3	50	D	30	161/36/24	OLTC	OT
	4	89.8	3	50	D	30	161/24	OLTC	
	4		3	50	D	130	161/22	Off-circuit	

Territory	No. of Tend.	Price Levels %	Ø	Hz	DW or AW	MVA	KV	Tap Changer	Pool
SAUDI ARABIA	6	107.8	3	60	D	30	115/66	OLTC	
SYRIA	5	97.0	3	50	D	50/50/15	230/66/15	OLTC	
	5	97.0	3	50	D	70/70/20	230/66/15	OLTC	
	7	134.76	3	50	D	40	65/10.5	Off-circuit	
LEBANON	11	134.0	3	50	D	30	78/6/11	Off-circuit	
MOROCCO	4	154.5	3	50	D	75	63/10.3	Off-circuit	
	8	127.5	3	50	D	40/40/20	150/63/11	OLTC	

No. of Tend. = Number of tenderers
Price level % = Price as percentage of cartel "reference price" (blank spaces indicate price not reported, for reasons unknown)
Ø = Phase
Hz = Hertz (cycles per second)
DW or AW = Double wound or Auto wound
MVA = Megavolt Amperes
KV = Kilovolt
Tap Changer = Type of equipment attached to the transformer
Pool = Type of agreement in effect: OT means Only Tenderer; PC, Pool Cancelled; SA, Special Arrangement; and blank spaces indicate standard agreement for Section H in effect.

VI. IBEMEP Cartel Accord Covering Transformers

REGULATION No. 2/67

Suggestions from the Sales Department to Board of Directors for the Regulation of Sales of Transformers above 7.5 MVA and/or 69 KV.

We propose the following program:

I
OBJECTIVE

Article 1: These regulations establish the rules to be observed in negotiations within the Brazilian internal market for transformers and auto-transformers with or without load tension regulators, with power above 7.5 MVA and/or with voltage above 69 KV.

II
MEMBERS

Article 2: The representatives of [companies] A, B, C, E, G, G, and I will be invited to participate in the program.

Representative D will participate only in negotiations for transformers up to 10 MVA, 138 KV.

III
SECRETARY

Article 3: The meetings will be conducted by a secretary to be chosen among employees or representatives of the members.

Article 4: Responsibility will be held by the secretary:

(a) to call regular meetings (Art. 6, 10, 14);

(b) to organize the meeting agenda;

(c) to conduct the meeting, co-ordinating the subjects under discussion;

(d) to file each meeting's notes, tables with bid results and, if available, results of private inquiries and negotiations;

(e) to receive the notification of inquiries or bids from members;

(f) to enforce the observance and fulfilment of these regulations;

(g) to give members information pertaining to Art. 7;

(h) to convene a meeting or make decisions as may be required in Art. 9;

(i) to convene a meeting as required by the sub-paragraph of Art. 9;

(j) to distribute up-to-date data on "shares" to members;

(k) to receive and distribute to each member complaints and requests for information originating from members;

(l) to cast a tie breaking vote if a committee or working group decision comes to a draw.

Article 5:   The secretary is forbidden:

(a) to take steps outside of his competence;

(b) to alter by innovation, change or termination, any of the dispositions of these regulations without the backing of the members;

(c) to take decisions on issues raised about which he has no knowledge or information;

(d) to participate in any activity outside of the coordination.

IV
MEETINGS

Article 6:   The meetings which will be convened by the secretary in São Paulo to discuss negotiations about transformers as mentioned in Article 1 of these regulations.

Article 7:   The members who have received consultation, inquiries, invitations to bid, or public notice will participate in the meeting.

Article 8:   It is compulsory that a member shows proof of the invitation or consultation, inquiries, or public notice if that is requested at the beginning of the meeting by any of the other members; sufficient proof may consist of a customer letter, a bid notice published in any official body, or any other means of confirmation.

Article 9: Representative members should attend the meetings mentioned in Article 6 of these regulations with all technical data and information on the subject under discussion; they should also be duly prepared to immediately take decisions on issues raised during the meeting.

Article 10: The meeting should take place within a maximum of seven days from the presentation of the offer.

Article 11: If any member is consulted after the day of the meeting, he will get in touch with the secretary to know the basis on which the offer is to be made.

1. Once each member has had a turn, the member who is in the situation described by the subject of this article will be included in his normal position.

2. If the situation anticipated in Paragraph 1 has not occurred, the member should give coverage.

3. If the late member obtains an extension of the bid, inquiry, or consultation, there will be a new meeting to discuss the subject again.

Article 12: It is forbidden to submit any offer without a previous consultation with the secretary as stated in Articles 7 and 11.

Article 13: Whenever the public notice, invitation for a budget, inquiry or consultation contains any demand contrary to these regulations or not covered by the regulations, the invited members will not accept or fulfill the said demand without a prior decision of the secretary, or before a meeting is held to discuss the demand.

1. The meeting requested by a member to discuss issues not covered by these regulations or contrary to them, as well as matters of the general interest, will be convened by the secretary.

Article 14: Whenever a member is late for the meetings covered by this title, there will be a leeway of 15 minutes before the meeting starts.

Article 15: Each member should participate in the meeting for its duration.

1. If a member cannot abide by above rule, he shall nominate another member to represent him with full responsibility.

Article 16: It is necessary that all members or their representative participate in all meetings convened.

Article 17: The deliberations reached in meetings convened as per Articles 6 and 13 will be final whenever backed up by the majority of the members convened.

Article 18: At the end of each meeting, minutes will be distributed.

V
OFFER

Article 19: The form in which an offer is to be made will be discussed in the meeting convened according to Article 6 of these regulations.

Article 20: Without detriment to the provision stated in the previous article, the offer should be clear in order to enable an accurate interpretation of price and other conditions agreed upon during the meeting.

Article 21: If an offer is to be made for complete installations including cabinet and other equipment, the price of the transformer or transformers will be presented separately.

　1. When the offer is for transformers jointly with other materials it is forbidden to include the expression "the request will be accepted only in case of total purchase," or equivalent expression.

Article 22: Only one manufacturing standard will be used in the offer, supplying of power figures in equivalent standards being forbidden.

VI
PRICE

Article 23: The prices will be agreed upon according to the meeting mentioned in Article 6.

　1. During the meeting convened, as per Article 6, the following items relevant to price also will be agreed upon: payment conditions, delivery site, readjustment, guaranty and validity.

　2. The following basic payment conditions will be generally observed:

I — 20% down
II — 60% after delivery
III — 20% within 30 or 60 days

3. Delivery dates, losses, and other transformer characteristics, will be determined by each member individually.

Article 24: The final sales' prices agreed upon during the meeting will include 2 percent payable by the winning member to a "reserve for combat purposes."

Article 25: It is compulsory that each member let the secretary know about all purchase requests he has received.

1. In case of doubt, the other members bidding on the same contract will be allowed to see the final terms of the purchase order received.

Article 26: By using purchase orders received, the secretary will keep a record of individual members credits in the "reserve for combat purposes."

Article 27: If the need for combat arises, it will be taken up first by the company that has accumulated the largest amount of reserves.

VII
ROTATION

Article 28: Rotation refers to orders in each of the product classifications.

1. The following are the classes and the participating members:
Class 1: Up to 10 MVA - 138 KV -
A, B, C, E, G, H, I
Class 2: From 10.1 to 20 MVA - 138 KV -
A, B, C, E, G, H, I
Class 3: From 20.1 to 30 MVA - 138 KV -
A, B, C, E, G, H, I
Class 4: Above 30.1 MVA - 138 KV -
A, B, C, E, G, H, I
Class 5: Up to 20 MVA - above 138 KV -
B, C, G, H, I
Class 6: From 20.1 to 30 MVA - above 138 KV -
B, C, G, H, I

Class 7: Above 30.1 MVA - above 138 KV -
B, C, G, H, I

The determination of the power of the transformers in above classification will be decided as follows:

(a) *Double wound transformers:* use nominal no-load power, that is without forced cooling; for single-phase transformers use no-load power of each single-phase unit.

(b) *3-winding transformers:* use one-half of the sum of no-load powers of the three windings.

Power = 0.5 (sum of the power of the three windings).

(c) *Auto-transformers:* use one-half of the sum of the powers of all the windings. The power of a winding is defined as the product of the highest voltage of this winding times the highest current it has to withstand.

Article 29: For each class, the rotation order will be modified after discussion in a meeting for each inquiry, consultation or bid.

1. This modification will consist of moving the letter that before the meeting occupies the first position in the class to the last position.

2. In the eventual case that an inquiry occupying the first position in the rotation is not participating in a bid, or consultation, for which a meeting is being held, the letter corresponding to that member that is in the winning position will be moved from its initial position to the last position in the class immediately after the member originally favored but not participating in the meeting.

Article 30: Whenever four or more members participate in a bid, inquiry or consultation, the members occupying the two last positions in any of the categories of the rotation will offer prices at least 5 percent and 10 percent respectively above the members in the next position.

VIII
PENALTIES

Article 31: Non-observance of any provision of these regulations, particularly where such conditions are expressly mentioned, will be considered an infringment; the same applies to the non-observance of prices, discounts and commissions, payment conditions, delivery dates without readjustment, rotation, price lists or any other acts undertaken by a member and whose effects, voluntary or not, are harmful to the other members.

Article 32: Upon determination by the majority of the members, the infringing member will be charged a fine corresponding to 20 percent of the total value of the accepted request.

Article 33: If the said member acknowledges the punishable mistake and withdraws or changes the offer before confirmation of the request, the fine described in the previous article will not be levied.

   1. The fine will be levied if the customer does not agree with the withdrawal or changes of the offer or any other reason arises that impeaches said change or withdrawal.

Article 34: Any denunciation or infringement shall be immediately brought to the attention of the coordinator and he will notify all the other members.

Article 35: For the purpose of the previous article, the coordinator will request prior clarifications from the alleged infringing member who will give his explanations during the first meeting to take place no later than 8 days after the notification, postponable for an equal length of time if the majority so decides.

Article 36: The subject will be debated whenever the parties have submitted their views during the meeting referred to in the previous article.

Article 37: For fast clarification and solution of the pending subject, all members must promptly submit any information even if in form of documents requested at the meeting through the coordinator.

Article 38: Following the debates on the question, there will be a secret vote.

Article 39: The member fined according to Articles 31 and 32 will be given the following options to pay the fine:

(a) Cash payments to be allotted to the contingency fund (article 44);

(b) Participate in the last position in those bids, inquiries or consultations for which he is classified in the first position either by rotation or eventual favorable situation, until foregone bids reach total of between two and four times the total value of the request accepted under infringment, until payment is fully covered.

Article 40: The infringing member will be given two working days to decide which alternative payment option to follow.

Article 41: If the option is for cash payment, the infringing member will have fifteen days to deposit the money in the contingency fund.

Article 42: If the option is for alternative b of Article 39, the member will be immediately placed under penalty.

Article 43: If the punished member does not make any statements about his options as per Article 40 it will be assumed that alternative b of Article 39 is chosen.

Article 44: The fine will go into the contingency fund.

Article 45: Under no conditions will any member punished according to this Article be allowed to forego payment of the fine.

    1. The punished infringing member will be excluded from agreements and conversations among the other members if he refuses to abide.

    2. The coordinator will schedule a top meeting to officially announce the exclusion of the non-abiding member and to deliberate about new directions to follow.

Article 46: The rule stated in the second paragraph of the previous article will also apply in the case of spontaneous exclusion sought by any member, whether or not a fine has been imposed.

Article 47: Even if there are no complaints for a period of 90 days, the coordinator will take advantage of an ordinary meeting being held after this period to discuss the subject giving a previous notice to members.

IX
IPI (TAX ON INDUSTRIALIZED PRODUCTS)

Article 48: The tax on industry will be added to the offer prices, the understanding being that "it is payable by the customer" except where customer is exempted for such taxes by law.

> 1. In the exceptional case described in this article, the invoice will contain the word "exempted" in lieu of the tax on industrialized products.

X
FINAL AND TRANSITORY DISPOSITIONS

Article 49: Whenever several bids, inquiries, or consultations need to be discussed during the same meeting, the chronological order of the presentation of the respective offers will be followed.

> 1. If the said bids, inquiries or consultations must be submitted on the same day, the discussion order will be determined by a draw.

> 2. Exceptions to the provision of this article and its first paragraph should be made if the bids, inquiries or consultations are all from the same company.

Article 50: In case any member leaves this program, he will be systematically combated by all the others who will alternate in the combat.

> 1. For the purpose of this article, the members will use the reserve established according to Article 24.

Article 51: The member that withdraws from this program will be allowed to return only with unanimous backing of the participating members and in accordance with the conditions that they set for such re-admisssion.

Article 52: The present regulations apply over the entire national territory.

Article 53: The present regulations will take effect on 8/28/1967.

Notes

INTRODUCTION

1. Quotes from the original complaint of May 9, 1977, drawn up by acting prosecutor-general Milton Menezes da Costa Filho.
2. *Movimento* (São Paulo), April 17, 1978.
3. See reports on the case in *O Globo* (Rio de Janeiro), August 5, 1974; and *Movimento*, April 17, 1978.
4. Copy of Official Registration Document, Ordem #10165, filed by IBEMEP on March 18, 1964.
5. Richard Newfarmer, *Transnational Conglomerates and the Economics of Dependent Development: A Case Study of the International Electrical Oligopoly and Brazil's Electrical Industry* (Greenwich, Conn.: JAI Press, 1980), p. 203.

CHAPTER ONE

1. The best source on early cartels is Roman Piotrowski, *Cartels and Trusts: Their Origin and Historical Development from the Economic and Legal Aspects* (London: Allen & Unwin, 1933). Also see Frederick Haussman and D. J. Ahearn, "Misconceptions about Cartels," *American Mercury*, March 1945.
2. Piotrowski, ch. 3.
3. Ibid., ch. 4.
4. George W. Stocking and Myron R. Watkins, *Cartels or Competition?* (New York: Twentieth Century Fund, 1948), p. 3. Also see *Dictionary of Political Economy*, vol. 1 (London, 1919), p. 229, cited in Ervin Hexner, *International Cartels* (Chapel Hill: University of North Carolina Press, 1945), p. 6; *Oxford English Dictionary*, (Oxford: Oxford University Press, 1933); and *Webster's New International Dictionary*, 2nd ed. (Springfield, Mass.: Merriam, 1934).
5. Hexner, p. 3.
6. George W. Stocking and Myron R. Watkins, *Cartels in Action* (New York: Twentieth Century Fund, 1946), p. 3.
7. Hexner, pp. 7–9.
8. Stocking and Watkins, *Cartels or Competition?*, p. 3.
9. Hexner, p. 24.
10. Stocking and Watkins, *Cartels or Competition?*, p. 15.

11. A colorful account of this period is found in Matthew Josephson, *The Robber Barons* (New York: Harcourt, Brace, 1934).

12. Richard Hofstadter, *The Age of Reform* (New York: Knopf, 1955), p. 243.

13. Great Britain, Reconstruction Ministry, *Report of the Committee on Trusts*, Cd. 9236, 1919, pp. 2, 18.

14. See Thorstein Veblen, *Imperial Germany and the Industrial Revolution* (New York: Huebsch, 1915).

15. Stocking and Watkins, *Cartels or Competition?*, p. 28; also see pp. 19–26.

16. Ibid., p. 29.

17. Robert Liefmann, "Die Unternehmerverbande," *Volkswirtschaftliche Abhandlungen der badischen Hochschulen* (Freiburg) 1, no. 1 (1897): 141–43.

18. Robert Liefmann, *Cartels, Concerns, and Trusts* (London: Methuen, 1932), p. 150.

19. Alfred Plummer, *International Combines in Modern Industry*, 3rd ed. (London: Pitman, 1951), pp. 226–27.

20. Ibid., pp. 160–62.

21. For the early years of the U.S. electrical industry, see U.S. Federal Trade Commission, *Electric Power Industries, Supply of Electrical Equipment and Competitive Conditions*, S. Doc. 46, 70th Cong., 1st sess., 1928; see also Oscar Silva, "A industria elétrica da lampada aos monopólios," *Opinião* (São Paulo), February 27, 1976; and Josephson, pp. 384–85.

22. Stocking and Watkins, *Cartels in Action*, pp. 322–23.

23. Stocking and Watkins, *Cartels or Competition?*, p. 31.

24. Ibid., p. 35.

25. Ibid., p. 57.

26. Rudolf K. Michels, *Cartels, Combines, and Trusts in Post-War Germany* (New York: Columbia University Press, 1928), pp. 34–57; see also Stocking and Watkins, *Cartels or Competition?*, pp. 46–7.

27. The best source on the Grand Alliance is the Complaint and Exhibits, including a copy of the Patents and Processes Agreement, filed on January 6, 1944, as part of the antitrust case *U.S. v. Imperial Chemical Industries, Ltd., et al.*, in U.S. District Court for the Southern District of New York, Civil Action. No. 24–13. The decisions in the case were rendered in *U.S. v. ICI*, 100 F. Supp. 504 (S.D.N.Y. 1951), and *U.S. v. ICI* 105 F. Supp. 215 (S.D.N.Y. 1952). For a summary of the Alliance see Stocking and Watkins, *Cartels in Action*, pp. 444–65; the legal case is summarized in Wilbur Lindsay Fugate, *Foreign Commerce and the Antitrust Laws*, 2nd ed. (Boston: Little, Brown, 1973), pp. 129–34.

28. Stocking and Watkins, *Cartels or Competition?*, p. 68.

29. Ibid., pp. 60–3.

30. For full details on the IG–Standard Oil–du Pont connections, see U.S., Senate, Special Committee Investigating the National Defense Program (the Truman Committee), *Investigation of the National Defense Program*, 77th Cong., 1st. sess.–79th Cong., 1st sess., pt. 11; also U.S., Senate, Committee on Patents (the Bone Committee), *Patents*, 77th Cong., 2d sess., pts. 1–10. Summaries of the matter are in Stocking and Watkins, *Cartels in Action*, pp. 87–113, 491–505; and Darel McConkey, *Out of Your Pocket* (New York: Pamphlet Press, 1947), pp. 83–94.

31. "Antitrust Policy and Full Production," *Harvard Business Review*, Spring 1942, p. 265; cited in Hexner, p. 143.

32. Anthony Sampson, *The Seven Sisters: The Great Oil Companies and the World They Made* (New York: Viking, 1975), pp. 78–80.

33. Stocking and Watkins, *Cartels or Competition?*, p. 269.

34. *New York Times*, September 9, 23, and 25, 1944.

35. Stocking and Watkins, *Cartels or Competition?*, pp. 343–44. See also Paul M. Goldberg and Charles Kindleberger, "Toward a GATT for Investment: A Proposal for Supervision of the International Corporation," *Law and Policy in International Business*, Summer 1970, which gives a good account of the political battle over the ITO proposal.

36. Earl W. Kintner and Mark R. Joelson, *An International Antitrust Primer* (New York: Macmillan, 1974), pp. 78–9.

37. Corwin Edwards, "The Impact of International Cartelization on International Trade," in H. Arndt, ed., *Die Konzentration in der Wirtschaft* (Berlin: Dunker & Humbolt, 1971).

38. For examples, see particularly Chapters 5 and 6 on fertilizers, dyestuffs, and man-made fibers.

39. For a general discussion of this strategy, see Heinrich Kronstein, *The Law of International Cartels* (Ithaca: Cornell University Press, 1973), particularly the chapter on "The Technological Cartel," pp. 43–76.

40. On aluminum, see ibid., pp. 92–5, 187–89; U.S., Senate, Committee on the Judiciary, Subcommittee on Antitrust, *Economic Concentration Outside the United States*, 90th Cong., 2d sess., pt. 7; 3651–58; and *The Economist*, October 30, 1971. For a detailed account of the aluminum cartel before the war, see Stocking and Watkins, *Cartels in Action*, pp. 216–73.

41. Organization for Economic Cooperation and Development, *Restrictive Business Practices of Multinational Enterprises*, Report of the Committee of Experts on Restrictive Business Practices (Paris: OECD, 1977), p. 7.

42. Ibid., p. 9; see also United Nations, Economic and Social Council, Commission on Transnational Corporations, *Transnational Corporations in World Development: A Re-examination* (New York: United Nations, 1978), p. 236.

43. United Nations, Department of Economic and Social Affairs, *Multinational Corporations in World Development* (New York: United Nations, 1973), p. 8.

44. U.N., ECOSOC, p. 36.

45. U.N., Dept. of Economic and Social Affairs, p. 13.

46. Ibid., p. 7.

47. See figures on growth rate of production under TNC auspices, ibid., p. 14.

48. See the discussion of centralization in Richard J. Barnet and Ronald E. Muller, *Global Reach: The Power of the Multinational Corporations* (New York: Simon & Schuster, 1974), pp. 40–4.

CHAPTER TWO

1. For example, see the article in the trade journal *World Water*, January 1980. When confronted with a detailed report on the IEA, its secretary-general, Mr. Derek Rose, claimed that the cartel was merely "an ordinary trade association which provides a meeting point and a forum for its members throughout Europe to discuss matters of common interest." In February 1980, a Brown Boveri executive, Erwin Bielinski, who is a member of the IEA council, denied that the association is an international cartel. That month Brown Boveri even called a news conference to make the same point. At the conference, Kurt Mirow was called a "notorious liar," and all journalists in attendance were given an automatic egg boiler as a present. By April, however, Mirow's documentary evidence was being circulated widely enough to make this posture increasingly untenable, and Derek Rose made the first public admission that the IEA is an export cartel. This was followed by a similar admission from Bernhard Plettner, chairman of Siemens, who stated in an interview in *Der Spiegel* (no. 20, 1980), "Well, to this I can only say that [the IEA] is an export cartel approved by the Bundeskartellampt [the German federal cartel office]."

2. Federal Trade Commission, *Report of the Federal Trade Commission on International Electrical Equipment Cartels* (Washington, D.C.: Government Printing Office, 1948).

3. Monopolies and Restrictive Practices Commission, *Report on the Supply and Exports of Electrical and Allied Machinery and Plant* (London: Her Majesty's Stationery Office, 1957). Hereafter MRPC (1957).

4. See Barbara Epstein, *Politics of Trade in Power Plant* (London: Atlantic Trade Study; Trade Policy Research Center, 1971).

5. For an excellent description of the early development of the heavy electrical equipment industry, see ibid., pp. 44–50.

6. George W. Stocking and Myron R. Watkins, *Cartels in Action* (New York: Twentieth Century Fund, 1946), pp. 326, 331–32.

7. Ibid., pp. 333–40. GE and Philips were convicted in the "incandescent lamp" anti-trust case, *United States* v. *General Electric Co. et al.*, 82 F. Supp. 753 (1949). Also see FTC, pp. 145–46.
8. United Kingdom, Board of Trade, *Survey of International Cartels and Internal Cartels*, vol. 2 (London: Board of Fair Trading, 1944–46, pt. 3, "Electrical Machinery and Apparatus") p. 52. Hereafter UKBT.
9. Stocking and Watkins, pp. 344–49; also UKBT, p. 54. The 20 percent figure is GE's calculation; the higher figures from 1935–39 are from the government's calculations in its antitrust complaint. GE's own figures for those years are somewhat lower.
10. Monopolies and Restrictive Practices Commission, *Electric Lamps: Second Report on the Supply of Electric Lamps* (London: Her Majesty's Stationery Office, 1968), p. 35. Hereafter MRPC (1968).
11. Stocking and Watkins, p. 354.
12. Ibid., p. 355.
13. Ibid., p. 359.
14. UKBT, p. 54.
15. *United States* v. *General Electric Co., et al.*, 82 F. Supp. 753 (D.N.J. 1949); see also *New York Times*, January 20, 1949.
16. We are indebted for this analysis to Richard S. Newfarmer. See his *The International Market Power of Transnational Corporations: A Case Study of the Electrical Industry*, United Nations Conference on Trade and Development, Doc. no. UNCTAD/ST/MD/13, 1978, p. 33.
17. Epstein, pp. 9–30.
18. For full details of INCA and early IEA, see FTC, pp. 13–48.
19. Epstein, p. 114; Newfarmer (UNCTAD), p. 33.
20. FTC, pp. 45, 57; MRPC (1957), pp. 29–31.
21. FTC, p. 57; MRPC (1957), p. 29.
22. MRPC (1957), pp. 90–101.
23. MRPC (1968), p. 58.
24. Richard Newfarmer, *Transnational Conglomerates and the Economics of Dependent Development: A Case Study of the International Electrical Oligopoly and Brazil's Electrical Industry* (Greenwich, Conn.: JAI Press), pp. 107–12.
25. MRPC (1968), pp. 22–3.
26. Rapport de la Commission Technique des Ententes et Positions Dominantes (CTE), no. 1193, *Entente entre fabricants des lampes électriques*, May 26, 1956, pp. 22–3; and Rapport de la CTE, no. 1193/67, *Entente dans l'industrie des lampes électriques*, April 22, 1966, p. 34. Cited in Frédéric Jenny and André-Paul Weber, *L'Entreprise et les Politiques de Concurrence* (Paris: Les Editions d'Organization, 1976), pp. 78–83.
27. *Business Week*, September 20, 1976.
28. Newfarmer, *International Market Power*, p. 106.
29. S. M. Dugar, *Law of Restrictive Trade Practices* (Delhi: Taxman, 1976), pp. 429–35, cited in Newfarmer, *International Market Power*, p. 106.
30. Newfarmer, *International Market Power*, p. 113.
31. Federal Trade Commission, *Report on the Supply of Electrical Equipment and Competitive Conditions* (Washington, D.C.: Government Printing Office, 1928), pp. 28–9.
32. UNCTAD, *Restrictive Business Practices: Studies on the United Kingdom of Great Britain and Northern Ireland, the United States of America and Japan* (New York: United Nations, 1974), pp. 64–5.
33. Heinrich Kronstein, *The Law of International Cartels* (Ithaca: Cornell University Press, 1973), pp. 296–301. See also *Hazeltine Research, Inc.* v. *Zenith Radio Corp.*, 239 F. Supp. 51 (N.D. Ill. 1965).
34. Kronstein, p. 300.
35. Monopolies and Restrictive Practices Commission, *Report on the Supply of Insulated Electric Wire and Cable* (London: Her Majesty's Stationery Office, 1952), p. 50; Ervin Hexner, *International Cartels* (Chapel Hill: University of North Carolina Press, 1945), p. 356.
36. This account of the ICDC is largely based on the article in the *Times*, April 7, 1975.
37. *The Economist*, March 15, 1975; *American Metal Market*, March 10, 1975.

38. FTC, p. 56.
39. MRPC (1957), p. 241.
40. Ibid., pp. 26, 31.
41. See Barbara Epstein and Richard Newfarmer, *International Electrical Association: A Continuing Cartel*, Report Prepared for the Use of the Committee on Interstate and Foreign Commerce and Its Subcommittee on Oversight and Investigations, U.S. House of Representatives, 96th Cong., 2d sess. (Washington, D.C.: Government Printing Office, 1980), pp. 47–9. We are indebted to this report for the organization of certain material in this chapter and in Appendix I.
42. Newfarmer, *International Market Power*, p. 57.
43. Epstein and Newfarmer, p. 620.
44. *Financial Times*, March 21, 1977; Newfarmer, *International Market Power*, pp. 68–9.
45. Newfarmer, *Transnational Conglomerates*, p. 150.
46. Ibid., p. 153.
47. Ibid., pp. 202–3.
48. Ibid., pp. 205–6.
49. Ibid., p. 206; *O Globo* (Rio de Janeiro), September 19, 1975.
50. *Electrical Week*, August 4, 1975.
51. James W. Vaupel and Joan P. Curhan, *The Making of Multinational Enterprise* (Boston: Division of Research, Graduate School of Business Administration, Harvard University, 1969), pp. 355–58.
52. Newfarmer, *Transnational Conglomerates*, pp. 213–24, 236–38.
53. Ibid., p. 192.
54. Ibid., p. 198. Also see Codima suit against Brown Boveri, Conselho Administrativo de Defesa Economica, Proceso No. 9, for an account of Brown Boveri dumping. A good summary of this case is contained in *O Globo* (Rio de Janeiro), August 5, 1974.
55. *Jornal do Brasil* (Rio de Janeiro), April 3, 1978; *Financial Times*, September 23, 1975.
56. The two firms were Walita S.A. and Lustrene S.A.
57. See deposition of João Mario Nigro in hearings of the parliamentary inquiry into multinational corporations (CPI das Multinaçionais), Brasília, June 26, 1975.
58. "In 1962, 65% of the 51 leadership positions were occupied by representatives of Brazilian-owned enterprises. By 1974, the much stronger organization had representatives from Brazilian enterprises in only 40% of the leadership positions." Newfarmer, *Transnational Conglomerates*, p. 174.
59. See Charles Bane, *The Electrical Equipment Conspiracies: The Treble Damage Actions* (New York: Federal Legal Publications, 1973), pp. 1–22, and app. 2; also *Fortune*, February 11, 1980.
60. U.S., Department of Commerce, *Market Share Reports*, Commodity Series, S.I.T.C. # 722.1, Electrical Power Machinery, for years 1964–68, 1973–77.
61. Epstein and Newfarmer, pp. 132–45.
62. U.S. Tariff Commission, "Large Power Transformers from France, Italy, Japan, Switzerland, and the United Kingdom," Determination of Injury in Investigations Nos. AA1921-86/90 Under the Antidumping Act, 1921, as amended, TC Publications 476 (Washington, D.C.: Government Printing Office, April 1972).

CHAPTER THREE

1. John M. Blair, *The Control of Oil* (New York: Pantheon, 1976), pp. 47–52.
2. Ibid., pp. 296, 385.
3. Anthony Sampson, *The Seven Sisters: The Great Oil Companies and the World They Made* (New York: Viking, 1975), p. 21. On the early years of the oil industry in Pennsylvania, see Ida M. Tarbell, *The History of the Standard Oil Company* (New York: McClure, Phillips, 1904), ch. 1; and John J. McLaurin, *Sketches in Crude Oil* (Harrisburg, Pa.: the author, 1896), chs. 5–10.
4. For the early years of Rockefeller and Standard Oil, see Tarbell, especially chapters 2 and 3; Allan Nevins, *Study in Power: John D. Rockefeller* (New York: Scribner's, 1953), chs. 2–9. (This biography was written with the cooperation of Standard Oil but

remains reasonably objective.); and John T. Flynn, *God's Gold: The Story of Rocke-feller and His Times* (New York: Harcourt Brace, 1932), pts. 3–5.

5. For details on the Rockefeller monopoly, besides the above sources, see United States Corporations Bureau, *Report of the Commissioner of Corporations on the Petroleum Industry* (Washington, D.C.: Government Printing Office, 1907).

6. Sampson, pp. 32–5; Blair, pp. 39, 127, 147–51.

7. Blair, pp. 32–3; see also Carl Solberg, *Oil Power: The Rise and Imminent Fall of an American Empire* (New York: Mason/Charter, 1976), pp. 71–9.

8. The basic source for the petroleum cartel through the 1940s is the Federal Trade Commission investigation begun in 1949 and headed by John M. Blair. This investigation produced the famous report, *The International Petroleum Cartel*, Staff Report of the Federal Trade Commission to the Subcommittee on Monopoly of the Committee on Small Business of the United States Senate, 82nd Cong., 2d sess., 1952. For its account of the Red Line Agreement, see pp. 51–69. Sampson's summary is on pp. 65–9; Blair's on pp. 31–4.

9. FTC, pp. 199–210.

10. Ibid., pp. 228–68.

11. Ibid., p. 241.

12. Ibid., p. 232.

13. Ibid., p. 242.

14. Ibid., pp. 313–20.

15. Ibid., pp. 280–97; for number of meetings, p. 291.

16. Ibid., pp. 280–97.

17. Ibid., pp. 352–72.

18. Ibid., p. 212.

19. See statement of Karl Crowley, in United States Temporary National Economic Committee, Investigation of Economic Concentration, *The Petroleum Industry, Hearings*, 76th Cong., 2d sess., 1939, pt. 14: 7591–7629. Besides the TNEC hearings, and the FTC report (pp. 210–18), the best source on the prorationing story is Erich W. Zimmerman, *Conservation in the Production of Petroleum* (New Haven: Yale University Press, 1957), pp. 130–35, 142–60, and 203–33. Zimmerman is particularly interesting because he is generally sympathetic to the oil industry.

20. Blair, pp. 158–60.

21. Zimmerman, loc. cit.

22. TNEC, p. 7596.

23. Blair, p. 163.

24. U.S., Congress, Senate, *Oil Supply and Distribution Problems*, A Final Report of the Special Committee to Study Problems of American Small Business, 81st Cong., 1st sess., 1949, p. 13.

25. Sampson, pp. 82–3.

26. FTC, p. 266.

27. *United States* v. *Standard Oil Co. (New Jersey) et al.*, Civil Action No. 86/27, Plaintiff's Statement of Claims, June 12, 1961, S.D.N.Y. Reprinted in U.S., Congress, Senate, Committee on Foreign Relations, Subcommittee on Multinational Corporations, *The International Petroleum Cartel, the Iranian Consortium and U.S. National Security*, 93rd Cong., 2d sess., 1974, p. 131.

28. Ibid., p. 132.

29. Sampson, p. 96.

30. FTC, pp. 117–18, 121.

31. U.S., Congress, Senate Committee on Foreign Relations, Subcommittee on Multinational Corporations, *Multinational Oil Corporations and United States Foreign Policy*, 93rd Cong., 2d sess., 1975, p. 48. Also see the rest of chapter 2 of this report, "The 1947 Aramco Merger."

32. Ibid.

33. This story is recounted in an addendum to the 1952 FTC report. When the report was first published, the addendum was omitted for reasons of national security. It was feared that Iraq's wrath on learning what the companies had been doing would cause unpleasantness. As a result this information remained secret until 1974, when it was

revealed by the Senate Subcommittee on Multinationals. See U.S., Congress, Senate, Committee on Foreign Relations, Subcommittee on Multinational Corporations, *Multinational Corporations and U.S. Foreign Policy*, 93rd Cong., 2d sess., 1974, pt. 8: 529–32.

34. Ibid., p. 531.
35. Ibid., pt. 7: 310.
36. Ibid., p. 83.
37. *Multinational Oil Corporations*, p. 80.
38. Blair, pp. 47–8.
39. Ibid., p. 79.
40. For this section we have relied chiefly on three sources: Sampson, ch. 6; *Multinational Oil Corporations*, ch. 3; and *International Petroleum Cartel.*
41. *International Petroleum Cartel*, p. 91. The author of the memo, Kenneth R. Harkins, remarks further: "In the light of the information we have in the cartel case, I do not believe that we can properly assume that the participants will market this oil in a lawful manner."
42. *Multinational Oil Corporations*, pt. 7: 297.
43. See particularly ibid., pp. 244–78.
44. Blair, p. 105.
45. Ibid., pp. 102–11.
46. Ibid.
47. Ibid., p. 72.
48. *Multinational Oil Corporations*, pt. 7: 110.
49. Ibid., p. 109.
50. Blair, p. 75.
51. See the memoranda from Emmerglick and Harkins in *International Petroleum Cartel*, pp. 89–94.
52. Blair, p. 75.
53. Ibid., p. 213. For a detailed analysis of oil price trends from 1957 to 1969, see M. A. Adelman, *The World Petroleum Market* (Baltimore: John Hopkins University Press, 1972), ch. 6, esp. pp. 182–91, which includes discussion of the Libyan production. Also see U.S., Congress, Senate, Committee on the Judiciary, Subcommittee on Antitrust and Monopoly, *Governmental Intervention in the Market Mechanism: The Petroleum Industry*, 91st Cong., 1st sess., 1969, pt. 1: 41–76.
54. Blair, pp. 216–18.
55. *Multinational Oil Corporations*, pt. 5: 100, 112–13; pt. 4 contains a "Chronology of the Libyan Oil Negotiations, 1970–1971" (p. 155), and Part 5 contains the full story.
56. Ibid., p. 260. Also see the rest of John J. McCloy's testimony.
57. Blair, pp. 227–29.
58. Ibid.
59. Ibid., p. 220.
60. *Multinational Oil Corporations*, pt. 5: 134.
61. Cited in Sampson, p. 161.
62. *Multinational Oil Corporations*, pt. 9: 167–91.
63. Blair, pp. 266–68.
64. Ibid., pp. 276–80.
65. *Multinational Oil Corporations*, ch. 7; Sampson, pp. 300–5; Blair, pp. 289–93.
66. Sampson, p. 301.

CHAPTER FOUR

1. This pattern of acquisition may be changing, but the trend as yet is in a very early stage. See *Business Week*, April 24, 1978, on oil company diversification.
2. *Engineering News-Record*, April 5, 1979.
3. Much of the documentation for this chapter can be found in the records of hearings before the Subcommittee on Oversight and Investigations of the Committee on Interstate and Foreign Commerce, U.S. House of Representatives. Hearings on Novem-

ber 4, 1976, were titled *International Uranium Supply and Demand* (95th Cong., 2d sess.). In 1977, hearings titled *International Uranium Cartel* (95th Cong., 1st sess.) were published in two volumes. The present reference is from *International Uranium Cartel*, 1: 457.

4. *International Uranium Cartel*, 1: 651.
5. See memorandum of the Australian delegation to the meeting, *International Uranium Supply*, pp. 344–51.
6. *International Uranium Cartel*, 2: 293.
7. Ibid., 1: 493–524.
8. Ibid., pp. 516–19.
9. The basic cartel document is reproduced in *International Uranium Supply*, p. 184. Also see *International Uranium Cartel*, 2: 10.
10. *International Uranium Supply*, p. 194.
11. Ibid., pp. 195, 202, 253.
12. *International Uranium Cartel*, 1: 564.
13. Ibid., p. 257.
14. Ibid., p. 290.
15. Ibid., p. 562.
16. A draft of the new rules can be found in Ibid., pp. 628–40.
17. Ibid., pp. 639, 669.
18. For an account of the price rises see a report by the Nuclear Exchange Corporation (Nuexco, Menlo Park, Ca.), "Significant Events in the Uranium Market, 1969–1976," published by Nuexco on October 15, 1976, reprinted in *International Uranium Supply*, pp. 363–74.
19. *New York Times*, July 9, 1978.
20. *International Uranium Supply*, p. 50.
21. *International Uranium Cartel*, 1: 131.
22. Ibid., p. 347.
23. *New York Times*, July 9, 1978.
24. For example, see letter from Gulf counsel Roy D. Jackson, Jr., October 11, 1973, reprinted in *International Uranium Cartel*, 1: 600.
25. Ibid., p. 132 et seq.
26. See review of these statements, Ibid., 2: 195–202. The minister's statement is on p. 200.
27. Ibid., p. 308.
28. Ibid., pp. 246–47.
29. Ibid., 1: 254–55.
30. Ibid., p. 460.
31. Ibid., p. 255.
32. Ibid., pp. 195, 552.
33. Ibid., 2: 117.
34. Ibid., 1: 594.
35. Ibid., 2: 108.
36. *International Uranium Supply*, p. 7 et seq.; *International Uranium Cartel*, 2: 336–42.
37. *International Uranium Cartel*, 1: 627.
38. Ibid., pp. 319–20, 329.
39. *International Uranium Supply*, p. 64.
40. *International Uranium Cartel*, 2: 76.
41. Ibid., 1: 347, 352.
42. Ibid., p. 420.
43. Ibid., p. 341.
44. Ibid., pp. 544–45.
45. Ibid., pp. 511, 567, 585–86.
46. Ibid., pp. 537–38.
47. Ibid., p. 550.
48. Ibid., p. 231.
49. Ibid., p. 475.
50. Ibid., p. 485.

51. Ibid., p. 491.
52. Ibid., p. 550.
53. Ibid., p. 190.
54. Ibid., p. 351.
55. Ibid., p. 422.
56. *New York Times,* June 3, 1978.
57. Ibid., March 27, 1979.
58. Ibid., December 4, 1979.
59. *International Uranium Supply,* p. 265.

CHAPTER FIVE

1. George W. Stocking and Myron W. Watkins, *Cartels or Competition?* (New York: Twentieth Century Fund, 1948), p. 112.
2. George W. Stocking and Myron W. Watkins, *Cartels in Action* (New York: Twentieth Century Fund, 1946), p. 425.
3. Corwin Edwards, *Cartelization in Western Europe* (Washington, D.C.: Department of State, Bureau of Intelligence and Research, 1964), pp. 24-5.
4. For this account of early pharmaceuticals we are indebted to a report by the United Nations Centre on Transnational Corporations, *Transnational Corporations and the Pharmaceutical Industry* (New York: United Nations, 1979), pp. 14-16.
5. Ibid., p. 110.
6. On this point see A. Cilingiroglu, *Transfer of Technology for Pharmaceutical Chemicals: Synthesis Report on Five Industrializing Countries* (Paris: OECD, 1975); and Sanjaya Lall, *Major Issues in Transfer of Technology to Developing Countries: A Case Study of the Pharmaceutical Industry* (New York: United Nations, 1975).
7. U.S., Congress, Senate, Committee on the Judiciary, Subcommittee on Antitrust and Monopoly, *Administered Prices,* 86th Cong., 1st and 2d sess., 1960–61, pts. 14–25.
8. Ibid., pt. 20: 11258.
9. Ibid., p. 11254.
10. Heinrich Kronstein, *The Law of International Cartels* (Ithaca: Cornell University Press, 1973), p. 112. For a full account of the Tolbutamide story, see the testimony of Dr. E. Gifford Upjohn, *Administered Prices,* pt. 20: 11005–84. The text of the licensing agreement is reprinted on p. 11266.
11. This was the figure cited by drug industry spokesmen; the committee considered it possibly somewhat exaggerated. U.N. Centre on Transnational Corporations, p. 72.
12. U.S., Congress, Senate, Committee on the Judiciary, Subcommittee on Antitrust and Monopoly, *Administered Prices: Drugs,* 87th Cong., 1st sess., 1962, p. 65.
13. Ibid., pp. 74, 143–44.
14. Ibid., p. 148.
15. Ibid., pp. 148–49.
16. *Oil, Paint and Drug Reporter,* March 11, 1968; *Wall Street Journal,* January 23, 1973.
17. *The Structure and Behavior of Enterprises in the Chemical Industry and Their Effects on the Trade and Development of Developing Countries,* Study prepared by UNCTAD secretariat with the assistance of Mr. R. H. Yates (New York: United Nations, 1979), p. 45. Also see *Journal of Commerce,* July 7, 1976; *European Chemical News,* July 9, 1976.
18. For example, see *Administered Prices: Drugs,* pts. 4 and 5; Paul A. Brooke, *Resistant Prices: A Study of Competitive Strains in the Antibiotic Markets* (New York: Council on Economic Priorities, 1975), p. 19 et seq.; U.N. Centre on Transnational Corporations, pp. 47–53.
19. Cilingiroglu, pp. 65–75.
20. See U.N. Centre on Transnational Corporations, p. 102; Lall; and various publications of the United Nations Industrial Development Organization, particularly *Assessment of the Pharmaceutical Industry in Developing Countries, Its Potential, and the National and International Action Required to Promote Its Development* (New York: United Nations, 1978).

21. For the full details of the quinine cartel, see U.S., Congress, Senate, Committee on the Judiciary, Subcommittee on Antitrust and Monopoly, *Prices of Quinine and Quinidine*, 1966–67, 89th Cong. 2d sess.–90th Cong., 1st sess., pts. 1 and 2. A good summary of the cartel can be found in John Blair's testimony, pt. 2: 180–223. A brief account can be found in UNCTAD, *Restrictive Business Practices: Studies on the United Kingdom of Great Britain and Northern Ireland, the United States of America and Japan* (New York: United Nations, 1974), pp. 57–61.

22. *Prices of Quinine and Quinidine*, pt. 2: 180–81.

23. UNCTAD, *Restrictive Business Practices*, p. 58.

24. Ibid., p. 59.

25. Ibid., p. 61.

26. *Oil, Paint and Drug Reporter*, October 28, 1968, and May 25, 1970.

27. UNCTAD, *Restrictive Business Practices*, p. 18.

28. Stocking and Watkins, *Cartels or Competition?*, p. 86. See also Stocking and Watkins, *Cartels in Action*, ch. 10.

29. W. J. Reader, *Imperial Chemical Industries — A History*, 2 vols. (London: Oxford University Press, 1970–75), 2:413.

30. Stocking and Watkins, *Cartels in Action*, p. 423.

31. Stocking and Watkins, *Cartels or Competition?*, p. 90.

32. *United States* v. *United States Alkali Export Association*, 86 F. Supp. 59 (S.D.N.Y. 1949). Also see Earl W. Kintner and Mark R. Joelson, *An International Antitrust Primer* (New York: Macmillan, 1974), p. 78.

33. *United States* v. *Imperial Chemical Industries, Ltd.*, 105 F. Supp. 215 (S.D.N.Y. 1952).

34. *United States* v. *National Lead Co.*, 63 F. Supp. 513 (S.D.N.Y. 1945), aff'd, 332 U.S. 319 (1947). Also see *New York Times*, July 12, 1945.

35. *Oil, Paint and Drug Reporter*, November 19, 1962.

36. For this account, see UNCTAD, *Restrictive Business Practices*, pp. 19–20; Organization for Economic Cooperation and Development, *Export Cartels* (Paris: OECD, 1974), esp. pp. 84–6, where the text of the agreement is reprinted; and UNCTAD, *Chemical Industry*, p. 31.

37. UNCTAD, *Chemical Industry*, pp. 31–2.

38. *Chemical Week*, October 15, 1960, and July 11, 1964. See also *United States* v. *American Cyanamid Co.* (BB. No. 1565) 60CN.3857 (S.D.N.Y. 1960).

39. Ibid.; see also *Oil, Paint and Drug Reporter*, October 10, 1960; *New York Times*, October 6, 1960.

40. *New York Times*, October 6, 1960; *Chemical Week*, October 15, 1960.

41. *New York Times*, July 2, 1964; *Chemical Week*, July 11, 1964.

42. *Chemical Week*, April 2, 1975; *Wall Street Journal*, May 28, 1976.

43. Stocking and Watkins, *Cartels in Action*, pp. 505–6; Ervin Hexner, *International Cartels* (Chapel Hill: University of North Carolina Press, 1946), pp. 308–12.

44. Stocking and Watkins, *Cartels in Action*, pp. 507–10.

45. *Oil, Paint and Drug Reporter*, August 11, 1969, and September 29, 1969.

46. *Chemical Marketing Reporter*, July 31, 1972.

47. UNCTAD, *Chemical Industry*, p. 39.

48. *Chemical Marketing Reporter*, December 23, 1974; *New York Times*, July 19, 1974, and October 19, 1974; *Wall Street Journal*, November 17, 1976.

49. For early fertilizer cartels, see Stocking and Watkins, *Cartels in Action*, ch. 4; Hexner, *International Cartels*, pp. 262–70, 323–30; and United Kingdom, Board of Trade, *Survey of International Cartels and Internal Cartels 1944–1946* (London: Her Majesty's Stationery Office, 1946), pp. 89, 98, 102.

50. See the account of the U.S. cartel in Stocking and Watkins, *Cartels in Action*, pp. 147–54.

51. Hexner, *International Cartels*, pp. 263–64; U.K. Board of Trade, pp. 99–100.

52. Hexner, *International Cartels*, pp. 267–68; Alfred Plummer, *International Combines in Modern Industry*, 3rd ed. (London: Pitman, 1951), pp. 94–100; U.K. Board of Trade, pp. 102–3.

53. The sources in note 52 disagree on the dates.

54. Plummer, p. 99.

55. *New York Times*, May 16 and 17, 1940.
56. Edwards, p. 29.
57. UNCTAD, *Chemical Industry*, pp. 36–7.
58. Edwards, p. 28.
59. *Oil, Paint and Drug Reporter*, October 4, 1965.
60. UNCTAD, *Restrictive Business Practices*, p. 80.
61. Ibid., pp. 80–1.
62. Ibid.; *Chemical Week*, April 17, 1965.
63. *Oil, Paint and Drug Reporter*, February 24, 1964.
64. Ibid., May 4, 1964.
65. Ibid., October 4, 1965.
66. Ibid., July 26, 1965.
67. *Wall Street Journal*, May 2, 1979.
68. *The Economist*, August 25, 1962.
69. London *Times*, June 24, 1968.
70. Edwards, p. 30; *The Economist*, August 25, 1962.
71. UNCTAD, *Chemical Industry*, p. 34.
72. BMWI-Tagesnachrichten No. 6705, February 28, 1973, edited by the German Ministry of the Economy; cited in Juergen Raushcel, *Die BASF: Zur Anatomie eines Multinationalen Konzerns* (Cologne: Pahl Rugenstein, 1975); pp. 215–16.
73. July 25, 1963.
74. U.S., Congress, Senate, Committee on the Judiciary, Subcommittee on Antitrust and Monopoly, *International Aspects of Antitrust, 1967*, 90th Cong., 1st sess., 1967, pp. 106–8.
75. *Common Market Law Reports*, January 2, 1979, p. 16.
76. Ibid., pp. 24–25, 29, 37.
77. Ibid., p. 15.
78. Stocking and Watkins, *Cartels in Action*, p. 516.

CHAPTER SIX

1. George W. Stocking and Myron W. Watkins, *Cartels in Action* (New York: Twentieth Century Fund, 1946), pp. 172, 182.
2. For accounts of these negotiations and the early steel cartels, see Ervin Hexner, *The International Steel Cartel* (Chapel Hill: University of North Carolina Press, 1943), pp. 70–80; and Stocking and Watkins, pp. 182–86.
3. Hexner, pp. 144, 251.
4. Ibid., pp. 171–99; Stocking and Watkins, pp. 205–10.
5. Stocking and Watkins, p. 215.
6. See Corwin Edwards, *Cartelization in Western Europe* (Washington, D.C.: Department of State, Bureau of Intelligence and Research, 1964), p. 61.
7. See descriptions in Heinrich Kronstein, *The Law of International Cartels* (Ithaca: Cornell University Press, 1973), pp. 134–35; and UNCTAD, *Restrictive Business Practices: Studies on the United Kingdom of Great Britain and Northern Ireland, the United States of America and Japan* (New York: United Nations, 1974), pp. 13–14.
8. UNCTAD, p. 14; Stocking and Watkins, p. 189.
9. London *Times*, October 11, 1966.
10. See accounts of the case in *The Economist*, March 6, 1971; *Business Week*, March 6, 1971; and Organization for Economic Cooperation and Development, *Export Cartels*, Report of the Committee of Experts on Restrictive Business Practices (Paris: OECD, 1974), p. 38.
11. London *Times*, September 3, 1968.
12. UNCTAD, p. 15.
13. *Business Week*, September 3, 1966.
14. For example, see the testimony of Professor Egon Sohmen in U.S., Congress, Senate, Committee on the Judiciary, Subcommittee on Antitrust and Monopoly, *Economic Concentration*, 1968, 90th Cong., 2d sess., pt. 7: 3447–8.

15. *Business Week*, September 3, 1966.

16. Mark Green, *The Closed Enterprise System* (New York: Grossman, 1972), p. 231.

17. For example, note the conflicts that developed in 1980 when recession exacerbated the overproduction problem. The highly cartel-minded EEC commissioner of industry, Viscount Etienne Davignon, moved for a mandatory production cut by Eurofer members. The Germans and Italians, however, resisted, calculating that their relatively efficient plants would benefit most from a competitive battle. Finally, in October 1980, the EEC voted for mandatory cutbacks of 18 percent, with certain German products exempted. The *New York Times* (October 31, 1980) called this an "immense new mandatory steel cartel," but in reality it was simply the old cartel with stronger teeth.

18. On the Bresciani, see *The Economist*, December 17, 1977; *Business Week*, March 27, 1978; *New York Times*, October 9, 1980.

19. C. H. Ward-Jackson, *A History of Courtaulds* (London: Printed at the Curwen Press for Private Circulation, 1941), p. 112.

20. *International Combines in Modern Industry*, 3rd ed. (London: Pitman, 1951), p. 35.

21. Stocking and Watkins, p. 512.

22. Ibid., p. 513; Plummer, pp. 37–9; Hexner, pp. 380–82.

23. Clair Wilcox, *Competition and Monopoly in American Industry*, Temporary National Economic Committee: Investigation of Concentration of Economic Power Monograph, no. 21 (Washington, D.C.: Government Printing Office, 1940), pp. 202–3.

24. *New York Times*, July 7 and May 13, 1937.

25. Wilcox, pp. 203–4.

26. Hexner, p. 382; *The Economist*, April 29, 1939.

27. Great Britain, Monopolies Commission, *A Report on the Supply of Man-Made Cellulosic Fibers* (London: Her Majesty's Stationery Office, 1968), pp. 18–19.

28. Ibid., p. 19.

29. Ibid., p. 20.

30. OECD, pp. 34–35; *The Economist*, April 8, 1972; *Chemical Marketing Reporter*, April 17, 1972.

31. *Chemical Marketing Reporter*, February 12, 1973.

32. Ibid.

33. *Chemical Week*, January 3, 1973. The U.S. market was excluded from all these agreements.

34. *Chemical Marketing Reporter*, February 12, 1973.

35. *New York Times*, August 10, 1977.

36. *The Economist*, November 13, 1971, and October 7, 1972; *Chemical Week*, March 8, 1972.

37. *New York Times*, May 17, 1978; *European Chemical News*, February 26, 1979.

38. *New York Times*, November 10, 1978; *European Chemical News*, December 24/31, 1979.

39. *European Chemical News*, February 26, 1979.

40. *Chemical Week*, February 6, 1980.

CHAPTER SEVEN

1. An excellent history of the regulated U.S. ocean shipping industry, with particular reference to the conference system, can be found in the Report of the Antitrust Subcommittee of the Committee on the Judiciary, U.S. House of Representatives, entitled *The Ocean Freight Industry*, 87th Cong., 2d sess. (Washington, D.C.: Government Printing Office, 1962), esp. ch. 12, "Conclusions and Recommendations."

2. Sources critical of government misregulation include Roger G. Noll, *Reforming Regulation* (Washington, D.C.: Brookings Institution, 1971); Arthur Belonzi et al., *The Weary Watchdogs: Governmental Regulators in the Political Process* (Wayne, N.J.: Avery, 1977); and Robert C. Fellmeth, *The Interstate Commerce Omission: The Public Interest and the ICC* (New York: Grossman, 1970).

3. U.S., Department of Justice, *The Regulated Ocean Shipping Industry* (Washington, D.C.: Government Printing Office, 1977), p. 6.
4. *New York Times*, October 1, 1967.
5. Figure is from spokesman for Federal Maritime Commission, January 1980.
6. See *Ocean Freight Industry*, pp. 384–88; Justice Department, pp. 55–66; *The Economist*, April 11, 1964.
7. *The Economist*, April 11, 1964.
8. Alfred Plummer, *International Combines in Modern Industry*, 3rd ed. (London: Pitman, 1951), p. 65.
9. Ervin Hexner, *International Cartels* (Chapel Hill: University of North Carolina Press, 1945), p. 388.
10. U.S., Congress, Joint Economic Committee, *Discriminatory Ocean Freight Rates and the Balance of Payments*, 89th Cong., 1st sess., 1965, pp. 16–17.
11. See *Ocean Freight Industry*, pp. 12–17, 324–48.
12. On the Isbrandtsen case, see Justice Department, pp. 108–10; *Ocean Freight Industry*, pp. 212–15.
13. *Ocean Freight Industry*, p. 382.
14. Joint Economic Committee, p. 26; Justice Department, pp. 30–37; see also *Business Week*, April 18, 1964, for an account of the political battle over the dual rate question.
15. *New York Times*, September 26 and October 5, 1961.
16. Joint Economic Committee, p. 27.
17. Ibid., pp. 3–6, 22–4.
18. Ibid., p. 6.
19. Ibid., p. 9.
20. Ibid., p. 18.
21. Ibid., p. 19.
22. Ibid., pp. 16–17.
23. Ibid., pp. 2–4, 20.
24. Ibid., pp. 6, 31.
25. *The Economist*, December 19, 1964.
26. Joint Economic Committee, pp. 32–4; *New York Times*, December 16, 1964.
27. *The Economist*, March 9, 1968.
28. *New York Times*, August 21, 1968.
29. Ibid., September 15, 1967.
30. Ibid., July 26, 1968.
31. For example, see *The Economist*, September 19, 1970.
32. *The Economist*, July 19, 1975.
33. Ibid.; and *New York Times*, July 4, 1975.
34. *Business Week*, July 21, 1975.
35. *New York Times*, May 18 and November 25, 1976; see also Justice Department, p. 102.
36. For the story of the Sea-Land case, see U.S., Congress, Senate, Committee on Commerce, Science, and Transportation, Subcommittee on Merchant Marine and Tourism, *Illegal Rebating in the U.S. Ocean Commerce*, 95th Cong., 1st sess., 1977, pp. 25–31.
37. *New York Times*, November 25, 1976.
38. *Illegal Rebating*, p. 7.
39. Ibid., p. 33.
40. Ibid., p. 23.
41. See Sager's testimony, ibid., pp. 77–88.
42. For a summary of these investigations, see U.S., Department of Justice, *Report of the Task Group on Antitrust Immunities* (Washington, D.C.; Government Printing Office, 1977).
43. Justice Department, *Regulated Ocean Shipping*, p. 238.
44. Ibid., p. 68.
45. Ibid.
46. Ibid., pp. 71–81.

47. Ibid., pp. 106–22.
48. Ibid., pp. 131–34.
49. Ibid., p. 155.
50. Ibid., p. 167.
51. Ibid., pp. 169–74.
52. Ibid., pp. 175–89. See also the government's complaint in *United States* v. *Atlantic Container Line, Ltd. et al.*, Criminal No. 79-0021, Filed June 1, 1979, in U.S. District Court for the District of Columbia.
53. *U.S.* v. *Atlantic Container Line*, pp. 16–17.
54. Justice Department, *Regulated Ocean Shipping*, pp. 190–215.
55. For example, see *New York Times*, October 7 and 12, 1980.
56. Justice Department, *Regulated Ocean Shipping*, pp. 221–24.
57. Ibid., p. 240.
58. U.S., Congress, House, Committee on Merchant Marine and Fisheries, Subcommittee on Merchant Marine, *Closed Conferences and Shippers' Councils in the U.S. Liner Trades*, 95th Cong., 2d sess., 1978, p. 73.

CHAPTER EIGHT

1. See Organization for Economic Cooperation and Development, *Export Cartels*, Report of the Committee of Experts on Restrictive Business Practices (Paris: OECD, 1974); also UNCTAD, *Restrictive Business Practices: Studies on the United Kingdom of Great Britain and Northern Ireland, the United States of America and Japan* (New York: United Nations, 1974). The authors have examined the cartel register in the Bundeskartellampt (the West German cartel agency), Bonn.
2. Among the recent books to deal with this subject are Richard Barnet, *The Lean Years: Politics in the Age of Scarcity* (New York: Simon & Schuster, 1980); Mary Kaldor, *The Disintegrating West* (London: Allen Lane, 1978); and Alan Wolfe, *America's Impasse: Growth Politics in a No-Growth Economy* (New York: Pantheon, 1981).
3. We are indebted for this observation to Richard Barnet and Ronald Muller, *Global Reach* (New York: Simon & Schuster, 1974), pp. 287–89. For an account of this development as it relates to the most recent recession, see "The Recession: Now It's Sweeping Through Europe," *New York Times*, September 21, 1980.
4. See Robert Lekachman, *Economists at Bay: Why the Experts Will Never Solve Your Problems* (New York: McGraw-Hill, 1976); and Wolfe.
5. *Business Week*, March 27, 1978; *The Economist*, July 29, 1978.
6. On the proposal for a cartel in plastics, see *European Chemical News*, April 28, 1978.
7. *Business Week*, March 27, 1978.
8. George W. Stocking and Myron R. Watkins, *Cartels or Competition?* (New York: Twentieth Century Fund, 1948), p. 356.
9. Ibid., p. 146. Stocking's and Watkins's discussion of the tension between competition and the desire for market control is particularly cogent, and this book is indispensable reading for anyone wishing to evaluate the role of cartels in an economy theoretically based on a free market.
10. U.S., Congress, Senate, Committee on Commerce, Science, and Transportation, Subcommittee on Merchant Marine and Tourism, *Illegal Rebating in the U.S. Ocean Commerce*, 95th Cong., 1st sess., 1977, p. 85.
11. U.S., Congress, House, Committee on Interstate and Foreign Commerce, Subcommittee on Oversight and Investigations, *International Uranium Cartel*, 95th Cong., 1st sess., 1977, vol. 1, pp. 455, 458, 523.
12. See Stocking and Watkins, p. 136.
13. Barnet and Muller, p. 162.
14. See Chapter 5, particularly the section on pharmaceuticals, for sources. Also see Organization for Economic Cooperation and Development, *Restrictive Business Practices Relating to Patents and Licenses*, Report by the Committee of Experts on Restrictive Business Practices (Paris: OECD, 1972); and Constantine Vaitsos, "The Revision of the International Patent System: Legal Considerations for a Third World

Position," *World Development*, February 1976. For other U.N. studies on the licensing of patents, see UNCTAD, *Restrictive Business Practices*, TD/122/Supp. 1 (New York: United Nations, 1972); UNCTAD, *Transfer of Technology Policies Relating to Technology of the Countries of the Andean Pact: Their Foundations*, A Study by the Junta del Acuerdo de Cartagena (New York: United Nations, 1971); and UNCTAD, *Restrictions on Exports in Foreign Collaboration Agreements in India* (New York: United Nations, 1972). The first two of these UNCTAD studies are reprinted in the *Proceedings* of the Third United Nations Conference on Trade and Development, Santiago de Chile, 1972, vols. 2 and 3, respectively.

15. Stocking and Watkins, p. 223; Barnet and Muller, p. 351.
16. Heinrich Kronstein, *The Law of International Cartels* (Ithaca: Cornell University Press, 1973), ch. 3, esp. pp. 64–76.
17. See Stocking and Watkins, pp. 68–75; Ervin Hexner, *International Cartels* (Chapel Hill: University of North Carolina Press, 1945), p. 188.
18. See Cheryl Payer, *Commodity Trade of the Third World* (New York: Wiley, 1975), pp. 104–28; Statement by Joseph A. Greenwald, Assistant Secretary for Economic and Business Affairs, *Department of State Bulletin*, August 23, 1976; *New York Times*, October 6, 1979 (on rubber pact); and Kronstein, pp. 10–23.
19. This account is based on Payer, pp. 154–68; and Greenwald statement.
20. In 1979 and 1980 the members of the European fibers cartel carried out an intense and ultimately successful campaign for higher duties on European imports of American-made fibers. The Europeans charged that the U.S. goods had a price advantage of about 15 percent because price controls on oil in the United States allowed fibers producers there to buy petroleum feedstocks at an "artificially" low cost.
21. Richard Newfarmer, *The International Market Power of Transnational Corporations: A Case Study of the Electrical Industry* (New York: United Nations, 1978), ch. 2.
22. Stocking and Watkins, p. 234. The authors go on to remark, "The arrangement between du Pont and Imperial Chemical Industries . . . under which they jointly exploit the several South American markets, buttressed as it is by numerous cartel agreements involving other leading chemical companies, undoubtedly has retarded new investments in Latin America."
23. Carlos Doellinger and Leonardo Cavalcanti, *Empresas Multinaçionais na Indústria Brasileira*, Relatoria da Pesquisa, no. 29 (Rio de Janeiro: Instituto de Planejamento Económico e Social), p. 38. Also see Rubem Medina, *Desnacionalizacão: Crime Contra o Brasil?* (Rio de Janeiro: Editorial Saga, 1970); and Peter Evans, *Dependent Development: The Alliance of Multinational, State and Local Capital in Brazil* (Princeton: Princeton University Press, 1979), esp. chs. 2 and 3.
24. Barnet and Muller, p. 147.
25. See Juan V. Sourrouille, "The Impact of Transnational Enterprises on Employment and Income: The Case of Argentina," World Employment Programme Working Paper No. 7 (Geneva: International Labor Organization, 1976); L. Willmore, "Direct Foreign Investment in Central American Manufacturing," *World Development*, June 1976; and D. Chudinovsky, *Empresas Multinacionales y Ganáncias Monopólicas* (Buenos Aires: Siglo XXI, 1974). There have been remarkably few empirical studies of denationalization in Asia and Africa. One study of Nigeria concludes that multinational firms have not replaced local capitalists to any large degree but have certainly "pre-empted" local investment in many fields. See Thomas J. Biersteker, *Distortion or Development? Contending Perspectives on the Multinational Corporation* (Cambridge, Mass.: MIT Press, 1978), ch. 6.
26. Barnet and Muller, pp. 154–55, 408n.
27. January 15, 1970. The report is based on data from the empirical study by James W. Vaupel and Joan P. Curhan, *The Making of Multinational Enterprise* (Cambridge: Harvard University, Graduate School of Business Administration, 1969).
28. Newfarmer, pp. 84–5.
29. See Chapter 2. An article by Raymond Vernon found that "by the end of the 1960s almost 65 percent of 2904 subsidiaries of 396 U.S. and other transnational corporations in LDCs had been set up by acquisition rather than by new investments." The

quote and citation is from Sanjaya Lall, "Transnationals, Domestic Enterprises, and Industrial Structure in Host LDCs: A Survey," *Oxford Economic Papers*, July 1978. For data on Brazil and Mexico, see U.S., Congress, Senate, Committee on Foreign Relations, Subcommittee on Multinational Corporations, *Multinational Corporations in Brazil and Mexico: Structural Sources of Economic and Non-Economic Power*, prepared by Richard Newfarmer and Willard F. Mueller, 94th Cong., 1st sess., 1975.

30. Barnet and Muller, p. 164. See also note 14 above.
31. Ibid., pp. 164–65.
32. UNCTAD, *Restrictive Business Practices: Studies on the United Kingdom of Great Britain and Northern Ireland, the United States of America and Japan*, p. 28. Also see Great Britain Monopolies Commission, *A Report on the Supply of Metal Containers* (London: Her Majesty's Stationery Office, 1970).
33. S. M. Dugar, *Law of Restrictive Trade Practices* (Delhi: Taxman, 1976), p. 429.
34. See Constantine Vaitsos, "Employment Problems and Transnational Enterprises in Developing Countries: Distortions and Inequality" (Geneva: International Labor Office, October 1976), cited in Newfarmer, p. 94.
35. Barbara Epstein and Kurt R. W. Mirow, *Impact on Developing Countries of Restrictive Business Practices of Transnational Corporations in the Electrical Equipment Industry: A Case Study of Brazil* (New York: United Nations, 1977), p. 14.
36. Ibid., pp. 14, 31–3.
37. Barnet and Muller, pp. 158–59.
38. See UNCTAD, *Restrictive Business Practices*, E. 72.II.D.10 (New York: United Nations, 1972).
39. Barnet and Muller, p. 208. For an exchange concerning the significance of these data on overpricing, see "An Exchange on Multinationals" by Ronald Muller, Richard Barnet, and Raymond Vernon, *Foreign Policy*, Summer 1974.
40. See Ronald Muller, "The Multinational Corporation and the Underdevelopment of the Third World," in Charles Wilbur, ed., *The Political Economy of Development and Underdevelopment* (New York: Random House, 1973), pp. 139–46; Barnet and Muller, pp. 157–62; Raymond Vernon, *Storm over the Multinationals: The Real Issues* (Cambridge: Harvard University Press, 1977), pp. 154–61; also Sidney M. Robbins and Robert B. Stobaugh, *Money in the Multinational Enterprise: A Study of Financial Policy* (New York: Basic Books, 1973), pp. 91–2, 184–86. For a recent review of the empirical studies of the styles of transfer pricing, see Roger Y. W. Tang, *Transfer Pricing Practices in the United States and Japan* (New York: Praeger, 1979), chs. 2 and 5.
41. See note 14 above.
42. Barnet and Muller, p. 412.
43. UNCTAD, *Restrictive Business Practices: Studies on the United Kingdom of Great Britain and Northern Ireland, the United States of America, and Japan*, pp. 26–7.
44. Barnet and Muller, pp. 16–17, 259.
45. "Latin American Underdevelopment in the Year 2000," in Jagdish N. Bhagwati, *Economics and World Order: From the 1970s to the 1990s* (London: Macmillan, 1972), p. 249.
46. Barnet and Muller, ch. 9.
47. See the figures on growth of TNCs, Chapter 1. See also United Nations Economic and Social Council, (ECOSOC), Commission on Transnational Corporations, *Transnational Corporations in World Development: A Re-Examination* (New York: United Nations, 1978), pp. 34–54; Barnet and Muller, pp. 228–53.
48. See the detailed description of tax treatment of TNCs in Barnet and Muller, pp. 273–83, and notes thereto. Bergsten, Horst, and Moran, who are generally much more sympathetic to the transnationals than are Barnet and Muller, argue that the tax system does not favor foreign investment as much as is "commonly supposed." But even they admit that some TNCs are substantially favored and that the complexities of transfer pricing and tax havens allow them to evade taxes. See C. Fred Bergsten, Thomas Horst, and Theodore H. Moran, *American Multinationals and American Interests* (Washington, D.C.: Brookings Institution, 1978), ch. 6. On the struggle

over tax rates of corporations versus private citizens, see Philip Stern, *The Rape of the Taxpayer* (New York: Random House, 1972).

49. The most obvious current examples of this are the protectionist campaigns now being waged by the steel, auto, and textile industries.

50. Sources disagree, naturally, as to the relative importance of this development. The United Nations study *Multinational Corporations in World Development* (New York: United Nations, 1973), pp. 60–5, regards the huge liquid resources of the transnationals as a possible threat to a stable currency exchange system. Barnet and Muller agree, citing various examples, pp. 283–86. Bergsten argues that TNCs may actually contribute to the *stability* of the international monetary system because their "flexibility," that is, the huge liquid sums they control, helps the system adjust quickly to basic shifts in exchange rates. Bergsten does allow that massive movements of TNC funds can be a destabilizing factor in the short run, however. See Bergsten et al., pp. 272–88. Vernon, pp. 118–23, after reviewing the evidence, concludes, "Multinational corporations have the potential for contributing substantially to the instability of currencies. So far as anyone can tell, the potential has remained just that and has not so far been realized. But that conclusion generates only a limited amount of comfort for those who feel that one day the dam may burst."

51. The disagreement over the net effects of the "runaway shop" is even more extreme than on the issues outlined in notes 48 and 50 above. U.S. organized labor is convinced that foreign investment by U.S. transnationals costs American workers many jobs. See the study, "An American Trade Union View of International Trade and Investment, AFL-CIO," in *Multinational Corporations*, a compendium of papers submitted to the Subcommittee on International Trade of the Committee on Finance of the U.S. Senate (Washington, D.C.: Government Printing Office, 1973). The TNCs, on the other hand, claim that foreign investment actually *creates* large numbers of jobs for Americans in the parent firm headquarters, in the production of machinery, parts, and so forth, that are exported to the foreign subsidiaries, and in opening up new markets to American firms. See the study performed by the Emergency Committee for American Trade, "The Role of the Multinational Corporation in the United States and World Economies" (Washington, D.C.: 1973). Both of these studies are cited in Barnet and Muller, pp. 298–300. A more recent study cited by Bergsten suggests that the net effect has been the loss of a substantial number of jobs (p. 103). Other sources on this subject are Vernon, pp. 114–19; U.S., Congress, Senate Committee on Foreign Relations, Subcommittee on Multinational Corporations, *Direct Investment Abroad and the Multinational Corporations: Effect on the United States Economy*, prepared by Peggy B. Musgrave, 94th Cong. 1st sess., 1975; and two books edited by Duane Kujawa, *American Labor and the Multinational Corporation* (New York: Praeger, 1973), and *International Labor and the Multinational Enterprise* (New York: Praeger, 1975). Finally, an excellent brief account of the runaway shop as it affects the garment industry, which cites many other sources on the problem in general, including recent statements from the AFL-CIO, can be found in U.S., Congress, House, Committee on International Relations, Subcommittee on International Economic Policy, *Foreign Investment and American Jobs*, 94th Cong., 2d sess., (Washington, D.C.: Government Printing Office, 1976), pts. 1 and 2.

52. The best source on the political power of the oil companies in the United States remains Robert Engler, *The Politics of Oil* (New York: Macmillan, 1961), particularly chs. 12–16. Also see his more recent *The Brotherhood of Oil* (Chicago: University of Chicago Press, 1977).

53. See John M. Blair, *The Control of Oil* (New York: Pantheon, 1976), pp. 169–86.

54. Ibid., pp. 330–41.

55. Barnet and Muller, p. 256.

56. Ibid., p. 221; Engler, *Brotherhood of Oil*, pp. 184–92. See also Richard Barnet, *Lean Years*, pp. 32–4; and Donald L. Barlett and James B. Steele, "The Oil Went Thataway," in Robert Engler, ed., *America's Energy* (New York: Pantheon, 1980).

57. Barnet and Muller, pp. 266–67.

58. Ibid., pp. 28, 283–86; see also note 50 above.

CHAPTER NINE

1. For cartel law in Western nations, see various publications of the Organization for Economic Cooperation and Development: *Export Cartels* (Paris: OECD, 1974), *Annual Reports on Competition Policy in OECD Member Countries* (1978), and *Comparative Summary of Legislation on Restrictive Business Practices* (1978).

2. See OECD, *Restrictive Business Practices of Multinational Enterprises* (Paris: OECD, 1977), pp. 20–1; David A. Larson, "An Economic Analysis of the Webb-Pomerene Act," *Journal of Law and Economics*, October 1970; Ryan C. Amacher et al., "A Note on the Webb-Pomerene Law and the Webb Cartels," *Antitrust Bulletin*, Summer 1978; and Federal Trade Commission, *Webb-Pomerene Associations*, Staff Report to the FTC (Washington, D.C.: Government Printing Office, 1967).

3. Heinrich Kronstein, *The Law of International Cartels* (Ithaca: Cornell University Press, 1973), pp. 200–44.

4. See note 2 above. Also C. Fred Bergsten et al., *American Multinationals and American Interests* (Washington, D.C.: Brookings Institution, 1978), pp. 258–59; and UNCTAD, *Restrictive Business Practices: Studies in the United Kingdom of Great Britain and Northern Ireland, the United States of America and Japan* (New York: United Nations, 1974), pp. 78–9.

5. See OECD, *Restrictive Business Practices of Multinational Enterprises*, pp. 5, 68–9.

6. Bergsten, p. 264.

7. Ibid.

8. Note in this context the remark by Joel Davidow, former head of the Foreign Commerce Section of the Antitrust Division, that U.S. antitrust laws are "one of our most successful exports." Ibid., p. 270.

9. See the accounts of these negotiations in Earl W. Kintner and Mark R. Joelson, *An International Antitrust Primer* (New York: Macmillan, 1974), pp. 266–69; and Paul M. Goldberg and Charles Kindleberger, "Toward a GATT for Investment: A Proposal for Supervision of the International Corporation," *Law and Policy in International Business*, Summer 1970, p. 320.

10. Goldberg and Kindleberger, p. 306.

11. Bergsten, pp. 490–91.

12. Robert E. Smith, "Cartels and the Shield of Ignorance," *Journal of International Law and Economics*, June 1973.

13. Goldberg and Kindleberger.

14. *Columbia Journal of World Business*, November–December 1967.

15. *Journal of International Law and Economics*, December 1973.

16. Richard J. Barnet and Ronald E. Muller, *Global Reach* (New York: Simon & Schuster, 1974), p. 372.

17. For a good account of the development of "extraterritorial reach," see Kintner, pp. 21–7, 78–80. The cases are *United States* v. *American Tobacco Co.*, 221 U.S. 106 (1911); *United States* v. *Aluminum Co. of America*, 148 F.2d 416 (2nd Cir. 1945); and *United States* v. *United States Alkali Export Association*, 86 F. Supp. 59 (S.D.N.Y. 1949).

18. Mark J. Green, with Beverly C. Moore, Jr., and Bruce Wasserstein, *The Closed Enterprise System: Ralph Nader's Study Group Report on Antitrust Enforcement* (New York: Grossman, 1972), p. 238.

19. In this regard the landmark case is *United States* v. *Imperial Chemical Industries, Ltd.*, 105 F. Supp. 215 (S.D.N.Y. 1952), in which a U.S. court imposed penalties on British firms that were eventually voided by British courts. For a description of the case see Kintner, pp. 63–4.

20. See the full discussion of this extremely complex matter in Kintner, ch. 4.

21. Green, p. 239.

22. *New York Times*, December 4, 1979.

23. Green, p. 275.

24. Accounts of the traditionally painless antitrust penalties can be found in Green, ch. 5; Richard Posner, *Antitrust Law* (Chicago: University of Chicago Press, 1976), pp. 31–5; and Kenneth G. Elzinga and William Breit, *The Antitrust Penalties* (New Haven: Yale University Press, 1976), pp. 30–62.

25. See Green, pp. 164–67.
26. See Andrea Berger Kalodner, "Consent Decrees as an Antitrust Enforcement Device," *Antitrust Bulletin*, Summer 1978.
27. "A Statistical Study of Antitrust Enforcement," *Journal of Law and Economics*, vol. 13, 1970, cited in Green, p. 179.
28. Green, pp. 179–80; Kalodner, p. 277.
29. *Wall Street Journal*, June 4, 1979.
30. Elzinga and Breit, p. 134.
31. See Posner, p. 225.
32. Elzinga and Breit, p. 38.
33. Green, pp. 167–69.
34. Ibid., p. 176.
35. Kalodner, pp. 280–81.
36. Green, p. 204.
37. See Elzinga and Breit, chs. 4 and 5; Posner, pp. 228–32.
38. Green, pp. 214–17.
39. William Meinhardt, "Patentfragen bei Internationalen Kartellen," *Gewerblicher Rechtsschutz und Urheberrecht*, no. 1222, 1931. An excellent account of the development of corporate control over patents, and the resulting importance of patent cartel schemes to the dominance of the great firms in America, can be found in David F. Noble, *America by Design: Science, Technology and the Rise of Corporate Capitalism* (New York: Knopf, 1977), ch. 6.
40. Ward S. Bowman, *Patent and Antitrust Law* (Chicago: University of Chicago Press, 1973), pp. 53–63. See also Theodore L. Bowes, "Patent Law Reform and the Expansion of Provisions Relating to Licensing," *Loyola University of Chicago Law Journal*, Winter 1976.
41. In this connection see George L. Priest, "Cartels and Patent License Arrangements," *Journal of Law and Economics*, October 1977.
42. Note recommendations along these lines in Donald Turner, "The Patent System and Competitive Policy," *New York University Law Review*, May 1969.
43. George W. Stocking and Myron R. Watkins, *Cartels or Competition?* (New York: Twentieth Century Fund, 1948), pp. 293–94.
44. "Property Rights Theory and Patent-Antitrust: The Role of Compulsory Licensing," *New York University Law Review*, November 1977.
45. See James M. Wertzel, "Can Patent Properties Be Distributed Through Compulsory Licensing?" *APLA Quarterly Journal*, Summer 1973.
46. Bowman, pp. 243–49.
47. An interesting discussion of how to evaluate patent licensing agreements, particularly in relation to international cartels, can be found in Priest.
48. For example, see Peter O'Brien, "Developing Countries and the Patent System: An Economic Appraisal," *World Development*, September 1974; and Douglas Greer, "The Case Against Patent Systems in the Less-Developed Countries," *Journal of International Law and Economics*, December 1973.
49. O'Brien, p. 28.
50. "The Patent System and the Third World," *World Development*, September 1974. Also see Edith Penrose, "International Patenting and the Less-Developed Countries," *Economic Journal*, September 1973.
51. OECD, *Restrictive Business Practices Relating to Patents and Licenses* (Paris: OECD, 1972), p. 11.
52. "The Revision of the International Patent System: Legal Considerations for a Third World Position," *World Development*, February 1976, pp. 91–2.
53. United Nations ECOSOC, *Transnational Corporations in World Development: A Re-Examination* (New York: United Nations, 1978), p. 89.
54. O'Brien; Vaitsos.
55. U.N. ECOSOC, pp. 24, 89–90.
56. Ibid., p. 89; see also Richard Newfarmer, *Transnational Conglomerates and the Economics of Dependent Development* (Greenwich, Conn.: JAI Press, 1980), pp. 302–11; Barnet and Muller, pp. 207–8.
57. Barnet and Muller, p. 261.

58. See "Informational Requirements for the Control of Restrictive Business Practices Originating with Firms of Developed Countries," Report of the UNCTAD Secretariat, reprinted in *Antitrust Bulletin*, Winter 1975.
59. Ralph Nader, Mark Green, and Joel Seligman, *Taming the Giant Corporation* (New York: Norton, 1976), p. 63. This book contains an excellent brief account of the development of the law regarding the nature of the corporation. See also the classic study on the subject by A. A. Berle, Jr., and G. C. Means, *The Modern Corporation and Private Property* (New York: Macmillan, 1933); and James C. Bonbright and Gardiner C. Means, *The Holding Company* (New York: McGraw-Hill, 1932), esp. ch. 3.
60. U.S., Bureau of the Census, *Statistical Abstract of the United States* (Washington, D.C.: Government Printing Office, 1979), p. 573.
61. Nader, Green, and Seligman, p. 137.
62. Introduction to *Guide to Corporations: A Social Perspective* (New York: Council on Economic Priorities, 1974), p. ii.
63. The House Subcommittee on Domestic Finance of the Banking Committee has reported that it "presumes" a 10 percent share of a corporation's stock amounts to control, that 5 percent qualifies for control, and that 1–2 percent affords "tremendous influence." See Robert Sherrill, "Where Is the Cry of Protest?" *The Nation*, October 25, 1980, on oil company ownership.
64. Nader, Green, and Seligman, p. 174.
65. Barnet and Muller, pp. 279–80, 369.
66. Ibid., pp. 282–83. Also see Bergsten, pp. 89–90, 491–92.
67. See the account of this battle in Nader, Green, and Seligman, pp. 168–73.
68. Ibid., p. 176.
69. On this subject see ibid., pp. 161–65; Stanley Charles Abraham, *The Public Accounting Profession: Problems and Prospects* (Lexington, Mass.: Lexington Books, 1978), esp. pp. 145–60. The Abraham book describes the two government reports: U.S., Congress, House, Committee on Interstate and Foreign Commerce, Subcommittee on Oversight and Investigations, *Federal Regulation and Regulatory Reform*, 94th Cong., 2d sess., 1976; and U.S., Congress, Senate, Committee on Government Operations, Subcommittee on Reports, Accounting, and Management, *The Accounting Establishment*, 94th Cong., 2d sess., 1976.
70. Nader, Green, and Seligman, p. 163.
71. See Robert Chatov, *Financial Reporting: Public or Private Control?* (New York: Free Press, 1975), p. 296.

EPILOGUE

1. See Lynn Chadwick and William A. Dobrovir, "The High Cost of Baksheesh," *The Nation*, November 22, 1980.
2. Anthony Sampson, *The Seven Sisters* (New York: Viking, 1975), p. 316.
3. Richard J. Barnet and Ronald E. Muller, *Global Reach* (New York: Simon & Schuster, 1974), pp. 369–75.
4. For critiques of giantism in corporations, see ibid., pp. 347–54, 377–82; John M. Blair, *Economic Concentration: Structure, Behavior and Public Policy* (New York: Harcourt Brace Jovanovich, 1972); Graham Bannock, *The Juggernauts: The Age of the Big Corporation* (London: Weidenfeld and Nicolson, 1971), esp. pts. 1, 2, and 5; Edward Schumacher, *Small Is Beautiful: A Study of Economics as if People Mattered* (London: Blond and Briggs, 1973), pt. 4; Morton Mintz and Jerry S. Cohen, *America, Inc.: Who Owns and Operates the United States* (New York: Dial, 1971), prologue and ch. 1; and Ralph Nader et al., *Taming the Giant Corporation* (New York: Norton, 1976), chs. 1, 2, and 7. An interesting collection of material, particularly relating to the question of concentration and innovation, can be found in U.S., Congress, Senate, Select Committee on Small Business, *Small Business and the Quality of American Life*, A Compilation of Source Material on the Relationship Between Small Business and the Quality of Life, 1946–78, 95th Cong., 1st sess. (Washington, D.C.: Government Printing Office, 1977).

Index

Abscam, 184n
Accounting practices: corporations and, 236
Acheson, Dean, 30
Achnacarry Agreement, 24, 27, 71, 72, 73, 74, 84, 87, 210
ACNA, 139
Adelman, Martin, 229
Administrative Council for Economic Defense (CADE), 5, 9
AEG, 4, 5, 6, 8, 21, 38, 42
Africa, 212; and uranium industry, 98
Agency for International Development (AID), 143, 145
Agriculture: price supports for, 197
Aircraft industry, 165
Airlines industry, 166, 167, 183
Aktiebolaget Svenska Amerika Linien v. FMC, 180
AKZO, 136
Albright & Wilson, 134
ALCACE, 6
Alcan, 32
Alcoa, 27, 32
Alcoa (1945), 220
Algemeene Kunstztidje Unie (AKU), 160
Alkasso (1949), 220
Allen, R. K., 114
Alliance for Progress, 206
Allied Chemical, 137, 139
Allis Chalmers, 63
Aluminum industry, 22, 32–33
American Agricultural Chemical Co., 143
American Color and Chemical, 139
American Cyanamid, 122, 125, 135–36, 137, 139, 143

American Export Lines, 181
American Home Products Corp., 125, 126
American Petroleum Institute, 74
American Steel Rail Makers, 19
American Sugar Refining, 15
American Tobacco, 15
American Tobacco (1911), 220
American Viscose Company, 161
Andean Common Market, 231
Andean Pact, 205
Anglo-Persian Oil Company, 24, 69
Ansaldo San Giorgio, 6
Antitrust laws, 15, 23, 30, 32, 45, 60, 73, 75, 80, 84, 89, 95, 99, 105, 106, 107, 108, 114, 158, 159, 183, 213, 215; enforcement of, 116, 121; international, 216–19, 227; penalties under, 222–23, 224, 225
Antitrust movement, 15–16, 31
Antitrust Procedures and Penalties Act of 1974, 224
Antitrust proceedings, 9, 28, 29, 32, 37, 40, 41, 43, 45, 68, 76, 84, 86–87, 130, 132, 135, 139, 140, 143, 166, 181–82
APQ, 82–83, *table* 83, 86
Aramco, 79, 80, 82, 83, 89, 91
Armaments industry, 22, 241
Armour & Co., 143
Arno, 58
Arnold, Thurman, 28, 29
ASEA, 4, 5, 6, 8, 55, 58
Asia, 204; and fibers industry, 164
AT & T, 45, 46
Ateliers de Constructions Electriques Charleroi (ACEC), 5
Atlantic Container Line, 181
Atlantic Richfield, 95

313